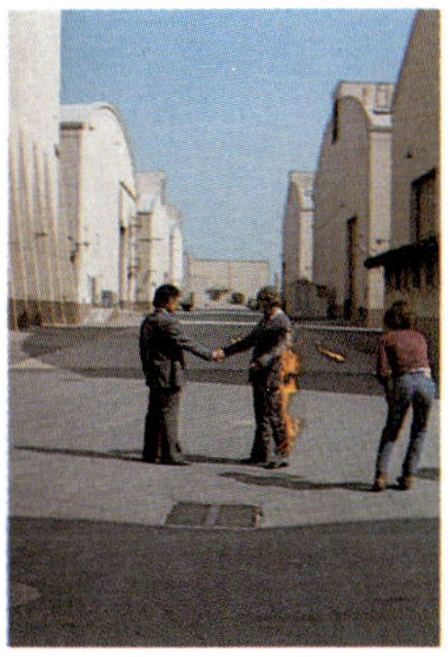 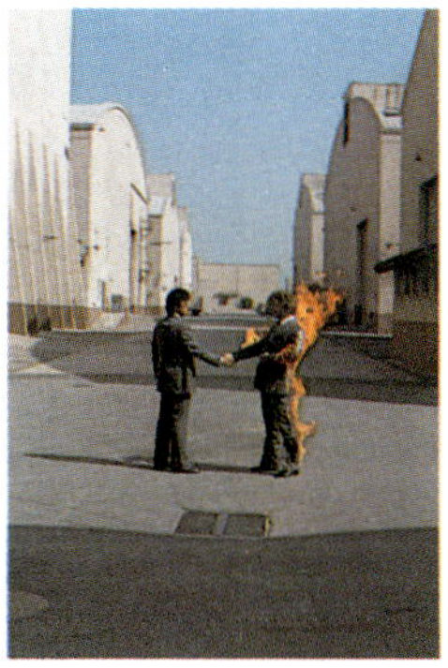

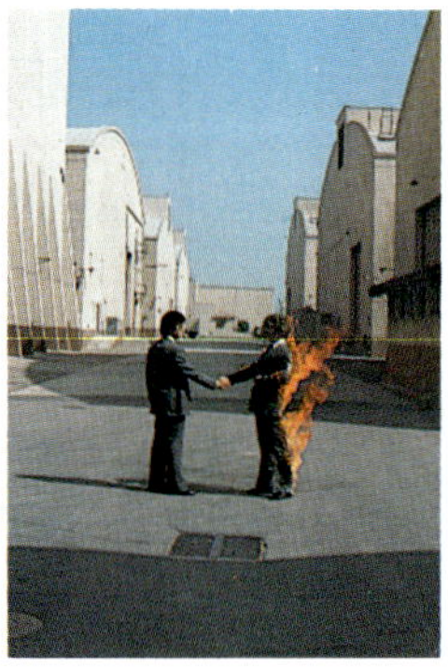 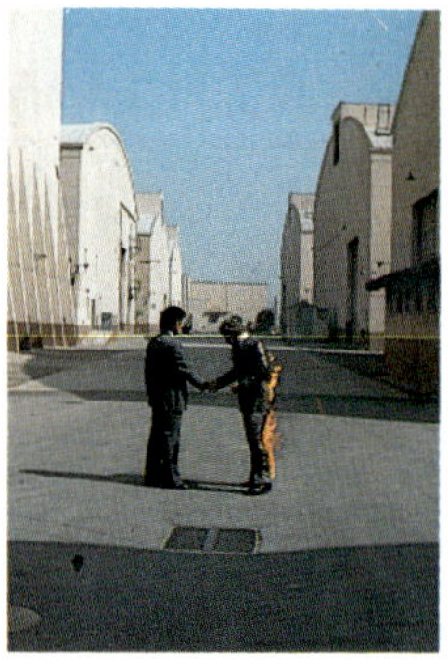

OUR GRATEFUL THANKS TO ARTISTS, MANAGEMENTS AND RECORD COMPANIES FOR THEIR KIND CO-OPERATION IN THE COMPILING OF THIS BOOK.

CREDITS AND INFORMATION REGARDING INDIVIDUAL ITEMS ARE IN THE APPENDIX.

AN ABC OF THE WORK OF

HIPGNOSIS

'WALK AWAY RENÉ'

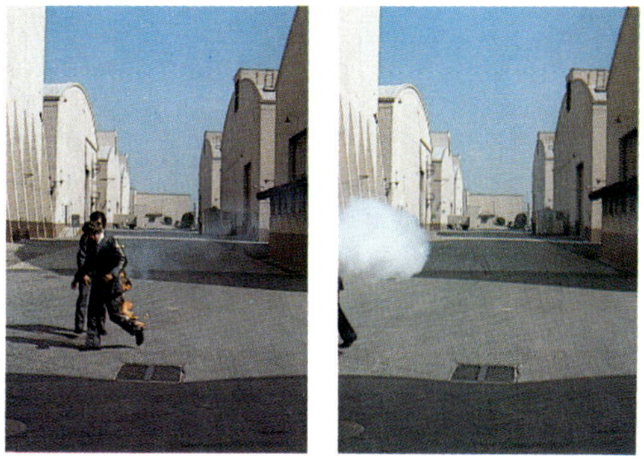

Paper Tiger

COMPILED BY HIPGNOSIS AND GEORGE HARDIE
TEXT BY STORM THORGERSON
DEDICATED TO VANJI

PAPER TIGER

A DRAGONS WORLD BOOK

DRAGONSWORLD LIMITED
LIMPSFIELD, SURREY RH8 0DY, UNITED KINGDOM

ISBN HARDBACK 0-905895-09-6
ISBN LIMPBACK 0-905895-08-8

Printed in Spain by
Printer Industria Gràfica S.A.
Sant Vicenç dels Horts 1978
Depòsito Legal B-16325-1978

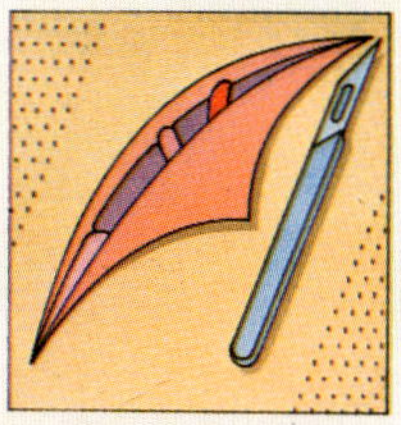

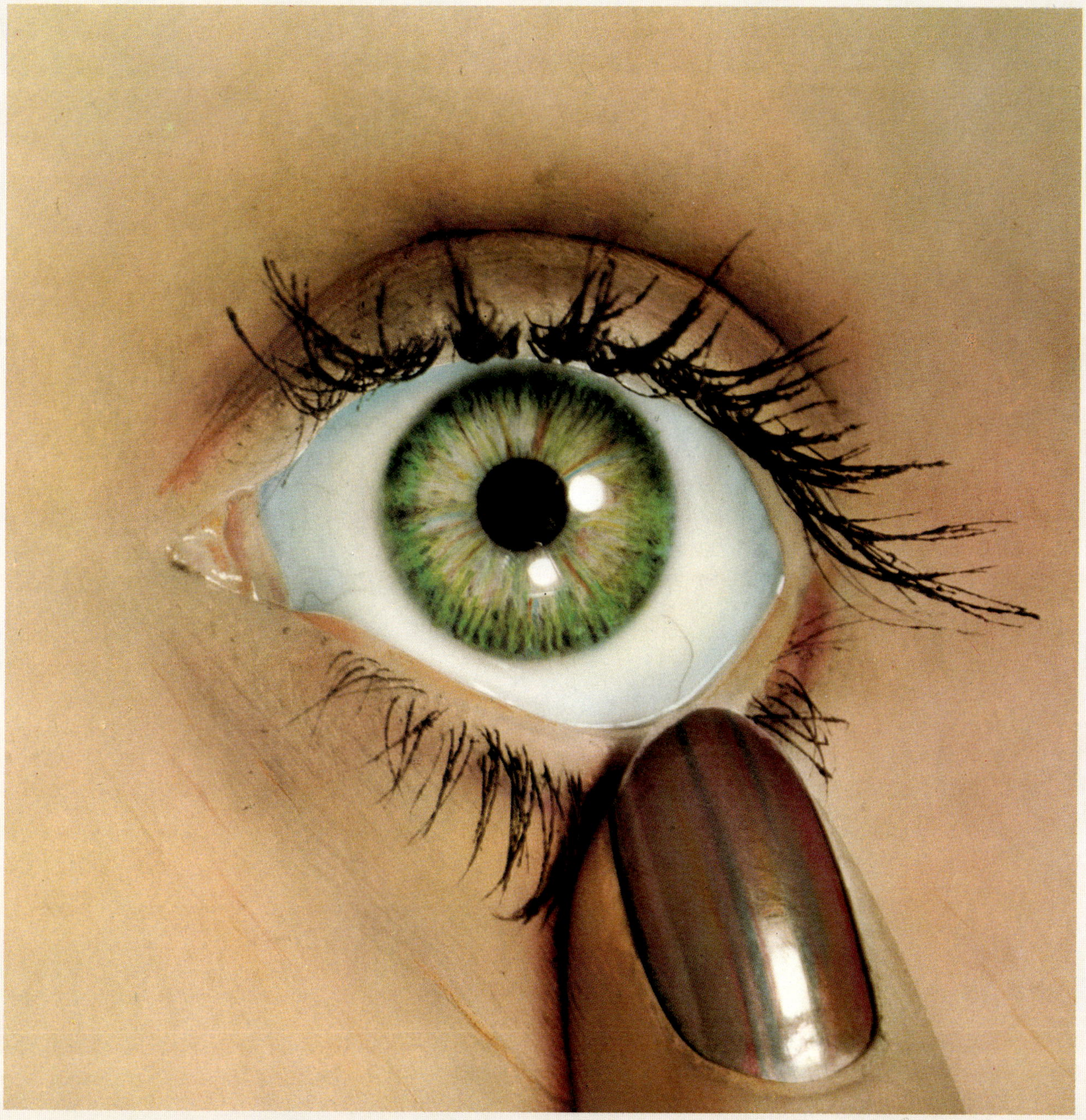

1975 PRETTY THINGS 'SAVAGE EYE' FRONT COVER

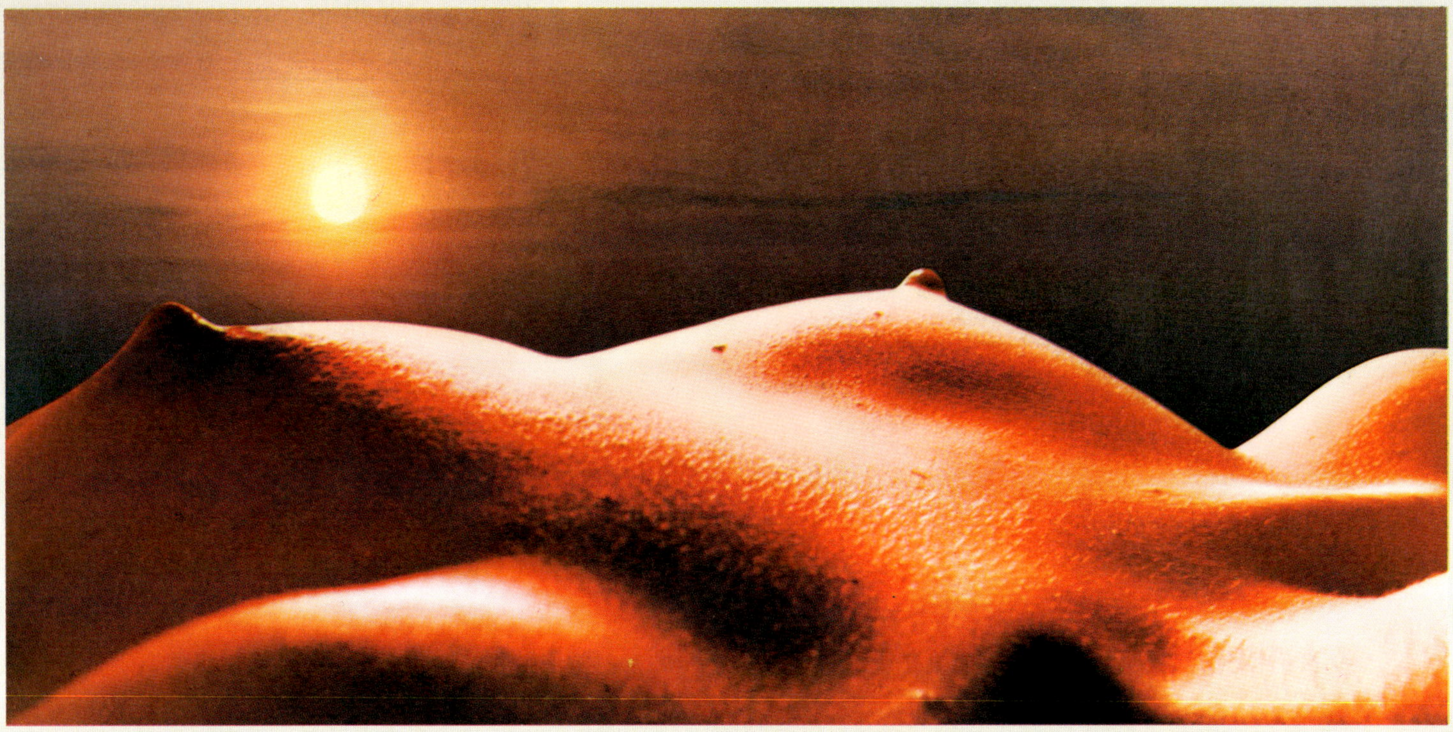

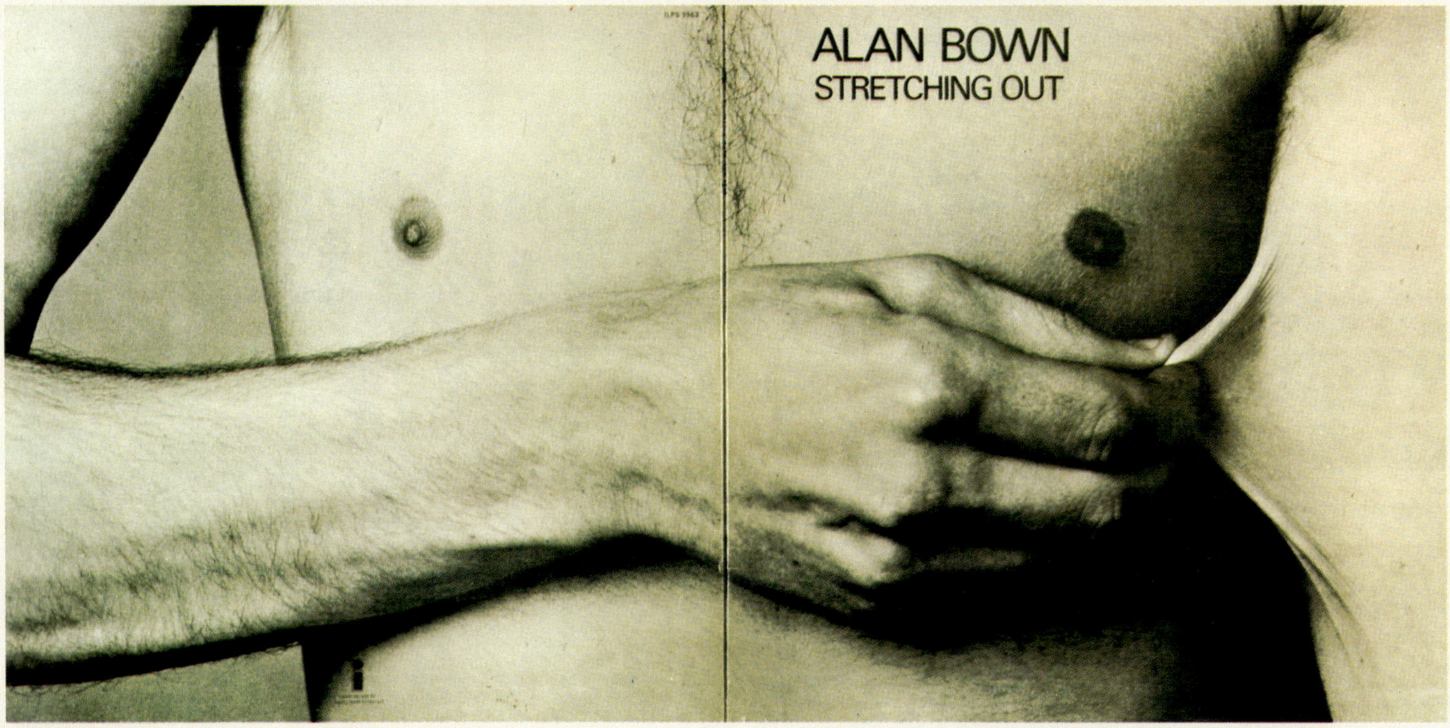

1970 COCHISE FRONT COVER

1971 ALAN BOWN 'STRETCHING OUT' FRONT COVER

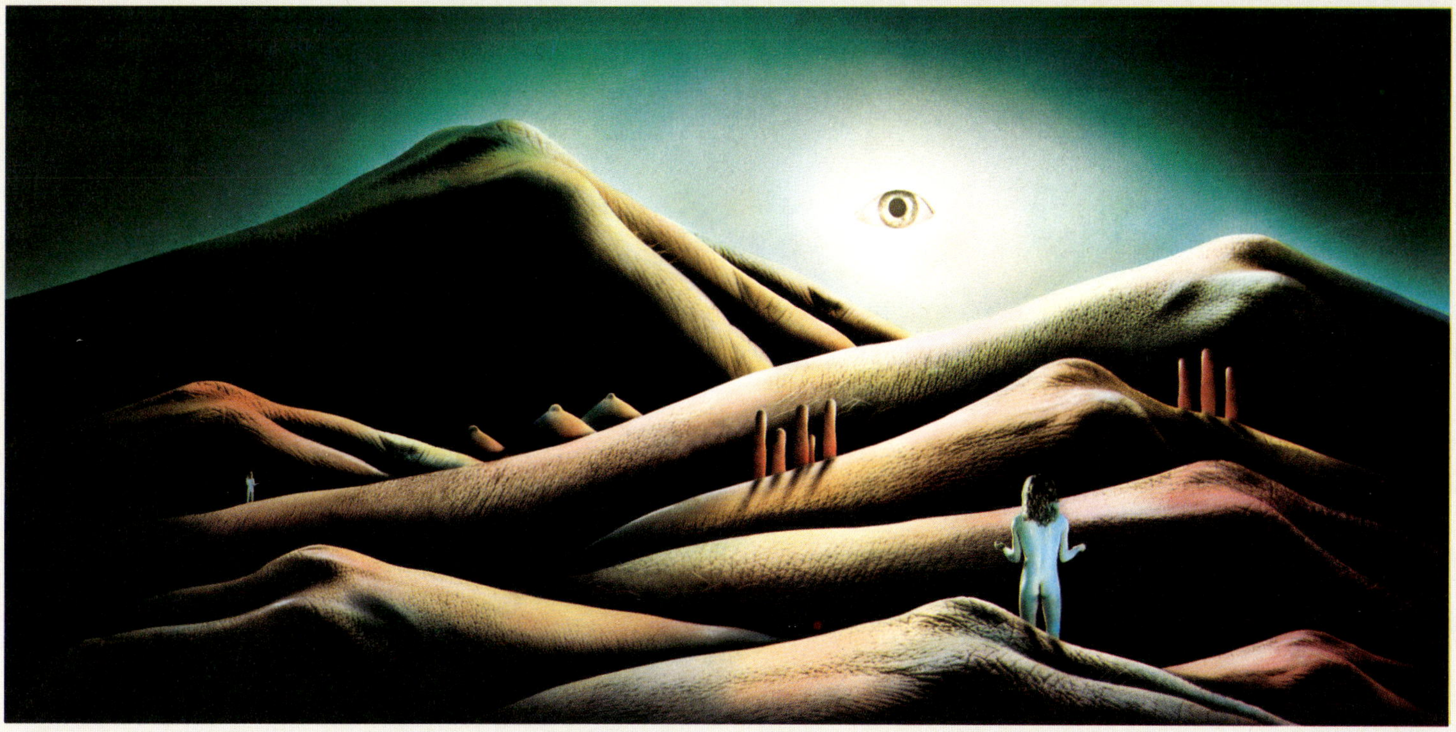

Hello to you. This is not the beginning chronologically. What we've done is to lay out the book alphabetically under various headings which loosely describe areas of our work. Sometimes these headings refer to particular kinds of imagery or to individual jobs, and sometimes they relate to other more general things like our past history. Most of the headings are, however, rather arbitrary and so all sorts of stuff tends to crop up in odd places — like right here for instance.

One of our preoccupations is with the human body. The pictures in this section are most particularly about detail and not about full figures. Montrose's 'Jump On It' is an attempt at turning a very real and sensual part of the body into an abstract geometrical shape by going in close and posing the girl in an exact way. Toe Fat uses anatomical detail in a montage designed primarily to shock the viewer. The breasts of Cochise simulate a landscape, non-terrestrial perhaps, whilst 'Savage Eye' is on the one hand simply impactful, and on the other a kind of dialogue. The eye belongs to someone who is telling you to mind your own business, or alternatively, is giving you a knowing and playful come-on. Alan Bown's 'Stretching Out' is a curious idea taken from some work of our friend John Blake — did you know skin stretched like that?

Our cover designs usually refer quite specifically to the records and we make a point of listening to the music in most cases and reading the lyrics if there are any. Toe Fat, however, was designed from an idea about telecommunication. In the distant future the evolution of psychic powers will render normal sense organs redundant. Hence they're absent. We see a head of contourless skin which houses the psychic transmitters and receivers. When we used a photo of an actual toe in the artwork the result was initially so strong that even for a heavy rock outfit it felt inappropriate. Why the client ever accepted it is beyond us, but it is *supposed* to be grotesque. Cochise wanted a straightforward lyrical picture but this lunar bodyscape felt more interesting by far than a real slice of pretty countryside. Pretty Things' 'Savage Eye' and Alan Bown's 'Stretching Out' are designs stimulated by the album titles. The bright red crotch for Montrose was originally completed for another

1973 FLASH 'OUT OF OUR HANDS' FRONT COVER

client who, it seemed to me, suffered from terrible sexual repressions. At the end he rejected it in a fit of pique. Montrose had already decided on their title 'Jump On It' and were keen to have the design. They weren't so keen when we submitted a disclaimer along with the artwork — a note to the effect that whilst appreciating the relevance of this title we lamented its complete lack of elegance.

In thinking up designs to be photographed the more methods of photography, printing and montage that are at your disposal the better. There are less limitations. If, however, straight photography is your pursuit then an exploration of a variety of methods could be a distraction. You may be dilettanteish about it, as perhaps we have been, and avoid exploring grain and film, or light and shade with due thoroughness. Thus we know little about photography in depth but have worked with the medium enough to know quite a bit about how to use it in making up pictures and realising fantasies. For example, the body for Cochise is infra-red film (no filter) developed as negative, not transparency, and printed as normal c-type. It was then montaged on to another c-type print of the sky, shot on normal colour negative stock. 'Stretching Out' is five by four black and white studio work, whilst Toe Fat is both collage (figures in background) and phased printing — the neck and toe are joined in exposing one negative and vignetting off at the join by hand movements that block off the light, but not in a definite line, and then exposing the other negative on to the same part but vignetting the other way. Ordinary c-type colour prints were used.

Montrose, Pretty Things and Flash are black and white photos that have been hand-tinted with photo-retouching dyes. These translucent dyes sink into the print, unlike paint, which lies on top. They are very intense, but because they follow the silver bromide of the print, becoming part of the picture, they can be used quite subtly. The dyes are applied by airbrush or ordinary bristle brush. They can be diluted with water, but cannot be washed out. This, in fact, entails a lengthy business of building up the colour bit by bit and since nobody in Hipgnosis can draw or paint we employ a retoucher — Richard Manning. He's responsible for the colouring on Montrose, 'Savage Eye' and others as well as for the black and white retouching on just about everything we've done in the last four years. We think he's excellent, if a trifle argumentative. But then he has good reason because we're forever looking over his shoulder asking him to add a bit here and add a bit there.

We've been fortunate with retouchers. Maurice Tate did Flash 'Knickers' and 'House on the Hill' (pg. 124) in inspired fashion. Phil Crennel coloured 'Houses of the Holy' and the Flash in this section, but we lost him owing to his adventurous eccentricity. He vanished in a barge to sail round England. Terry Day was the first, and perhaps the best, black and white retoucher. He was very helpful in the early days, but as his business expanded he got too pricey for us, and we got too mean for him.

I don't remember when we first became enthusiastic about hand tinting; maybe it was some old pictures of the Himalayas shown a while back in the Sunday Times. 'House on the Hill' was our first attempt and was such a mind blower that we've been keen ever since. (Too keen, perhaps, and done it at times when not totally appropriate.) Like everything else, we've learned about it as we went along. Flash 'Out of our Hands' is a black and white collage of several knuckles and fingers which is then photocopied (to get it on one print) and finally hand coloured. 'Savage Eye' is a black and white print, made sepia to soften it, and then hand coloured mostly with bristle brush. Montrose is black and white and very slightly sepiaed and then hand tinted with airbrush because of the large flat areas.

One can do a lot with hand tinting and it's not hard to do it 'impressionistically'. We've tended to do it 'expressionistically' or literally — that is to render colours that could be there in reality but which have a slightly unreal feeling, either by simulating old photos ('House on the Hill') or accentuating the expected natural colours (UFO 'Phenomenon'). This involves great attention to detail and exactness. Continual adjustments to hand colouring can cause a sleeve artwork to be delivered late. If one has to do it stage by stage one can only tell if it's finished when one has been at it a long time. The result is only as good as the tones in the original print, the skill of the retoucher and the feel or vision of the designer.

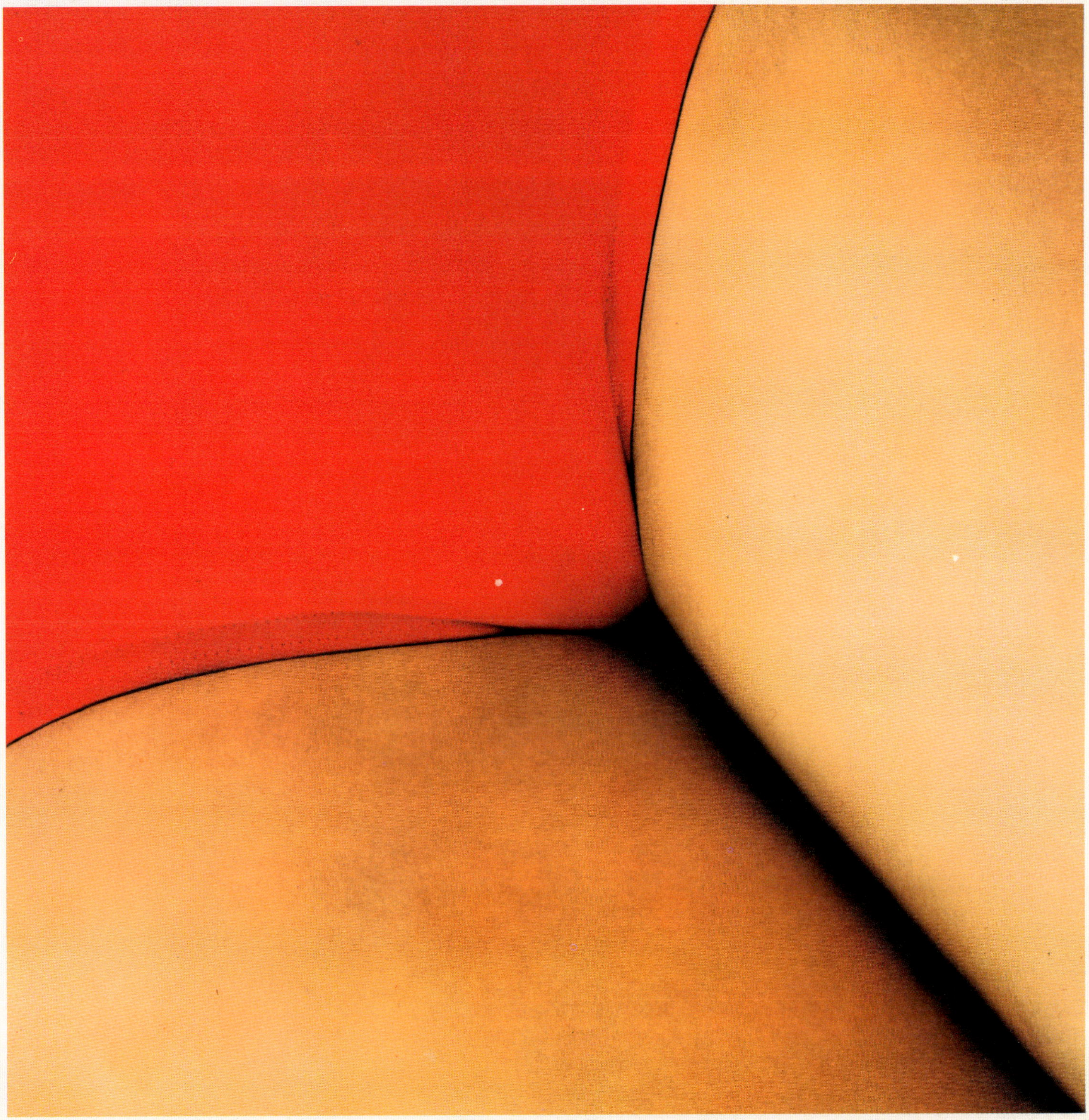

1976 MONTROSE 'JUMP ON IT' FRONT COVER

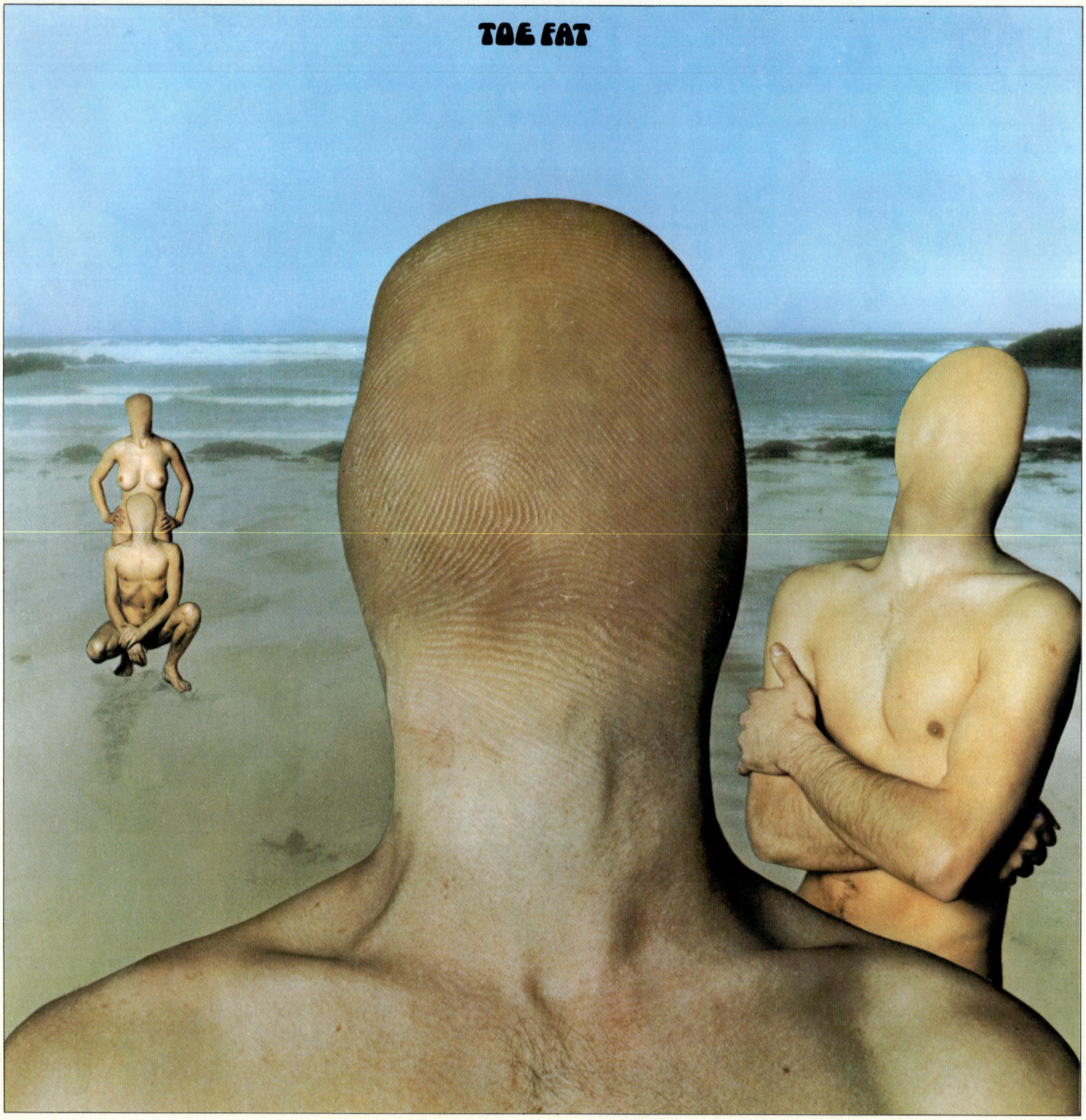

1970 TOE FAT FRONT COVER

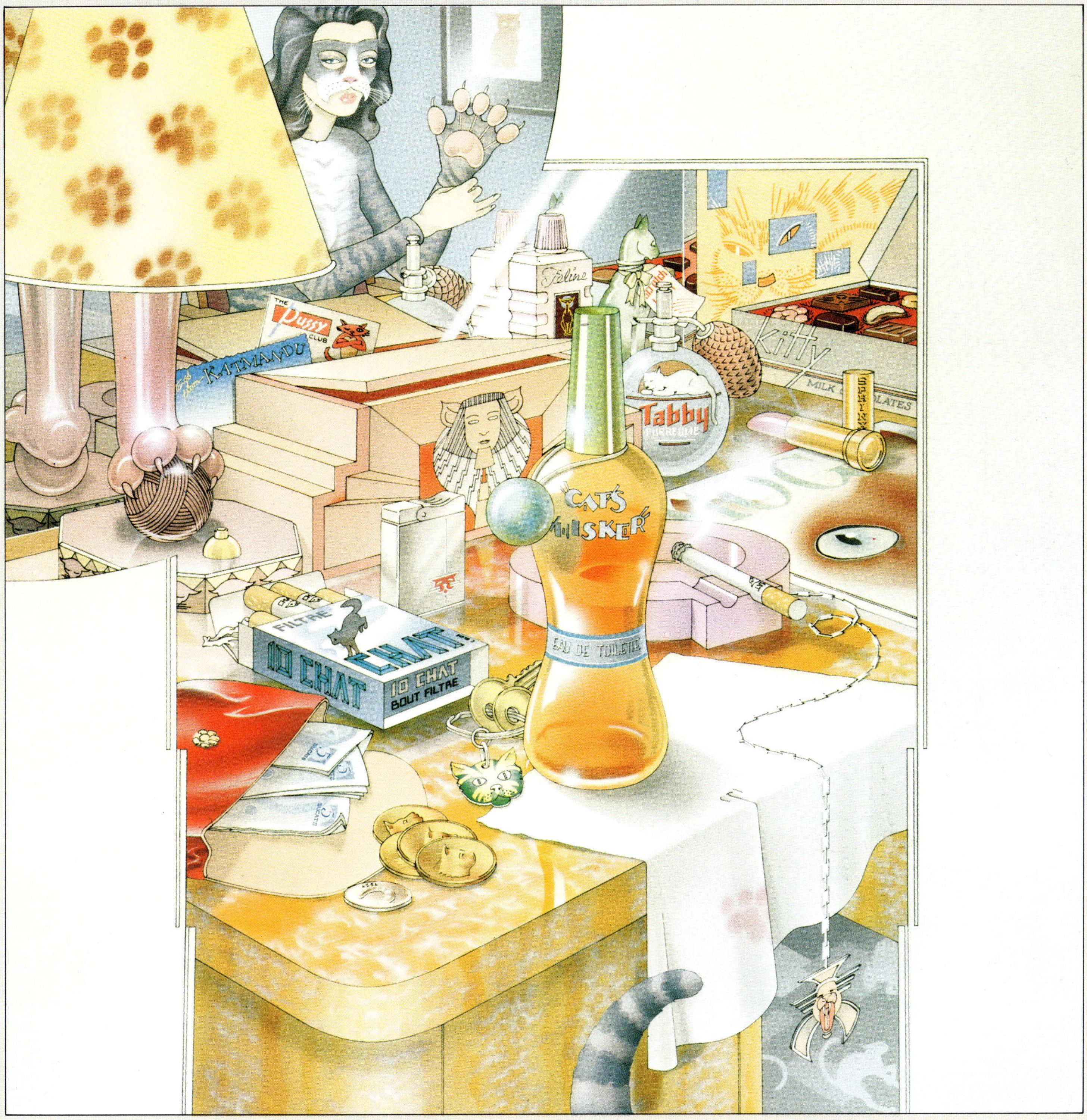

1976 AL STEWART 'YEAR OF THE CAT' ILLUSTRATION COLIN ELGIE FRONT COVER

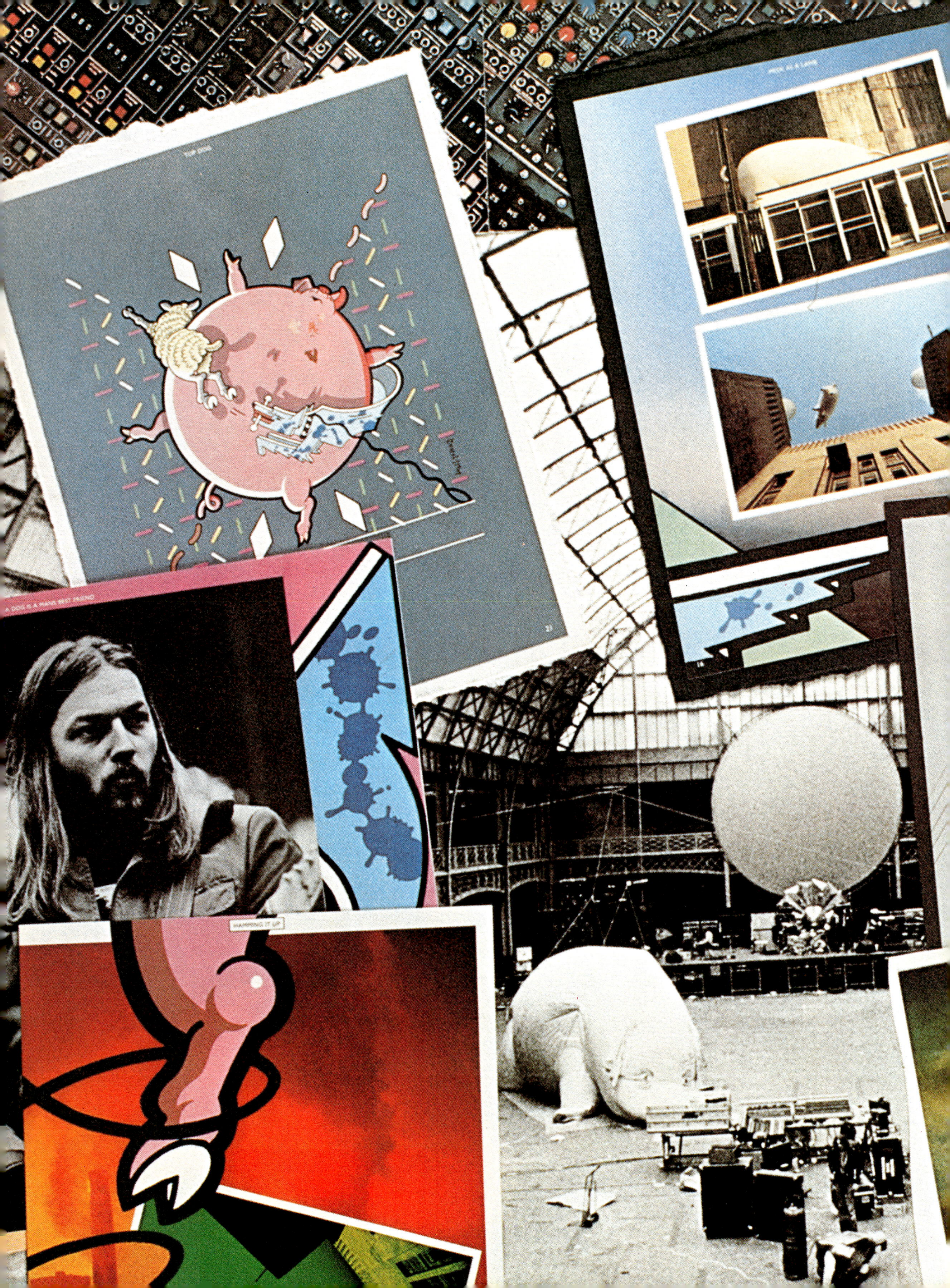

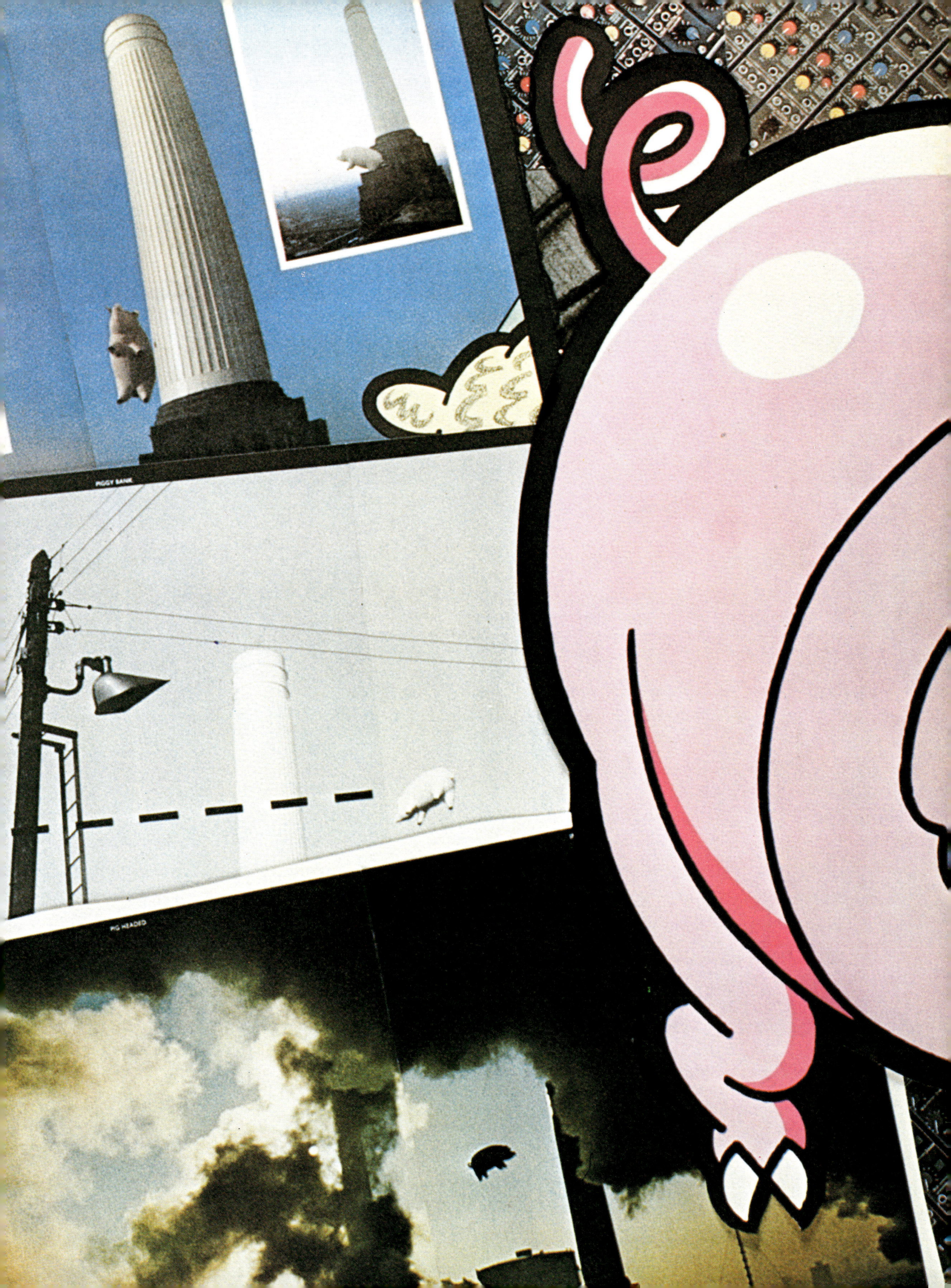

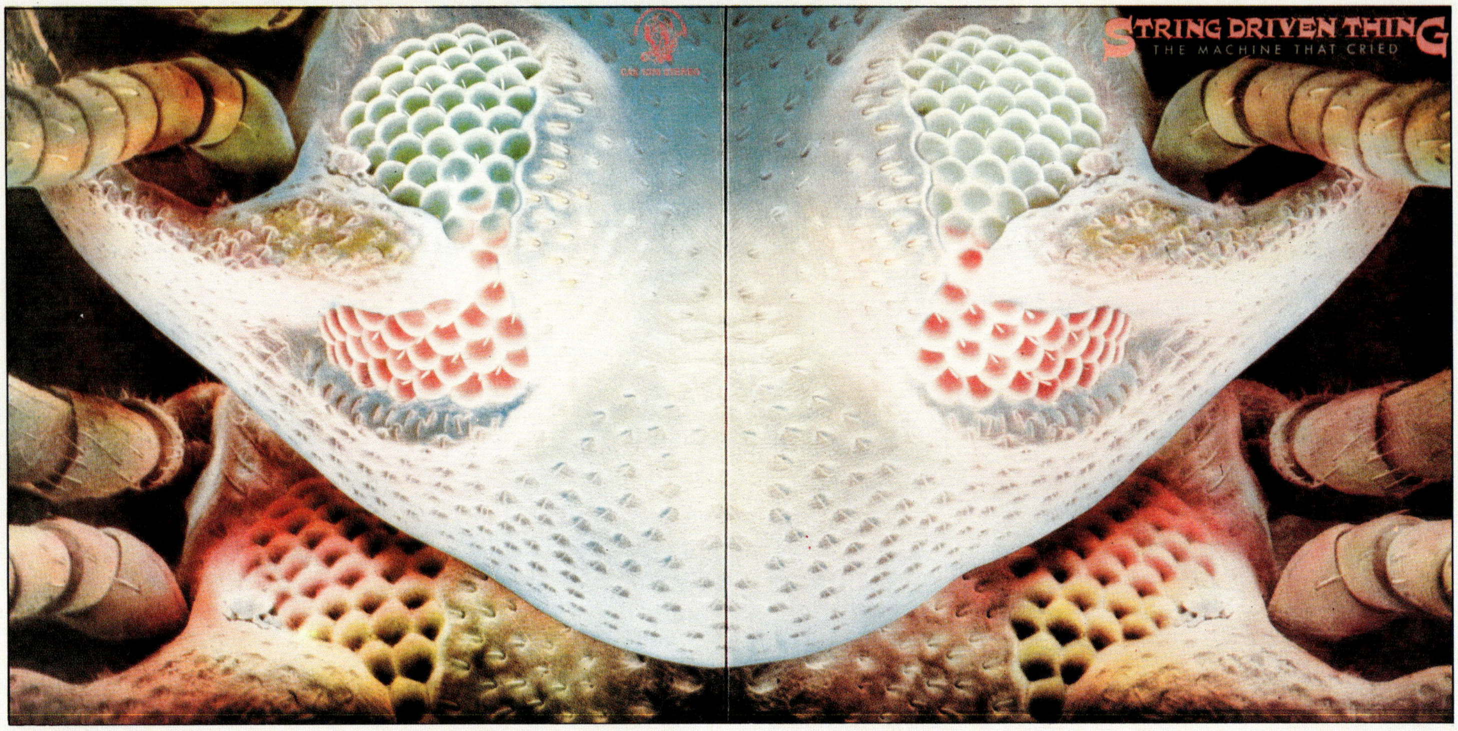

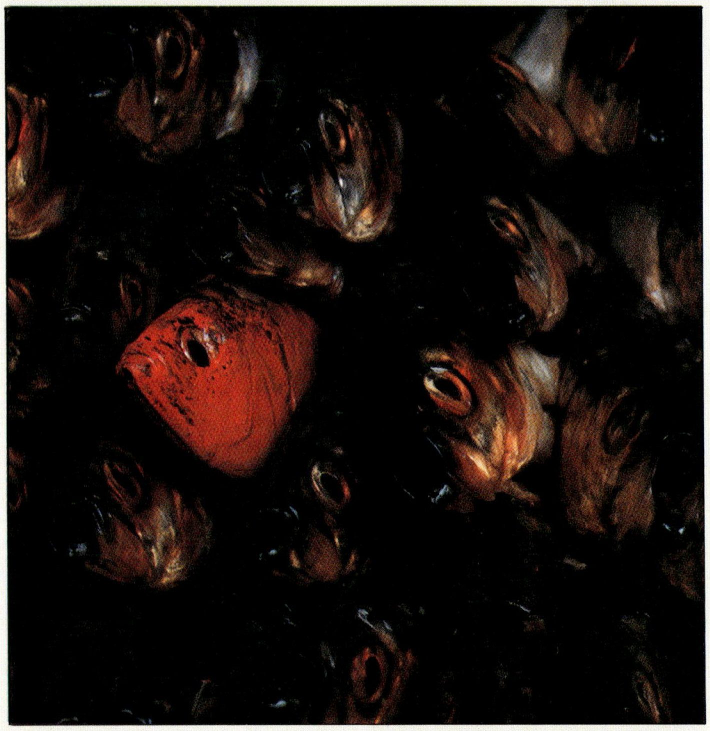

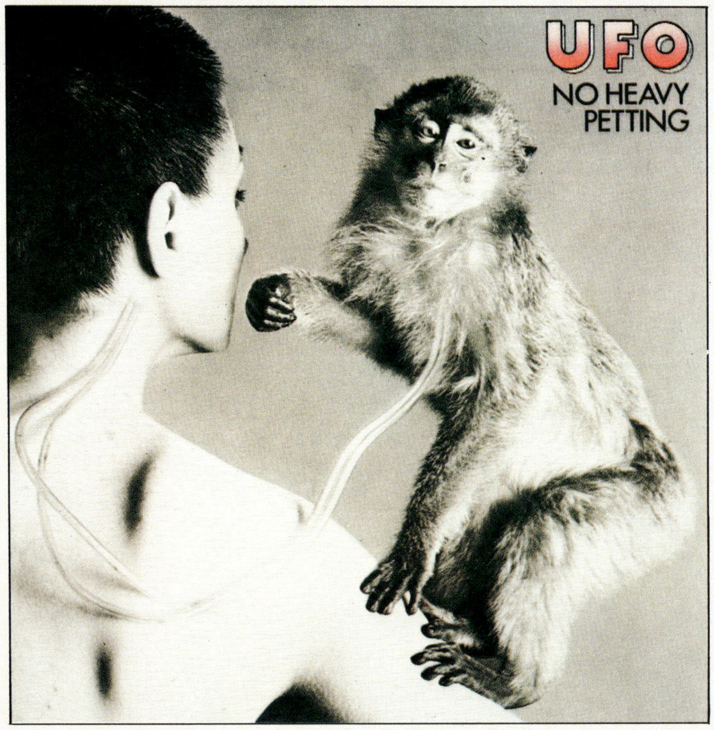

◁ PINK FLOYD 'ANIMALS' SONGBOOK

STRING DRIVEN THING UFO 9 DAYS WONDER

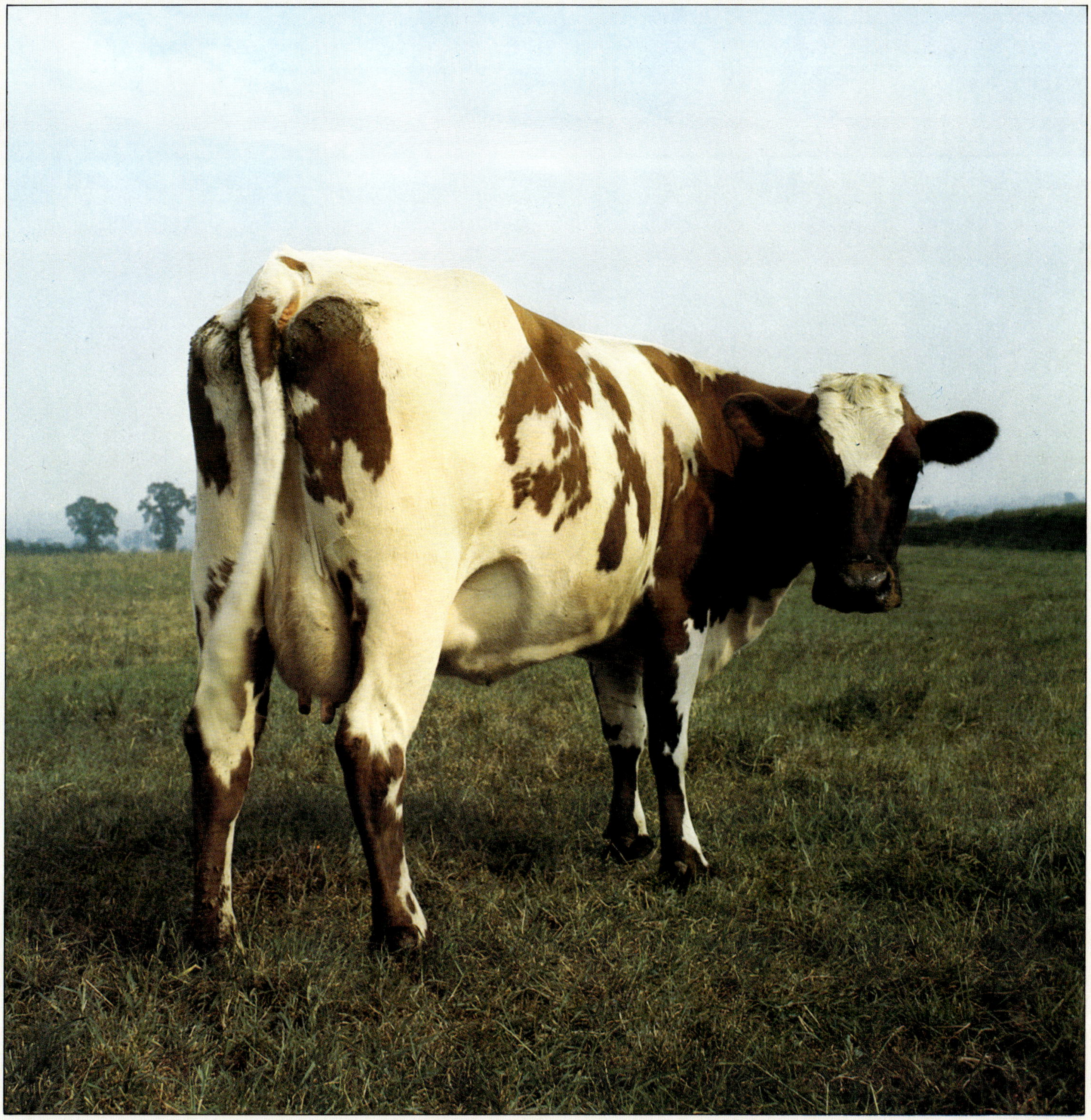

1970 PINK FLOYD 'ATOM HEART MOTHER' FRONT COVER

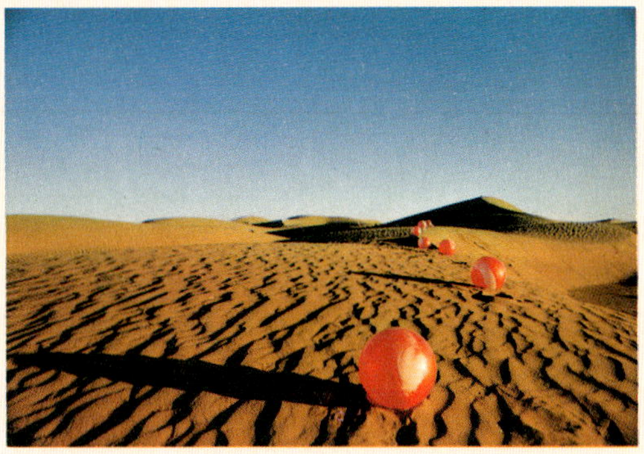

We've included several designs involving balls but I only want to talk about 'Elegy' for the Nice. I think this is one of the most vital of all pieces within the er . . . psychological development of Hipgnosis. The inspiration came from the music, late at night, and was a simple, spontaneous occurrence. The record evoked images of sparse landscapes. I imagined a desert but it felt too empty by itself and so was soon peppered with red balls, stretching as far as the eye could see, as if they covered the desert from end to end. And that's it. Charisma Records thought it bizarre, especially from the minute watercolour sketch which Po did, whilst Keith Emerson was very preoccupied with his music at the time and just told us to get on with it. So we were off to the desert. Our first job overseas, spending other people's money. It had better come out okay or we would be deep in the proverbial shit.

We felt like a couple of teenagers; riding the airways to mysterious Marrakech in Morocco, with sixty red vinyl footballs stowed in the cargo hold. They were, of course, deflated otherwise the air pressure drop at high altitude would have exploded them. When we landed in Marrakech the customs officer was very suspicious of our baggage. Sixty uninflated footballs for a photograph in the desert indeed! He didn't believe us for a moment and was beginning to wonder if we were in the business of importing goods for sale. He asked us for the appropriate papers but before we could reply his attention was fortunately diverted by a large film crew passing through at the same time.

The first night we stayed in the Mamounia Palace Hotel. It was decorated with tesselated floors, ornately carved ceilings and mosaic columns. Outside lay a luxurious garden of palm trees and lush tropical shrubs surrounding an underlit marble swimming pool. In the dining salon a pianist played whilst the guests were seated for supper. The clerk looked askance at our jeans and long hair. "You can't go in there without a tie", he said brusquely. Instead we sought food in the Medina, the market square, which was full of stalls, cafés, snake-charmers, dancers and hundreds of Arabs milling about, hustling noisily for food or money. We obtained the services of a young lad of nine or ten who not only kept the hustlers at bay but also installed us in a terraced restaurant overlooking the Medina. He arranged the food and then asked innocently, "Would you like two kilograms of kif?" Well, we declined, didn't we, because we were professionals now (?) and had to get on with the job.

Next morning we drove in our hired Renault estate car two hundred and fifty miles over the Atlas mountains to Zagora on the edge of the Sahara. If you want a desert, we thought, you might as well hit the biggest. The dunes were forty miles further on, across two sets of hills and an intervening plain or 'piste'. This 'piste' was dead flat and made up of zillions of small rocks. We checked out the dunes immediately and nearly got lost returning in the dark.

It had been cloudy that day. We needed to shoot the next day because we then had to return to Marrakech to catch the plane home. The tight budget didn't allow for days in the sun, nor time for experimentation. Fortunately, the next day was clear and sunny. We got up at dawn and hit the desert road. The art of driving across the piste was to go either below 60 m.p.h. and ride on the ground, or go over 60 m.p.h. and ride on top of the small rocks. Just our luck that the Renault would do exactly 60 m.p.h. flat out, and to go slower would take up too much time. After shooting the inside picture on the way, we arrived at the chosen spot around lunchtime. Back in Zagora the bicycle shop had inflated all the balls for us and they were packed jam tight in the back of the car. Red ones and striped ones, in case we fancied a variation. We parked the car and unloaded the balls. And it was truly amazing — the empty desert stretched away into the

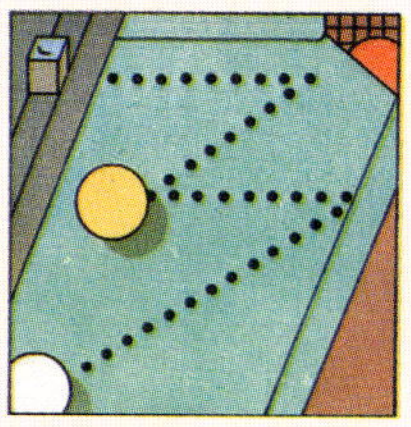

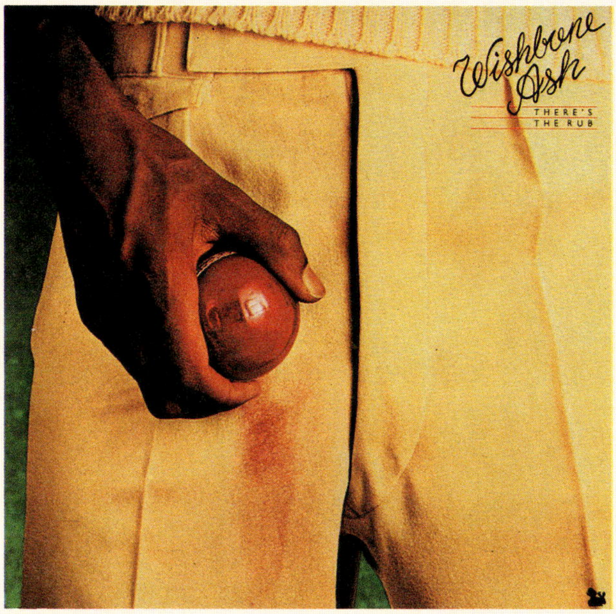

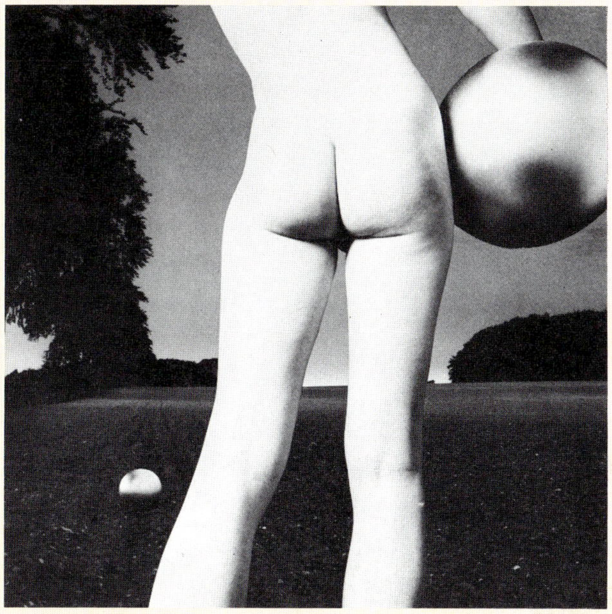

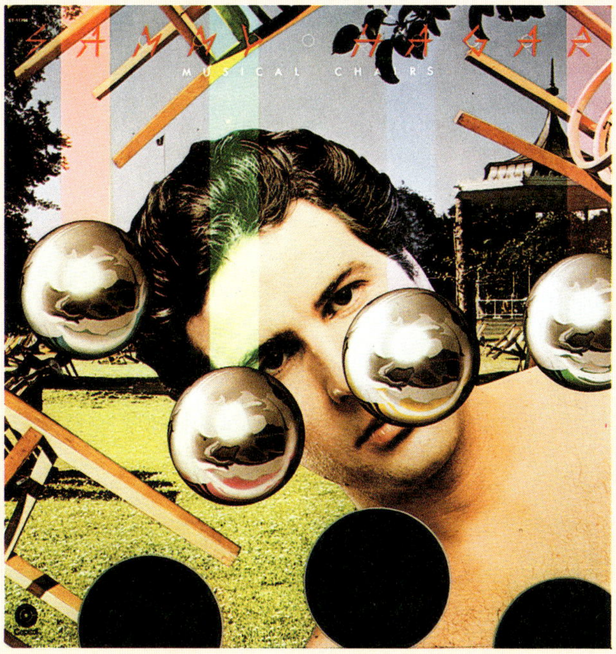

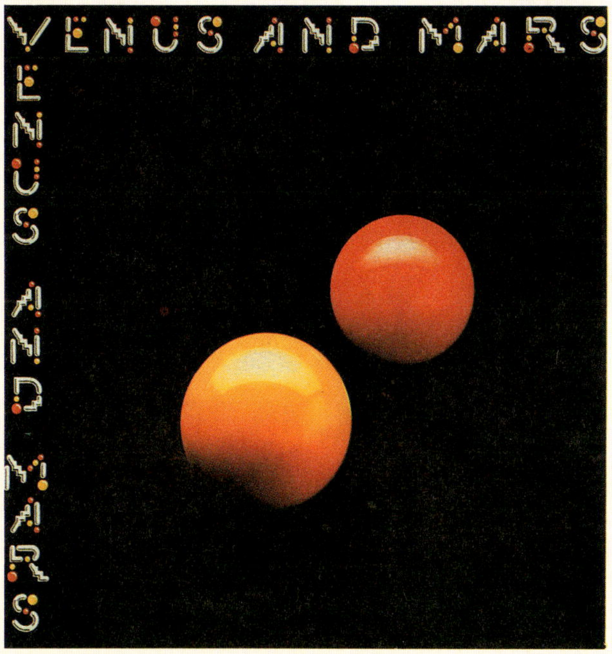

SAMMY HAGAR   WISHBONE ASH   WINGS   CREATION   1971   NICE 'ELEGY'   FRONT COVER ▷

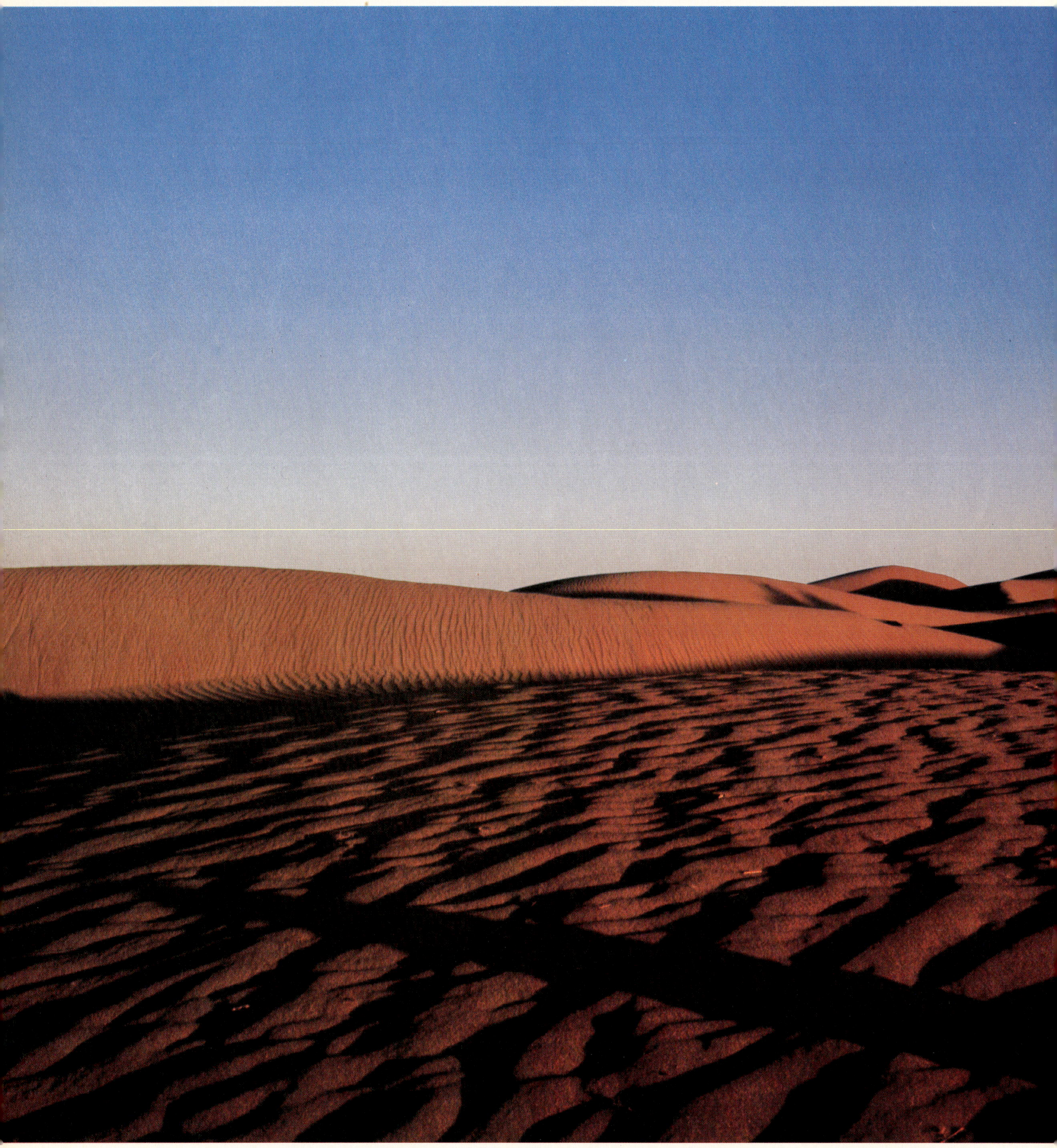

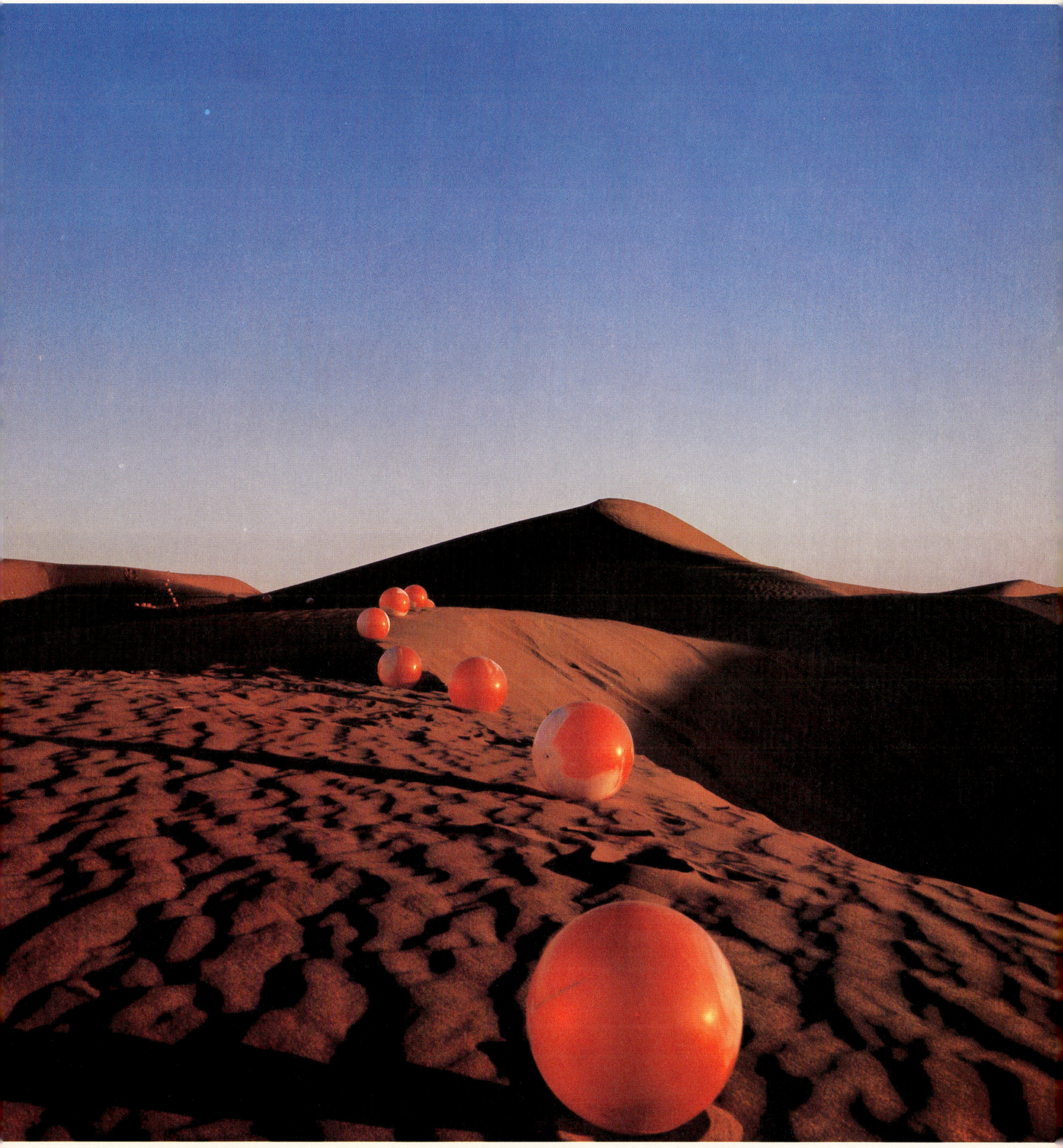

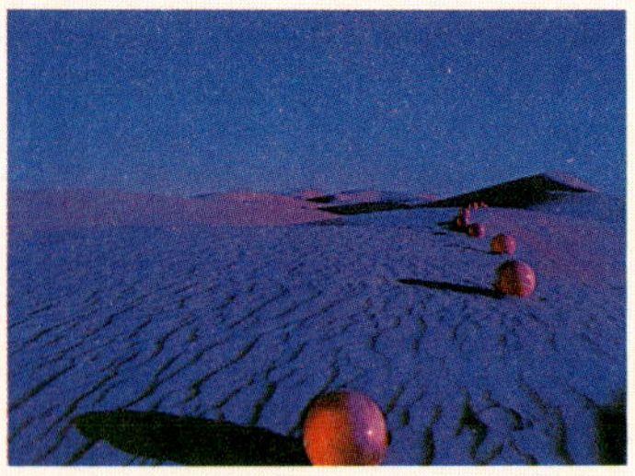

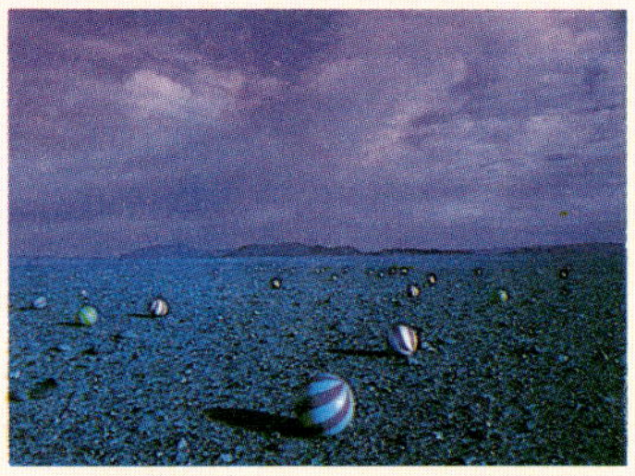

distance and in the foreground red and candy-striped balls were dotted all around. It looked more incongruous than we'd ever imagined.

The problem was to locate a beautiful set of dunes and to place the balls in a curved line. But how to position the balls without leaving footprints? Bright sparks that we were, we'd even thought of bringing a brush, to sweep away the desert! We wandered about desperately searching, hollering out to each other across the sand, kicking footballs up and down the dunes. But the sun was beginning to go down. Finally we found a spot where the balls could be placed on the rim of the craters and the down slopes of the dunes, thus leaving no marks, or ones that would be covered by collapsing sand. Po was arranging the balls when he fell over right at the end of the line (look closely and you can see). Time was running out. We were shouting at the top of our voices, "Third ball to the left", "Tenth ball to the right", in order to get a good line. Then we shot and the sun vanished. Gone, in a trice. Two rolls of film only. Phew!

But then the car got stuck in the sand as we tried to leave. Instant panic. Newspaper headlines would announce (in small print) that the skeletons of two young photographers were discovered in the desert. Miserable fate indeed. But the luck held and we got out somehow. We drove back hurriedly to the hotel, utterly wasted.

Next day was cloudy. We were about to leave when Po discovered he'd lost his prize leather jacket. Worst of all the hotel key was in it, the two languishing somewhere back amongst the sand dunes. And the hotel wanted £40 for the key. "Eez a very expensive, all ze way from Paris," they said. We had no money left. We mulled it over in the foyer, contemplating a quick runner when the gendarmes arrived and took us to the local nick. Oh no, stuck in a Moroccan jail for weeks and nobody, not even Charisma Records, would know where we were. And then the luck held some more. The police were charming, sharing mint tea and almonds on the verandah, chatting gaily of English politics. And then we were kindly bailed out by an American photographer, shooting swanky shots of new BMWs in the desert evening.

On our way again, but now time was short. The plane left the next day at noon and there were still the Atlas Mountains to cross. We'd been advised not to try it in the dark because they got very icy and misty, but we had no choice. And we were young and foolish.

I shall never forget it. More terrifying than Jaws, more horrifying than King Kong, more frightening than . . . we took regular nips from the bottle of whisky we'd brought to steady our nerves. Six thousand feet up, windy roads, pitch black, pockets of mist and cloud, icy corners and suddenly rambling oil tankers veering round bends driven by crazy Arabs smashed on kif. Praise to Allah that we made it and rolled into Marrakech at first light. I crashed out immediately and had the most violent nightmare of my life, reliving the mountain dash, careering off cliff roads, dying a thousand deaths and waking up drenched in sweat. I've not often been so scared, so physically terrified. All this for art I thought, we must be mad.

The sixty footballs couldn't go back on the plane because they were now inflated. Po reckoned to sell them, having a good nose for a bargain. Surprisingly the casbah was a dead loss. Then we tried the Jewish market with better luck. As we were unloading the balls from the back of the car, bouncing them into the shop, a gendarme on traffic duty began to get very curious. He left his post to the honking of horns and sauntered over. I thought this was it, busted for the illegal trafficking of footballs. He sidled round the back of the car and whispered sheepishly in my ear — could he buy one for his son? Well, said I, much relieved, of course he could. In fact, we'd give him a couple. We passed him later directing traffic with one ball under his arm, and the other sandwiched between his legs.

We hurriedly dumped the car back with the hire people, since it was by then totally ruined, and caught the plane home. And when the films were processed it looked terrific and Charisma liked it and Keith Emerson later confided that it was, perhaps, more together than the record. The private confidence that this whole adventure gave us I consider equalled only by the public confidence we derived from 'Dark Side of the Moon'. I mean, it all worked out okay, and no-one was more surprised by this than ourselves. The inference seemed to be that if you go somewhere amazing you'd got a good chance of taking a really satisfying picture.

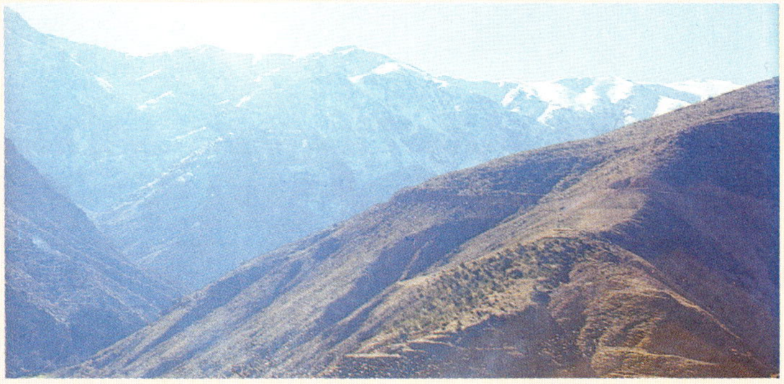

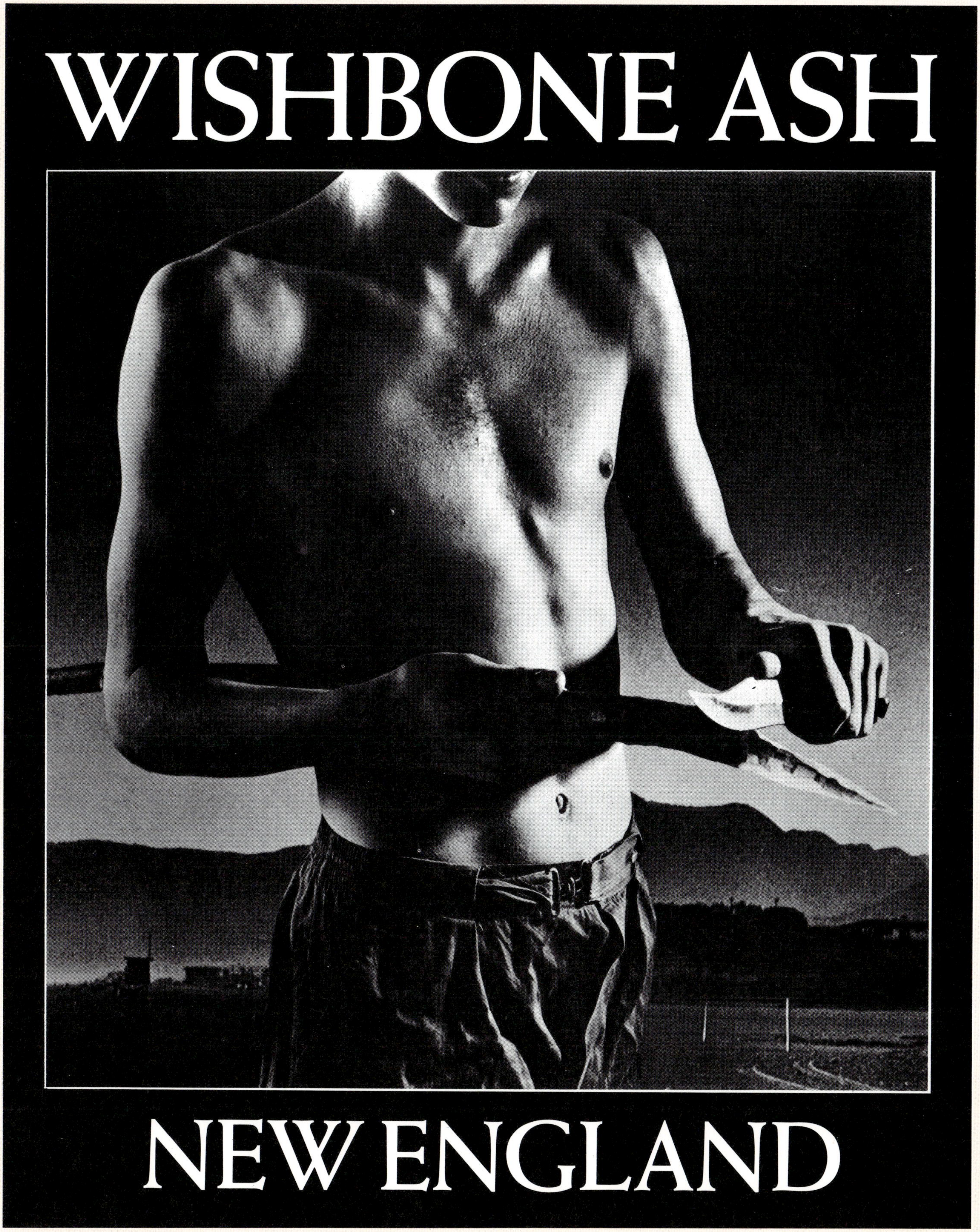

1976 WISHBONE ASH 'NEW ENGLAND' POSTER

1972 FLASH FRONT COVER ▷

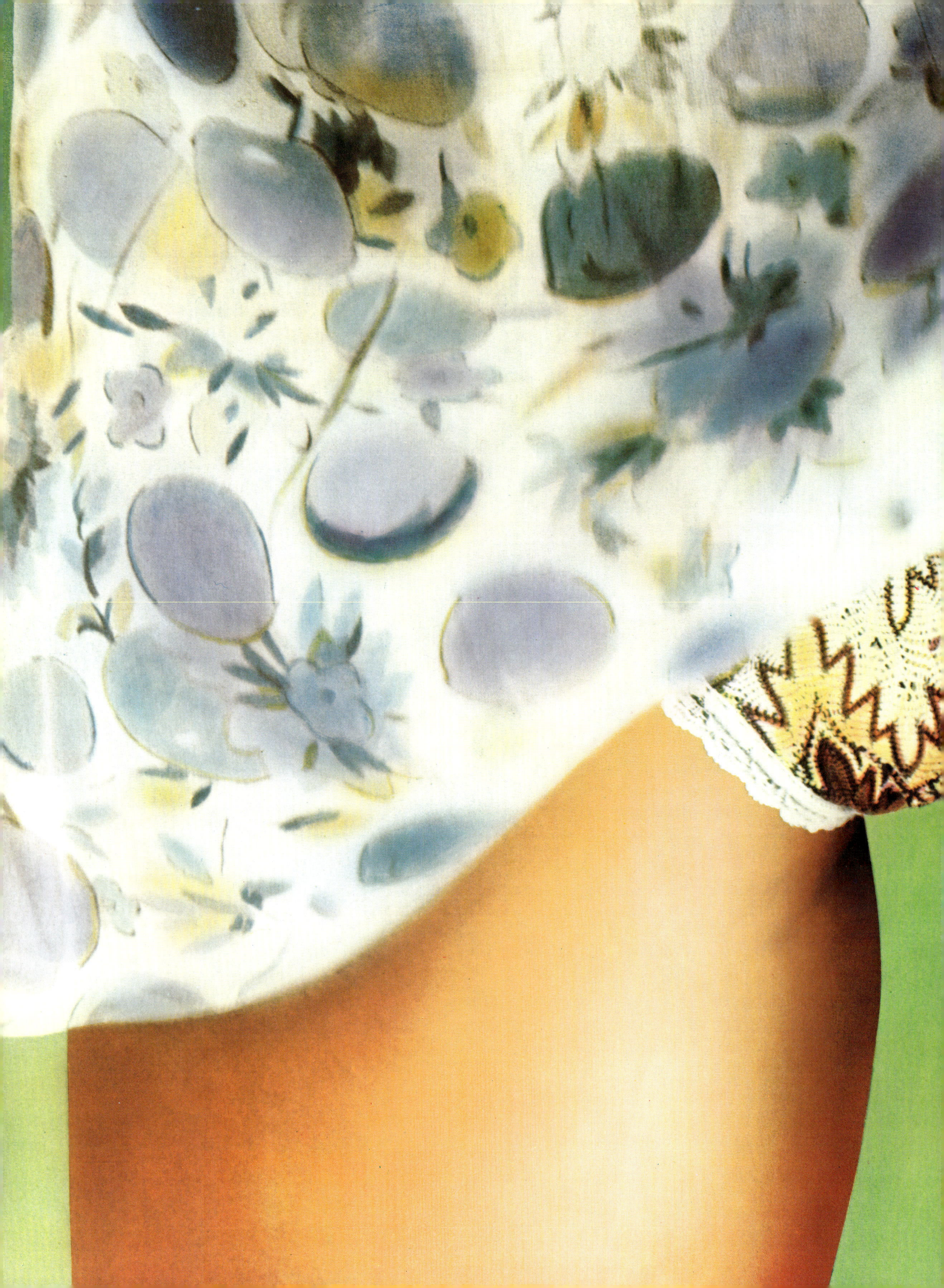

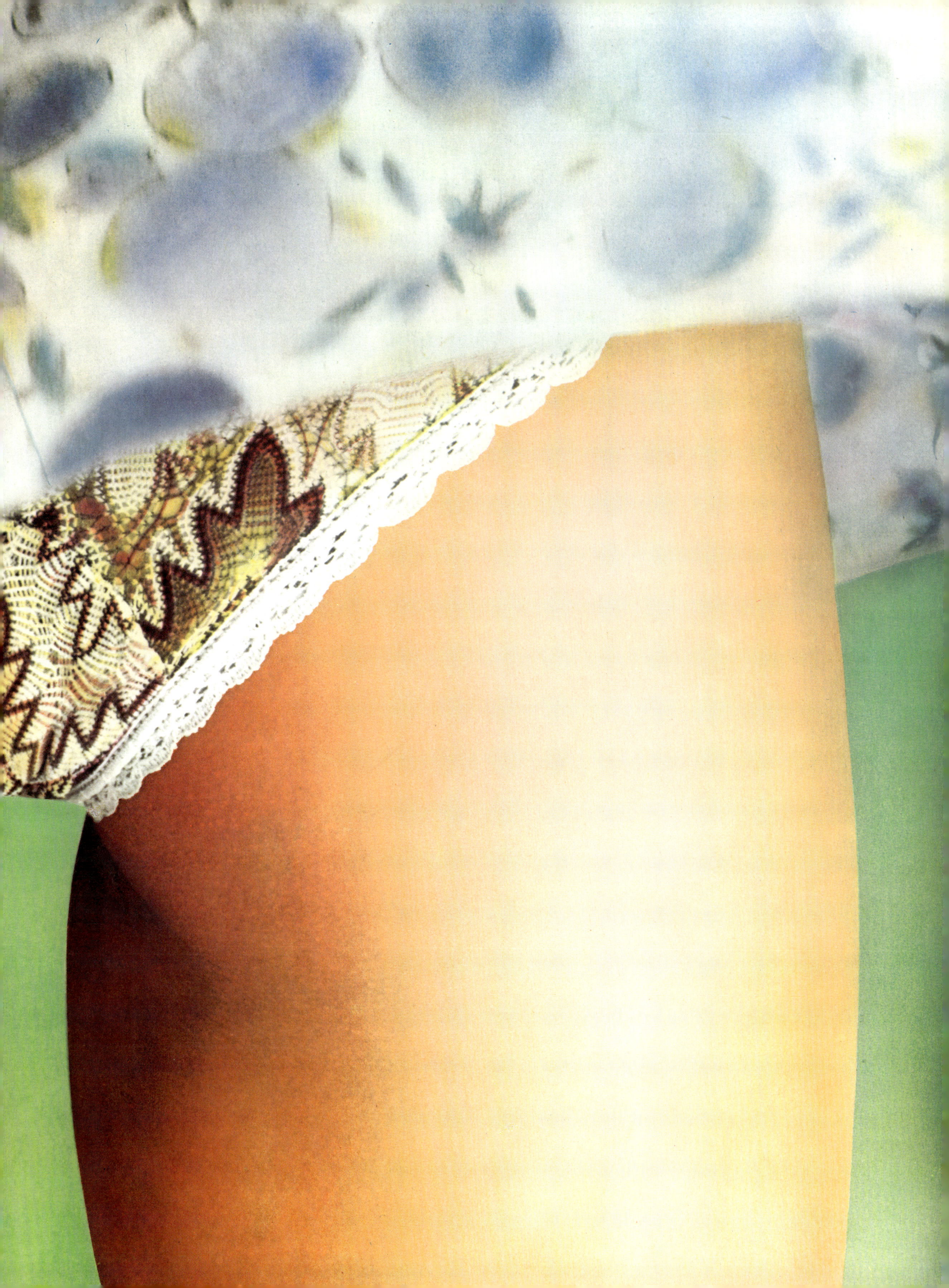

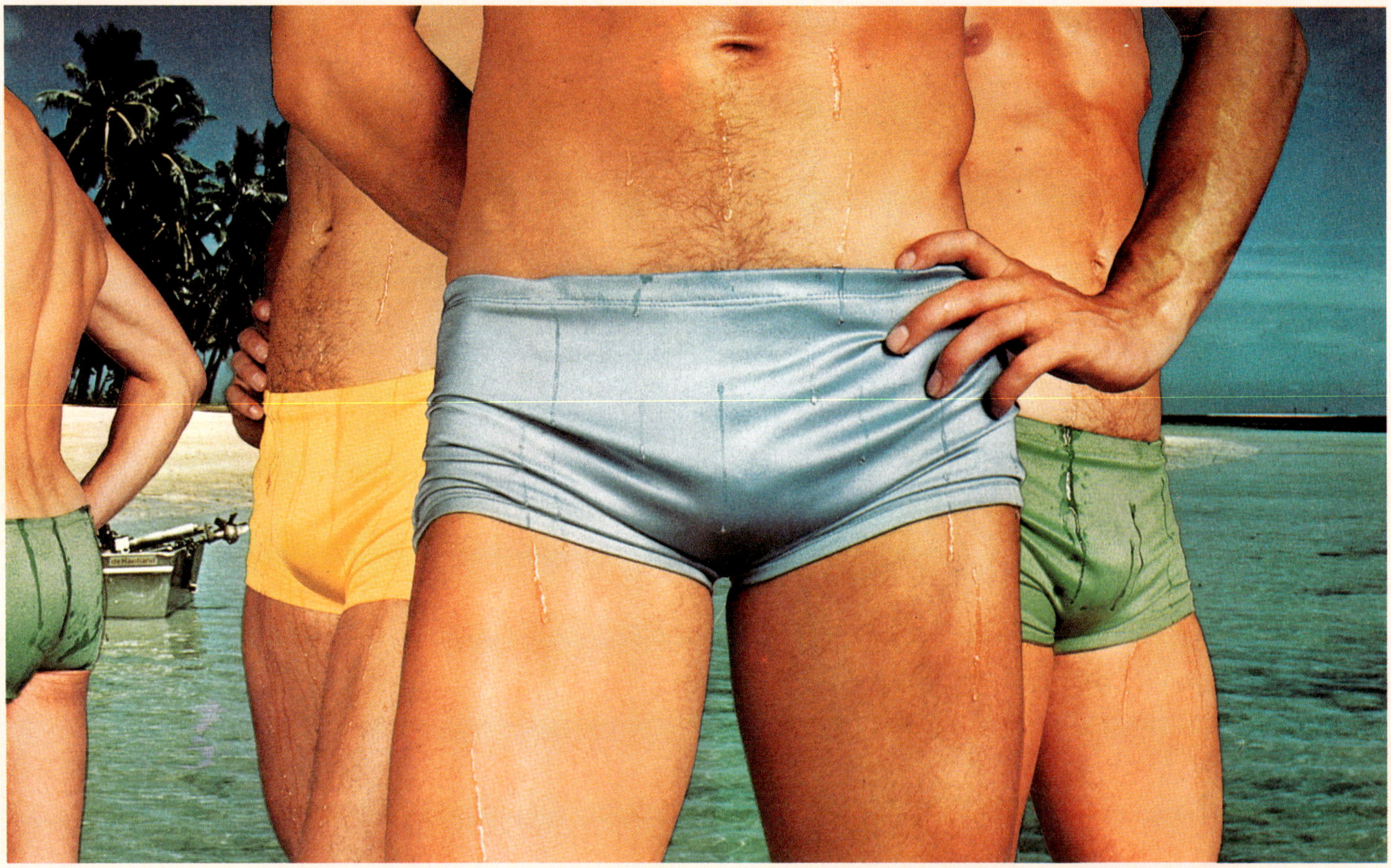

1975 WINKIES FRONT COVER

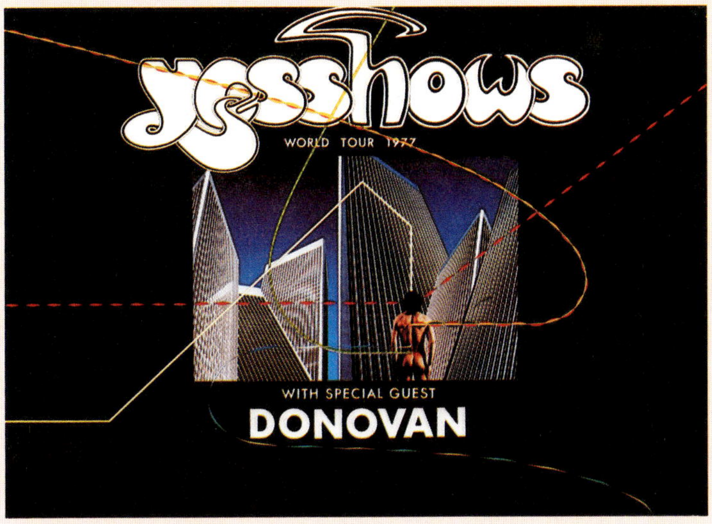

Yes' 'Going For The One' is a montage made up from colour reversal prints — prints taken straight from $2\frac{1}{4}''$ ektachrome transparencies. The lines are drawn in black and white and then reversed out mechanically from the montaged background and printed in specified tints, i.e. percentages of the primary printing inks. The poster for 'Dark Side of the Moon' is a 35mm infra-red transparency. The photograph was shot in the afternoon using a yellow filter and underexposing. Quatermass is comprised of a montage of black and white prints and a reversed double print, i.e. the building was exposed on one half of the paper whilst shielding the other, and then printed on the second half whilst shielding the first exposure. It was shot in the afternoon just after a shower. 'Oakdown Farm' is photographed on negative colour film and then printed on ordinary c-type paper but exposed through a neg bag, placed adjacent to the negative itself in the enlarger. This accounts for the mottled screen effect. 'Song Remains The Same' for Led Zeppelin is an illustration by George Hardie.

For those of you who don't know, montage is the sticking together of two or more prints, one over the other, and is not to be confused with superimposition, which is the exposing of two or more negatives on the one print (or the same negative more than once). With superimposition one image is placed on top of another and you can see both at the same time. In montage you can only see the one image, though it may comprise several parts. Now, the great things about montage are that it's easy, there are no rules and it's great fun. Images change abruptly on the addition of other images. Most obviously, you can bend reality. Pictures that may associate emotionally but not fit literally (follow perspective etc.) give an impressionistic kind of result when montaged, like Steely Dan's 'Can't Buy A Thrill' (not ours) or Wishbone Ash's 'Front Page News'. Images that are joined tightly (keep perspective) provide for the realistic rendition of the impossible or the unlikely, for instance 'Houses of the Holy' (pg. 34), UFO (pg. 80), Uno (pg. 45) and Yes in this section.

We prefer montage that more or less follows perspective. Winkies (pg. 24) is, in fact, a montage. Three separate blokes could stand like that but it's not likely — so we took three individual photographs of the same bloke. By shooting one at a time we could concentrate on getting the stance right and the droplets of glycerine positioned where we wanted them on the body. If we design a piece that can only be done by montage we photograph according to initial drawings and preliminary tests. It's also a good technique for keeping all the ingredients of a picture sharp. The focus of a lens will only carry so far.

The Yes sleeve shows a futuristic city which could just about exist, but only just. Many photos were taken of the skyscrapers (Century City in Los Angeles) from many different angles. They had been photographed previously in black and white so we had some idea of what was needed. After examining the colour transparencies we obtained a large number of colour prints in order to cut them out, stick them together, rearrange them and then cut out still more and replace some with others. This shuffling process can last days, taking long intervals to scrutinize the results carefully before deciding on various changes, only to examine them all over again. It's often these shufflings that make or break a piece — by moving one part a quarter of an inch this way and then using a slightly darker or smaller print alongside it and then recutting it, one can greatly improve the end result. The joy of all this cutting up and sticking down and then rearranging is that you gradually build up a composite piece over which you can exercise a lot of discretion. The only limitations are your imagination and the photos with which you start.

Now, when you're doing a montage (or collage) using existing material you just have to hunt about a lot. Such montage is a piece of cake — just take some magazines, a scalpel and some glue and cut out and stick together whatever you fancy. We don't do this, in fact, for we prefer to shoot specific photos that are intended to fit specific designs. But we have to be very careful to photograph the separate parts appropriately — that is to bear constantly in mind the lighting and the perspective. Wrong lighting and perspective can sometimes gel very nicely but usually do not. So long as control is in your hands you can do what you like, and repeat anything if it looks as though it's going to screw things up. But it can cost a lot of money, especially when several different locations and a mountain of printing are necessary.

We've done a lot of montage primarily because it's the only way we can execute half the ideas we come up with.

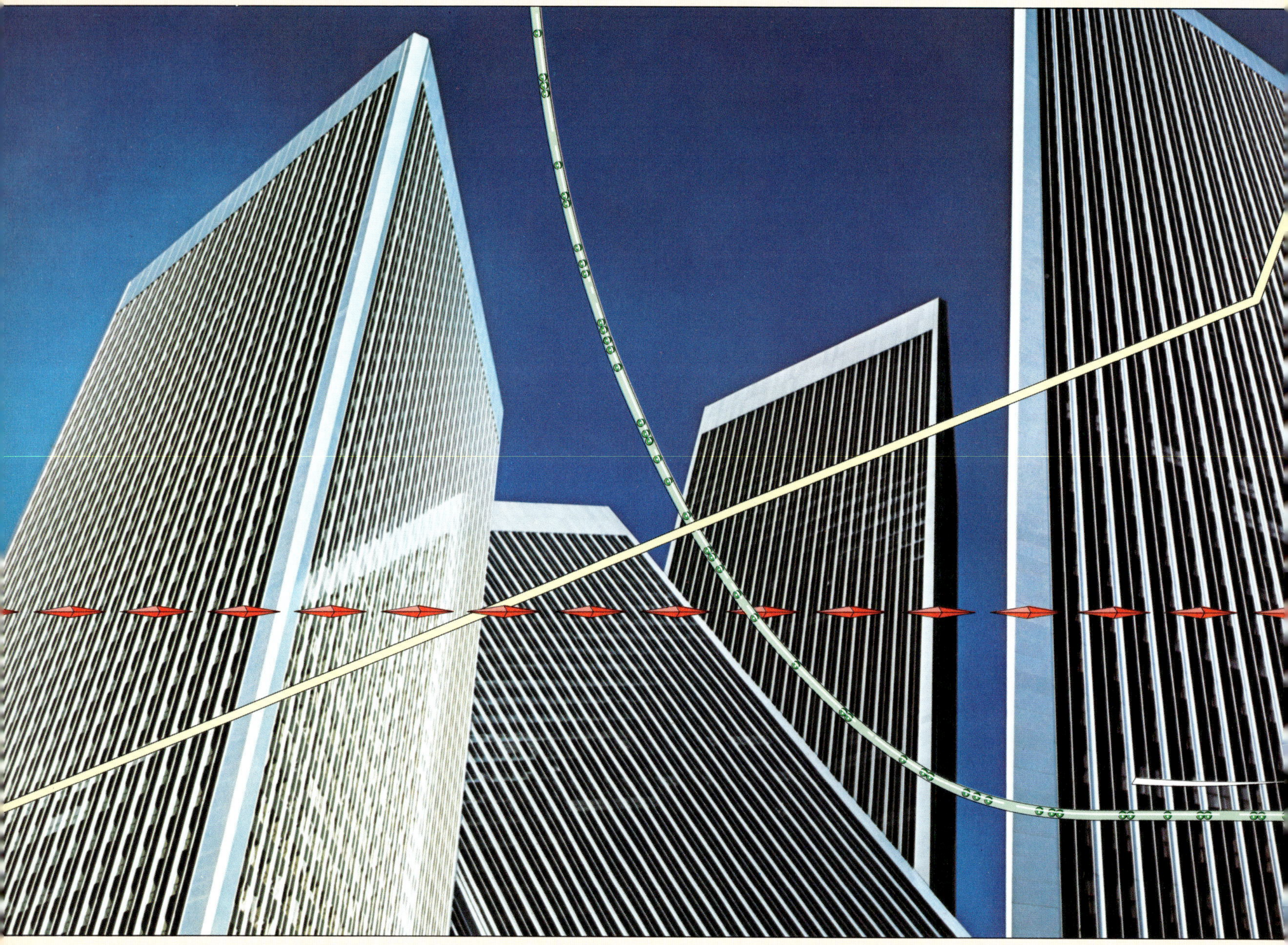

1977 | YES 'GOING FOR THE ONE' | FRONT COVER TRIPLE

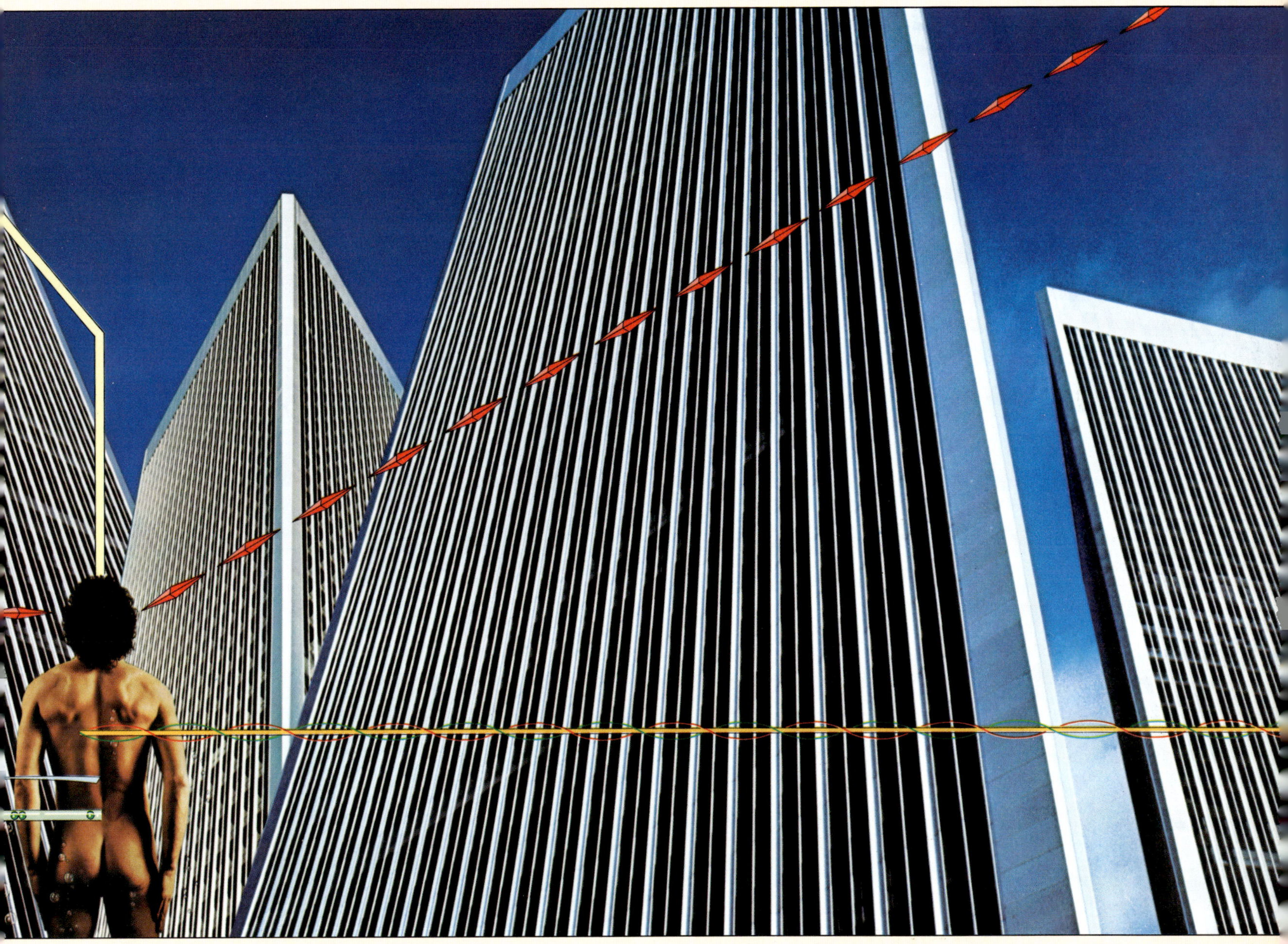

It's like a sort of photo painting — we can construct many of our fantasies, like a futuristic city, or repeated imagery or invisible capes (Uno) by this method. An illustrator can, theoretically, draw anything he cares to think of, from the labyrinths of his inner mind to the Rings of Saturn. We can't photograph like that directly but montage gets us someway towards this.

'Going For The One' is composed of five shots of buildings with the man stuck on top, against a sky comprising a mixture of photographed sky and airbrush retouching. Uno is composed of two identical shots except that the second one has the figure in it. This second print is positioned in exact register to the first and dry mounted on top of it. Alternate squares of the cape are then cut out to let through the background. For UFO 'Force It' we constructed our own bathroom set, at great cost and inconvenience to the nation, but found that the focus would not carry from the front to the back. All the foreground taps, shower hoses and bidet are separate prints, cut out and stuck over the background, but in the positions they would have occupied had it been one shot. The couple is male and female. 'Houses of the Holy' is a montage because we couldn't get all the necessary models. There are only two children in fact, photographed in different places from exactly the same camera position. The prints are then cut out round rock lines and replaced on a same size master print of the entire background. It is then re-photographed, retouched and hand coloured.

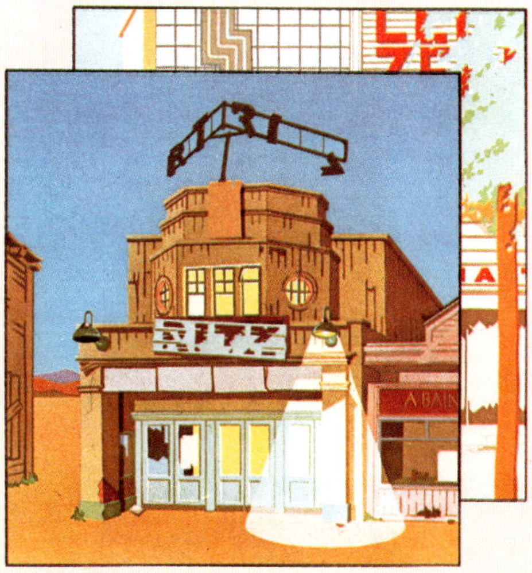

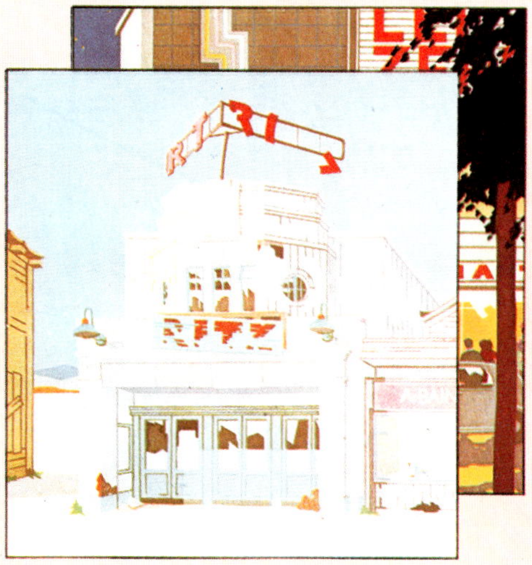

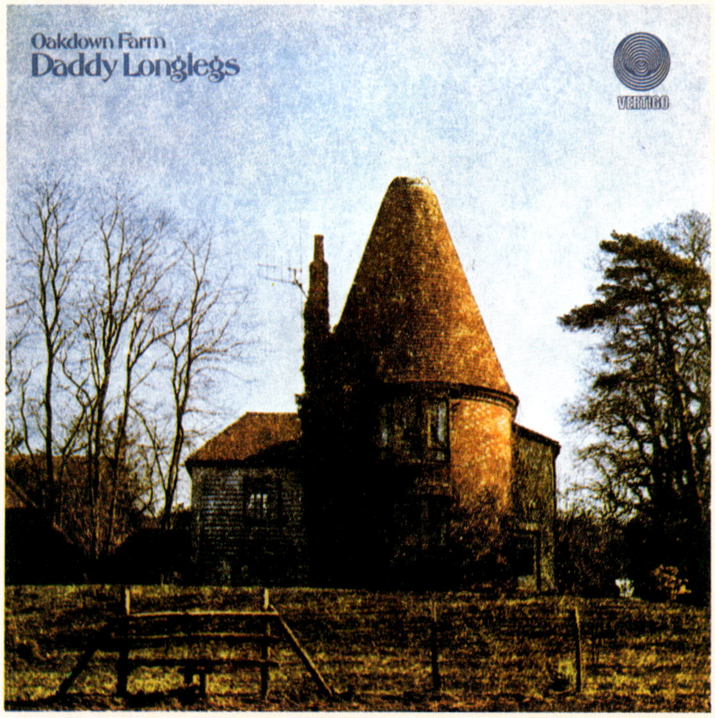

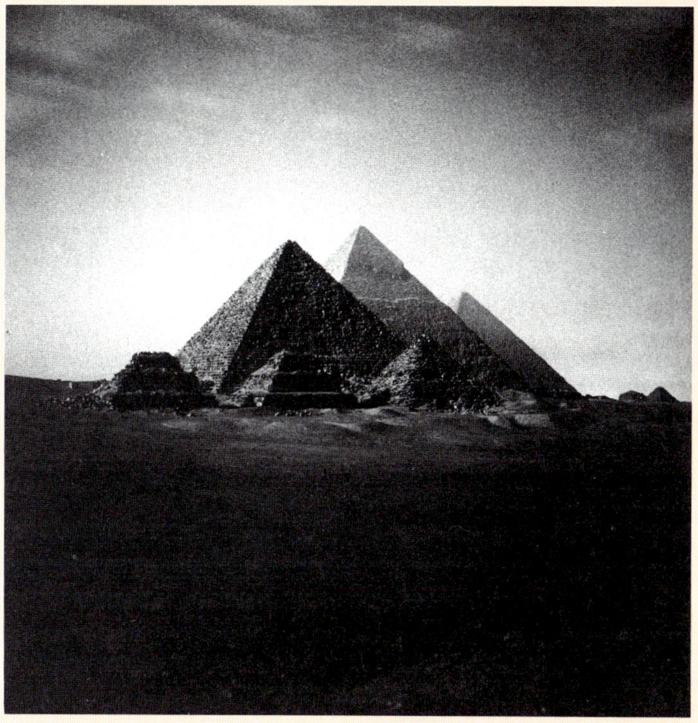

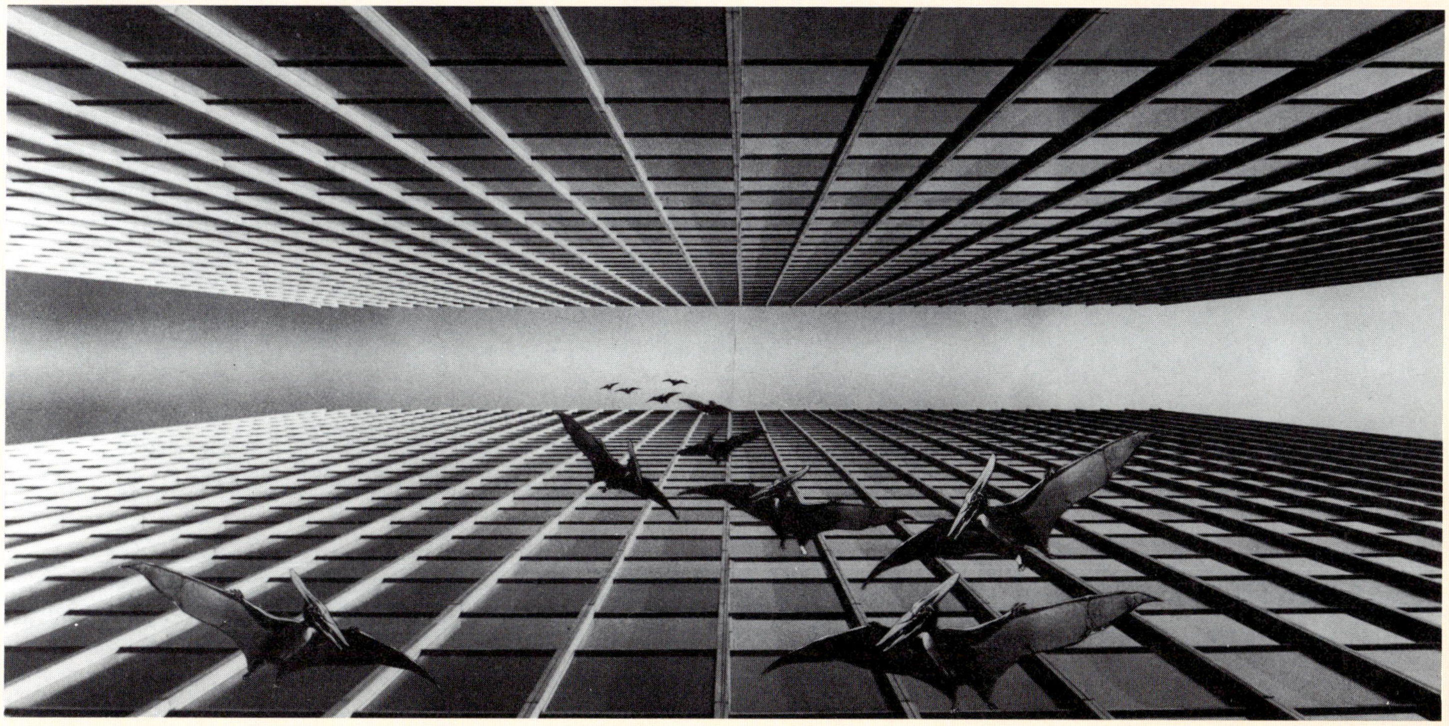

DADDY LONGLEGS PINK FLOYD (ADVERTISEMENT) QUATERMASS

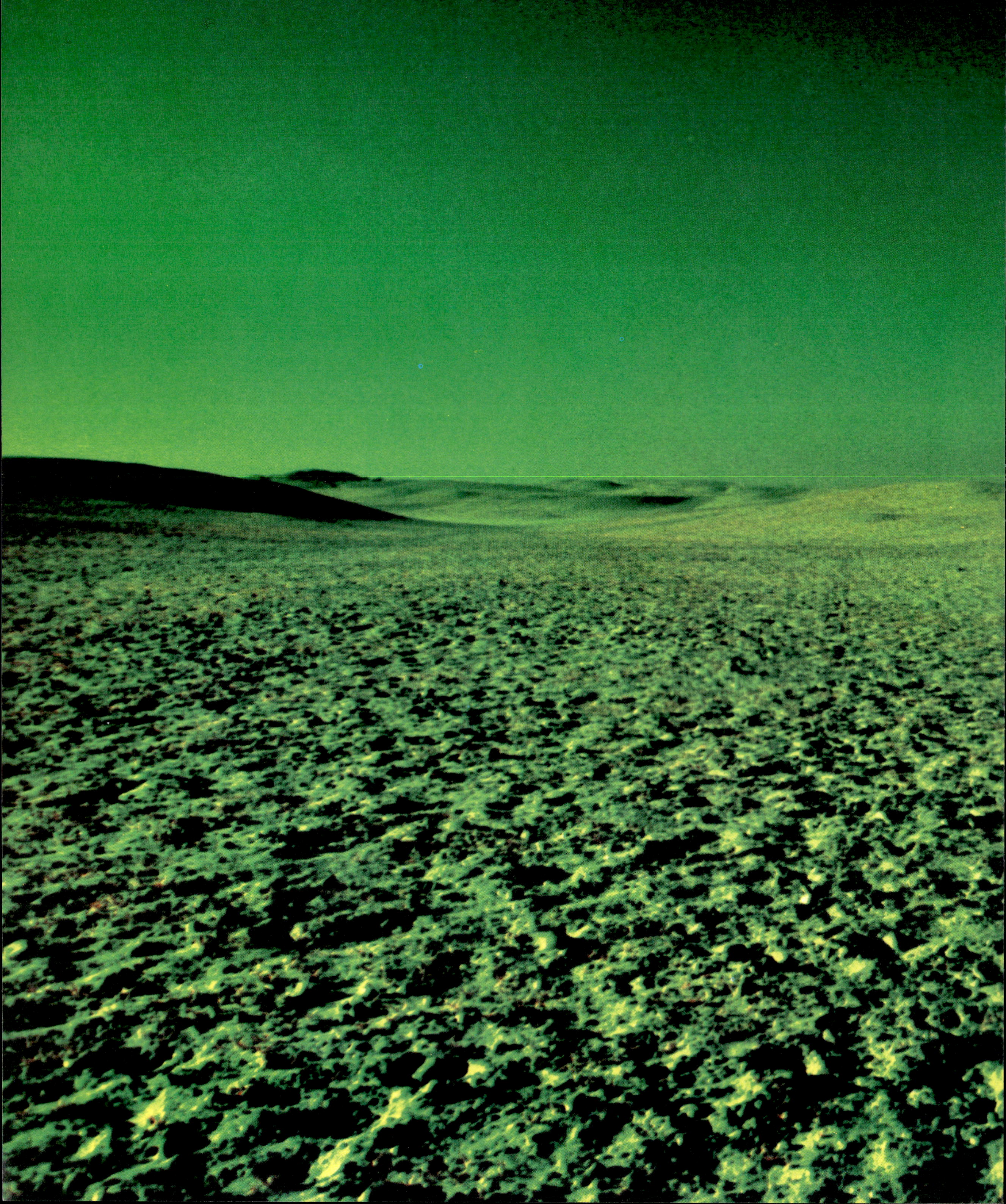

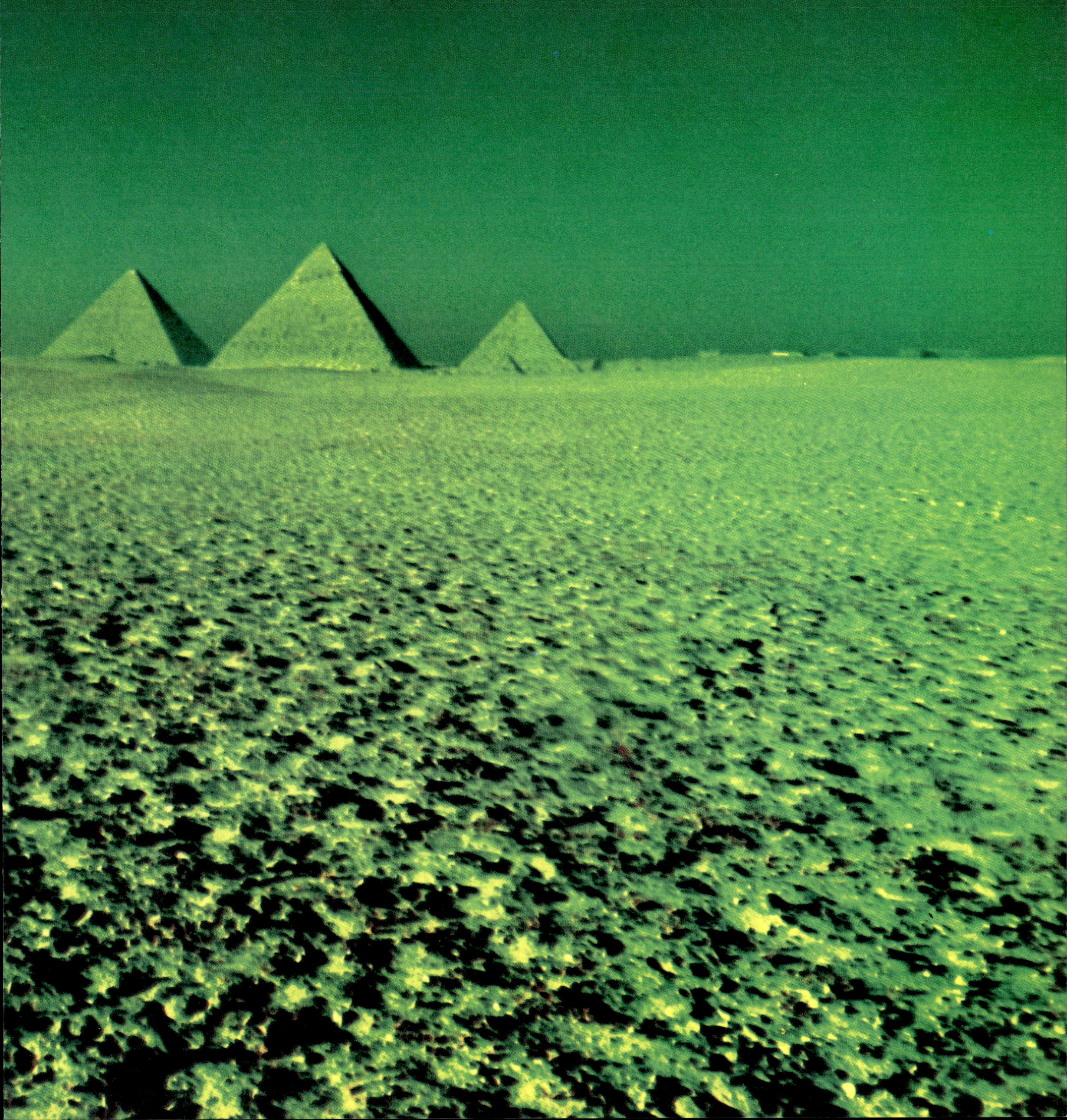

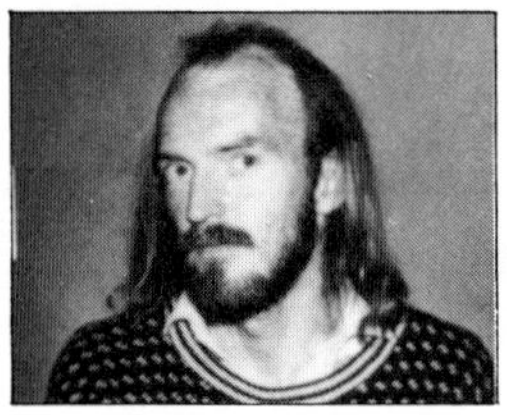

BRUCE ATKINS
PREVIOUS ASSISTANT

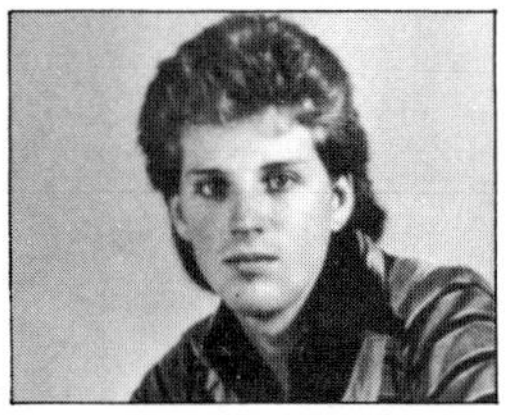

HOWARD BARTROP
PHOTOGRAPHER

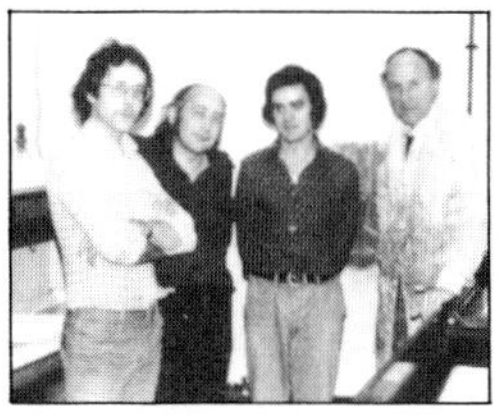

SIMON BELL
DYE TRANSFER PRINTER

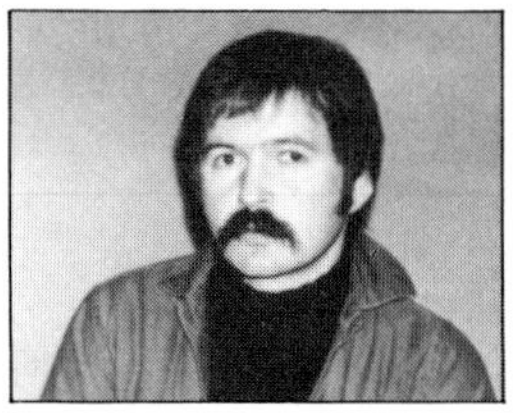

JOHN BLAKE
FRIEND

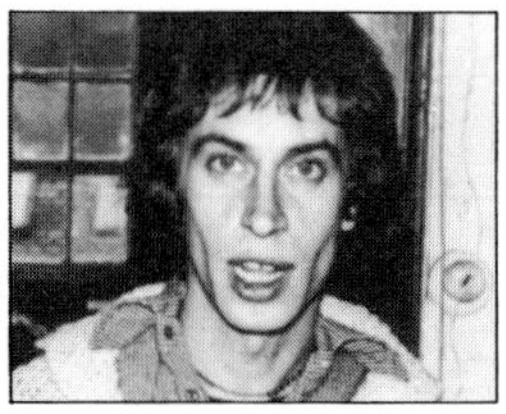

ROB BRIMSON
PREVIOUS ASSISTANT

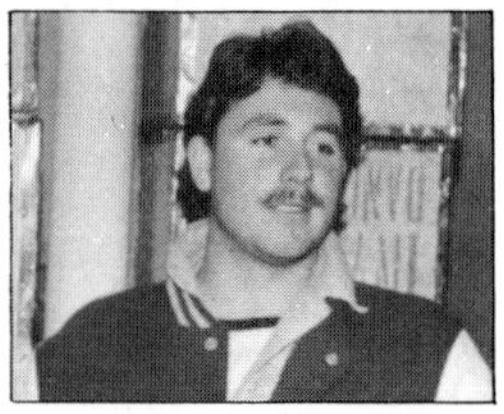

ALWYN CLAYDEN
ASSISTANT DESIGNER

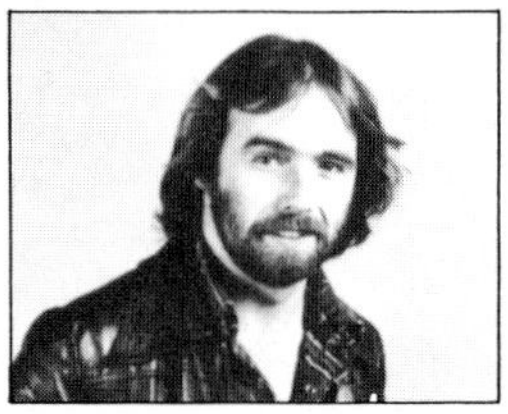

JEFF CUMMINS
PAINTER

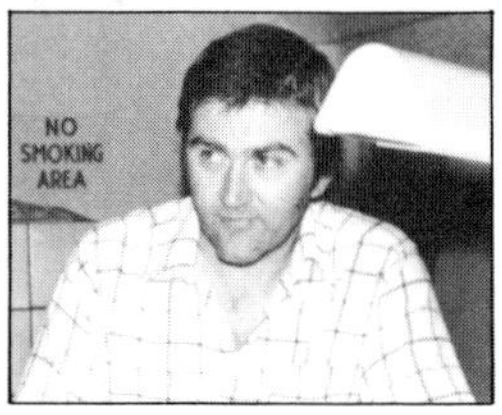

TERRY DAY
PHOTO RETOUCHER

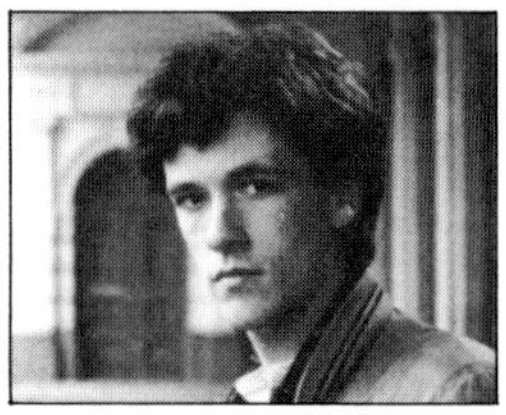

RICHARD DRAPER
PRESENT ASSISTANT

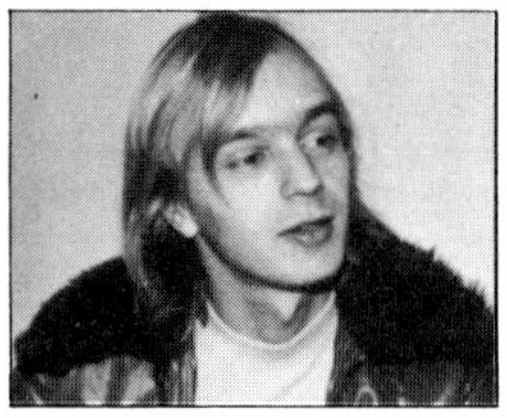

COLIN ELGIE
ILLUSTRATOR

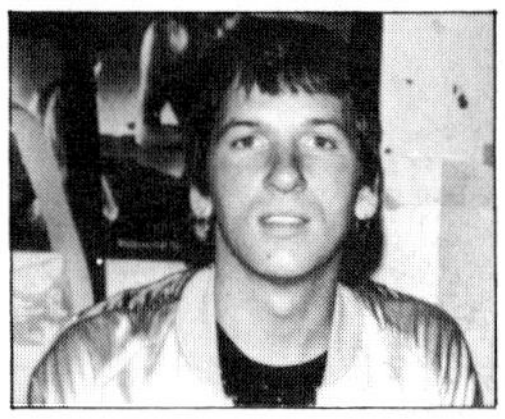

EMO
FRIEND AND MODEL

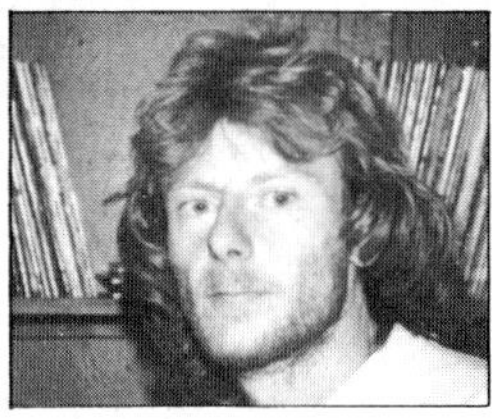

RICHARD EVANS
DESIGNER

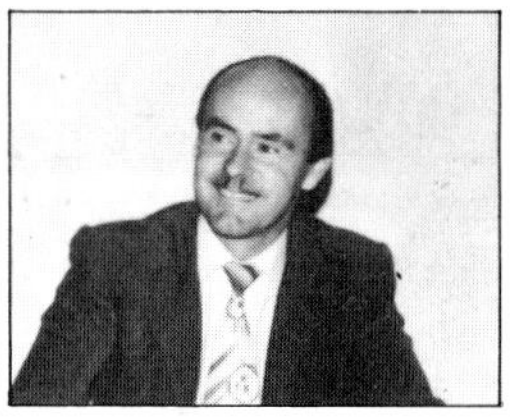

GEOFF HALPIN
DESIGNER

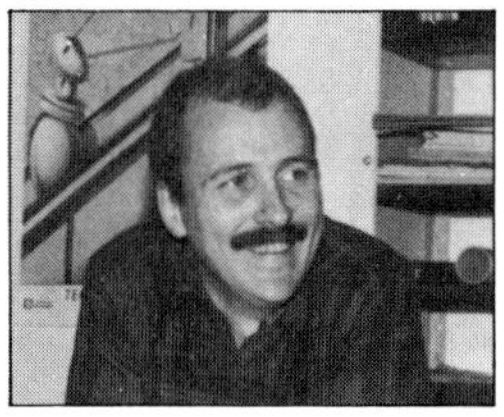

GEORGE HARDIE
DESIGNER

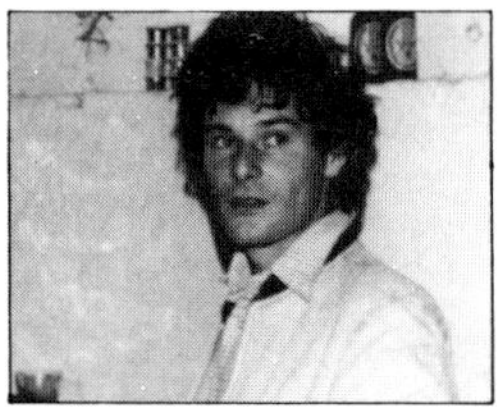

BUSH HOLLYHEAD
DESIGNER

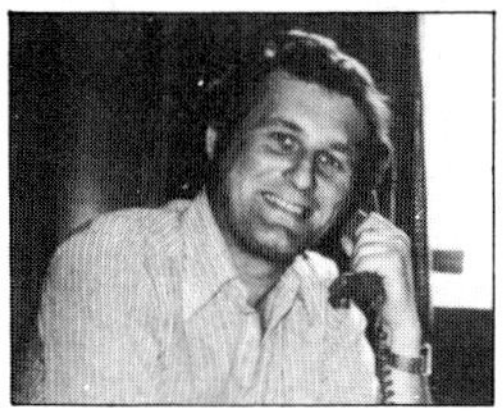

SPENCER JAY
COLOUR PRINTS

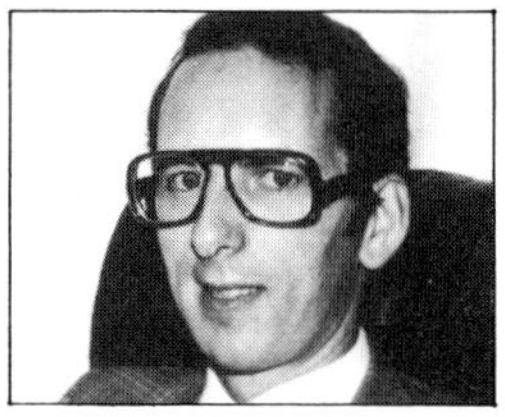

R. JOHN
ACCOUNTANT

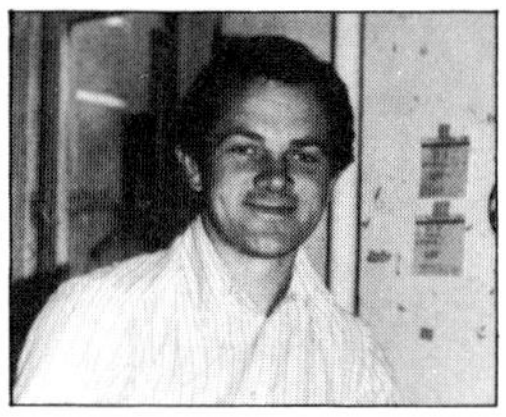

RICHARD MANNING
PHOTO RETOUCHER

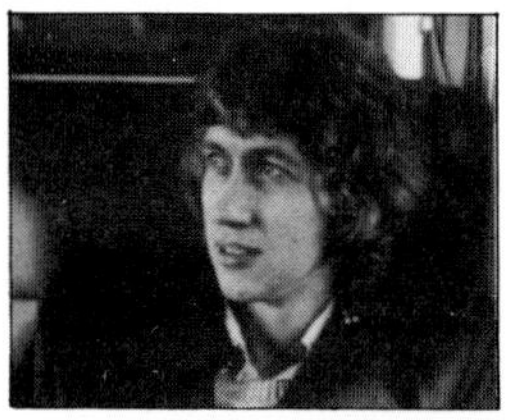

COLIN MITCHELL
COLOUR PRINTER

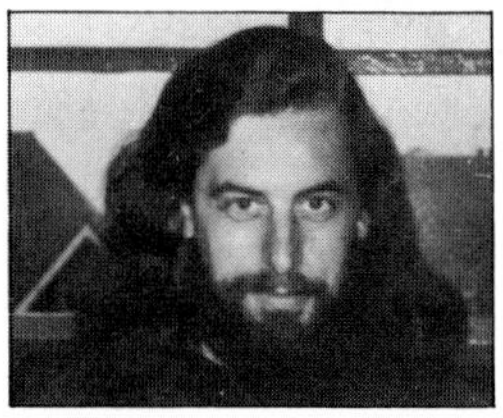

PONJI
FRIEND AND HELPER

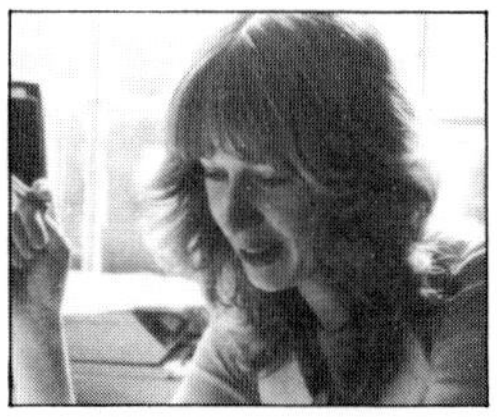

JUDY REYNOLDS
SECRETARY TO BOOK

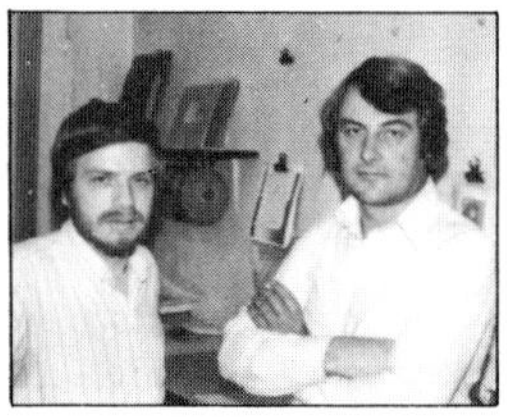

RON/DEREK
PHOTO PRINTERS

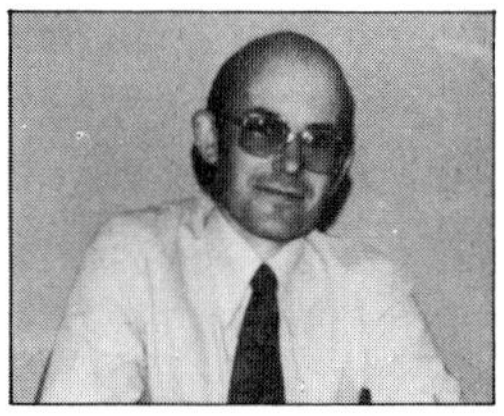

J. ROYAL
INSURANCE ADVISER

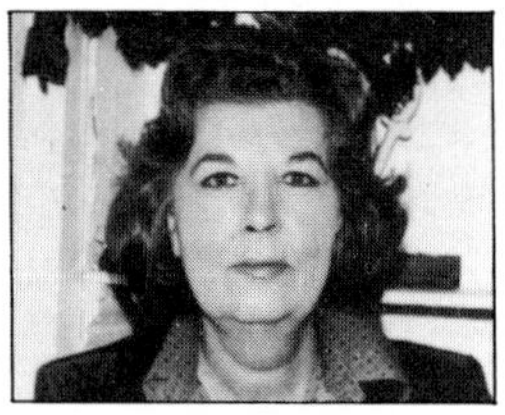

RUTH
PHOTO PRINTS

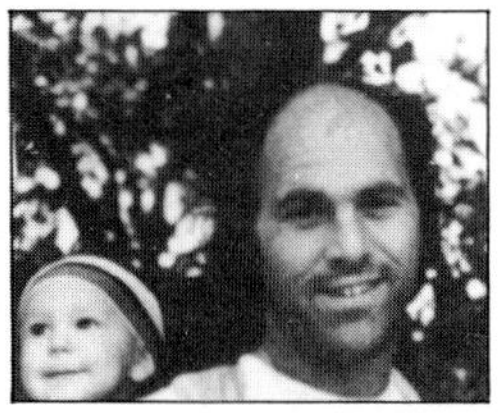

JEFF SMITH
USA CONTACT

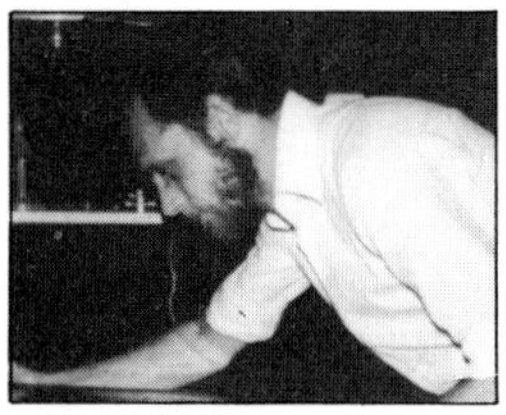

TIM WAKELY
DYE TRANSFER PRINTER

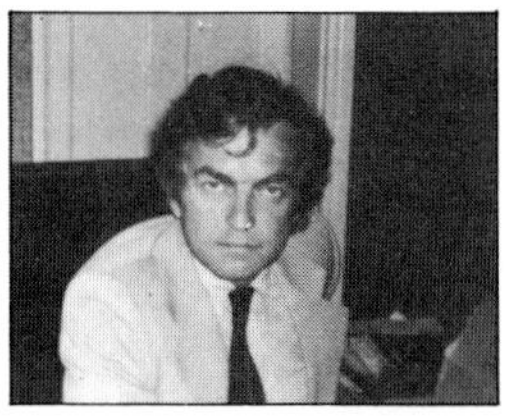

SIMON WAKEFIELD
SOLICITOR

◁ 1973 PINK FLOYD 'DARK SIDE OF THE MOON' POSTER

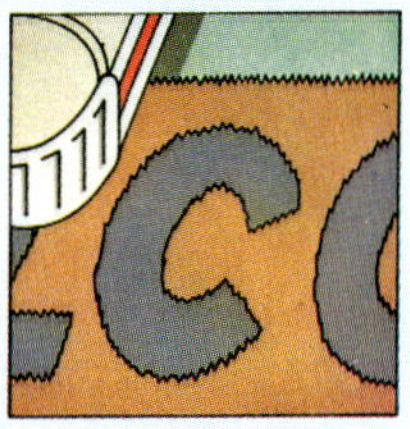

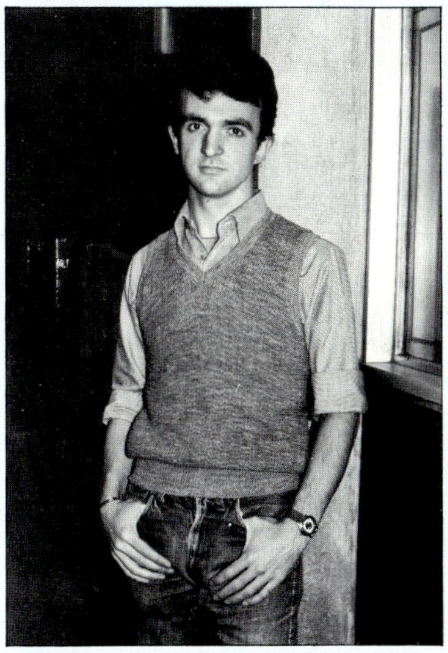

PETER

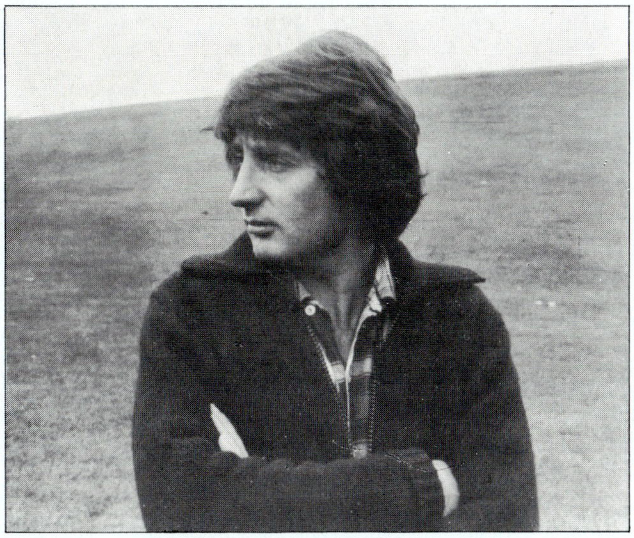

STORM

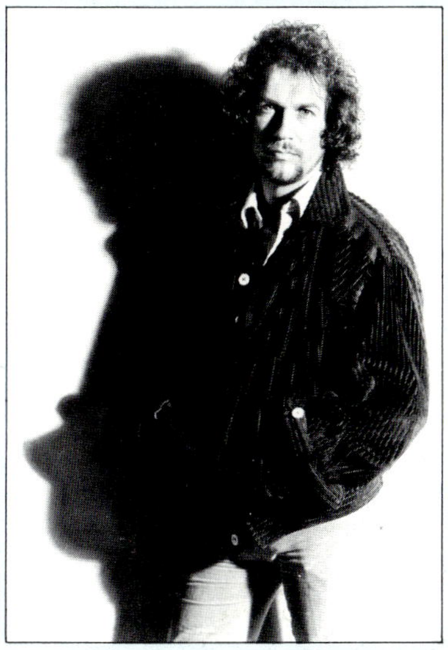

PO

Hipgnosis is Aubrey Powell, Peter Christopherson and Storm Thorgerson.

Aubrey Powell

Born September 23, 1946 in Sussex. Educated at Kings School, Ely, Cambridgeshire then London School of Film Technique. Left school and worked as blue-button clerk in Stock Exchange, bus conductor, waiter, on the dole, window dresser and assistant scenic designer in films and television. Interested in many things, especially those related to pleasure seeking.

Peter Christopherson

Born end of February 1955 in Leeds. Youngest in large academic family living in Wimbledon and later in Durham. Educated at Chorister School and later at Quaker co-ed boarding school at Ackworth. After A levels in sciences went briefly to State University of New York, in Buffalo studying fiction writing, computer programming, theatre design and video.

Returned to London Summer of '74 and joined Hipgnosis as junior assistant. Now joint partner. In spare time Director of Industrial Records, member of Casualties Union, technician for Throbbing Gristle and working on a number of projects with painter John Harwood.

Storm Thorgerson

Born in '44 in Potters Bar, Middlesex. Father away fighting the Hun. Schooled at Summerhill, Brunswick Primary, Cambridge and Cambridge High School for Boys. B.A. (Hons.) from Leicester University in English and Philosophy (1963-1966) and M.A. from the Royal College of Art, London (1966-1969).

Worked in the Newspaper Business (paper round), the Catering Business (college waiter), Posts and Telecommunications (Christmas postman), British Rail (temp porter) and Architecture (one week on building site).

Keen on tennis, squash, swimming, snooker, sex, drugs and rock 'n roll. Resuscitation by acupuncture. Lives alone with his son Bill, aged 6.

On the opposite page are many of the people who help Hipgnosis to function. It is particularly necessary to mention George Hardie of NTA Studios for continual collaboration in design and organisation, and for all his graphic work; also Colin Elgie for his illustrations and graphic work; and thirdly, Richard Manning for his photoretouching and hand-colouring. They all work freelance.

To these and the others, our sincere thanks. I never realised so many people were involved.

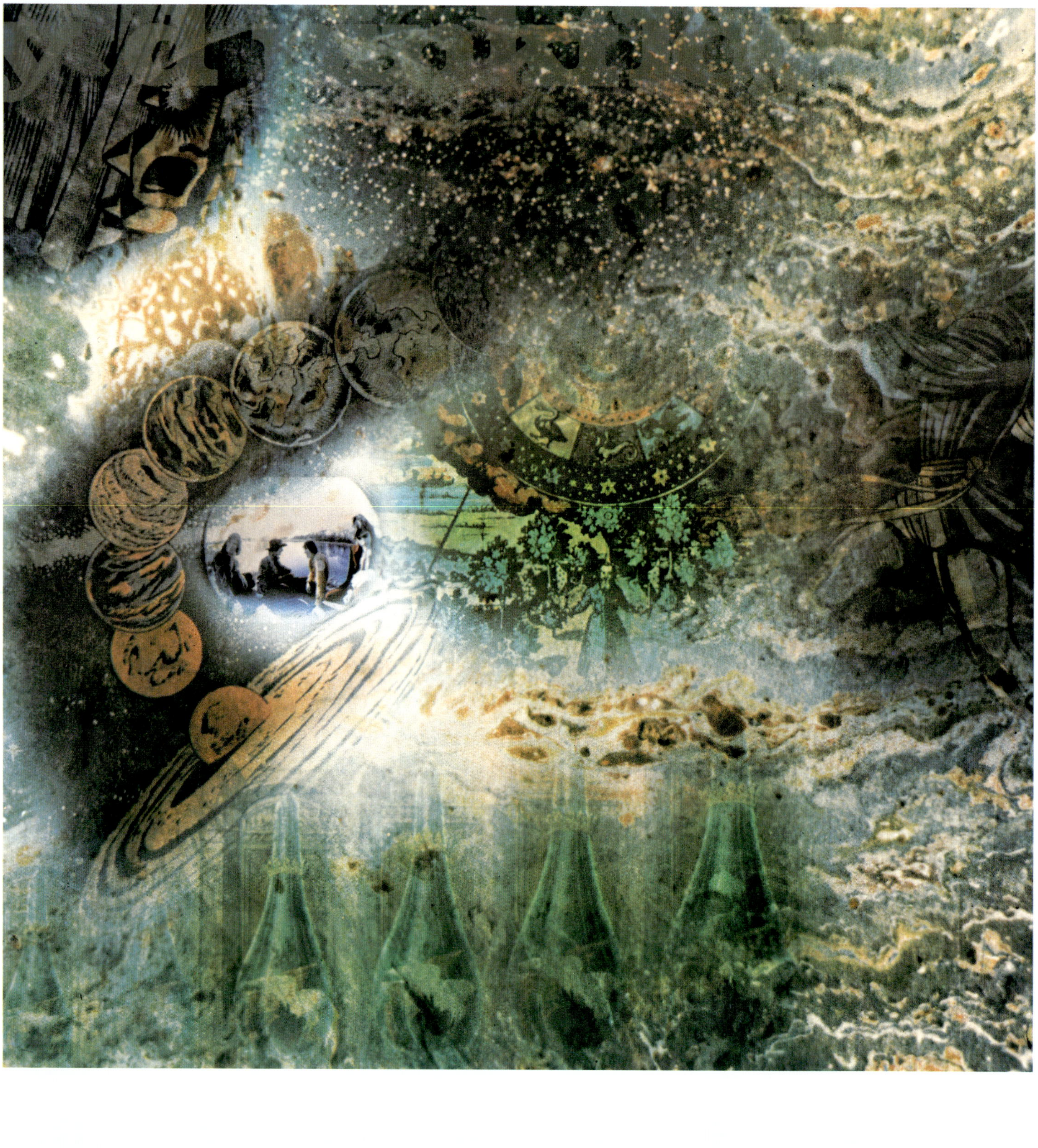

1968 | PINK FLOYD 'SAUCERFUL OF SECRETS' | FRONT COVER

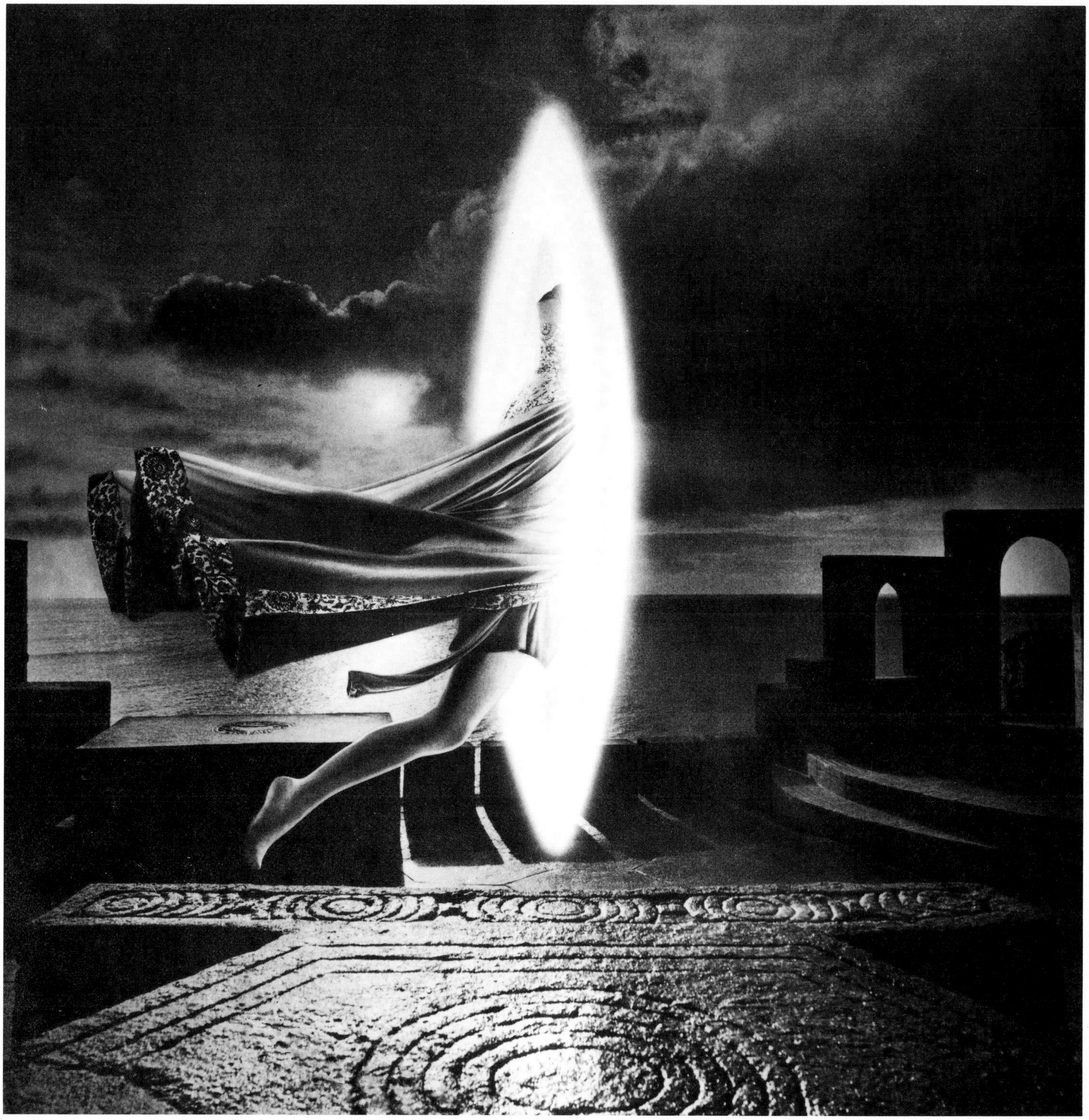

1973 AL STEWART 'PAST, PRESENT & FUTURE' FRONT COVER

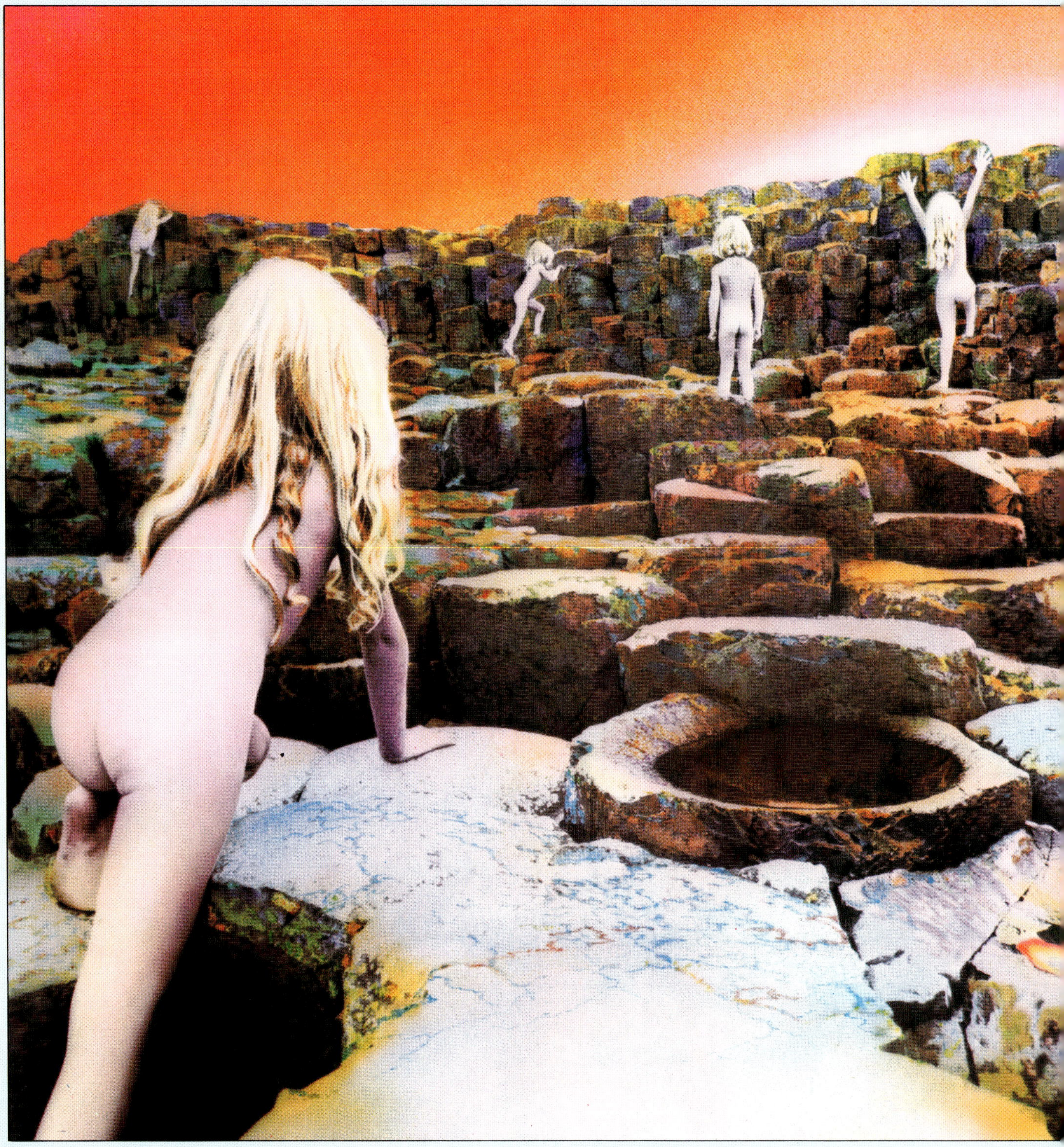

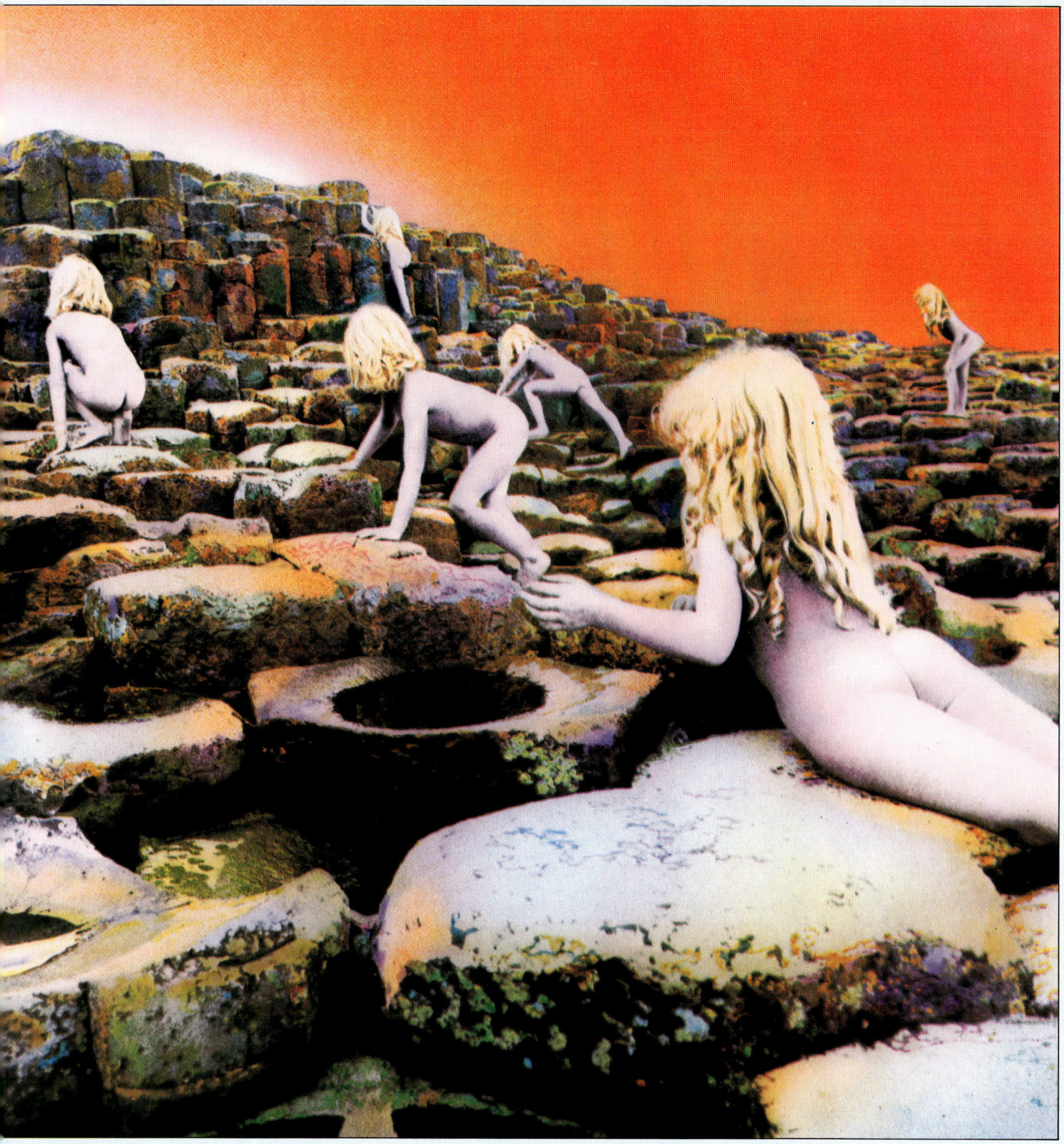

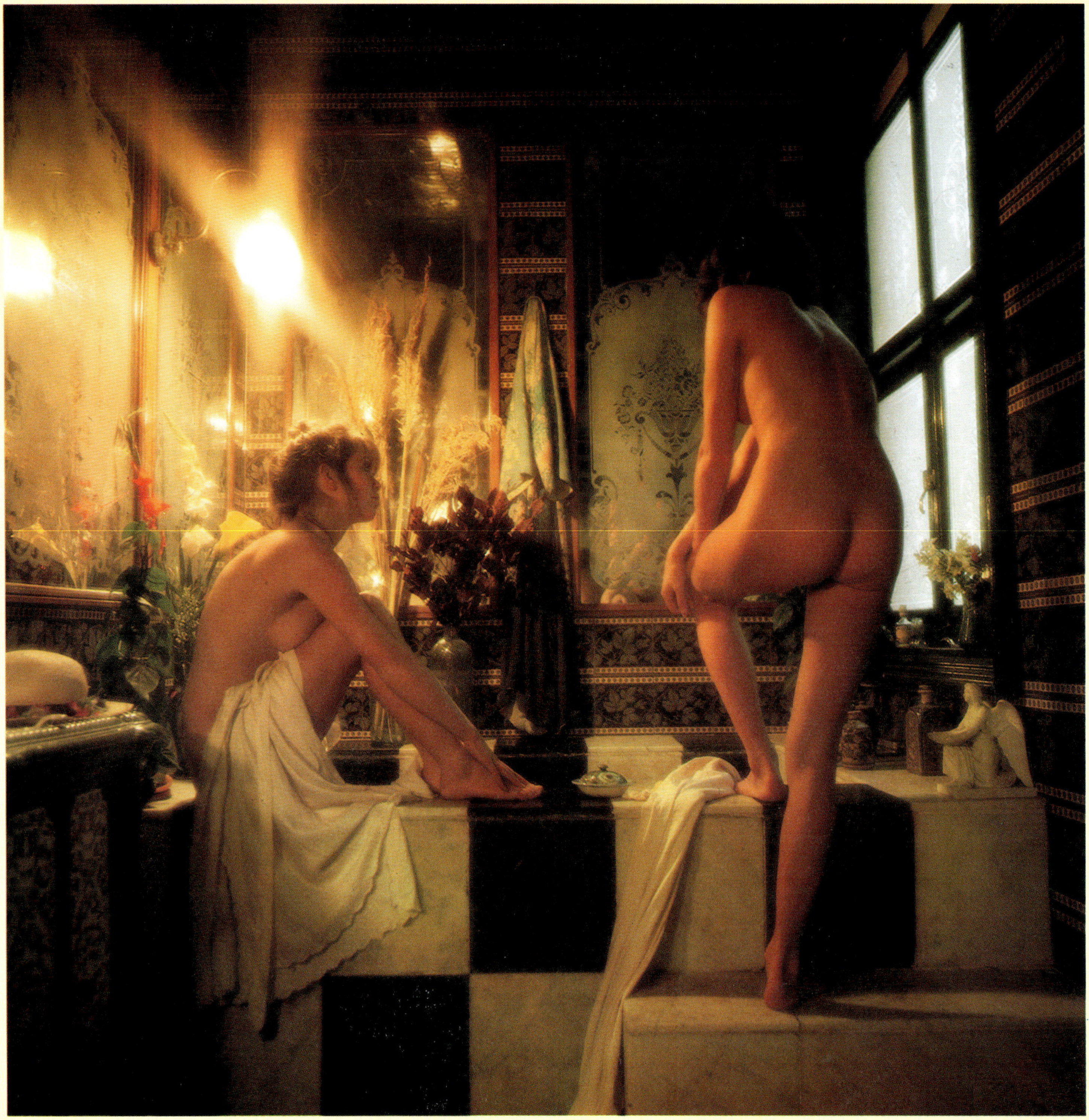

◁ 1973 LED ZEPPELIN 'HOUSES OF THE HOLY' FRONT COVER HUMBLE PIE 'THUNDERBOX'

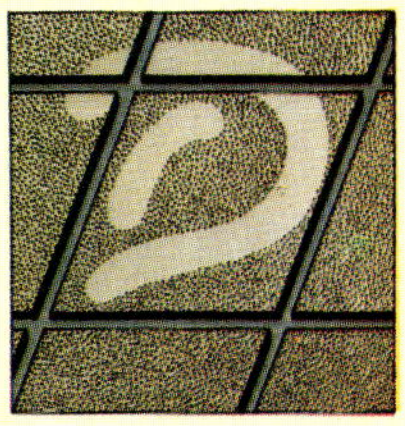

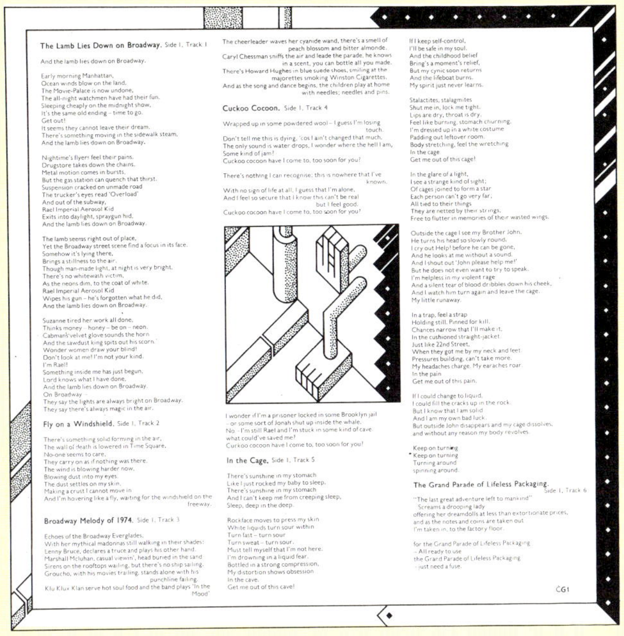

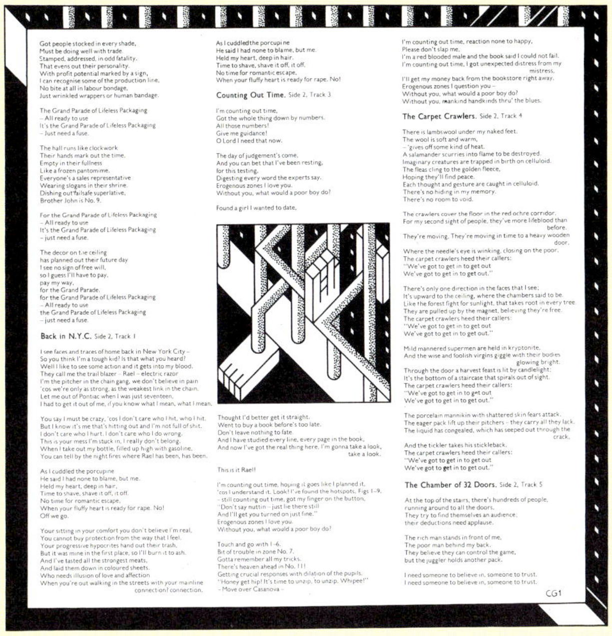

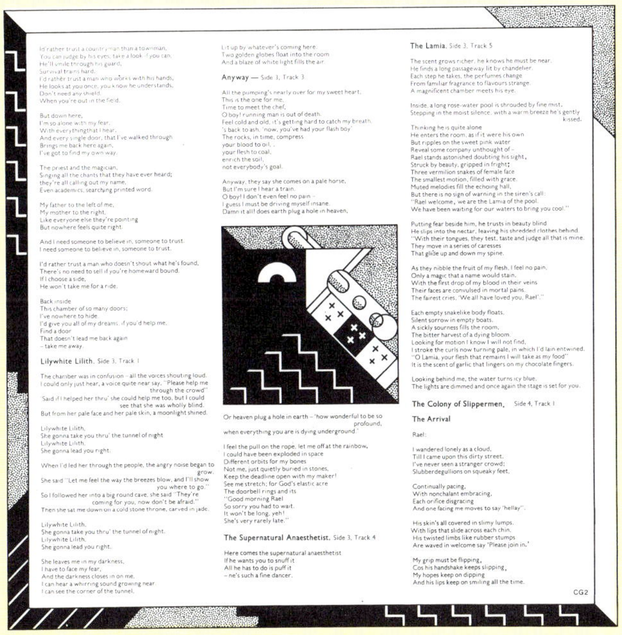

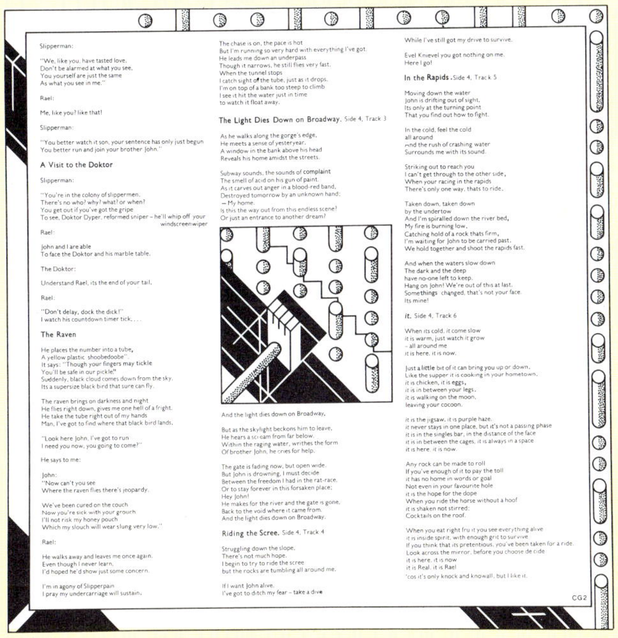

1974 GENESIS 'LAMB LIES DOWN ON BROADWAY' ILLUSTRATION GEORGE HARDIE DUST JACKET

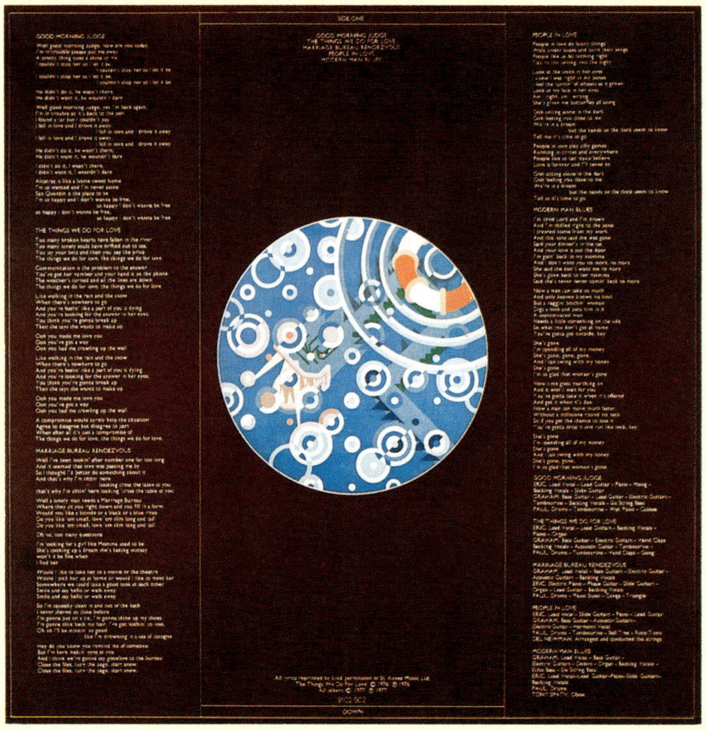

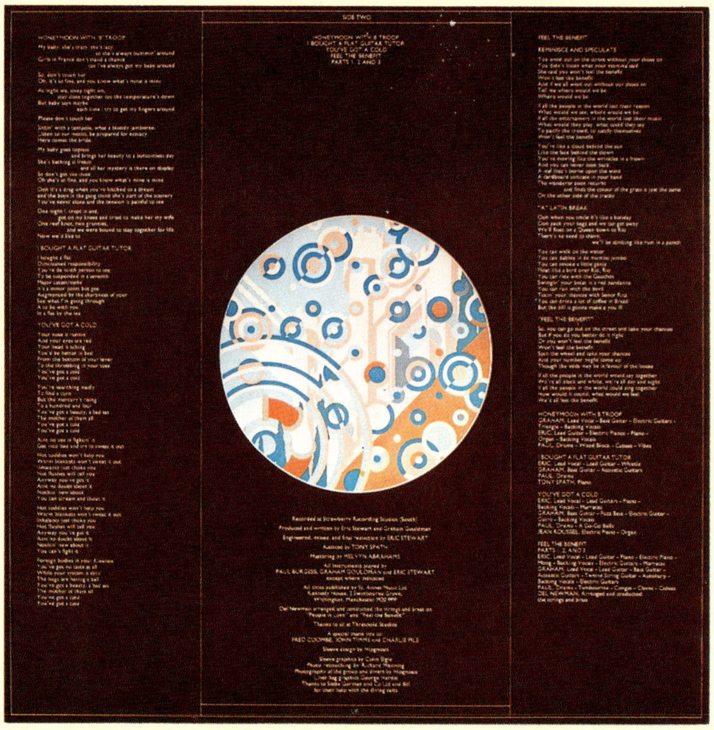

A dust jacket is sometimes called a liner bag or inner sleeve. It is the bag which holds the record itself and it fits snugly inside the outer board sleeve or album cover. Most records have them but they are often plain white or bear a standard design which advertises the record company and other records on the same label. It is a good idea to have dust jackets made of polythene lined paper or treated card in order to protect the record efficiently and reduce accumulation of static dust. The examples shown here have been specifically designed for certain records and relate to the outer sleeve design by continuing the same thematic or graphic motif.

Genesis is drawn by George Hardie and though it is different in style from the cover it still refers to parts of the story on the album. 'Venus and Mars', also by George, uses the idea of snooker balls as a basis for an abstract pattern. 'Wings Over America' comprises a sequence of graphic representations of a door opening — the gauge registers the increasing amount of light that emerges. Montrose and Pretty Things continue visual threads from the front sleeve, whereas Humble Pie is an integral part of a cover which shows a dye cut keyhole — the girls in the bathroom are what one sees through the keyhole. However, the photo by itself is much nicer, I think, than the sleeve, which was regretfully smutty. The soft focus is achieved by using a piece of muslin cloth stretched tight across the lens whilst shooting.

1977	10CC 'DECEPTIVE BENDS	ILLUSTRATION GEORGE HARDIE	DUST JACKET

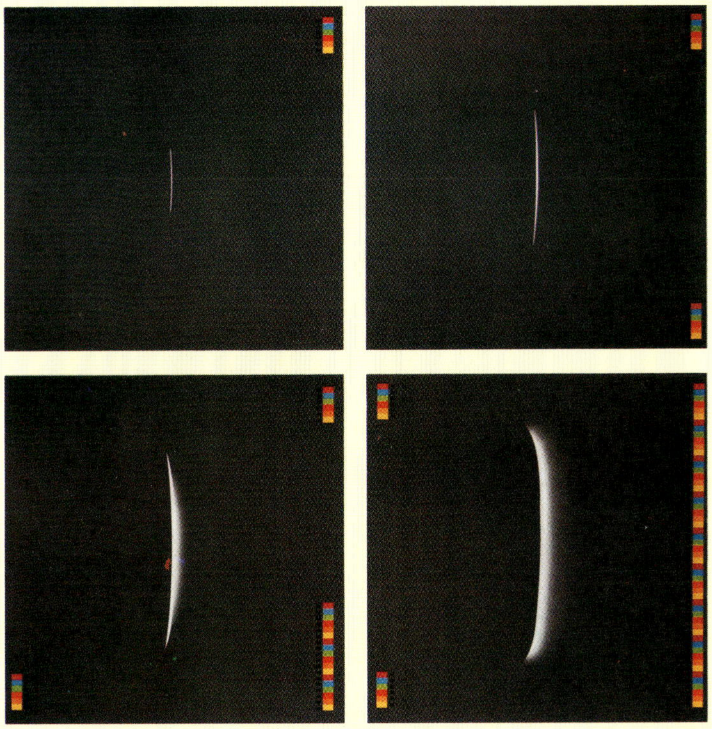

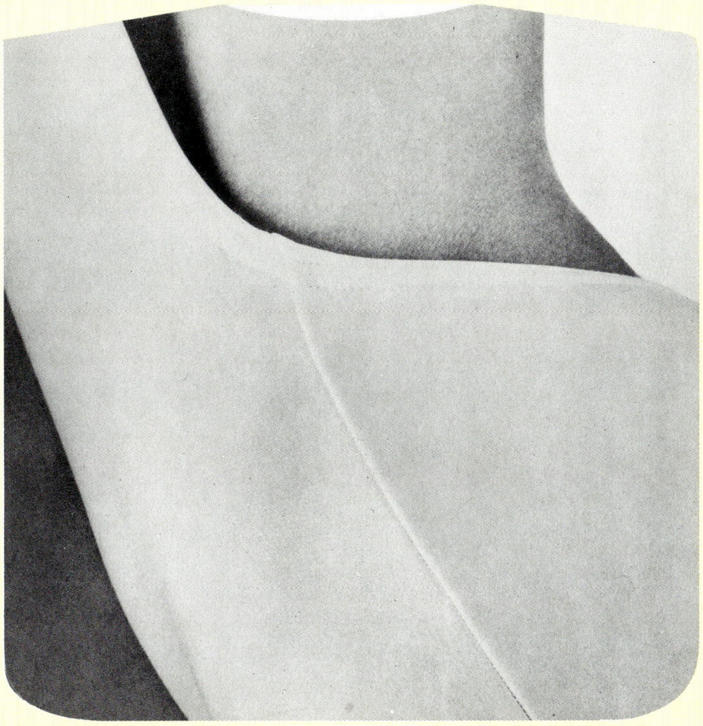

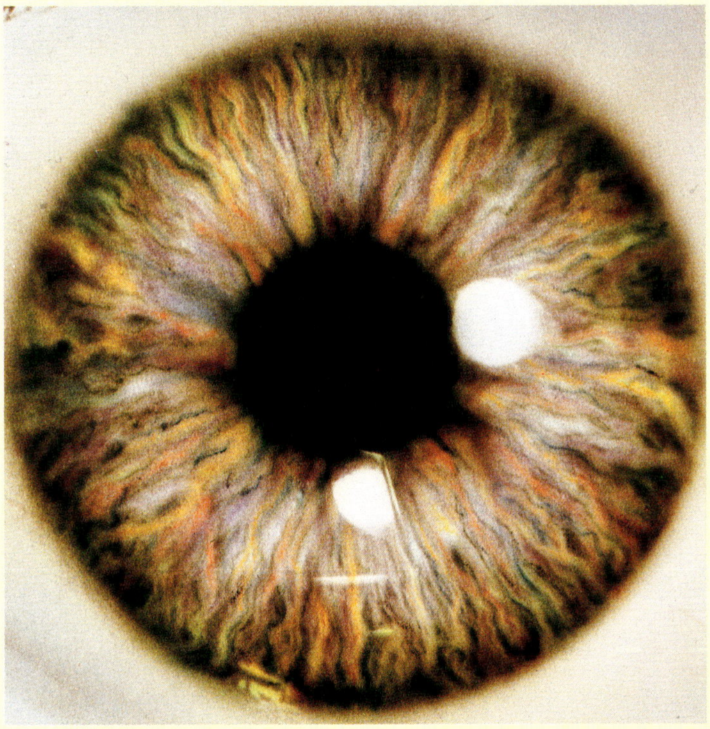

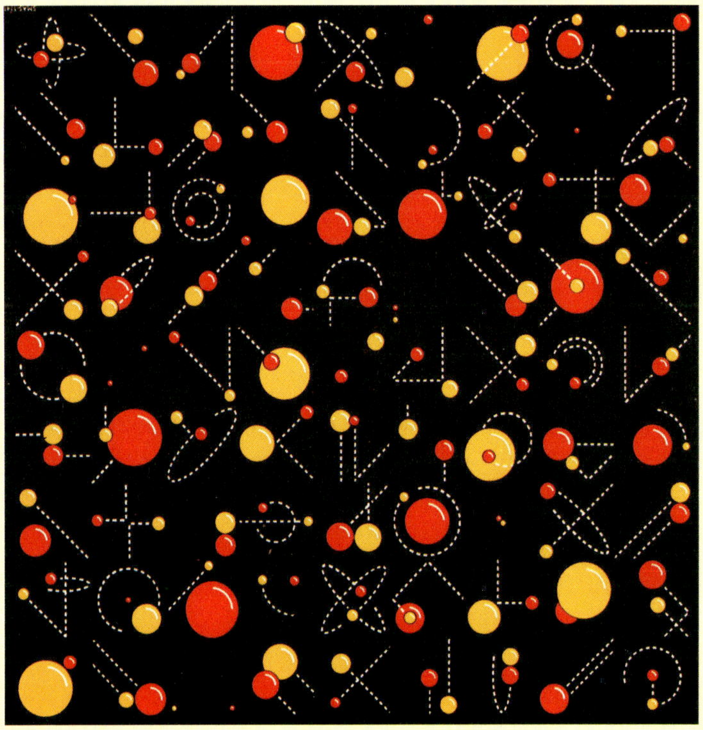

WINGS MONTROSE PRETTY THINGS WINGS

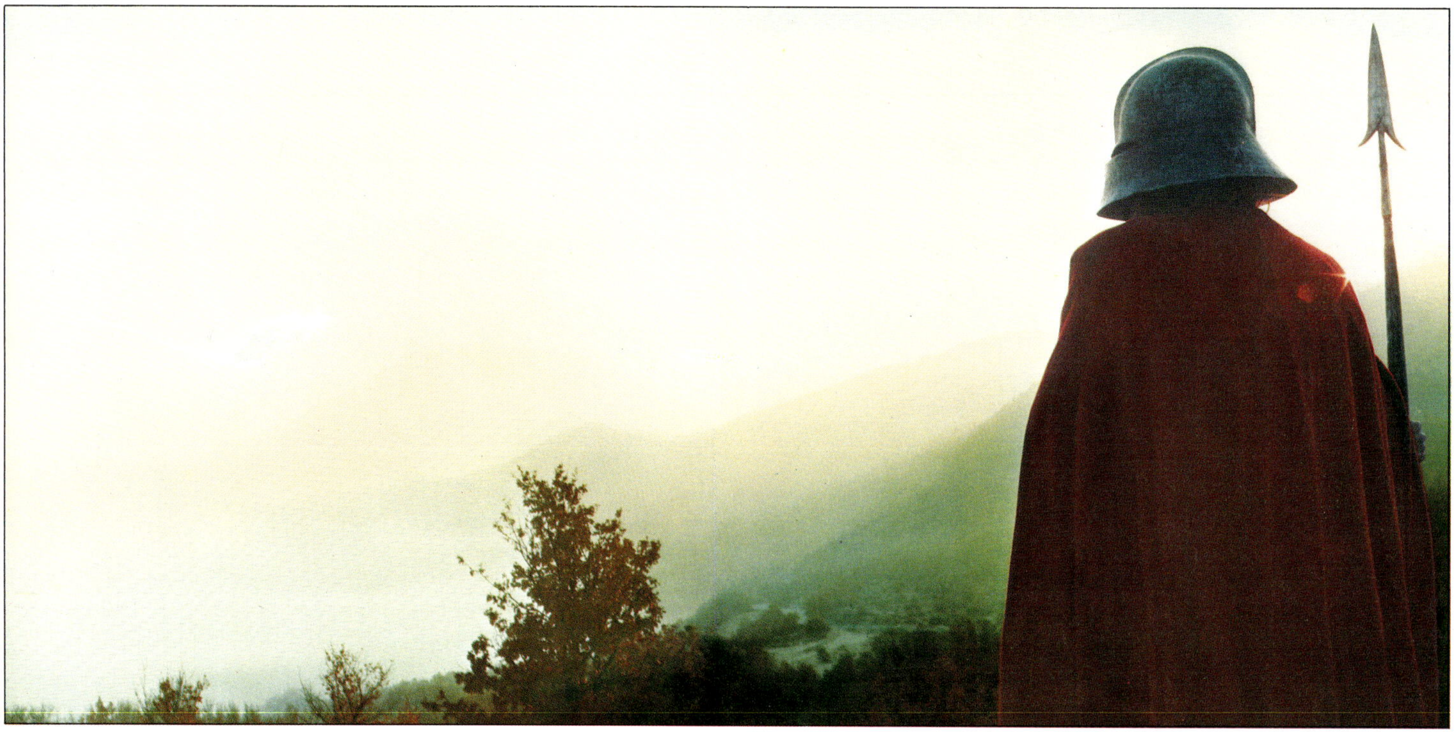

Apart from the fact that Our Man in Morocco is about to be rolled by some menacing Arabs, it's funny how all those different points match up and seem to make a pattern. This pattern is something we at Hipgnosis were lucky enough to discover after months of research. It is, of course, a computer programme for the cosmic key (the key to the knowledge and power of the universe). Long ago alchemists and mystics would do that — hide messages in the geometric substructure of a picture to keep it beyond the understanding of novices. Such novices would, no doubt, misuse it to the detriment of us all — children playing with adult toys can be a very dangerous business. Brand X invested their music with mystical clues and likewise their cover. What they knew was simply too powerful and too magical for ordinary senses. It had to be passed on in stages, in disguised forms, otherwise a recipient might be catapulted to higher regions prematurely and be scared half out of his wits. And if you believe that, you'll believe anything.

Uno is an encounter between the past — the hill carving and the future — the caped figure. It is also a montaging trick inspired by something we saw in a children's book. The poster for the Rolling Stones on page 94 uses the same device but executed in black and white rather than colour prints and subsequently hand tinted. 'Argus' for Wishbone Ash is also a meeting between the past (the soldier) and the future (the saucer). Black Sabbath is quite the opposite and reveals our sentimental streak. This time the encounter is one of love at first sight. Robots of the imminent future may not really be so humanoid as to fall for each other but if they do then they might well show it with laser beams and squirts of lubricating fluid. The inner spread for 10cc is not strictly an encounter but rather the avoidance of one. It's a paranoid nightmare about going to a crowded party and being totally unable to talk to anyone — better to be on the blower than face somebody directly. 10cc themselves are in there somewhere as are the characters from the front cover (pg 123).

These pictorial encounters are exciting and taxing in their own way but seldom as emotionally involved as real life ones. Well, I should hope not. Art is no substitute for life. Paul McCartney looked so like The Paul McCartney that I was taken aback. I was standing in the presence of a Beatle, and though I thought I was over the 'star bit', I

1972 | WISHBONE ASH 'ARGUS' | FRONT COVER

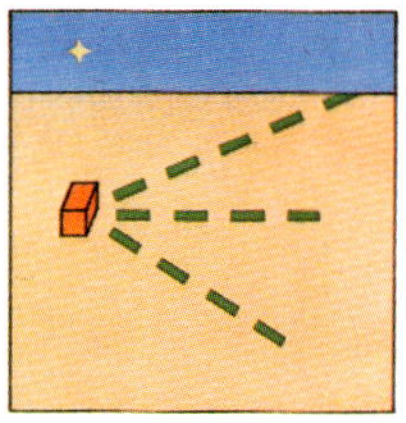

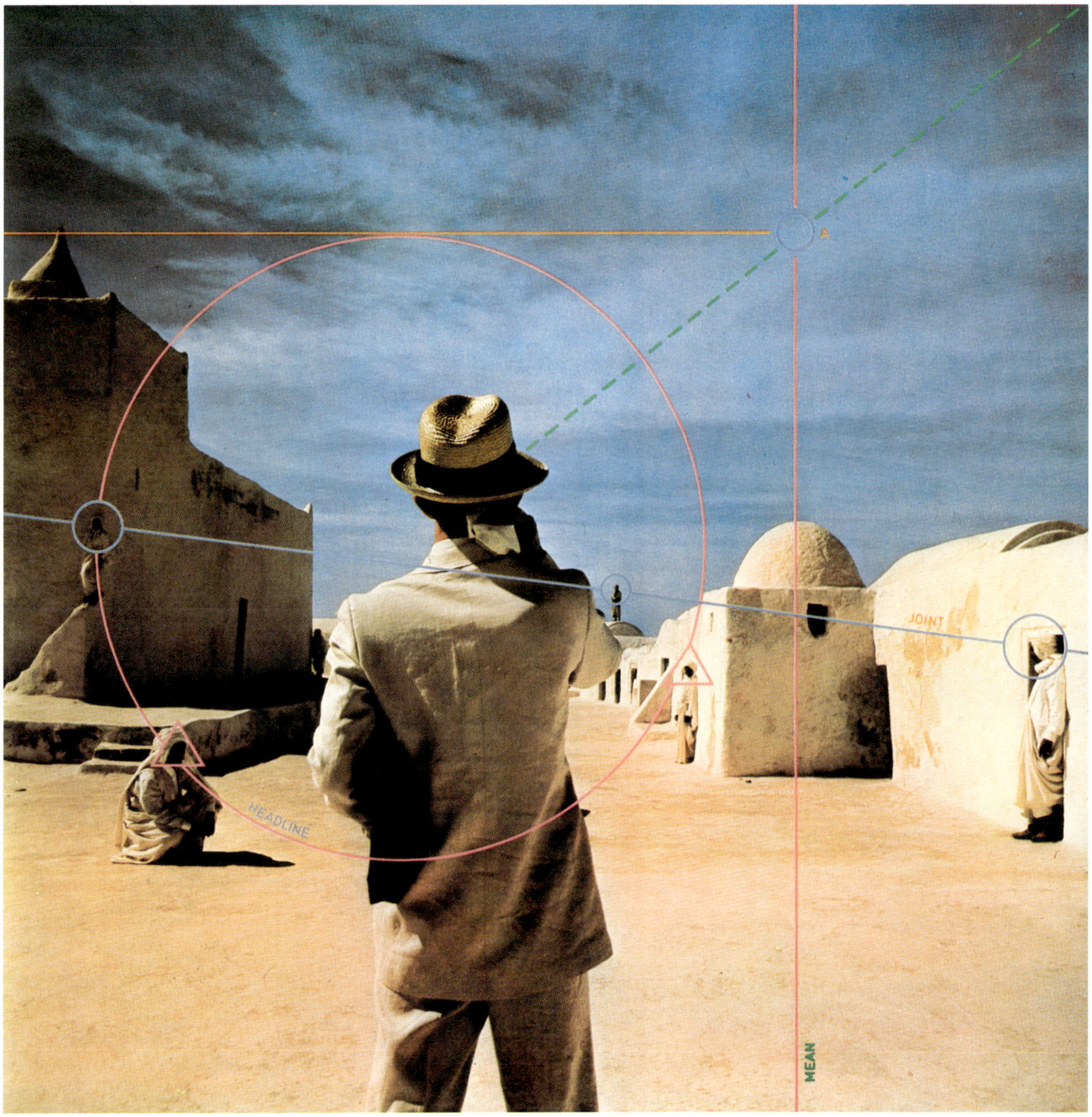

1977 BRAND X 'MOROCCAN ROLL' CO-DESIGN GEORGE HARDIE POSTER

was mistaken. I found it difficult to stop looking at him. He was explaining his idea for 'Band On The Run'. I didn't care for it that much but I kept quiet because I fancied being a groupie for once in my life. I saw myself riding around in his white Rolls, having tea in his kitchen and so on; and that's what happened. I organised his cover, worked conscientiously as an art director and it all turned out fine. Two years later and two sleeves later, we had a totally different encounter. The original concept for the 'Wings Over America' sleeve was an idea of his and was so unstimulating that in the end even he admitted it. He called Po and me round to his house at eleven at night and asked us straight out what we thought of the cover. We asked him if he really wanted a serious discussion about such matters and he said he did. So we told him it was boring, and that the previous covers hadn't been particularly noteworthy either, and that sleeve design could be an intricate business and so on and so forth. He accused us of colluding on previous sleeves (and he was right) and how would he know what was really going down if we didn't tell him straight? Then we said well, he wasn't the easiest person to say that to and he said okay, but what do we do now? So we designed a sleeve there and then by going over the album and discusing what he wanted to get across.

We have now worked with many different artistes and are no longer so subject to feelings of awkwardness when in their presence. Nevertheless, it can still get us, like the time we first met Mick Jagger. We were crammed into the control room at Olympic Studios feeling shy and uncomfortable. I was surprised both by his height, or rather his lack of it, and by his unfriendliness, like he was doing us a big favour, which didn't help our nervousness at all. Steve Harley, on the other hand, was really charming and not at all (at least not to us) the rampant ego I suspected. The Shadows were equally charming, but when they visited our studio a few years back, it was a bit embarrassing. We'd grown up to the sounds of Cliff and the Shadows. Hank and Bruce arrived and stood about aimlessly before asking where the lavatory was. We, personally, have this completely foul habit of urinating in our handbasin in our washroom at the back because the gents is out of the room and down some stairs and often locked, and because we're disgusting people. So I says to Hank that normally guests go downstairs but old regulars and mates do as we do and pee in the sink. There was a moment's silence. Then they said sure, might as well do it in the sink. The nervousness vanished and it was one of the most relaxed photo sessions we've ever done.

Two of the most disturbing encounters involved Syd Barrett. We were close friends in our late teens in Cambridge. Hipgnosis was asked to do the sleeve for a repackaging of his two solo albums so I went round to photograph him. He was living in Chelsea Cloisters at the time, which is a sort of permanent hotel. I knocked on the door and told him who I was and he just said go away. That was all. Not so much as a hello. I came back three more times at ten minute intervals but there was never another word from inside the room. On another occasion, about two years later, I was at Abbey Road Studios with Pink Floyd whilst they were recording 'Wish You Were Here'. 'Shine On' was being played back in the control room. Roger and Dave were singing about Syd (or nearly so) when suddenly he walked in! Nobody had seen him for over two years. He was fat, wore a white trenchcoat, white shoes, carried a white plastic bag and had had his head shaved, and he look unbelievable. Where had he been for so long and how come he'd suddenly arrived whilst that particular song was being recorded?

Capital Records once rang us and told our assistant that Sammy Hagar, ex-lead singer of Montrose, was in London with his band. They rang us again and left a message on the awful recording machine saying the band had arrived and were in Abbey Road Recording Studios. We were flattered — the Band, Dylan's Band, were asking for us! Our assistant had failed to give us the full message. We steamed up to Abbey Road and were introduced to Sammy Hagar by his producer whom we knew. We chewed the fat for a while and went indoors and talked some more about the sleeve design. We were still under the impression that we were seeing *the* Band. We kept looking about for Robbie Robertson or Richard Manuel. We continued to be sociable and chatty with Sammy Hagar but in fact we thought he was the roadie. After about three quarters of an hour it began to dawn on us that all was not as we thought. Neither of us said anything for fear of being impolite or of looking very silly. In fact, we didn't realise that we were both under the same illusion until we got out of the studio and cracked up laughing on the doorstep — not at Sammy, but at ourselves for a stupid yet very surreal mistake.

Olivia Newton-John was more dishy than I'd ever expected; Roy Harper was funnier and Peter Grant was more scary. The meeting with Uriah Heep resembled a barbiturate contest. Bad Company were more impervious but more humorous than I'd anticipated, whilst Peter Gabriel was more unsure of himself, etc.etc. Doing pictures is what it's about but encountering all kinds of musicians in all kinds of places and in all kinds of conditions has been enjoyable and interesting, and it would be dishonest to deny it. Rock and rollers are good, bad and indifferent like the rest of us. And they can be gossiped about like the rest of us, if not more so. And gossip is the backbone of our Great British Empire, as we all know. Personally, of course, I think gossip is degrading.

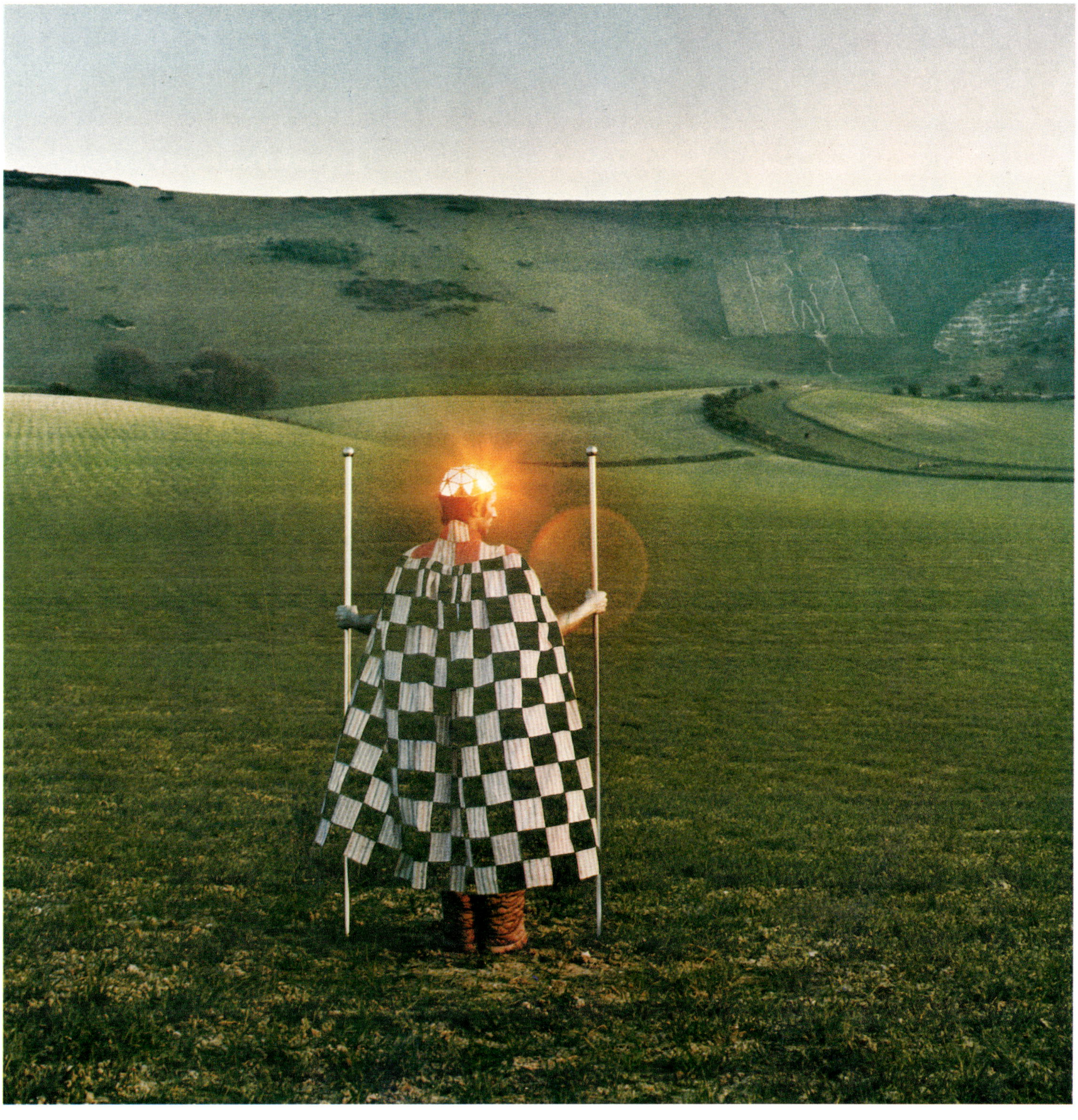

1974 UNO FRONT COVER

1975 10CC 'HOW DARE YOU' INNER SPREAD ▷

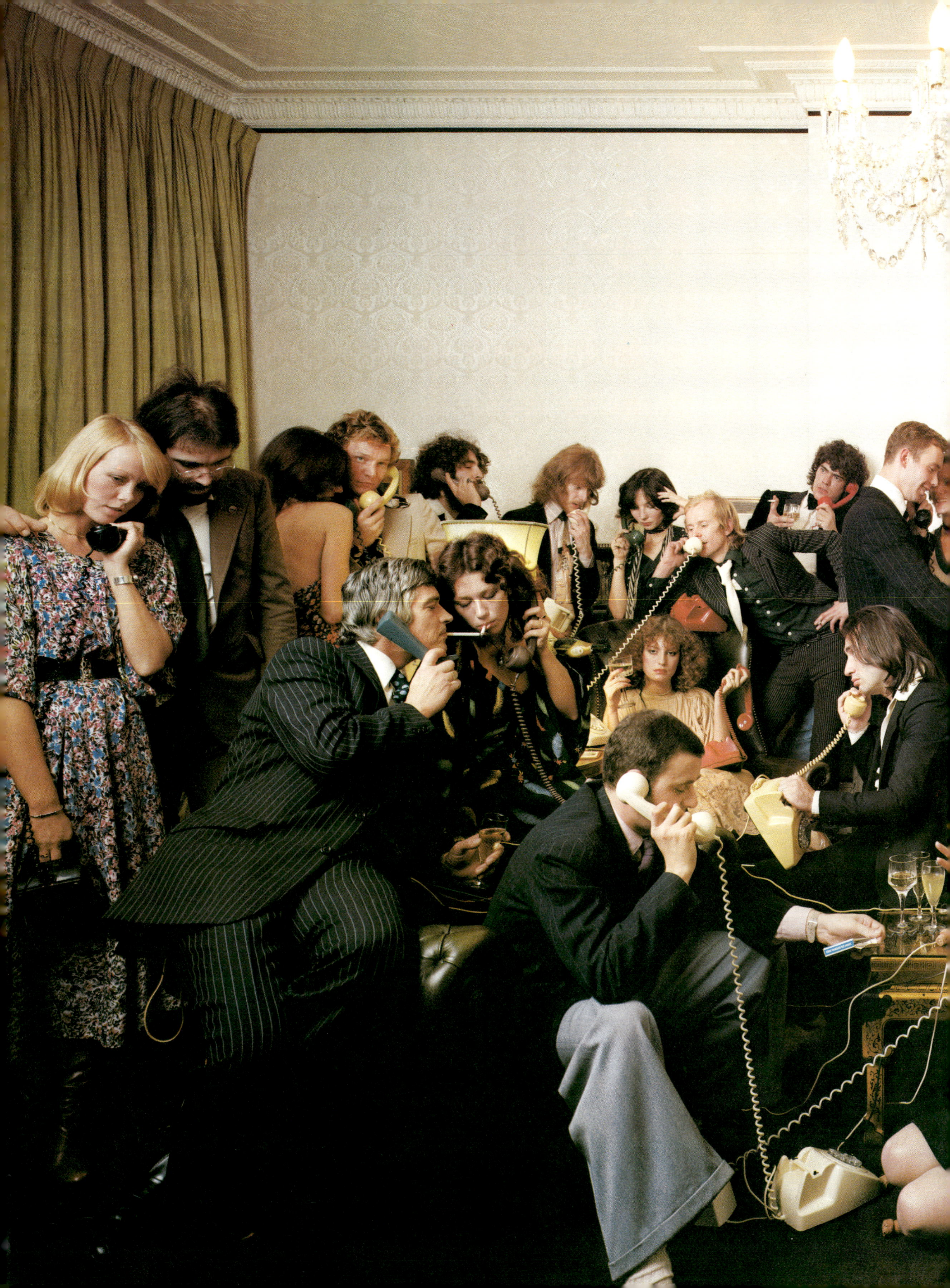

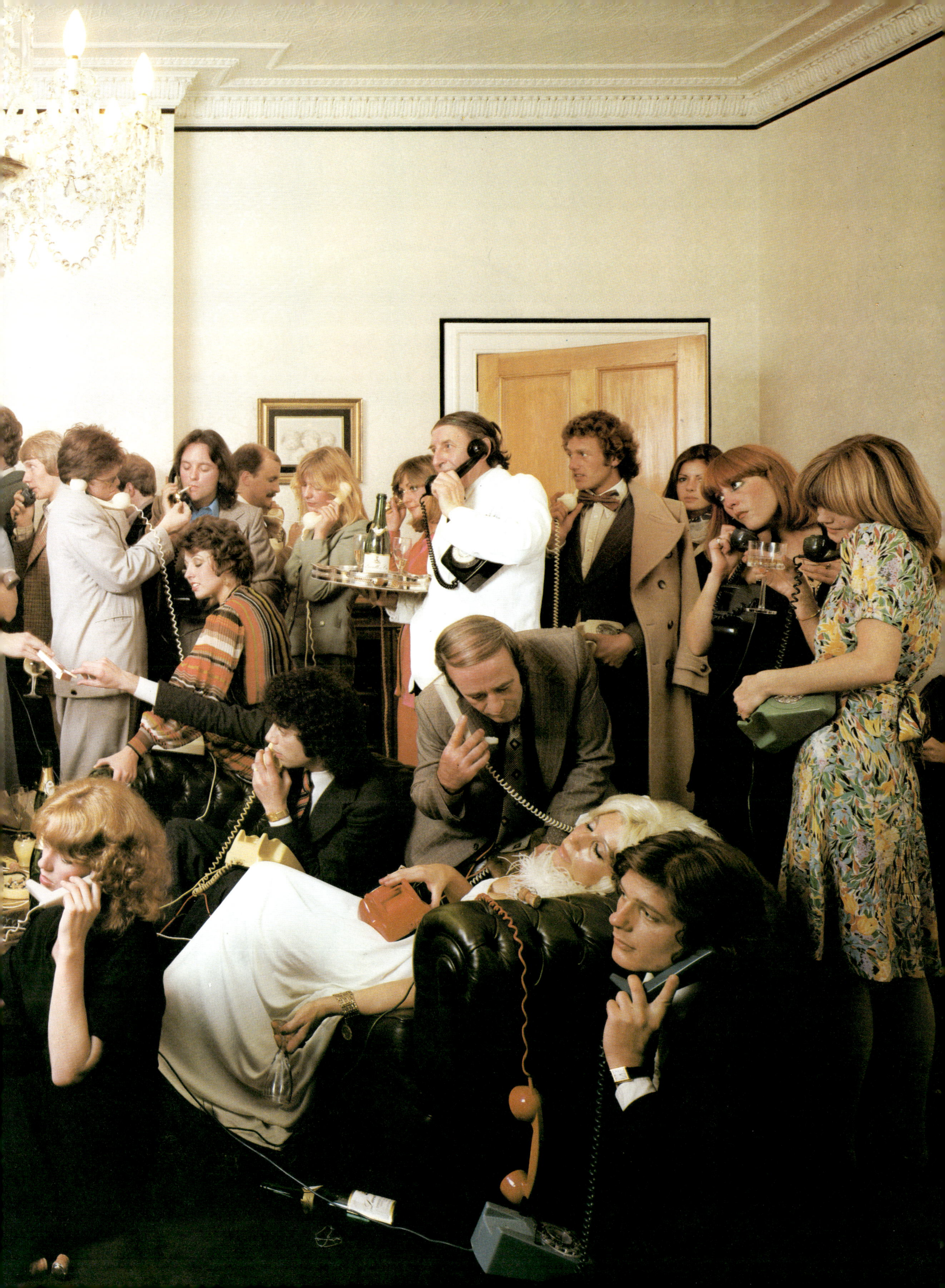

BLACK SABBATH

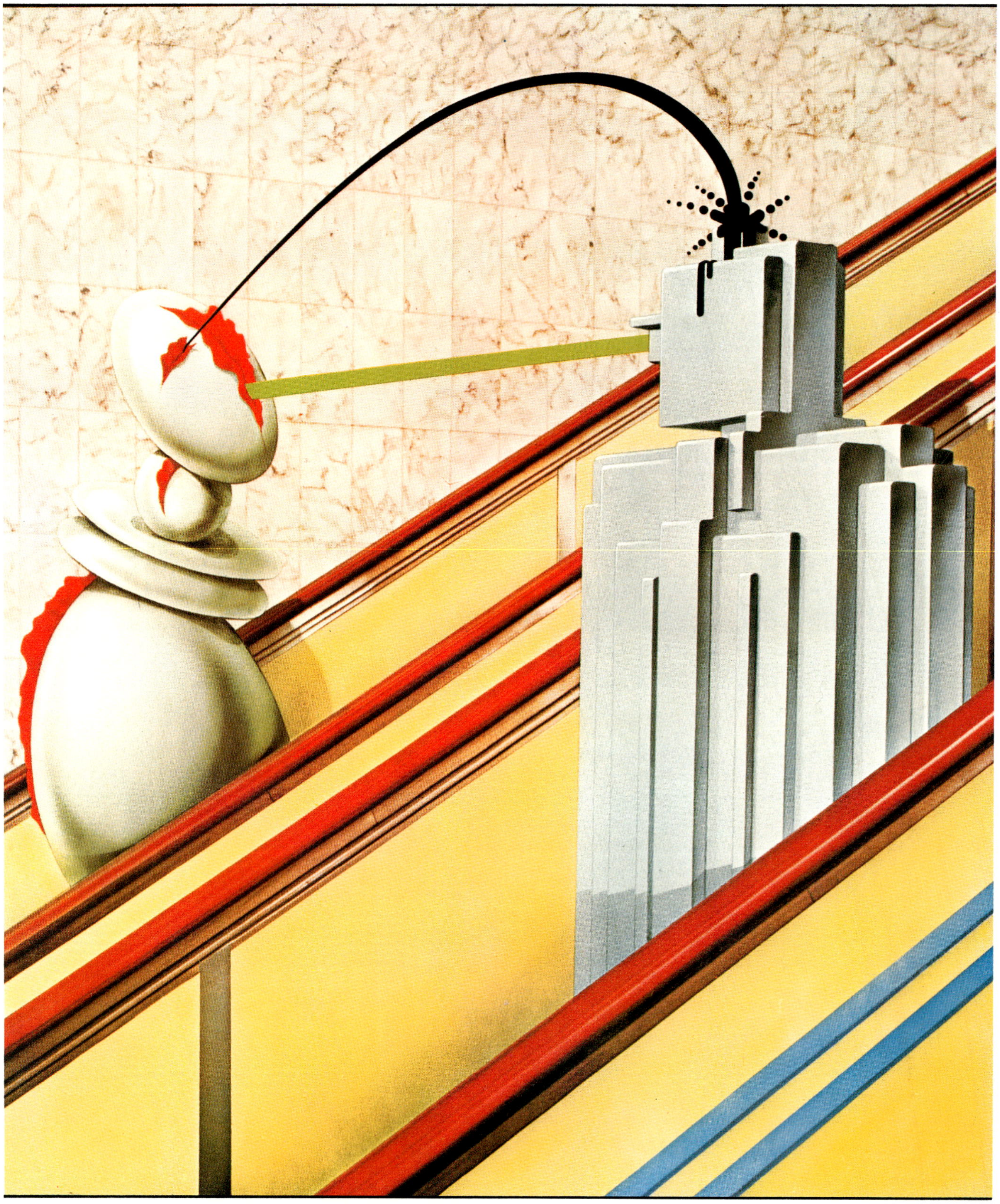

TECHNICAL ECSTASY

1976 BLACK SABBATH 'TECHNICAL ECSTASY' FRONT COVER

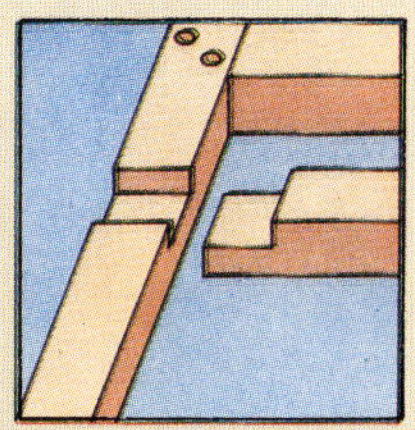

One of the more distressing events in our past took place when we worked for the Rolling Stones on 'Goatshead Soup' about four years ago. They decided to go with an idea about satyrs, in which the heads and chests of the band would be vignetted photographically onto the bodies of horses and goats. (On reflection, I don't think it was a great idea; David Bowie and Roger Daltrey have tried it on sleeves in the years that followed but it still hasn't been worth it.) The design entailed shooting the Stones themselves dressed in leotards. We hired a big studio thinking ours was a bit small and scruffy for the 'greatest rock and roll band' in the world. We stocked up with crates of beer and soft drinks for the band, and Jack Daniels scotch for Keith. We set up the lights and waited.

And we waited. Getting more and more nervous by the minute. Po was in a world of his own, rushing about furiously, fussing over details, trying to get everything just right. Not one of us felt relaxed. Three hours later the Stones finally arrived. Already our time was running out. And then to our horror Keith refused to be photographed in a leotard; he thought it silly. Now, I think he's very entitled to his opinion but why hadn't anyone told him earlier what we were going to do? So there was Keith arguing with Mick in the dressing room doorway, looking as black as night and as though he hadn't slept in a week. An hour of embarrassing inactivity passed — it felt terrible, all our worst paranoid fears come true. Finally Keith agreed and posed, actually with more enthusiasm than the others, but the moment had gone. Needless to say they later rejected the idea; nor did they like any of the publicity shots that they had asked us to take. Not surprising, but deeply disappointing.

Allan Clarke's second solo album was an artistic blunder of our own making. He stressed the need to convey the idea of co-operation on his album — of the musicians all helping each other, trying to build a single successful entity. We suggested a gymnastic sculpture like the human pyramid. Allan wasn't exactly bowled over by this idea but went along with our enthusiasm. We shot the thing twice, once with girls and once with boys. We reckoned that the gymnasium itself would be pretty striking, and then when one thinks of all those lovely young girls (or boys) in gym slips and aertex . . . it fairly takes the breath away. Well, we were wrong; very wrong. The whole thing looked charmless. Cap in hand we had to tell Allan that it was crummy. And we were the ones who had told him that it was going to be great.

I once shot a studio photosession of the Pretty Things and omitted to check the flash setting on the camera lens. It was on manual, not on flash and thus the shutter wasn't synchronized with the light. No illumination, no exposure. Two hours hard endeavour and absolutely nothing on the film. Blank, blank. You should've seen the group's faces. But of course you couldn't, because nothing came out. The burning man on 'Wish You Were Here' (see W) wore an asbestos suit under his ordinary suit. The asbestos stretched over his head and he wore a wig. He was literally set on fire, but the first time we did it the wind was blowing the wrong way, and so the flames licked round the front and burnt his moustache. Yikes!

For Wishbone Ash 'Argus' (pg. 42) we told the band and manager how we wished to shoot a picture of this timeless warrior at the mouth of a magnificent gorge, waiting patiently for the arrival of the space visitors. We described in breathtaking terms the Gorge du Verdun in Provence, Europe's answer to the Grand Canyon, and how the warrior, motionless as a sentinel, would look remarkable in relation to the vista around him, the jagged rocks, the rising cliffs and the floor of the plain behind, stretching magically into the distance. (We envisaged the warrior in medium long shot.) Don't sound so bad, does it? Well, the Gorge du Verdun *is* incredible. The trouble was that it was too incredible. A sheer knife cut two thousand feet deep, straight through the floor of an alpine valley. Hills rise above it and then suddenly it drops, miles and miles down to a tumbling river. We drove from

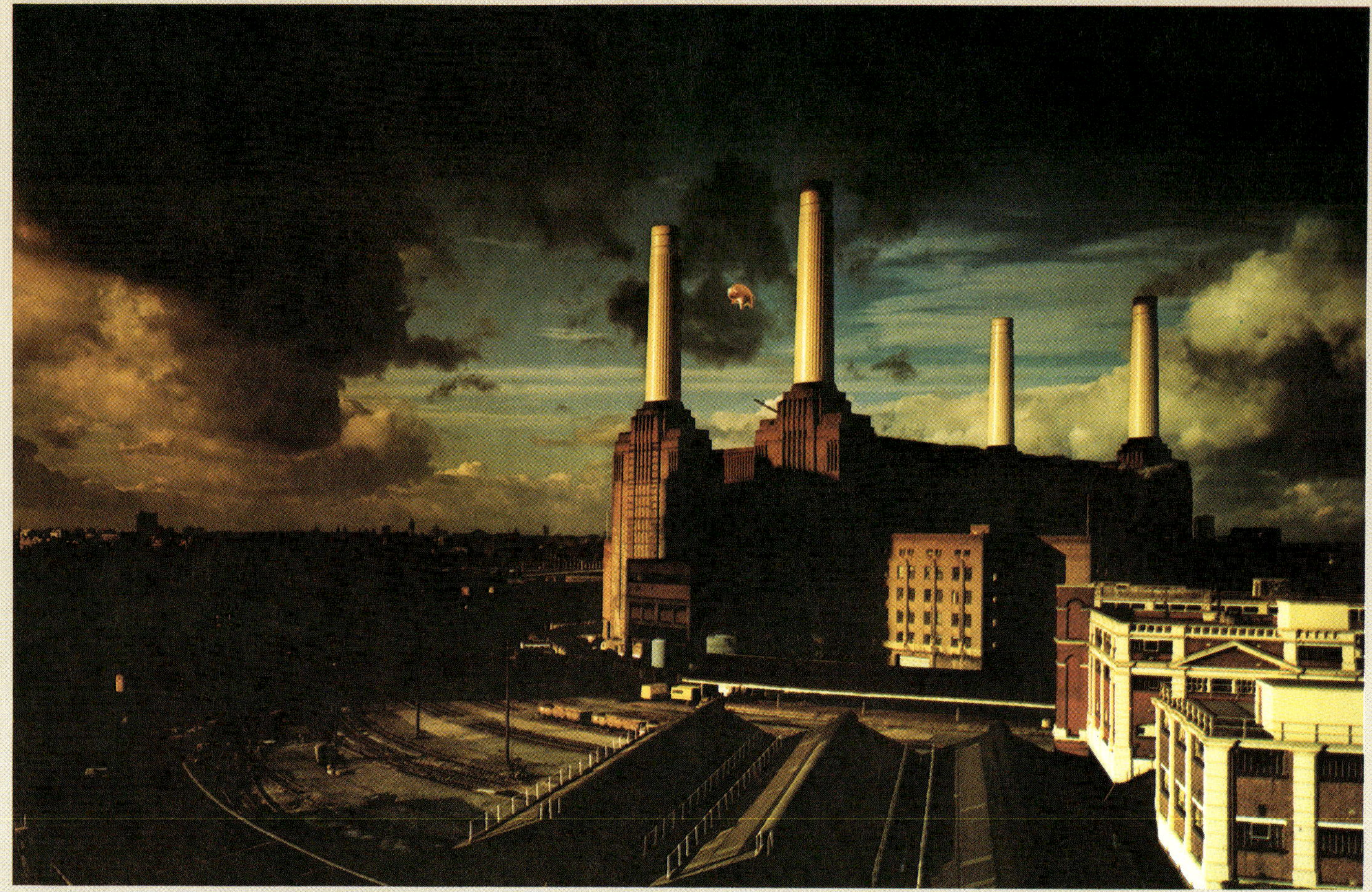

one end to the other and back again, but it was much too frightening. We simply didn't dare go near the edge. We chickened out. Next day we got up at dawn and photographed the cover by the side of the road! A fairly ordinary scene but the light was good and, in fact, it was an improvement to have the warrior close to. Going to the South of France had cost plenty and though the client was very keen on the final result it could've been shot in the Cotswolds, or Hampstead Heath at a pinch. But we didn't tell him that.

The most publicised fiasco was the Great Pig Escape, early 1977. Pink Floyd had rejected our suggestion for their 'Animals' cover in favour of the Pig hovering over Battersea Power Station. Despite serious misgivings about such a notion (shades of Monty Python and the Goodies — was it not intrinsically silly?) we offered to shoot the pictures and put the cover together. Contrary to our advice the band didn't want the pig 'stripped-in' (see pg. 52) which would allow us to photograph the pig anywhere, but wanted it shot for real, the pig actually floating above the power station. Thus the forty foot zeppelin was crated to London and assembled on location. Timetable as follows:—

Day 1. Still camera crew of eleven positioned at all good vantage points, plus eight man film crew, helicopter, roadies, group and manager, and one marksman with telescopic rifle to gun down the Pig in case it should escape and fall on someone's noggin (an insurance problem). Much puffing and blowing, many gas cylinders etc. but the pig was not launched. A beautifully moody sky, perfect photographic conditions, apart from being a bit chilly.

Day 2. Eleven still cameramen, eight man film crew, helicopter, one or two of the group, manager but no marksman (?). Pig launched successfully on bright clear morning. Hauled slowly up side of building, everyone snapping away. Near the top, betwixt the towers, a fateful gust of wind. The pig turned suddenly, broke mooring cable and lurched rapidly towards the heavens. No one had told the marksman to return. The pig sailed away and was lost from sight in five minutes. Absolute horrors. All that time and money and it had simply disappeared in front of our eyes. The police trailed it to thirty thousand feet and then gave up, the cowards. That evening, the dirigible came down on a Kent farm. The farmer was reported to have said he thought it "a bit unusual"! Actually the Press made a bundle out of the whole thing: "flying pig interrupts international flight patterns", "weird UFO spotted", "flying pig heads for home" (it was made in Holland). But the Floyd don't give up that easily and the roadies rescued it from Kent, repaired the puncture and we started again.

Day 3. Only four or five still photographers this time, plus depleted film crew but everything went really well. Pig stayed in position perfectly and everyone clicked away, the helicopter zoomed about, and we were all delighted.

The band were equally delighted. The material, movie and still, was fine (as it shoud've been after three whole days), but there was a snag. As if the whole event hadn't been enough of a fiasco, and very funny at that, it transpired that the band liked the sky and power station from Day 1 (but there was no pig) and the pig from Day 3, but the sky was boring. Well, well. What could we do but strip it in after all? Pig from Day 3 dropped into sky of Day 1 and retouched. It *is* true that we were seen to smile somewhat when they decided to do that.

An entirely different set of problems are the personal ones. Hipgnosis was burgled twice. Once on location when the entire camera collection was snitched from our parked car. This was back in 1971 and was disastrous for the head. We hadn't been going long and the theft was a psychological bombshell. The second burglary was very strange. About two years later our mate John Blake rang me at home. "Your front door is off its hinges." Someone had been through it like Desperate Dan. No messing with locks or anything, just straight on through. But the burglar had failed to find the cameras. In his frustration he had thrown our paper work all over the office, had done a crap on the floor, and had ripped a proof of Cochise off the wall and torn in into little pieces.

The Americans didn't like the naked couple on Toe Fat (pg. 10). The rumour was that they took them off and replaced them with a lamb, of all things. Birth Control (pg. 136) was considered so offensive by Roman Catholic women working in the packing factory, that they threatened not to handle it. We were surprised that they knew what it was. Flash 'Knickers' was banned in Franco's Spain and allegedly 'Houses of the Holy, was thought immoral and depraved in Kansas. Fumble's manager thought he was going to get a picture of fumbling at a teenage party and we forgot to tell him that we'd changed it to a quiet scene in front of the telly. He wasn't amused. The Winkies was felt to be too provocative by Chrysalis USA, Montrose was described as male chauvinist, no one knew what 'Presence' was all about, Edgar Broughton was labelled disgusting and degenerate by EMI's marketing manager and 'Wish You Were Here' was hated by the industry for its black shrink wrap — there's no pleasing some folks.

There were two pictures in 'Nice Pair' that had to be abandoned for legal reasons. The first was a photo of Floyd Patterson painted pink. He wasn't amused either. The second was the front window of a shop with venetian blinds. It was, in fact, a dentist in Hammersmith. But dentists are not allowed to advertise — it's contrary to professional ethics. On the window was inscribed the dentist's name . . . W. R. Phang.

When we were doing 'In Deep' for Argent (below), we told them that the idea would only be interesting if it were the band themselves submerged in the pool. They agreed whole-heartedly and so the following week we all turned up at the swimming pool at Crystal Palace. Running beneath the pool edge was a corridor with windows that looked into the pool itself. We positioned the camera appropriately and waited for the band to jump in the deep part. They dived in on cue and everything was going smoothly until Po in the corridor below started shouting that one of the band had not submerged enough, and was not visible in the camera. That was all very fair, but he was also failing to surface enough. We dived in and hauled him out to the safety of dry land, spluttering like an expiring fish. The unfortunate gentleman survived alright but was so shaken by the experience that the roadies rushed him home to recuperate. Much as I was impressed by his selfless endeavours on behalf of the group's promotion, I was, nonetheless, amazed that he had failed to tell us that he couldn't swim a stroke.

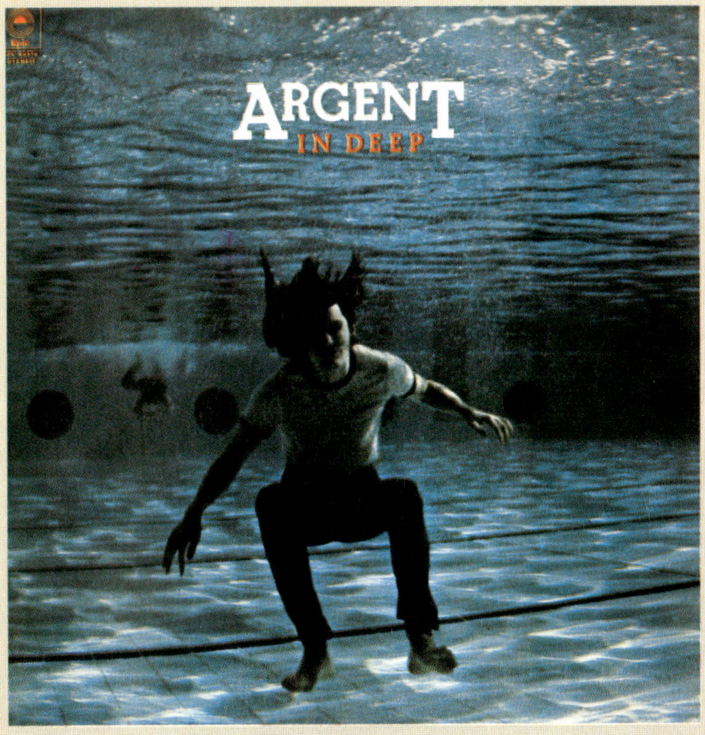

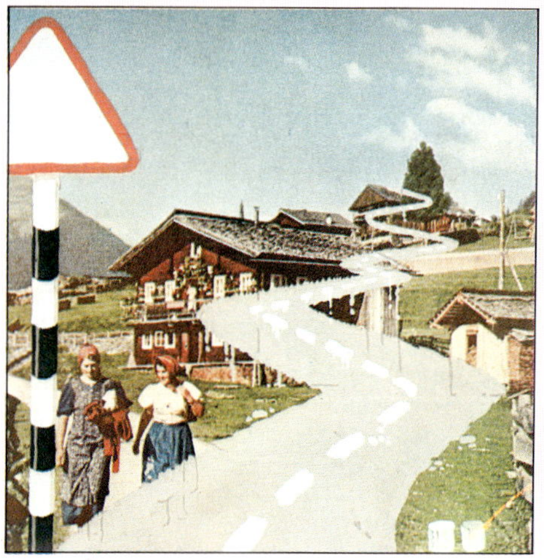

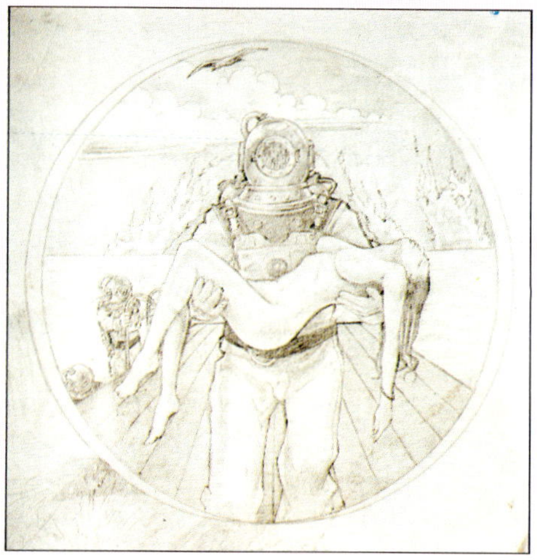

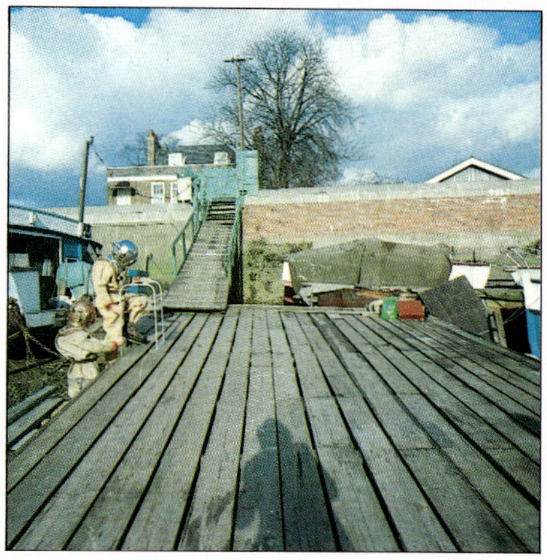

The stages of doing the sleeve for 10cc's 'Deceptive Bends' were basically the same as for most jobs though slightly more involved because of the complexity of the final artwork. These stages are as follows:— a) Commission; b) Brief and first meeting with the band; c) Roughs and second meeting with the band; d) Shooting; e) Artwork; f) Finishing.

The Commission

When 10cc were with Jonathan King, it was he, rather than them, who first came to us for 'Sheet Music'. By the time 'Deceptive Bends' was being recorded we had come to know 10cc and had designed three previous sleeves. They rang us up and said come round to listen to four songs that had been recorded and to chat about the sleeve.

The Brief

At the time (December 1976) 10cc had just split in half. Eric Stewart and Graham Gouldman were continuing 10cc and the record was their first attempt alone. They felt that a positive and romantic image was appropriate. They'd decided on the title, taken from some road signs on the way to their studio in Dorking and they'd composed four tracks which they played me. Included was 'Good Morning Judge' and 'The Things We Do for Love' so it sounded not totally unlike the 10cc we had known. They had no specific notions of their own, either about the visuals or about the packaging. There was serious talk about whether their faces should be on the front of the sleeve (the Americans had been pressing for this) but they considered that this was too egocentric, especially since they had just lost half the band. It hadn't been a feature before so it didn't seem worth pursuing now.

The Roughs

On the way home from the studio the first night that I'd seen Eric and Graham, I got to thinking about 'Deceptive Bends' as a phrase. I began to free associate and make simple connections and deductions. I cast aside anything to do with bends and curves in the road as too obvious. I rejected any ideas about deceiving the viewer with things that were bent but looked straight as idle trickery. As a result of this I considered the other possible meanings of bends . . . and the bends of a diver came easily to mind. I thought immediately of those diver's suits from the 20's or 30's and how amazing they look, not only for their bizarre metallic helmets but also for the whole 'monster' feeling that they evoke. Since you can't see either the face or the body you've no idea what the occupant really looks like. And then it wasn't long before I felt that the deception of 'Deceptive Bends' referred to the person in the picture, not to the person looking at it. The diver is deceived by his own bends and so fantasizes freely. Since the band wanted a positive design it had to be an up-lifting fantasy—such as emerging from the waters of the deep with his arms full of treasure. Perhaps he'd imagined himself rescuing the girl of his dreams from a watery death. I felt that this image would

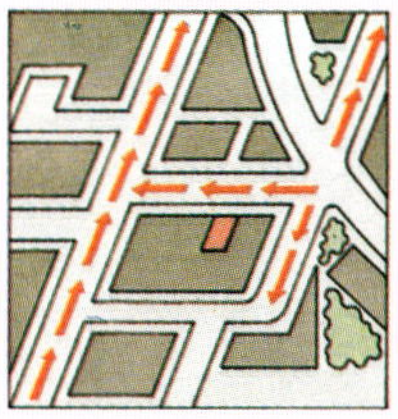

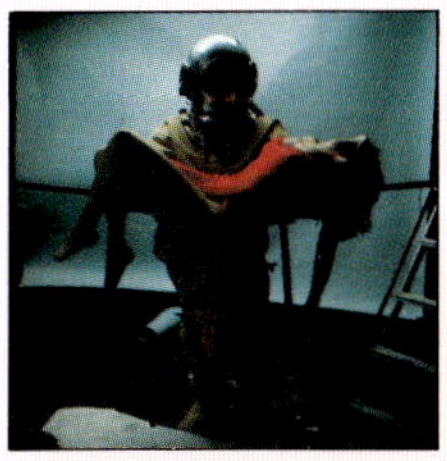

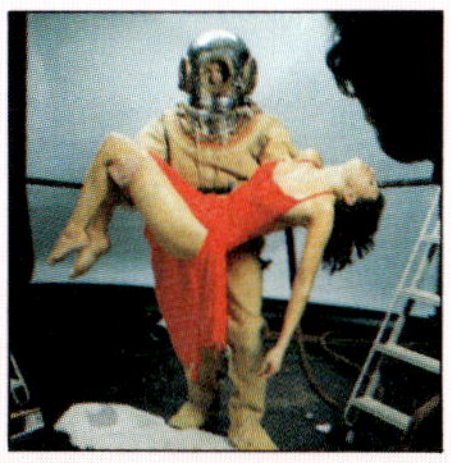

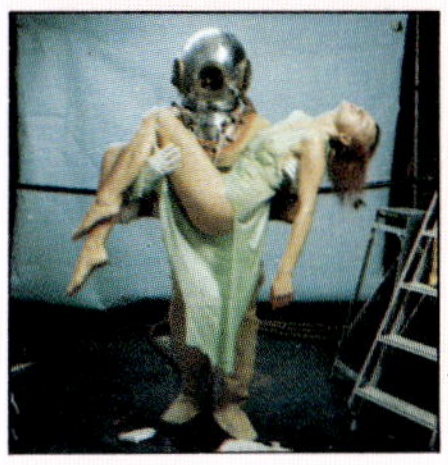

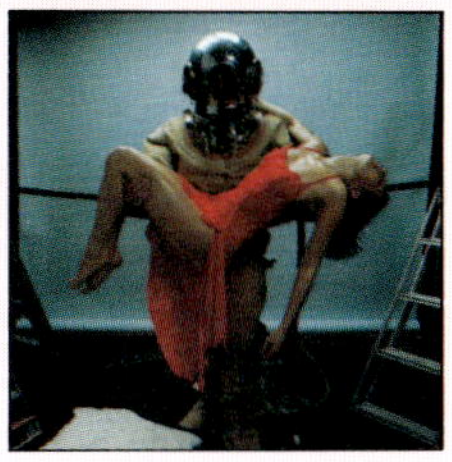

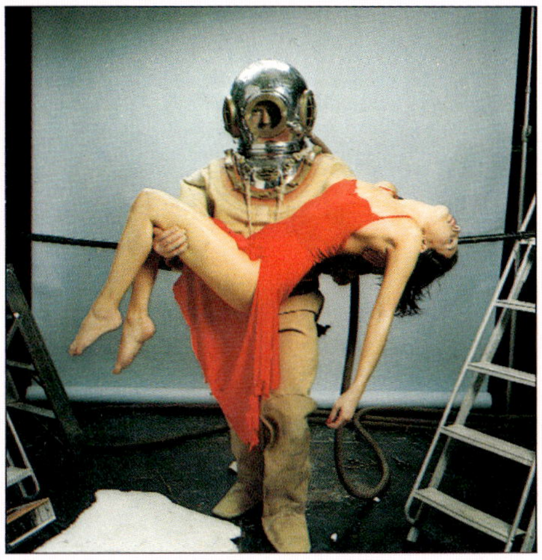

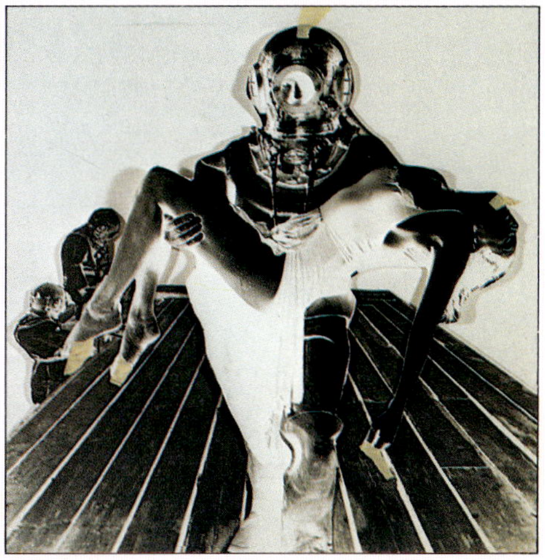

possess an heroic myth quality. Privately we may see ourselves as heroes, rescuing our sweethearts from fires, earthquakes and any number of terrible fates and it was this mythic feeling that appealed to me most. When I 'saw' it I visualised it in a circular frame (like the diver's mask). The border around it on the sleeve might well be illustrated but the central image had to be photographic, otherwise it would be too clichéd and too like a hundred comic book covers we've all seen before.

During the next month we had several meetings and came up with other possibilities, including some roads! They were drawn out as pencil or paint roughs and taken back to 10cc. This second meeting with the client is a fairly nerve racking affair because if they don't like anything we either have to start over again or are given the gentle elbow. Fortunately Eric and Graham were very keen on at least two ideas, the diver and one other. They asked us how certain things might actually end up and what colours we had in mind. They removed ones they considered inappropriate until they were left with the two, and then finally the one. We hit a ticklish spot here because Eric wanted to change the jetty into a road. This debate about the road was just plain awkward for about an hour. I personally couldn't see it. Eric gracefully gave way and the word was go.

The Shooting

Having agreed a budget with Phonogram (10cc's record company) we began to organise the actual photography. We decided against staging the idea as one complete event because there would be too many uncontrollable variables. Instead we would do it in bits and join them together later. As far as the shooting of covers is concerned 'Deceptive Bends' was relatively straightforward, though lengthy. We had decided to hire a studio specially, rather than use our own, so that we would have enough space to set up lights, dress and make-up models, organise diving apparatus and keep the boys comfortable and happy. At about 11 a.m. Peter picked up the diver and met with Po at the studio. The next hour or so was spent setting up the basic shooting configuration, grey backdrop, position and intensity of lights etc. After a short argument we settled on a large 'fishfryer' pointing down and slightly forward behind the diver's head and a smaller but stronger light in front and to the right of the camera. At this stage we usually take numerous polaroid test shots to see what it looks like on paper (often very different to what one thinks one sees in real life!) As a result of seeing these we added a couple of large white reflector boards to the left of camera to lighten up the shadows.

Once the diver was in his suit it was discovered that although he was no weakling the suit was so heavy that he could only lift and hold the lady with a lot of difficulty. Since we usually take ages faffing about with the camera it was consequently necessary to support the girl in some

HELMET, PRINTS OF DENMARK STREET

way. We rigged a bar just in front of him upon which to rest his arms. (Even with this he was pretty tired by the end of the day). The pictures were shot using a Hasselblad $2\frac{1}{4}''$ format camera.

To give us more of a choice later on we shot the front picture twice over with different girls wearing different dresses. Then the band arrived about 3 p.m. After a little make-up and appropriate hair wetting they were photographed for the back of the sleeve. Then we shot the lone diver who appears behind them. At the same time, we were filming the front picture of the diver and the girl on 35 mm. movie film in case it should be needed for a TV commercial. It takes a lot of time trying to make sure that for each different picture everything is how you want it, from the basic camera angle down to how wet the girl's legs are. We finished the whole of this session about 10.30 p.m. The jetty was photographed a couple of days later on location—by the Thames in Hammersmith. (The sea and sky pictures were procured from photo libraries but only after a long and arduous search,and only after we'd seen prints of the studio session).

The Artwork

When all the transparencies came back from processing there was a sigh of relief. But then there were furious debates as to which pictures should actually be used. (Some of the alternatives are shown here.) Using reversal prints, small scale mock-ups of the finished thing were made to give us a better idea of how it was looking. Eric and Graham popped in to select their own photos and to cast their votes on the front cover. By a lengthy process of elimination, by identifying the different faults with different pictures, we eventually chose the final ones. This is often a compromise because one sees good points in one photograph that are simply missing from another. Primarily, I think, we looked for a clearly stepping forward pose for the diver and a good curved (deceptive bend) shape to the girl, so that she looked really limp. Of secondary importance was the way the girl's dress fell, how her legs, shoulders and breasts looked and how her head hung. Lastly, we examined the head of the diver, searching for one which was looking very definitely toward the viewer. In addition, the lighting and focus needed to be spot on. When you consider all these points you can appreciate the necessity for shooting a lot of film.

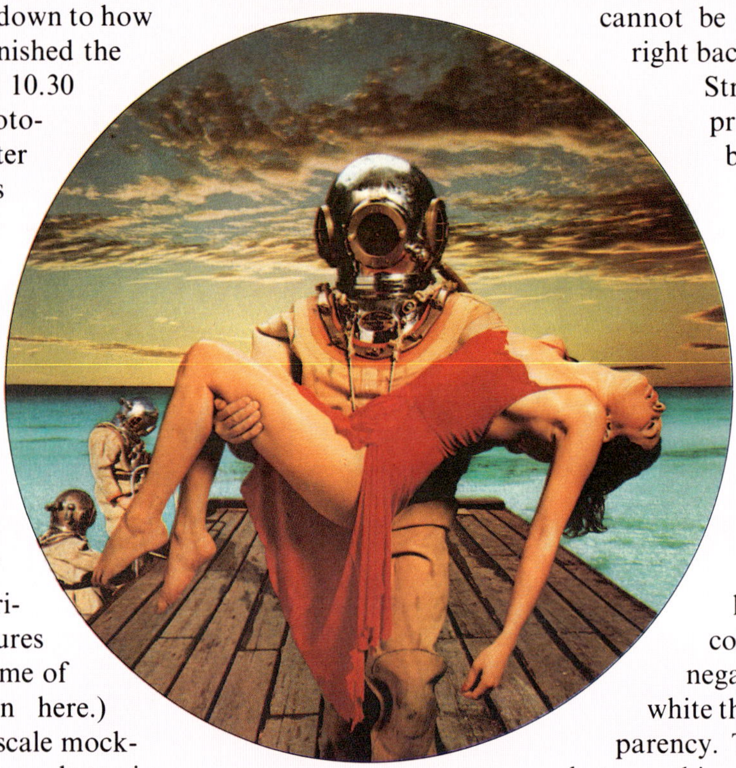

By using black and white negative prints taken from the actual transparencies we plan to use, we montaged a finished composition, oversized, in order to preserve the quality when the artwork came to be separated. This terminal composition could either be montaged or stripped-in finally using the selected colour pictures. Montage often requires copying on to one print and then retouching in order to prevent the overlapping elements causing shadows when the artwork is separated for the actual cover. Strip-in, however, gives a first generation combined print on a single surface and so avoids copying and the risk of unwanted colour variance and loss of focus. This advantage is partially offset by the composition being fixed—once decided and stripped-in for real it cannot be altered other than by going right back to the beginning.

Strip-ins involve dye transfer prints and are consequently bright and strong but very expensive. Initially the chosen transparency is separated into three black and white negative films which correspond to three colours (the dyes) namely magenta, yellow and cyan which when recombined give the full colour range of the original.

Each negative bears the photographic image in relation to the proportion of its colour in the original; the cyan negative represents in black and white the amount of cyan in the transparency. The image on the negative is photographic or silver based. The next stage is to contact the negatives on to positive films or matts which are gelatin based and bear the image in relief. The individual matts are soaked in the three dyes and then rolled on to the printed paper one after the other in exact register depositing their proportion of dye. A strip-in is achieved by contacting two sets of negatives from two transparencies on to a single set of matts whilst masking out the areas not required. Thus the matts will carry the required combination of images and the resultant print only needs the join or strip marks to be retouched. 'Deceptive Bends' is a four part strip—sky, sea, jetty, and diver and girl— and it called for some very careful retouching work by Richard Manning.

The complete pictures was given the thumbs up by 10cc. But the border remained a problem, mostly because it was virtually impossible to see it with the finished picture in the

1977 | 10CC 'DECEPTIVE BENDS' | FRONT COVER

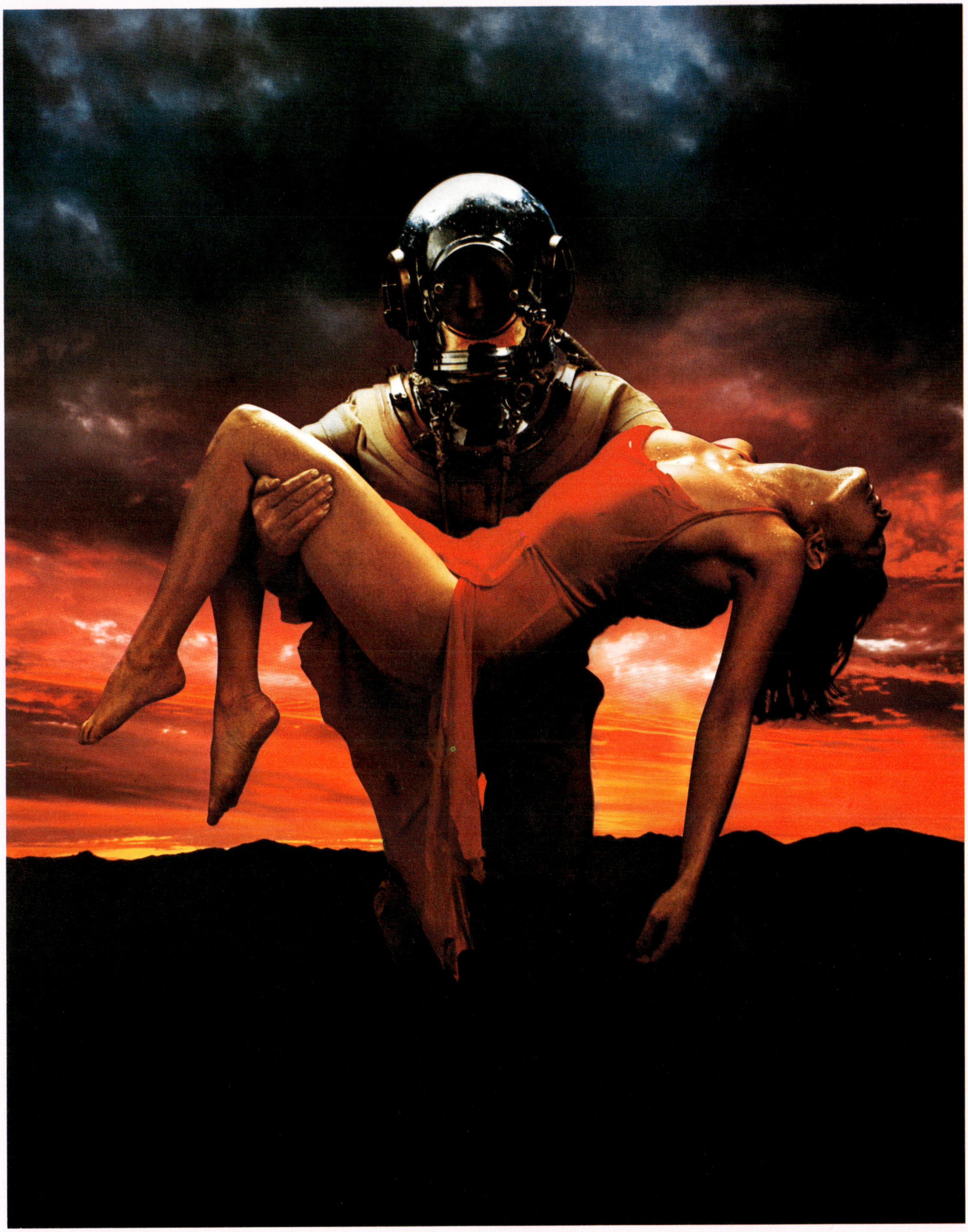

1977 | 10CC 'DECEPTIVE BENDS' | POSTER

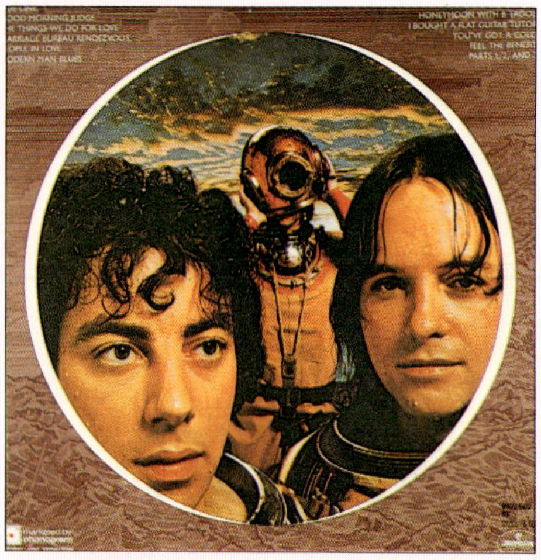

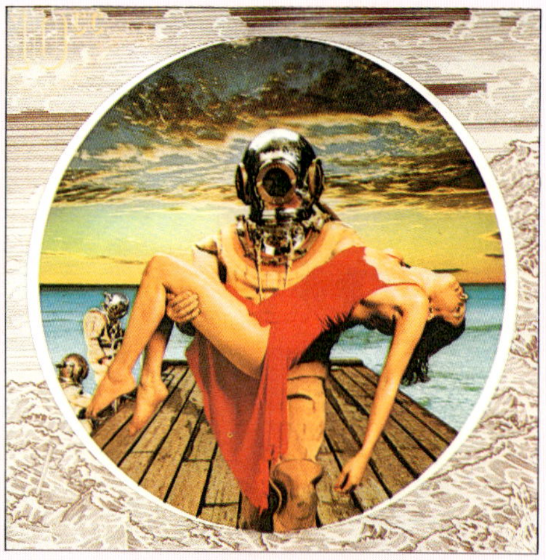

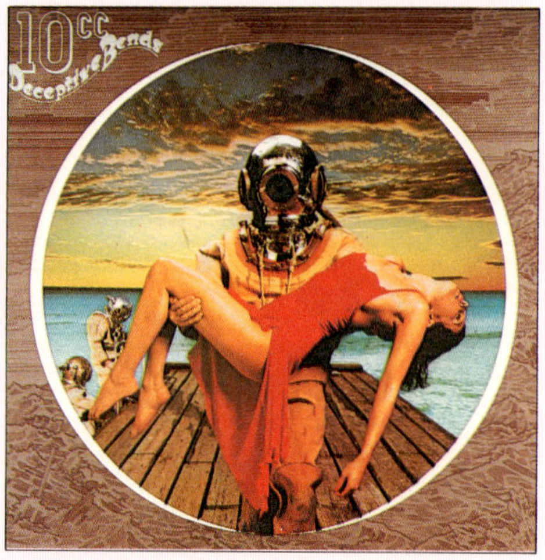

middle of it. We tried all sorts of colours and types of illustration. A plain border didn't work nor would a photographic one. It didn't want to be too colourful or too dull. In the end Colin suggested a pen and ink line drawing. It was executed in black and white and then requested to be printed in pale green. (Although it may seem odd we've chosen to show the poster large here rather than the sleeve. It was, of course, done at the same time and in the same way).

The Finish

The end is in sight. The record company is clamouring for the artwork, when suddenly we notice some blemish, or some minute piece of retouching that still needs to be done. At this juncture, the cover artwork is in many pieces—the pictures, front and back, the border, the lettering and the mechanical. This last piece indicates how the other pieces are to fit together on the final sleeve. In addition, there are some credits, logos and record numbers which are pasted down on this mechanical. The several pieces are labelled and covered with protective paper. Each item carries copious notes which inform the separator and printer about how it all joins up. Since this 'mark-up' is detailed and potentially confusing we endeavour to speak to the printer personally.

The separation of the artwork and the printing of the actual sleeve are vital to us in so much as if these processes are not performed as efficiently as possible, our work can look terrible when it reaches the public. And we don't want that if we can possibly avoid it. The first proof of 'Deceptive Bends' was awful. It was done again and the border colour altered from green to a maroon. The second proof was alright and the printing got under way. But then another calamity befell us—the red printing plate was weak in density. The over inking of the other plates, in order to compensate for this weakness, produced a dreadfully lurid result. Horrors. But 50,000 copies had to be done to meet shipping schedules after which the record company agreed to change plates and start over again. All this takes up time and destroys valuable brain cells. 'Deceptive Bends' began at the end of December 1976 and the printed sleeve appeared in April 1977.

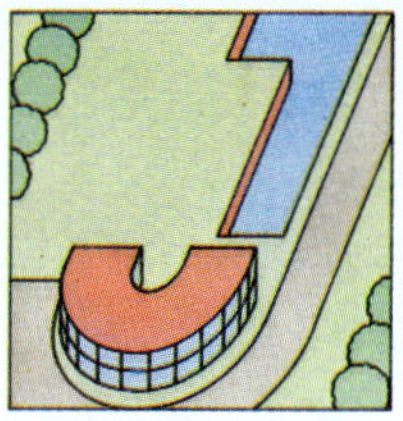

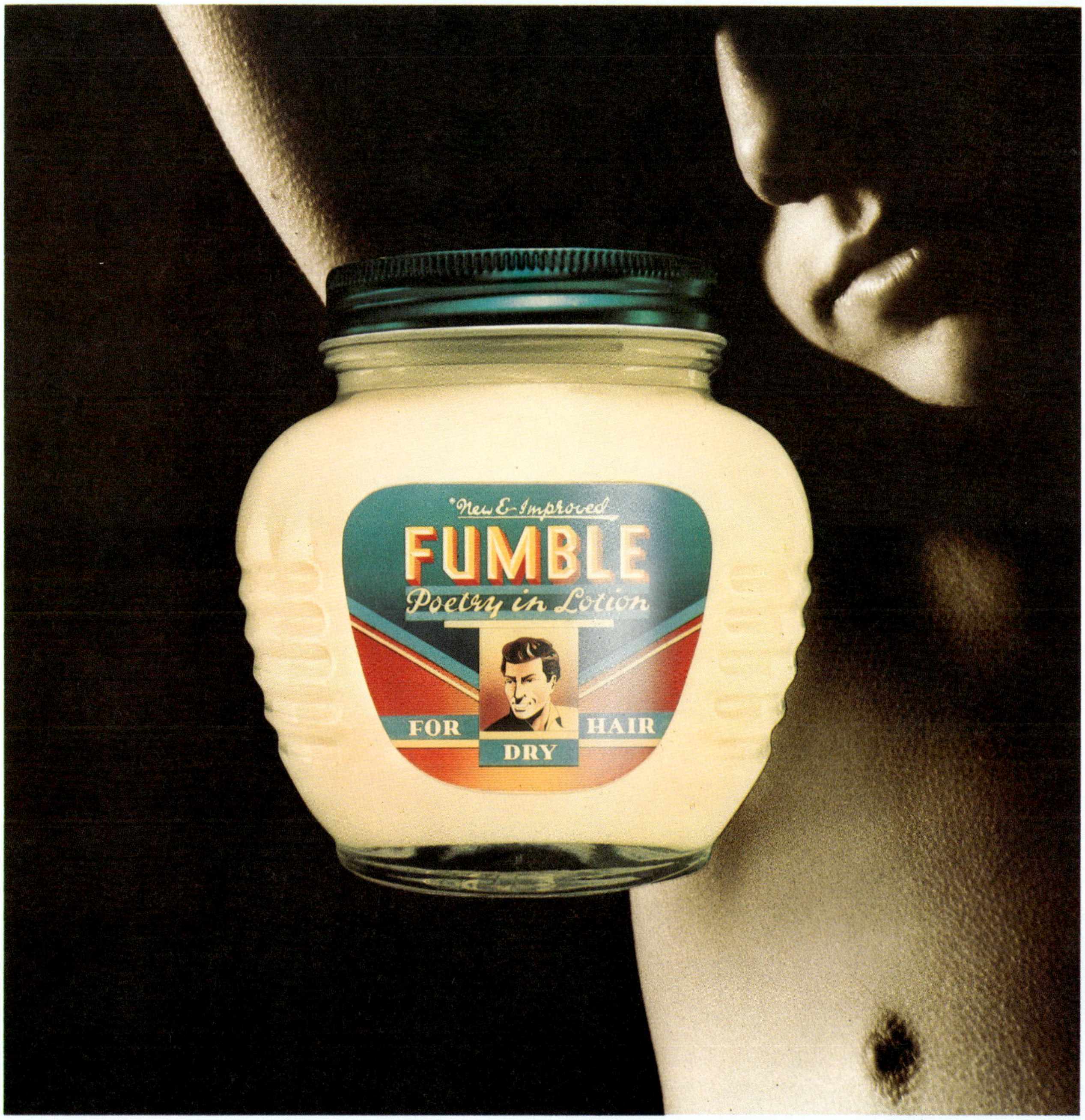

1974	FUMBLE 'POETRY IN LOTION'	FRONT COVER

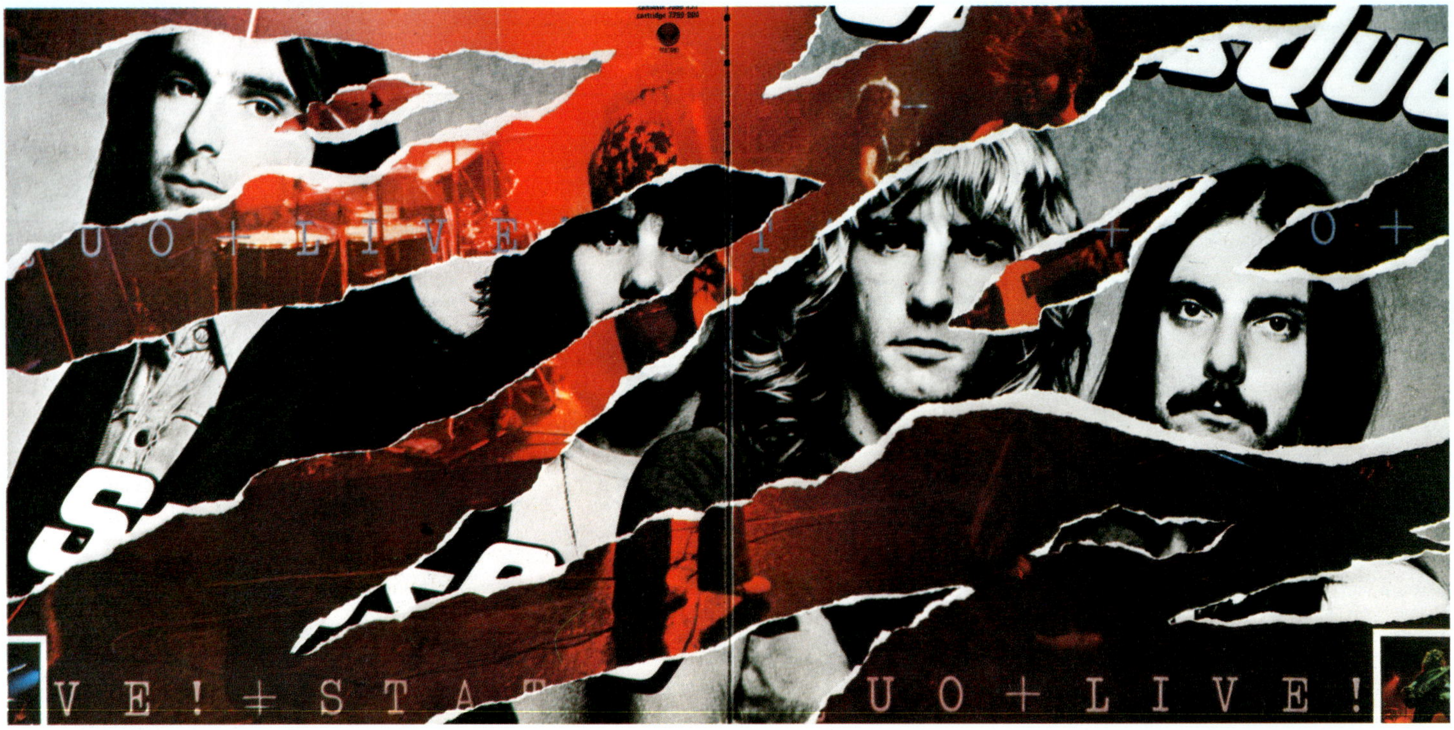

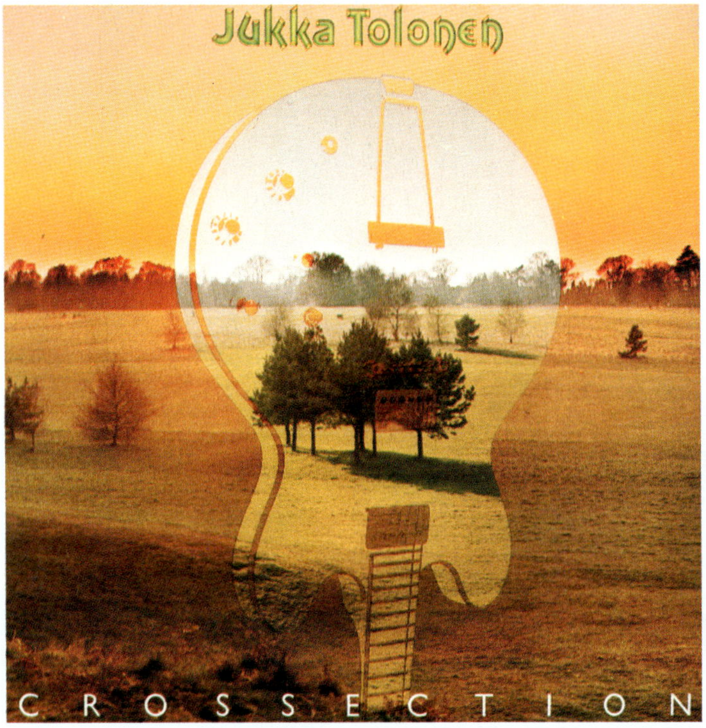

Designing for live albums is a thorny problem because it feels so predictable to use a live photograph and so obscure and uncommercial not to. In the face of this perplexing double bind record companies usually choose to play it safe. Consequently, most live sleeves are the same, and most of them are tedious — a live photo that often feels more dead than alive. Status Quo is a juxtaposition which attempts to avoid this pitfall. The idea comes from three things — firstly, the situation on street walls where posters have been pasted on top of each other and when one is ripped by fans or the ravages of time so another beneath may be partially seen. Secondly, the tearing is a decisive but unprogrammed action, appropriate to the energy of a live recording. And lastly, the design is a variation on a double level theme wherein an attempt is made to present two partial images in the same picture, but to leave enough of either picture visible so that the eye can fill in the rest. Hopefully, it means you don't see both pictures clearly at the one time. For Quo two posters were newly designed and printed up as actual items. The tearing was then done for real (about twelve times).

1977 STATUS QUO 'LIVE'

1975 JUKKA TOLONEN 'CROSS SECTION'

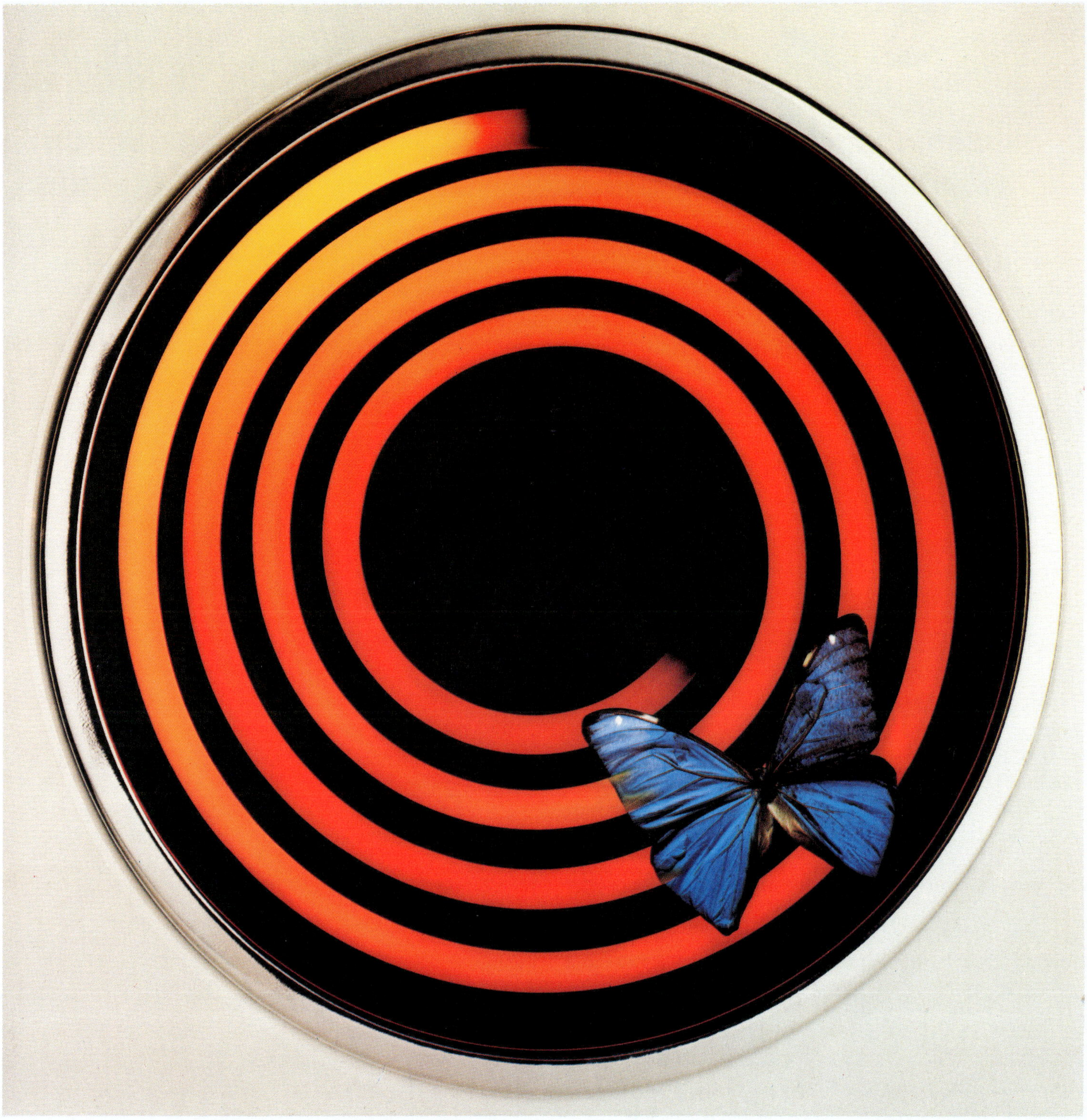

1975 SOLUTION 'CORDON BLEU' PHOTO H. BARTROP FRONT COVER

(I suggested that Colin wrote this section because he knows more about graphics than I do.) Though Hipgnosis are most widely known for their photographic covers they have collaborated closely with a number of designers and illustrators. Projects have included sleeve design, record labels, lettering, logos, stickers, T-shirts and so on. Among those involved have been George Hardie and Bush Hollyhead from NTA Studios, Richard Evans, Humphrey Ocean, Joe Patagno, Geoff Halpin, Geoff Cummings and myself, Colin Elgie.

These contributors encompass a wide range of styles from hard-edged abstract, through whimsical fairytale to realist. Subject matter has varied from diagrams ('Dark Side of the Moon'; 10cc 'How Dare You') to still life ('Year of the Cat'; 'Original Soundtrack') and from date box packaging ('Live Dates') to mythology (Swansong).

First it seems pertinent to explain how Hipgnosis operate in their lesser-known capacity as art directors. The illustrator or designer for a particular job is chosen for the 'appropriateness' of his style or thinking. There is usually one designer working on a job but sometimes two work together with Hipgnosis ('Tales of Mystery and Imagination'). The designer is involved in the job from an early stage, attending group meetings to discuss the brief and ideas. There tends to be a lot of argument but sooner or later a decision is made and roughs of the ideas are drawn up.

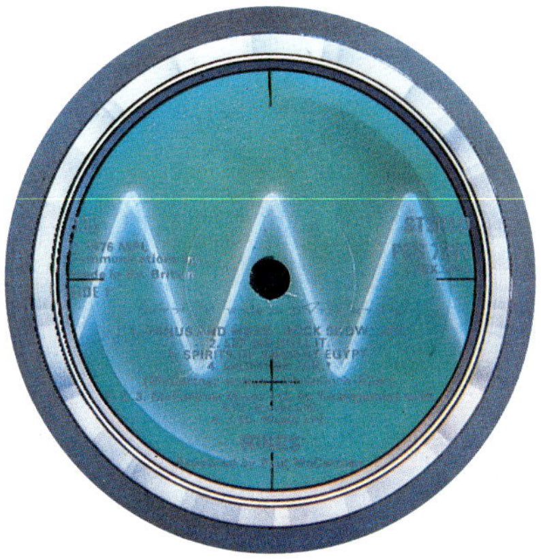

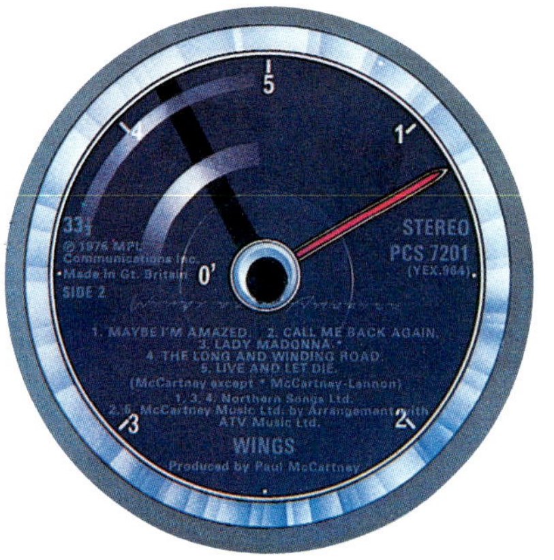

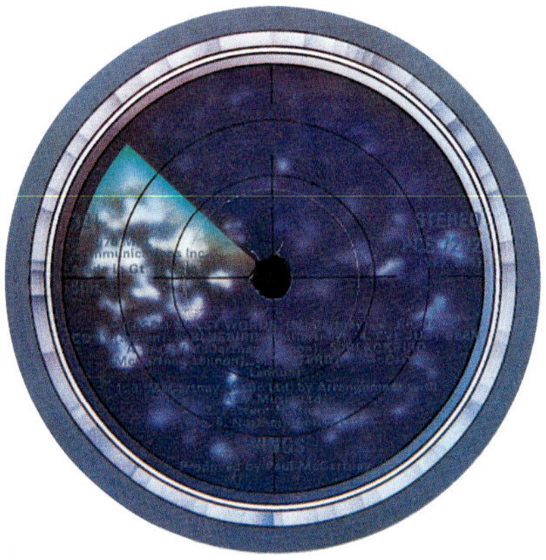

In most cases the roughs aren't exactly the kind of thing you'd hang on the wall; it is sufficient for them to get the idea across. Roughs for lettering and logos tend to be done in rapidograph pen with gouache or crayons while cover designs usually take the form of pencil drawings with examples of style to be used attached. These roughs are often accompanied by written explanations.

On acceptance of one of the ideas, the rough is then transformed into an artwork from which the covers are made. I've tried to give an idea of how different designers use the various tricks of the trade and at the same time to give a brief description (written as for beginners) of some of the techniques and processes used.

With the Mooncrest record label for B & C Records something bold and graphic was called for. The design had to be visually strong and recognizable whilst remaining romantic. After a few preliminary discussions, we submitted about five roughs; some things to do with moon-madness and sea-scapes (mostly with fairly literal meanings based around the word 'Mooncrest'). The client finally bought the painting of the three planets in a line which was taken indirectly from 2001. The image was eventually used as a corporate identity, that is on letterheads etc. The artwork was done with an airbrush using ink and gouache.

The airbrush is a small spray gun, delicate and precise. It has a receptacle which holds the paint mixture (gouache, watercolour, ink or dye can be used) which feeds into a central reservoir. By contracting a lever with your forefinger, compressed air is forced through the central reservoir, mixes with the paint and emerges as a fine spray from the nozzle. The artwork is covered by a transparent low-tack adhesive film and the areas to be coloured are carefully cut out with a surgical scalpel. The paint is then sprayed evenly over the exposed area to produce a flat tone, or more heavily in one area than another to produce gradations of tone. The masking film is then carefully removed without damage to the painting, and another mask is positioned and cut out for the next colour.

The Swansong label, also extended into a corporate identity, was airbrushed by Joe Patagno who used crayons to heighten the colour. The airbrush is also the major tool of the retoucher and much of Hipgnosis' photographic work involves retouching to some degree or other (see Rays of Light). Another spray job was 'Year of the Cat' (pg. 11). The idea, which came from George and Peter, was to imply obsession by multiple references to one object. Starting with this I worked out the contents of the picture. It's 1951 (the year of the cat in the Tibetan calender). The lady in the mirror is obsessed by cats and

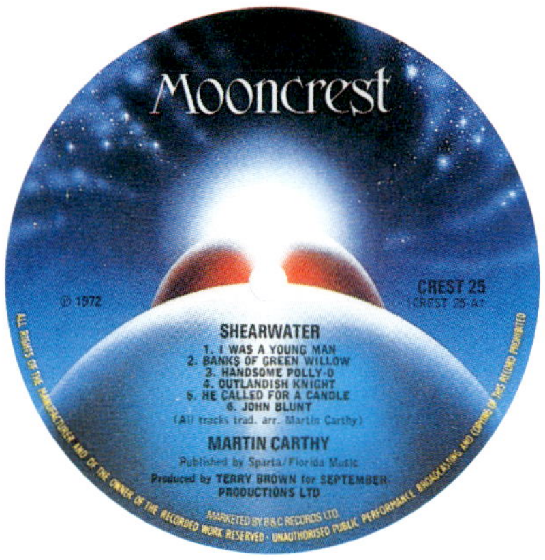

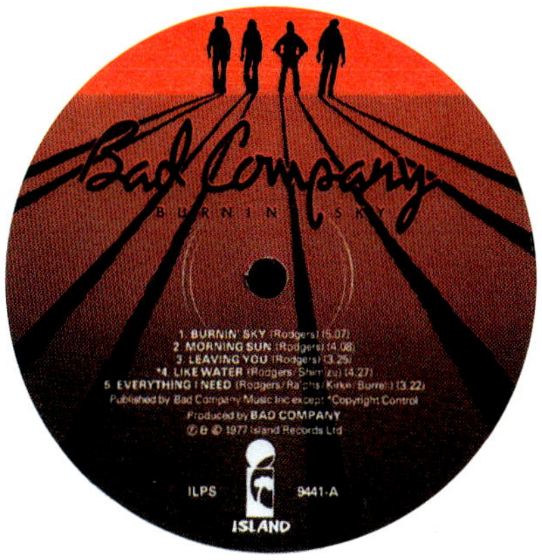

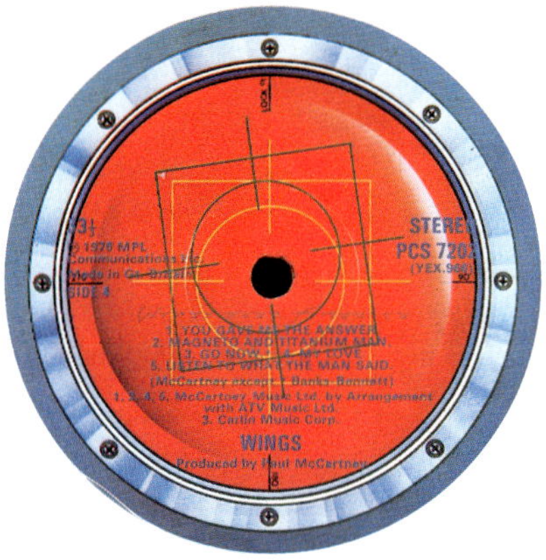

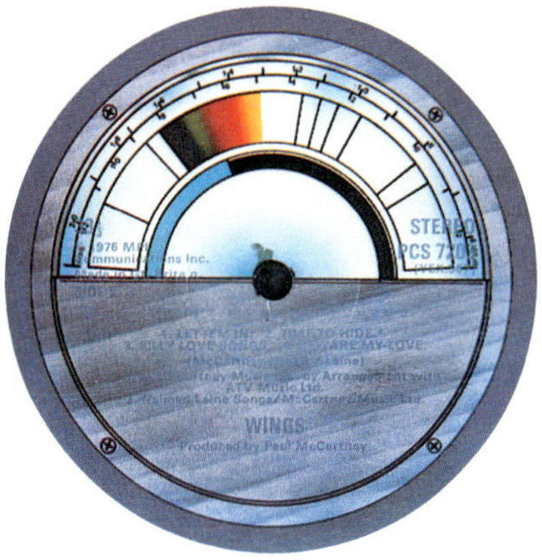

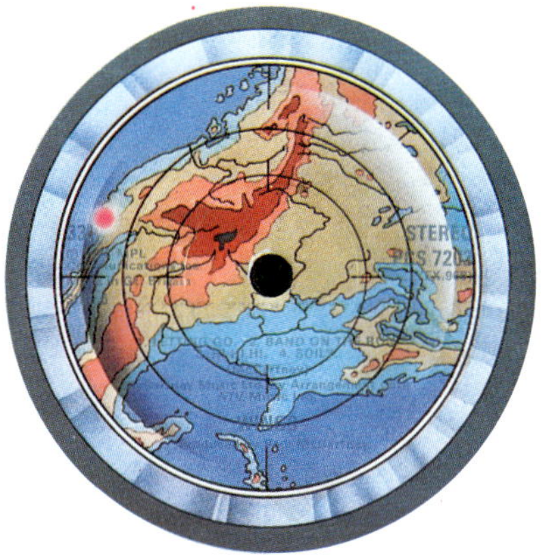

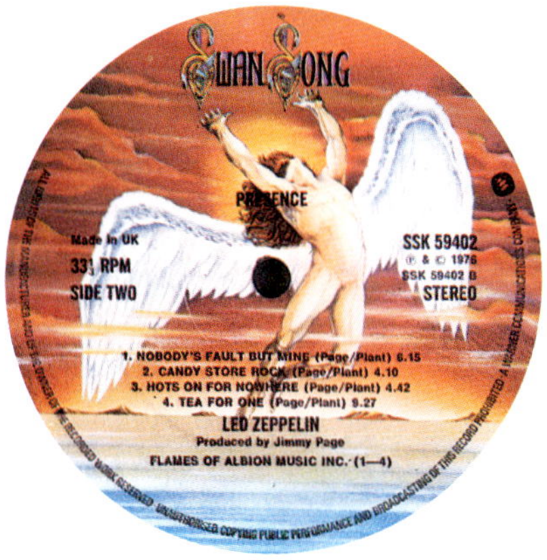

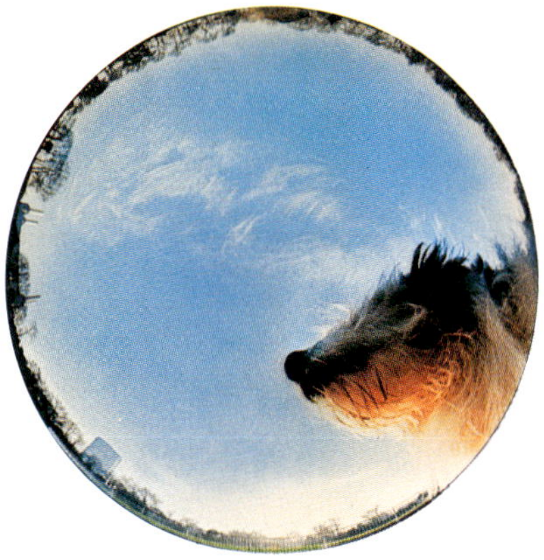

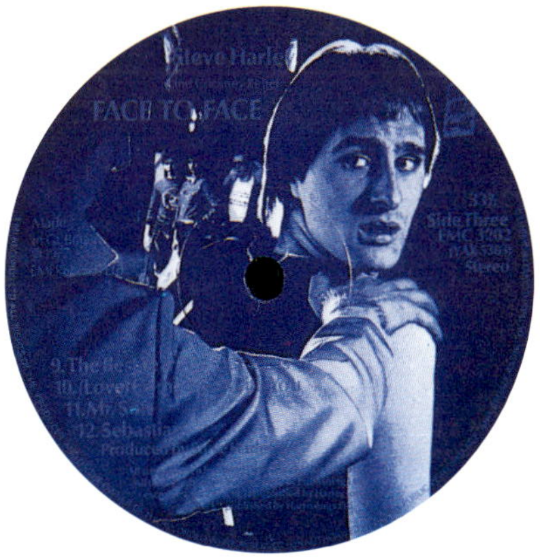

VARIOUS LABELS

cat-like things. Her dressing table is covered in objects and decorations that refer to cats or parts of a cat. She is preparing for a fancy dress ball — hence the cat suit. First I drew a line version in rapidograph, then I airbrushed an 18″ square photographic line print done on Kentmere paper. Using prints has two advantages. Firstly you don't have to do your line drawing again if you make a mistake. Secondly you have a line with a width to cut masks to. Kentmere paper has several advantages over ordinary photographic paper. It looks like drawing paper. It's absorbent so that it takes gouache applied with a brush as well as sprayed. The cut marks show much less. Photographic prints used in this way must be very carefully washed to avoid discolouration.

Keylines can be used in two ways. Firstly as part of an artwork to separate one colour from another ('Year of the Cat' or George Hardie's 'Dark Side of the Moon' sticker), or to separate colour from photographs (George's bicycle parts for the Knebworth poster). Secondly they can be used mechanically. Keylines are drawn in black on an overlay which is positioned in relation to the main picture artwork. A separate artwork or lettering piece can thus be 'dropped-in' photographically by the printer. The area outlined by the keyline, or the keyline alone, or both, can then be 'reversed out' of the main picture (i.e. reduced to white) and finally replaced by chosen colours specified as percentages of the four printing colours (Steve Harley lettering). Storm and George have used keylines as part of the design in Yes 'Going for the One', Brand X 'Moroccan Roll' and 'Finding A Path' from the Beatles story.

Richard Evans' labels for 'Wings Over America' are a combination of airbrushing and drop out keylines. Conceptually they are an extension, along with the dust jackets, of the cover idea. The realism in the pencil drawing of 'The Original Soundtrack' by Humphrey Ocean was achieved by imitating photorealist techniques. A photograph of the cutting room equipment was first taken by Storm and was then painstakingly copied as a pencil drawing. The editing screen area was laminated with shiny varnish (only visible on actual cover) using a keyline artwork overlay. Lamination is done by the printer after the printing of the four colours and is one of many available surface techniques. Choice of the board on which a picture is printed is important, as is the surface texture (from plain through to heavy canvas) and the surface finish (matt, varnished or laminated in ascending order of glossiness). The embossing used to give surface texture can be employed for only part of the picture (just as the varnishing was on 'The Original Soundtrack'), to raise, say, the lettering or a relevant part of the picture.

Artworks are still often done as straight paintings on

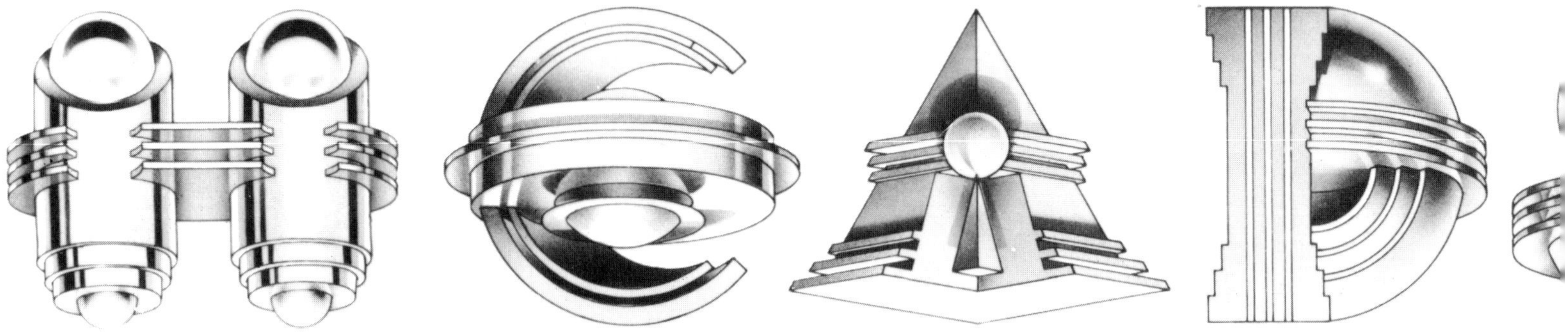

1975 HEADSTONE FRONT COVER

specially finished board. George Hardie's dust jacket for 'How Dare You' (pg. 123), his cover for 'Tales of Mystery & Imagination' (pg. 131) and his illustrations for 'The Song Remains The Same' are examples of painting in gouache without keylines. In nearly all cases lettering and logo artworks are prepared separately from the main artwork. This is done to give the designer the chance to alter the position, size and colouring of the lettering even after the printing films have been made. Films are made of both artworks, the lettering one being given a keyline and 'dropped in' onto the main artwork as explained.

Quite often it becomes difficult to see how a piece of lettering affects a design when the two exist as separate theme from trade union banners of the early part of the century).

Science Fiction has inspired a number of designs, among them 'Headstone', 'Hawkwind' and Alan Parsons' 'I Robot'. The 'Headstone' lettering was originally devised for Al Stewart's 'Modern Times' but was eventually rejected on the grounds that it was too individual and too strong for the photograph. The lettering on 'Hawkwind', designed by Geoff Halpin, is given scientific connotations with its use of graph paper and letter forms made out of electrical circuit symbols. 'I Robot' brings to mind the kind of electrical display panels found at airports.

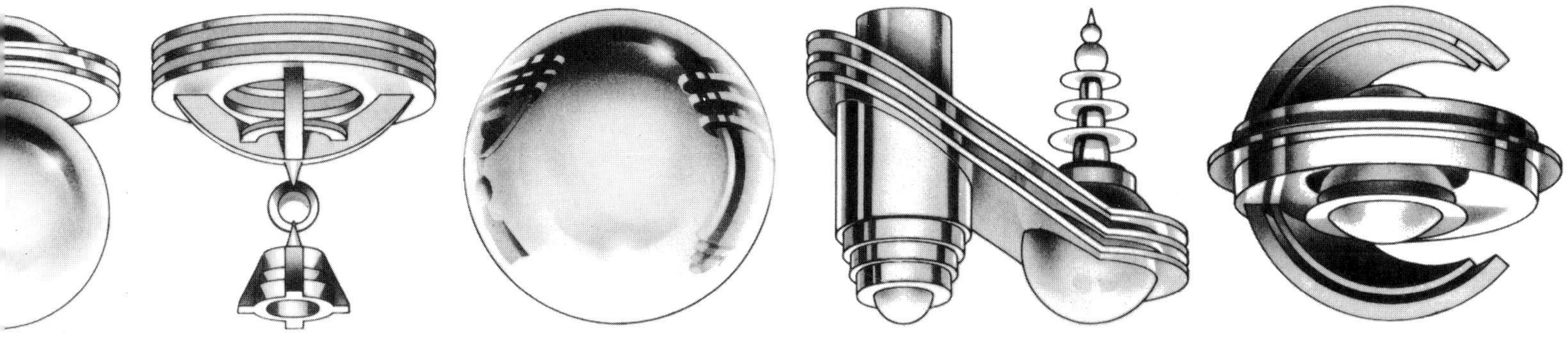

artworks. In order to 'see' and be able to alter the two combined, a print of the lettering artwork is made on acetate to size, it is then coloured with gouache and positioned over the artwork.

Logos and graphics have been culled from a number of popular sources and are often used to evoke a certain time or recreate a particular style. 'Fumble' for example, makes use of shapes from the fifties. 'Poetry in Lotion' is a pastiche of hair cream labels of the same era. The graphics on 'Lunch' complement the front cover photograph which dates from the 1930s. Art Nouveau has often been utilised in covers like 'Caravan', 'Houses of the Holy' (Bush Hollyhead) and 'Climax Chicago' (which takes its

The design of lettering must satisfy a number of needs. Firstly, it must be legible and be in a position on the sleeve so that browsers in shops can see it clearly (for this reason logos are nearly always put at the top of a sleeve). Secondly, it should work with the picture on the sleeve. Thirdly, it has to be bold enough and interesting enough to be used on its own in its various other roles (on advertisements and posters).

Legibility versus imagination is the great arguing point with lettering. These arguments can always be referred to Joe Public. George's Blue Mink 'Fruity' passed the EMI Cleaning Lady Test but his 'Uno' could not be read by the Man in the (Denmark) Street, and so was adjusted.

1975	HEADSTONE	FRONT COVER

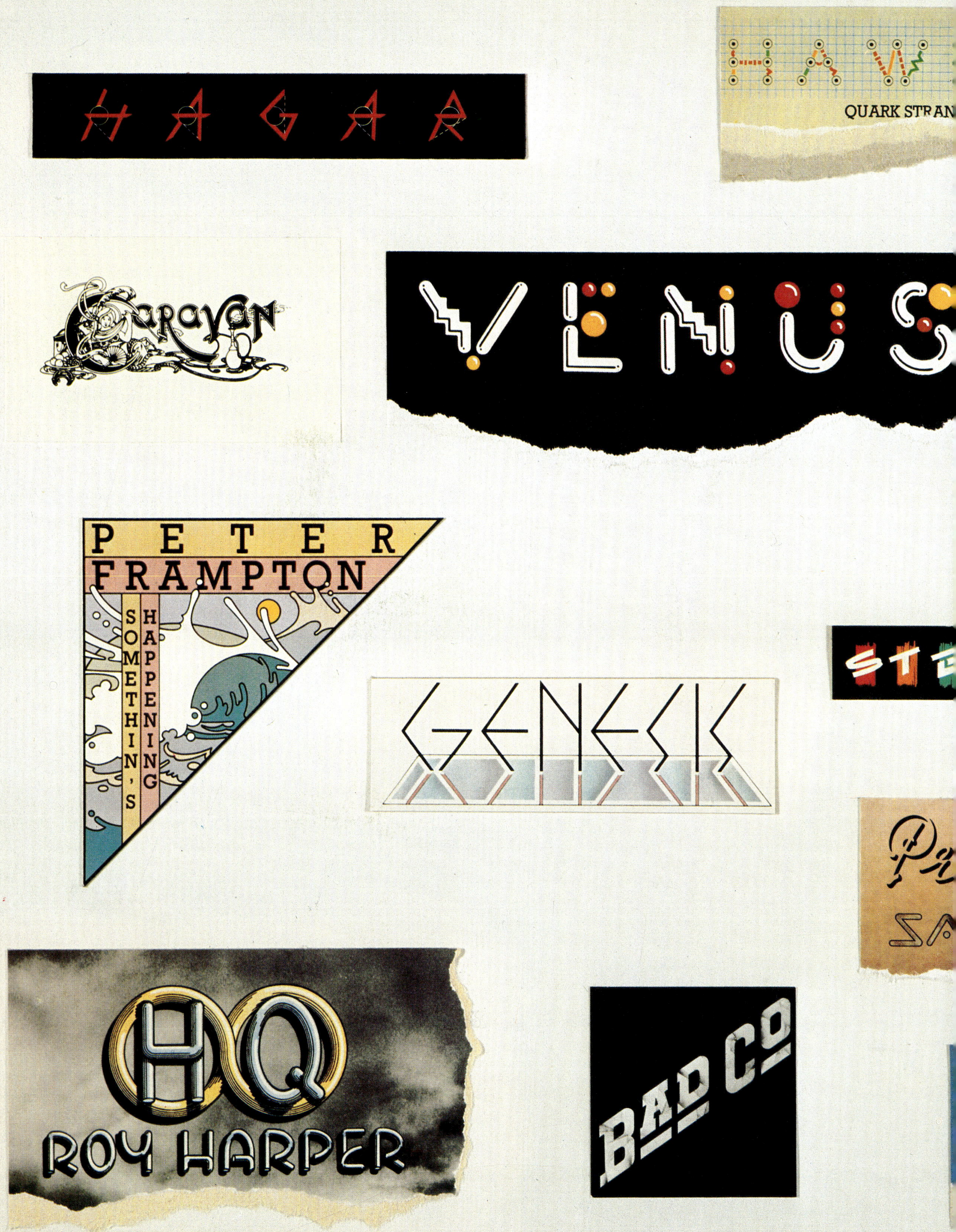
HAGAR
QUARK STRAN
Caravan
VENUS
PETER
FRAMPTON
SOMETHIN'S
HAPPENING
GENESIS
HQ
ROY HARPER
BAD CO

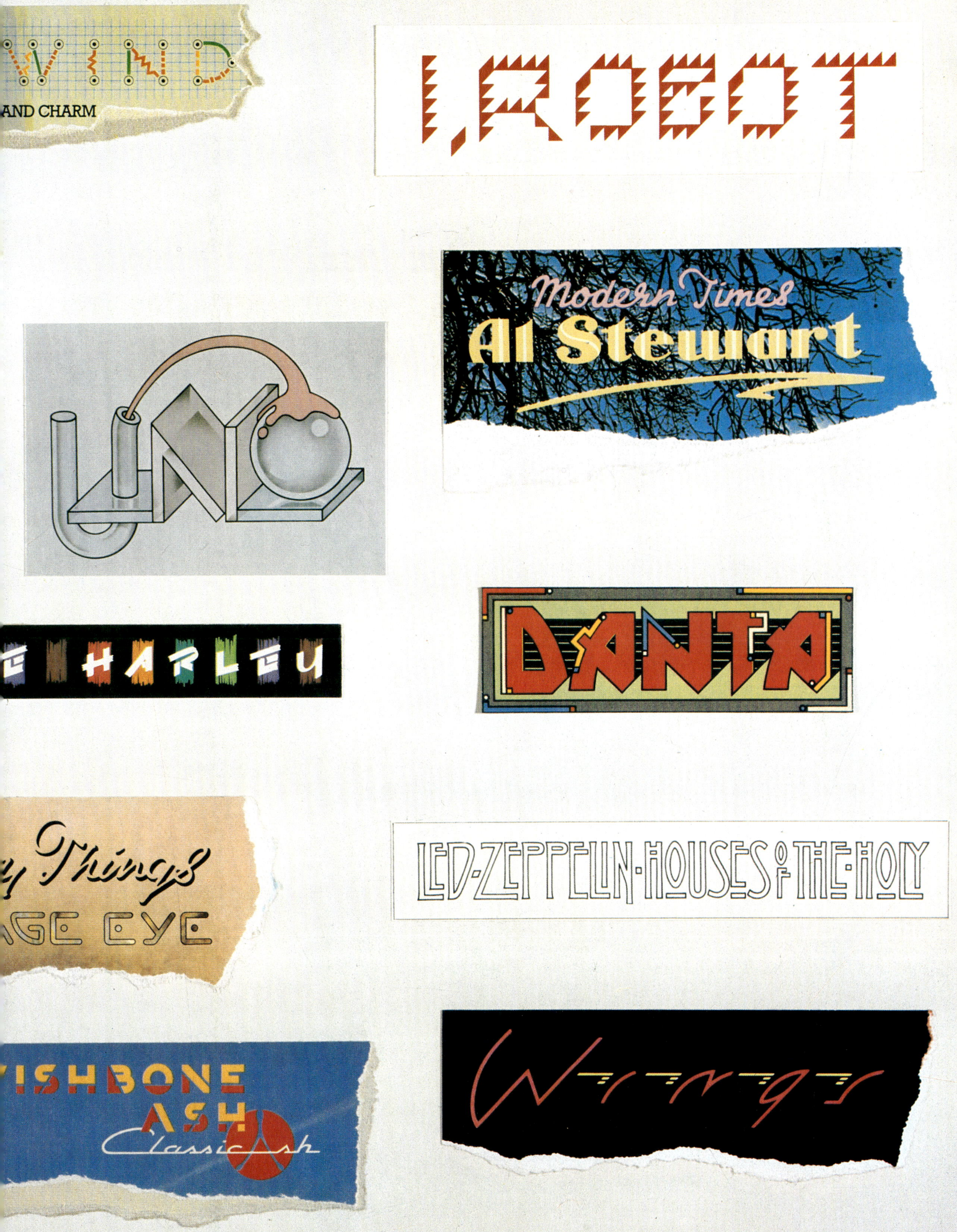

WIND
AND CHARM
I, ROBOT
Modern Times
Al Stewart
UNO
HARLEY
DANTA
Things
GE EYE
LED-ZEPPELIN-HOUSES OF THE-HOLY
ISHBONE
ASH
Classic Ash
Wings

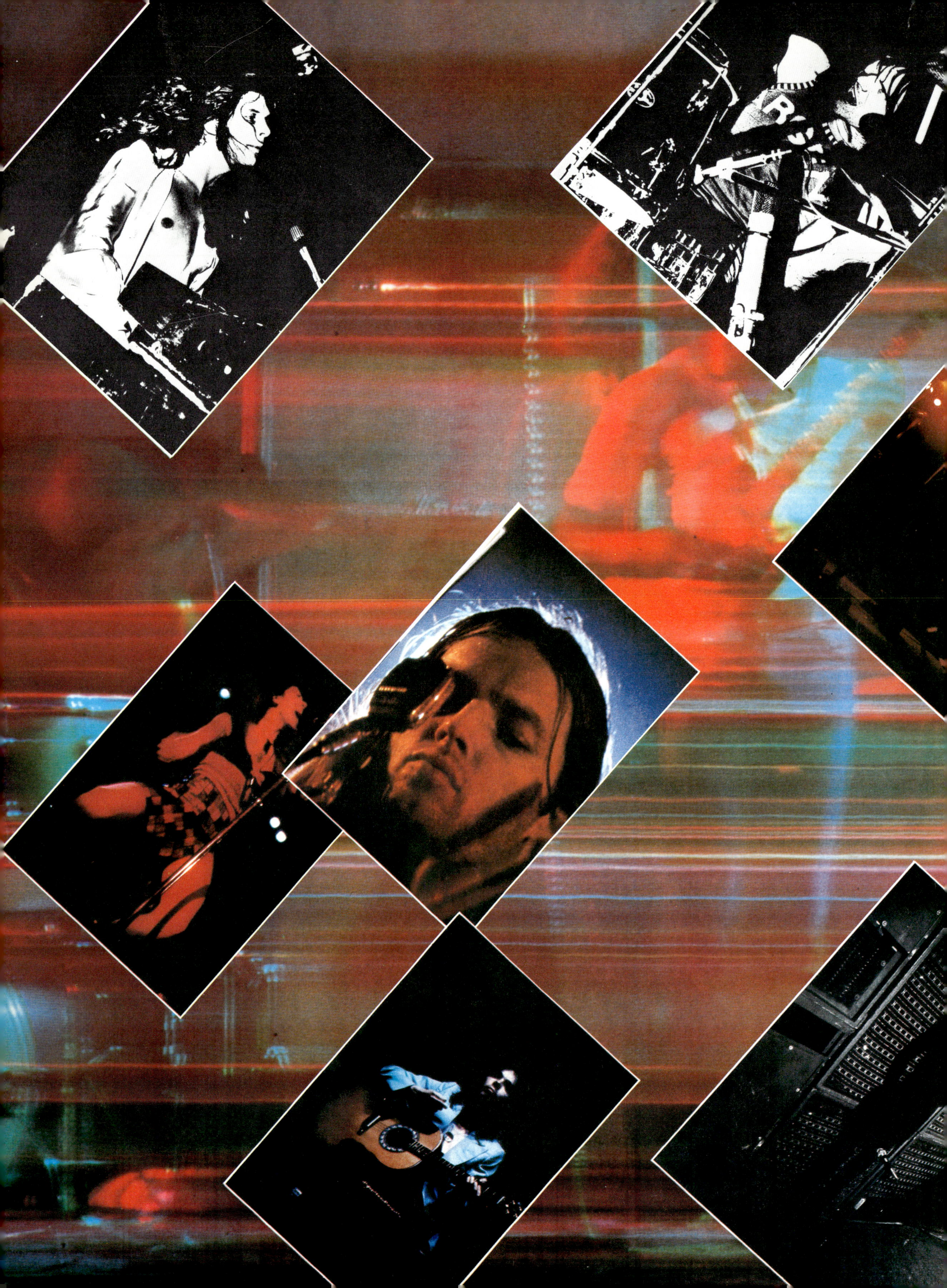

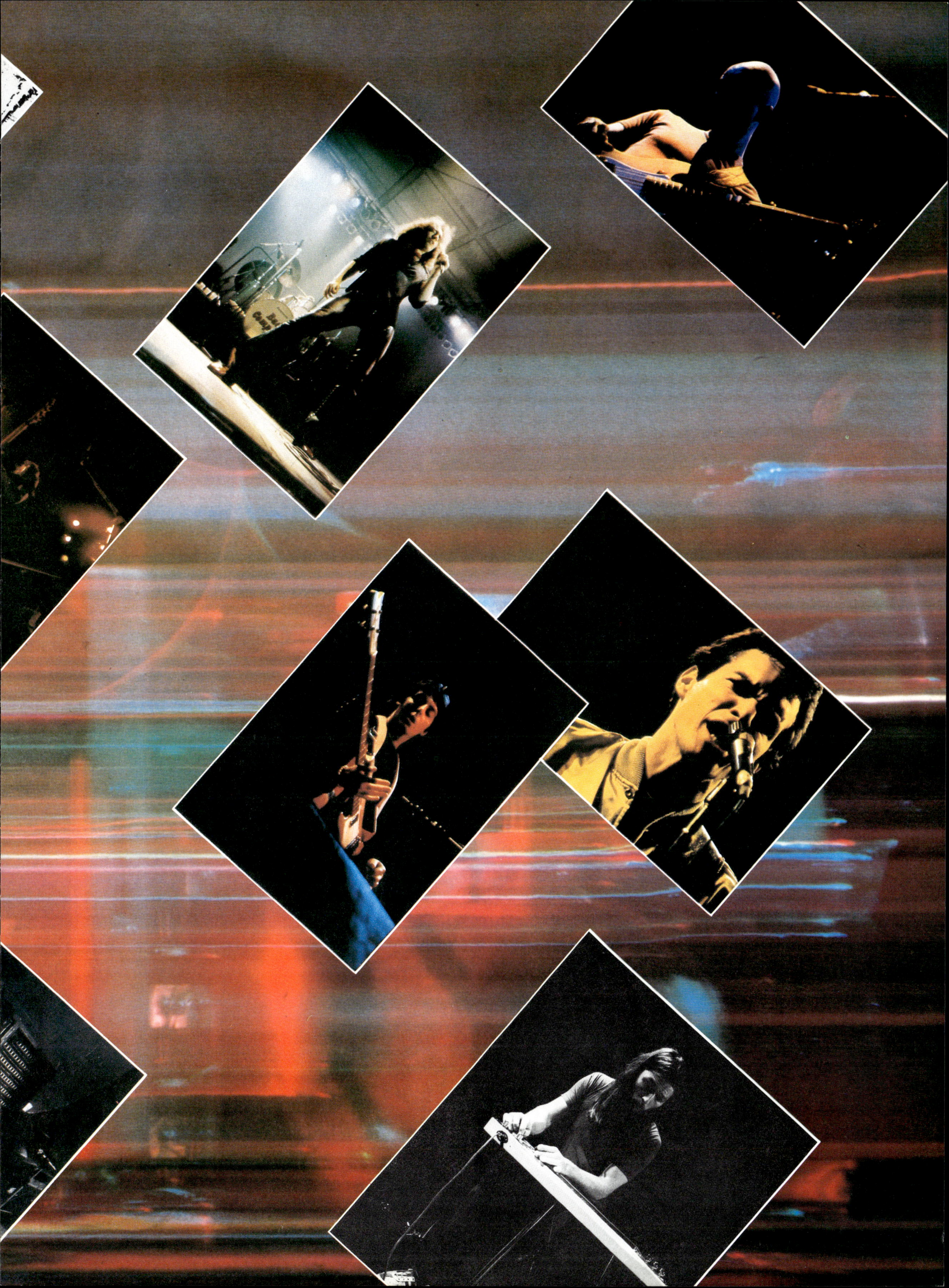

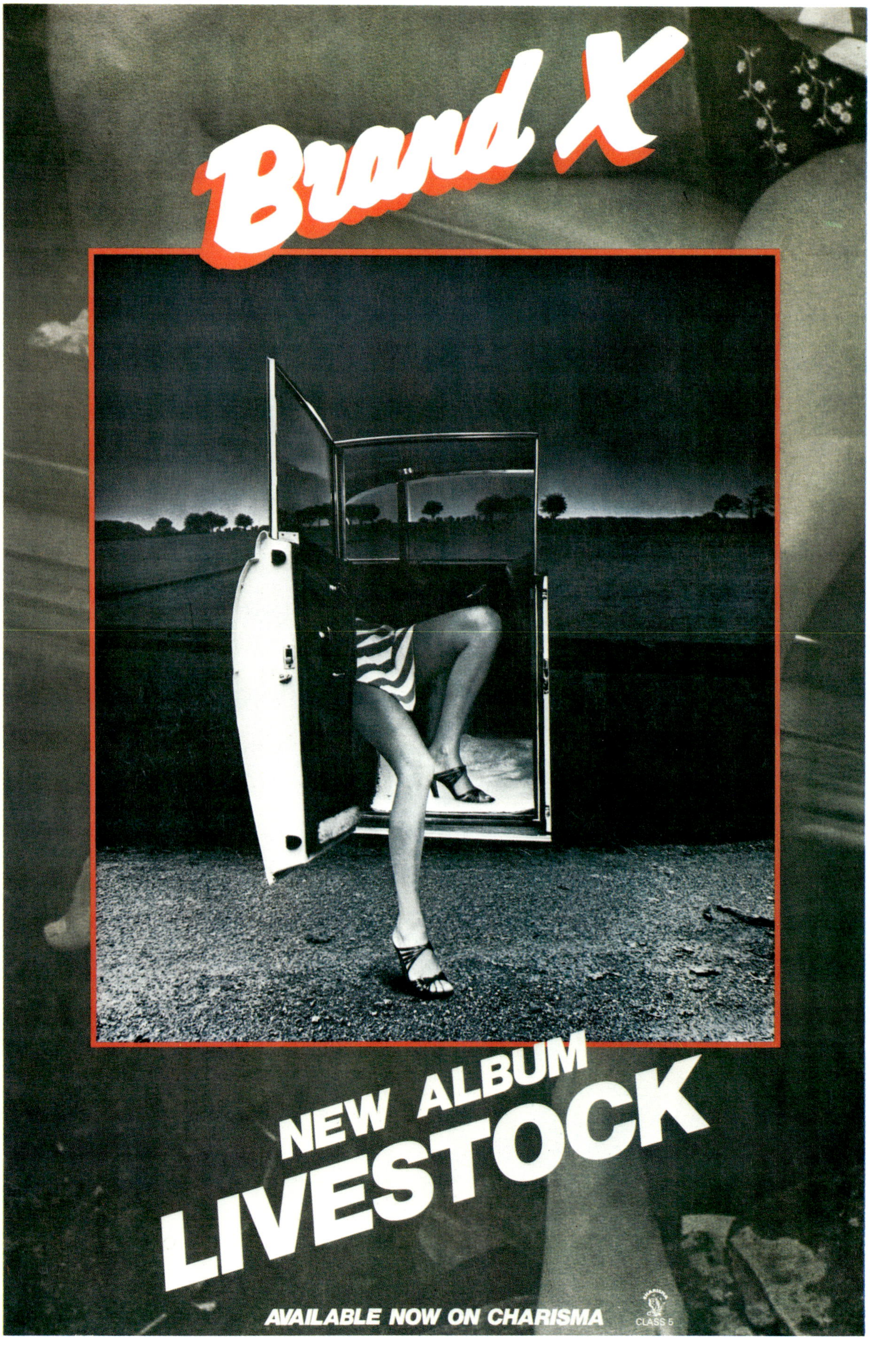

◁ LIVE PHOTOS

1977 BRAND X 'LIVESTOCK' POSTER

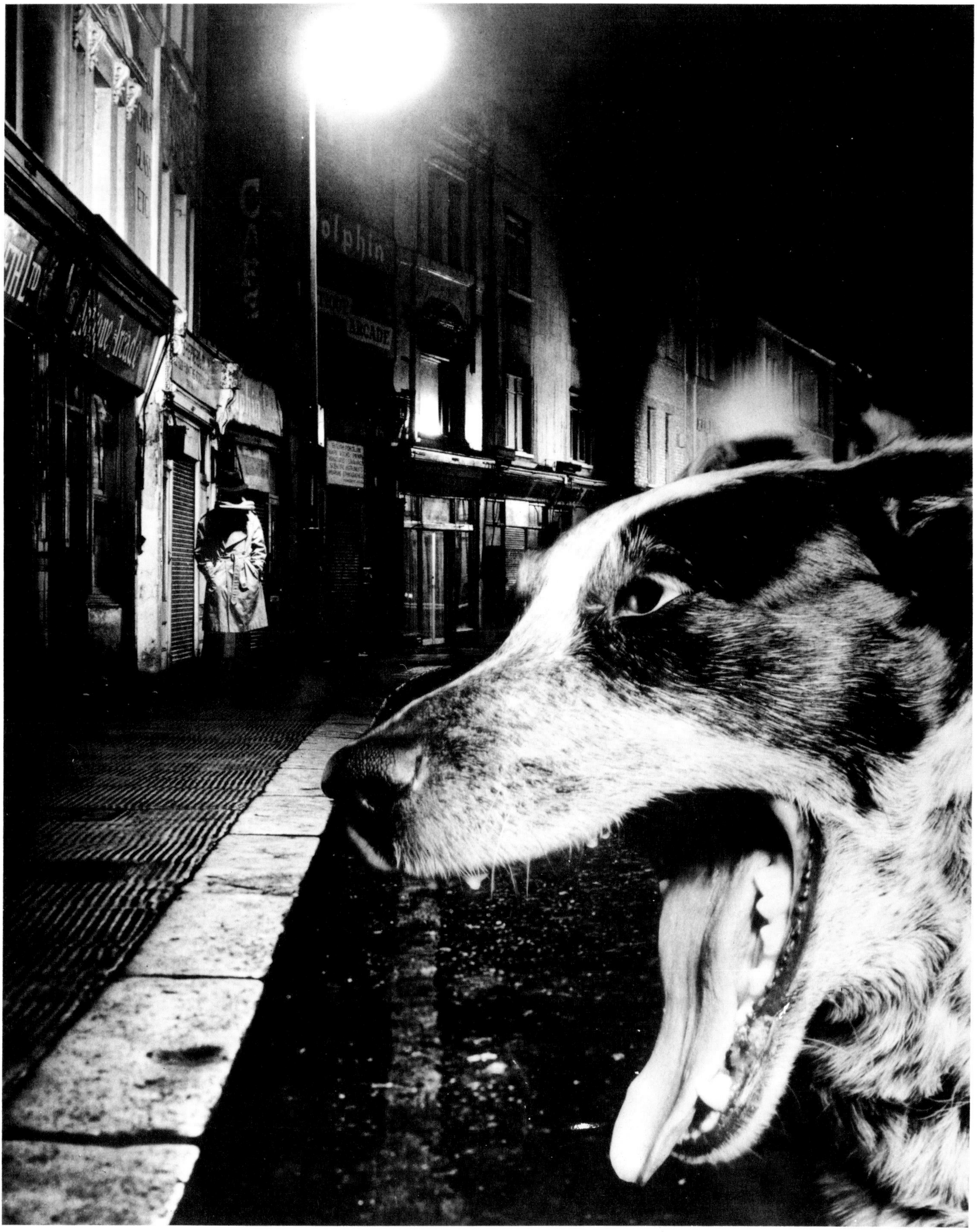

1976 | LUMIERE & SON 'DOGS' | POSTER

Bread, lolly, mozzala, scratch, potatoes — actually Lumiere & Son have no money to speak of, and the designs shown here have been done for nothing. Lack of funds also accounts for these pictures being in black and white. Lumiere & Son are a theatrical outfit directed by Hilary Westlake and David Gale. The latter is an old friend of mine and is the wittiest person I've ever met. Their shows are grotesque, surrealistic, didactic, often very funny and sometimes very rude. The two designs included here are 20″ x 30″ posters done to advertise and promote two of their works. Dogs is a simple montage — the dog stuck on the picture of a deserted street in London's Notting Hill. The second is a single shot taken in the studio by flashlight, using the actors who were to appear in the actual show.

Though they liked the result they were, I guess, grateful for small mercies, especially if it didn't set them back too much. (Their dramatic performances are not of a nature that lures the general public in their millions.) However, in the majority of instances the client is paying us for a design, and might feel he has some right to expect certain things. In some cases he feels it's his right to *demand* certain things. It's all a bit tricky really. I mean, if one is paying for something it's not so unusual to want it to be okay, to try to ensure that it's worth whatever one is paying. But if we, or any designer, were to allow dictation we may not, in the end, do what we think is right or good. And if the client is hiring us — purchasing a piece of our design facility — he is, in essence, buying what we think is good, not what he does. Because that's what we offer. In fact, it's the best that we can offer.

If the client can design it himself then all weli and good, and he can hire us perhaps to put his design together. But this needs to be stated up front so that all parties know what's going on and don't get too confused. (Confusion follows often enough without there being any extra.) If it's clear then we, or any designer, can decide if putting it together is what we want to do. There are paste up and layout studios who will do this service gladly. We are not one of them. Our hands are too shaky. Well, this is normally the case, unless funds are very low and payment of food and rent are required. We'll also do it for mates, or for clients with whom we have a solid relationship.

In the end it makes no sense to hire a plumber and then fix the sink yourself. But it often sounds so pompous when we say it that some clients consider us obstinate, or conceited, or both. In all honesty, we are best at doing our own designs and, in being true to that, we're being true to the client, whether or not he sees it that way.

Now, this is definitely problematic in rock and roll where there exists an above average number of people who reckon they know all about this and that, especially designing visuals. If they're forking out money they might feel they have a right to make changes to a design. But then if we think we know about design and the changes seem unpalatable to us, you have on your hands a situation known as A Difference of Opinion. You have An Argument. And you have Aggravation. It's not to say though, that the designer must close his ears to all suggestions, especially those from what he may pompously feel are uninformed sources, because some suggestions might be pretty good. We have worked in close collaboration with Howard Werth and Audience. Led Zeppelin and 10cc for example, have made constructive suggestions that have improved jobs. Perhaps the performers themselves are the best judge at least of what's appropriate for them and what most aptly represents their music.

The notion that payment entitles the payer to exercise power — that money talks — is one of the most tiresome aspects of the music business. We feel we have to resist this sometimes in order to complete work that we can believe in at the time and especially later. One of the most frightening things about it is not so much those who act out this dogma but rather those who subscribe to it. And although we've done that on only a couple of occasions we certainly don't feel too good about it.

Sleeves *are* important to a band, and then on the other hand they're not. The monies involved vary a lot. A cover does not cost any particular amount. Some record companies, in the face of this variance, endeavour to impose arbitrary budgets on every sleeve design. If it should cost more then the extra is to be met by the band or artistes. We do work to fixed budgets, but we more often invite the client to pay what he likes, trusting that he'll pay a reasonable evaluation of the job. It may sound naive, but it works surprisingly well and cuts down the number of arguments, there being more than enough of these about the design and about schedules. Sometimes, we estimate and tell the client once the idea has been agreed upon. And now. fortunately, we sometimes charge for showing our hand, for roughs, though this cost is absorbed in the overall budget if an idea is accepted.

The variance in cost is related mostly to the complexity of the artwork and the time invested in doing it. If an artwork like 10cc's 'Deceptive Bends' comprises expensive strip-in dye transfers etc. then it's bound to end up costing more than a single shot, like 'Savage Eye'. Photography is a costly procedure — artwork can cost thousands of pounds to execute, especially if distant locations are involved, or complex props or lots of models are needed. We cannot do some extravagant or bizarre things without somebody paying for it. Thus if the band is wealthy it can afford more, but this 'more' is not related to the goodness of the design, only to its nature. 'Deceptive Bends' cost about six and three-quarter grand but took six weeks, two photographers, one graphic designer,

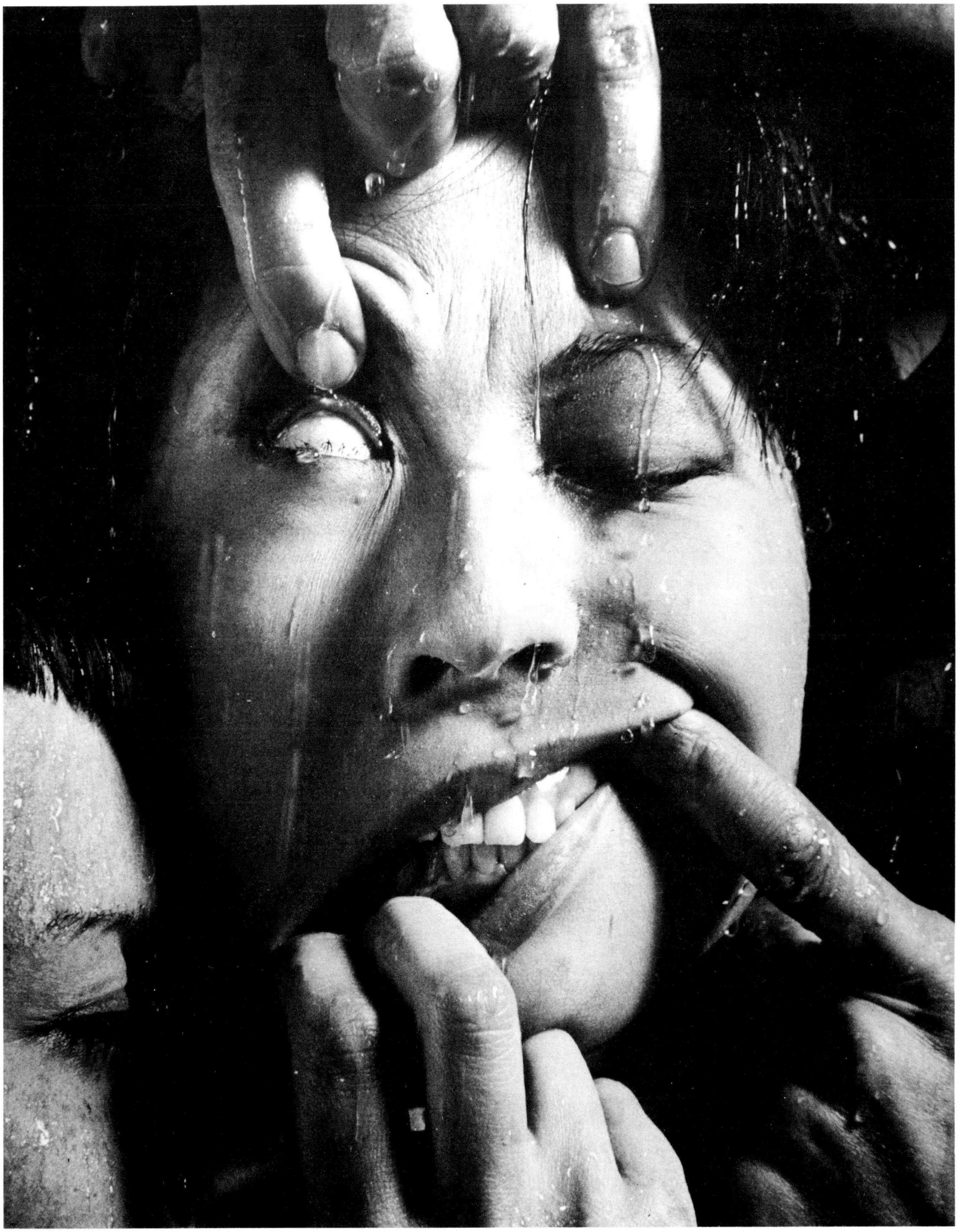

1977 LUMIERE & SON 'PASSIONATE POSITIONS' POSTER

one art director, one retoucher, thirty rolls of film, two models, etc. etc. 'Cordon Bleu' cost approximately £650, took one photographer and one retoucher and two weeks to complete. I don't think one is better than the other; just different. The following prices are approximate and include all expenses:— Quatermass cost £125 (in 1968), Dirty Tricks £750, Brand X £1100, whereas 'Silk Torpedo' was £1800, Bad Company £3500 and Yes £7000. The other factors determining the cost are going to be what the group can afford (or the company on their behalf) and what the designer may think he's worth. When we started we took what we could get. Having some kind of reputation allows us to quibble more if we think we are being ripped off, but then rock and roll is so subject to trend that what holds good for now may not be the case in a year. As a freelance outfit we're at the mercy of the market, of supply and demand. If we had little or no work we might get cheaper. We probably would. You've got to eat, haven't you?

The important thing to remember is that sleeve design costs all sorts of amounts. Considering that usually between half and two thirds of any of our budgets go on costs, on necessary (artistically necessary) expenses, and that these costs vary alarmingly from design to design, it's not so surprising. We'll do a sleeve from £100 to £10,000. There is no fixed sum.

And perhaps it's also worth remembering that this cost is measurable, in part, against the number of sleeves produced. The unit cost. A £100 sleeve for a record selling 10,000 is in this sense more extravagant and costly than one costing £5000 which sells two million copies. In addition, the cost of printing a design upon the actual cardboard construction is less than the cost of the board, and about the same as the make up of that board into a sleeve. When you buy a record in a single jacket this is the approximate cost breakdown as of November '77 (for a run of ten thousand or more):— LP retail £3.50, LP wholesale £2.16, cover 8p of which board, make up and finishing is 6p and colour printing is 2p. Origination costs for the cover design are about £500 for separation plus whatever is the design fee, and are paid by the record company and/or artiste usually from royalties.

Mind you, in my more perverse moments I think two grand for a sleeve design seems an awful lot. But then again, can art be priced? Is time circular?

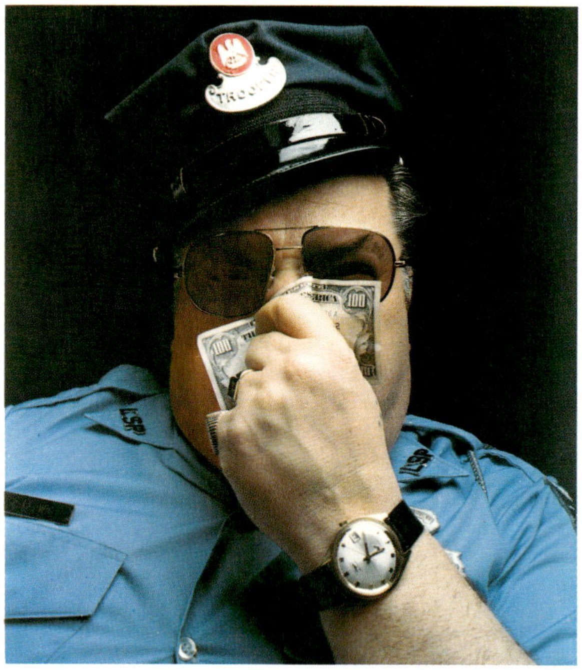

SAY FEES

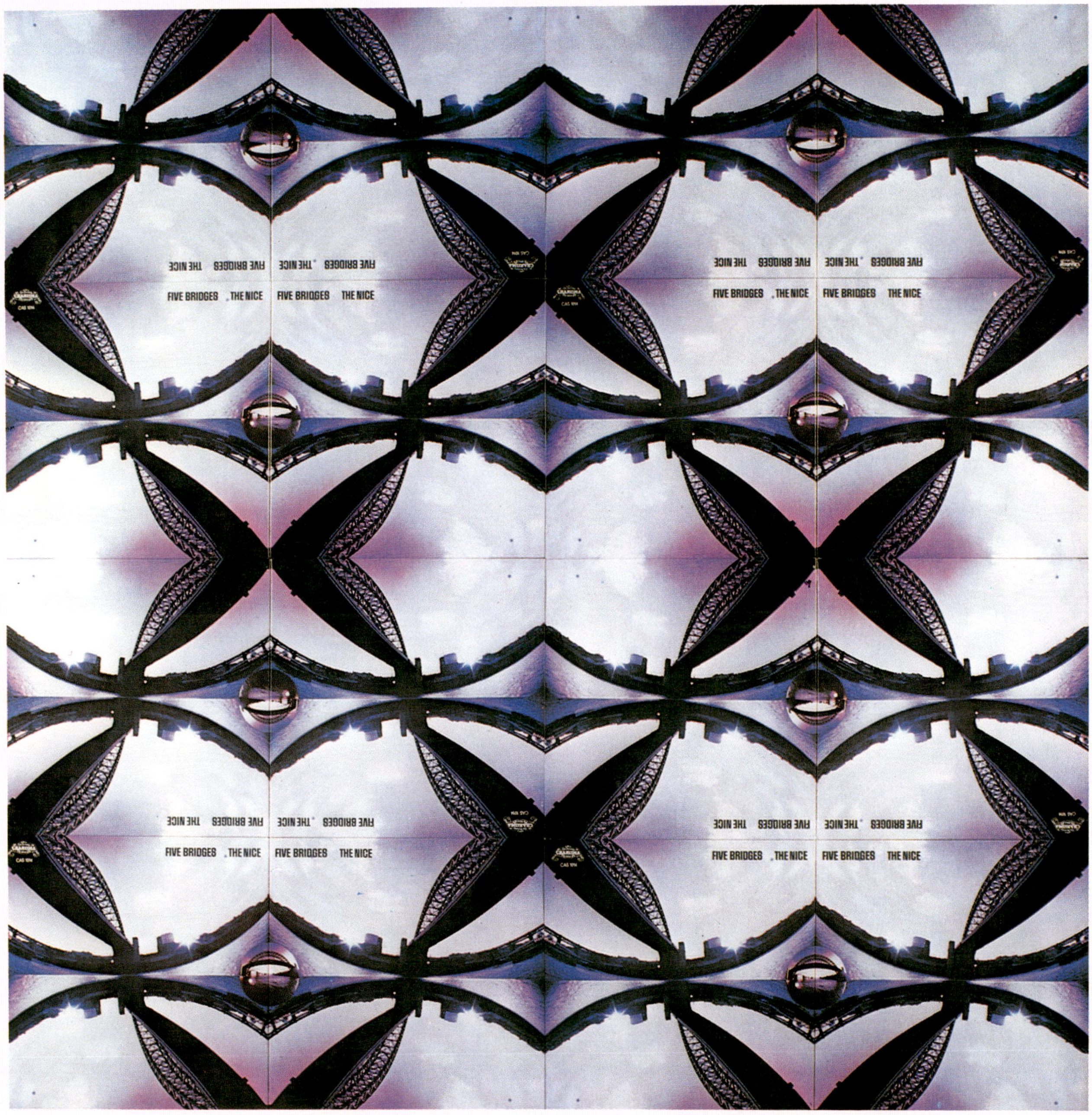

1970 NICE 'FIVE BRIDGES' FRONT COVER

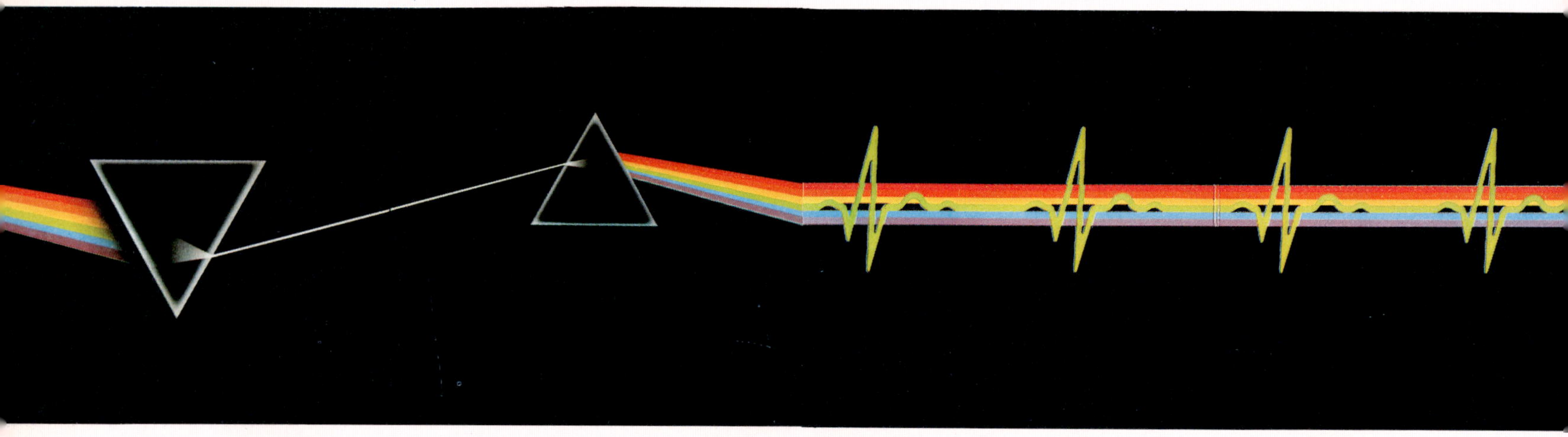

These record sleeves have been designed to work as well when seen joined together forming a mandala or pattern as they do when seen as single units. This is, of course, unlikely to happen to the individual person in private, but it may happen in shops, concerts or other places where the group or their records are being promoted. The patterns included here are quite simple yet quite striking when viewed from a distance. If one imagines that the reduction of these pictures is equivalent to viewing the full size ones in a shop window as you pass, you can see how effective they might be. The thing that always surprised us with the number of times this facility was ignored. It is a specific example of designing covers for the actual process of merchandising which is not something we often consciously do. However, one of the nice things about it is that it need not alter the effectiveness of the single sleeve nor the integrity of the design. It's a self-imposed limitation on the brief.

Working within a brief is really only problematic when the brief is very narrow and/or very unclear. Otherwise it's a question of predilection — in what way does a designer or artist like to work? Perhaps fine artists do, in fact,

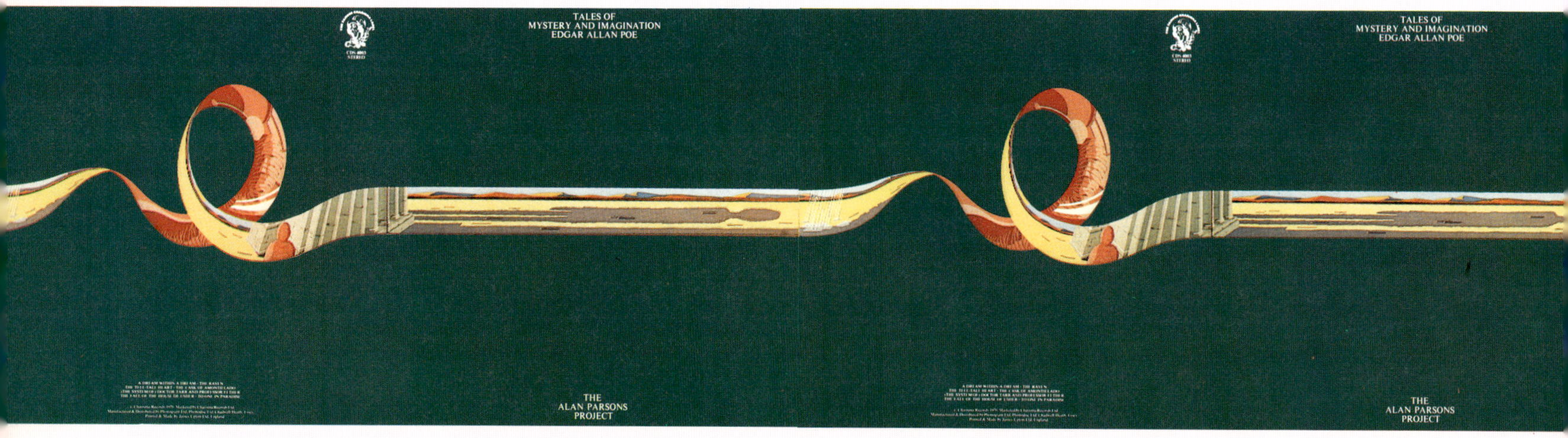

1973 PINK FLOYD 'DARK SIDE OF THE MOON' GATEFOLD COVER

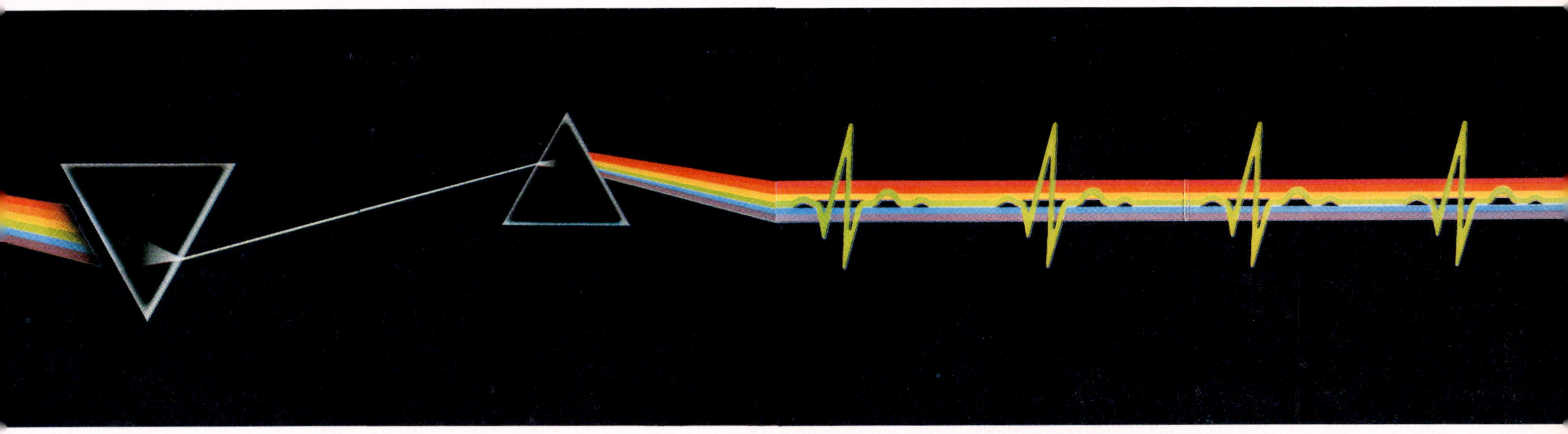

paint or photograph what *they* choose, from thoughts and feelings they possess — they provide their own brief. A commercial artist usually works according to briefs set by other people, namely the clients. The commercial artist also works to other people's timetables, but only to other people's tastes to the extent that he allows them to interfere. The non-commercial artist normally takes the same ostensible reward (money) and may end up working to timetables, whether they be subconscious drives or the Paying of The Rent, that are just as pressing.

Commercial art versus non-commercial or fine art is a continuing debate that seems to me a bit confused. An evocative picture or design can appear anywhere from galleries to supermarkets. The main difference is that there are commercial criteria and marketing values that make some commercial designs successful but which never apply to fine art. But then such a design is not what should perhaps be called good, or evocative. It should be seen clearly, and appreciated accordingly, as an efficient selling thing. It can be admired perhaps for its cuteness or effectiveness, and consequently valued highly by those parties concerned with such matters, like the merchandis-

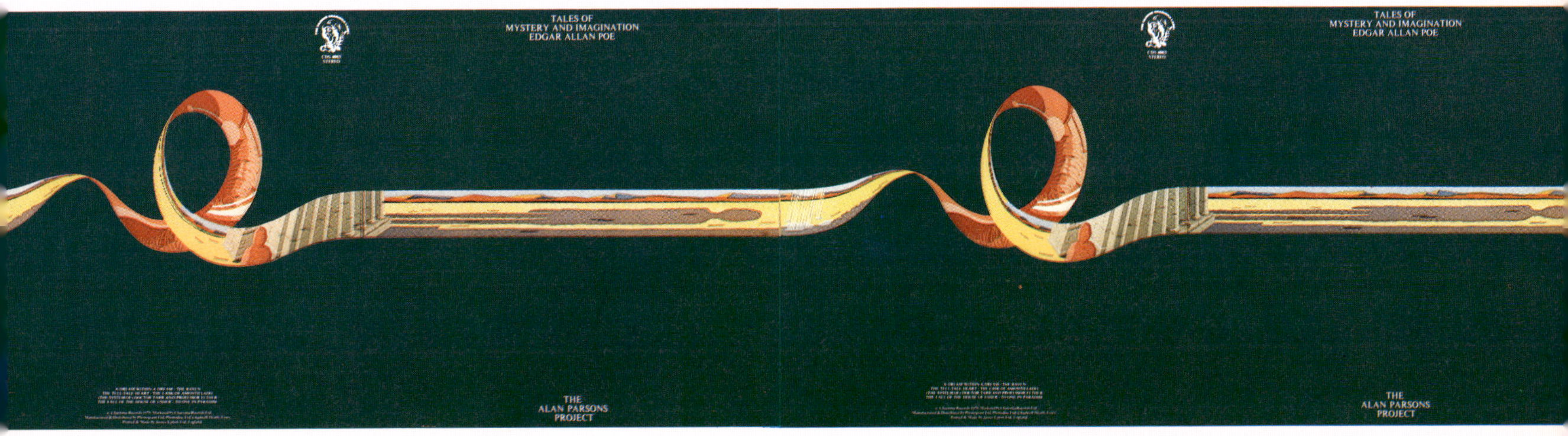

1975 ALAN PARSONS 'EDGAR ALLAN POE' GATEFORD COVER

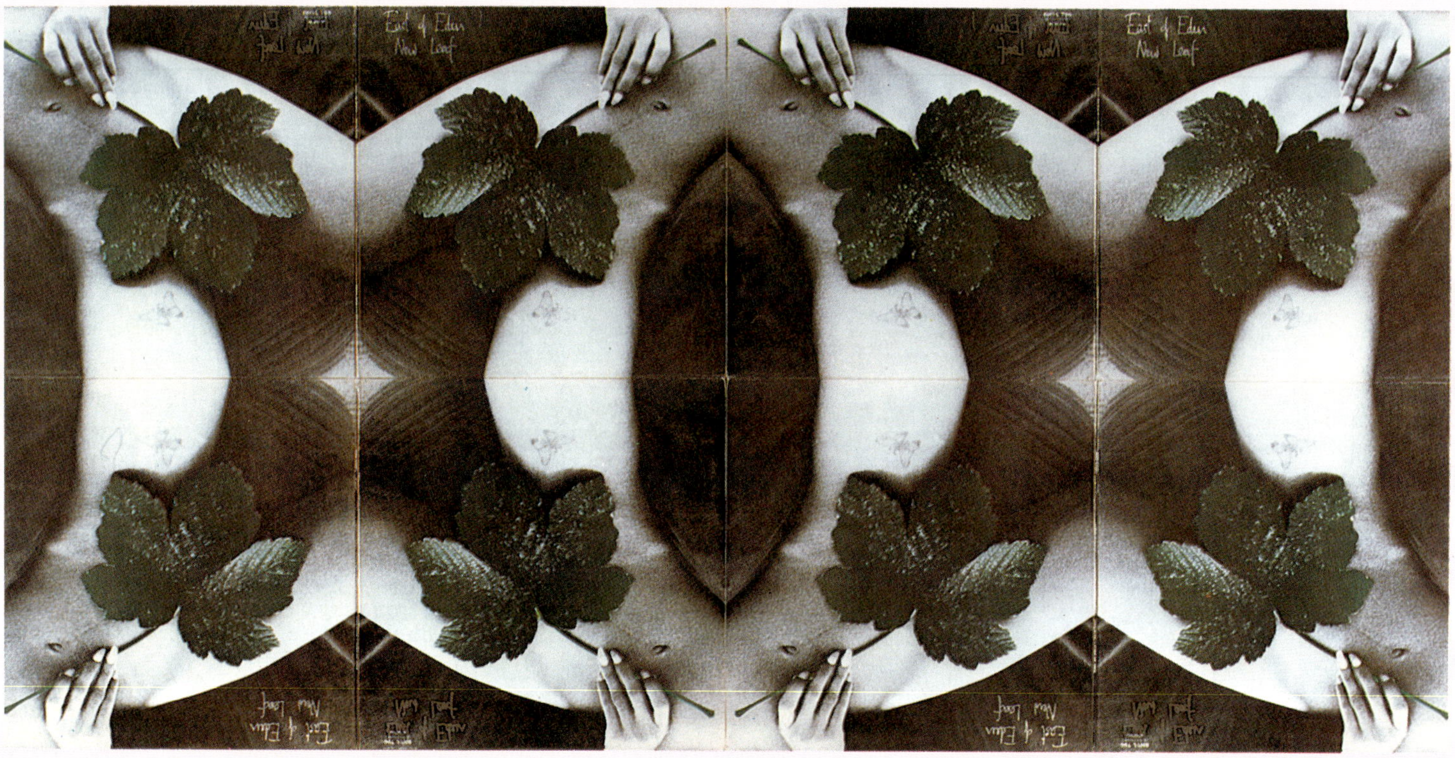

ing division of a record company. It hopefully means little to the rest of us (see Tasteless).

Commercial no more equals bad or lesser than non-commercial equals wonderful or greater. Album sleeves are not necessarily an important entity in themselves other than as a diverting barometer of fads and fashions; but a haunting album sleeve is potentially as good as any other visual, be it painting or patchwork. Their diversity of design occurs because they have an intrinsically wider realm than most commercial design — they refer directly or obliquely to an infinite variety of music and its performance. Apart from this they make no extra special claim upon the senses. They do not set out to alter your life as the music of the Beatles or John Coltrane might do in the end. Nor do they assert themselves as greater than or even compatible with any other particular field. To exalt or denigrate an album cover design just because it's an album cover is as daft as disliking Hamlet because it's a play, or loving the poems of Ezra Pound only because of his fascist leanings. Record covers are pictures and illustrations; they are seen as such and maybe should be responded to as such. Dali painted posters for French Railways and Mucha designed posters to advertise beer. Norman Rockwell and Maxfield Parrish worked almost exclusively as commercial artists, painting magazine covers. Any particular distinction between commercial and non-commercial art seemed not to intrude upon the lives of such eminent gentlemen and perhaps need not disturb the rest of us. But I regret to say it does disturb me and other designers too, I think, especially when prospective clients treat us like automatons or pieces of machinery, and expect designs to pop out at the push of a button. If only that were the case! Press here for instant surrealism, there for Art Nouveau, and right here for whatever style is now in vogue.

1971 EAST OF EDEN 'NEW LEAF' PHOTO GABI NASEMAN FRONT COVER

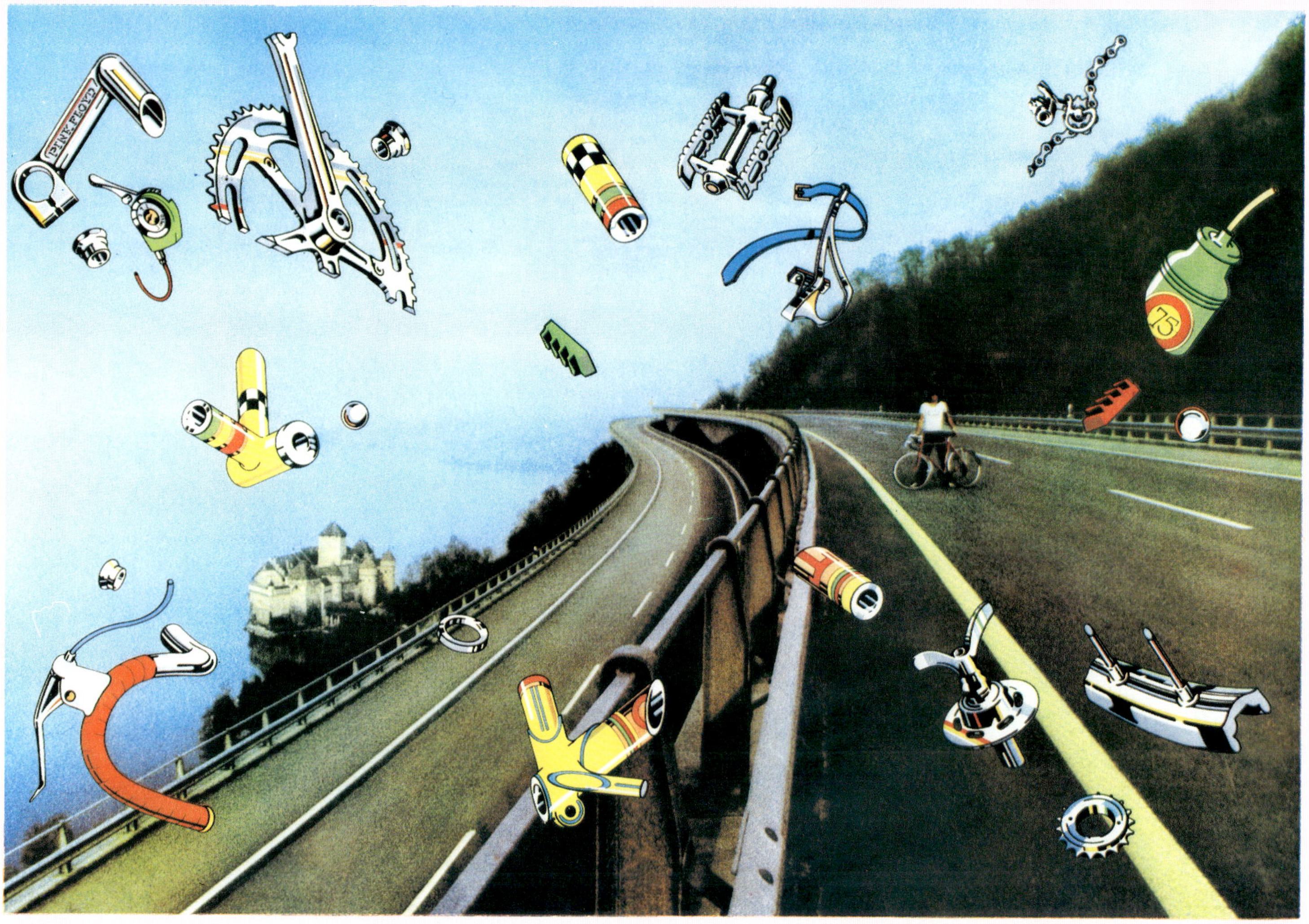

1975 | KNEBWORTH 'BIKES' CO-DESIGN GEORGE HARDIE | POSTER

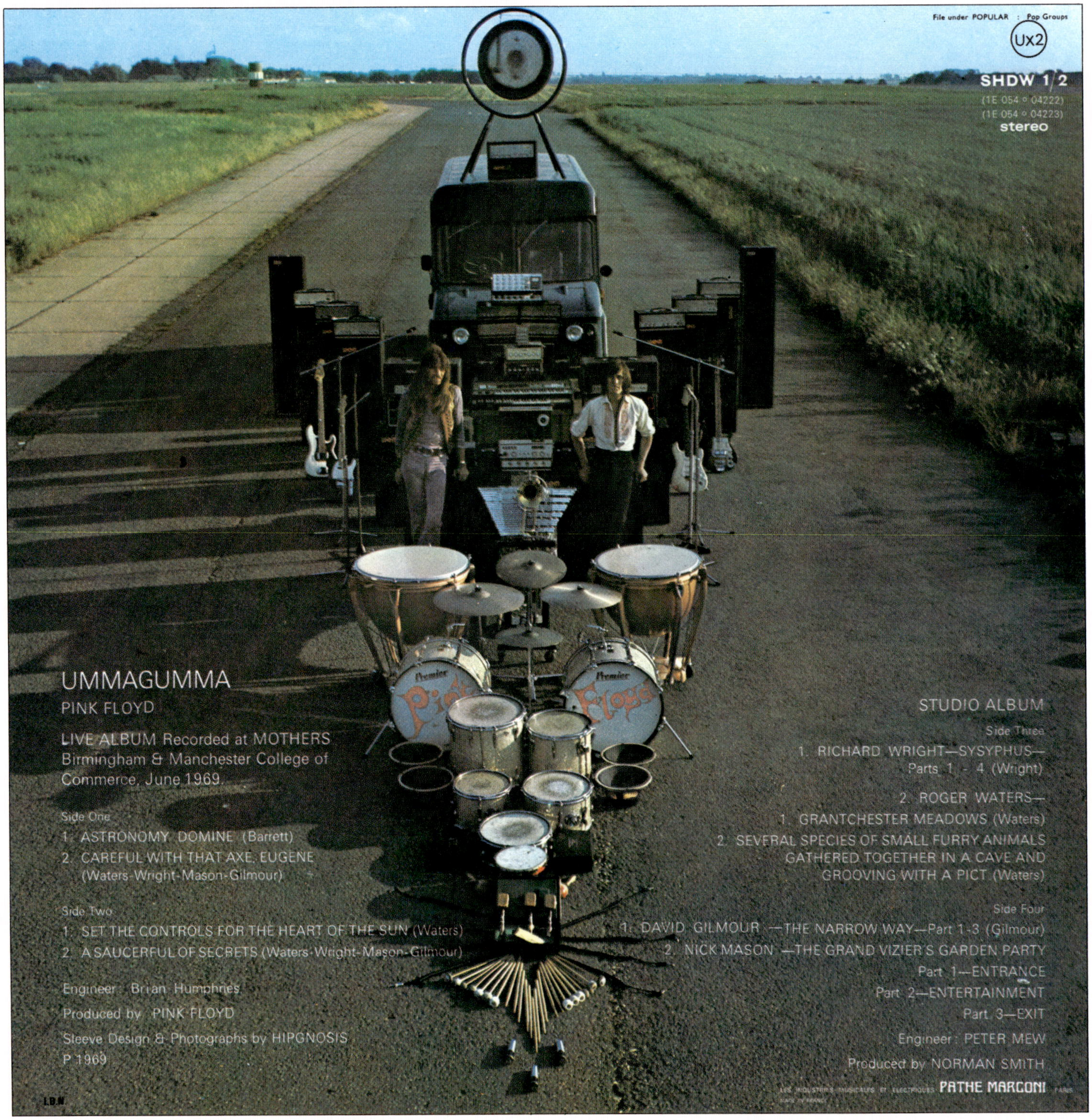
File under POPULAR : Pop Groups
UX2
SHDW 1/2
(1E 054 o 04222)
(1E 054 o 04223)
stereo
UMMAGUMMA
PINK FLOYD
LIVE ALBUM Recorded at MOTHERS Birmingham & Manchester College of Commerce, June 1969.
Side One
1. ASTRONOMY DOMINE (Barrett)
2. CAREFUL WITH THAT AXE, EUGENE (Waters-Wright-Mason-Gilmour)
Side Two
1. SET THE CONTROLS FOR THE HEART OF THE SUN (Waters)
2. A SAUCERFUL OF SECRETS (Waters-Wright-Mason-Gilmour)
Engineer: Brian Humphries
Produced by PINK FLOYD
Sleeve Design & Photographs by HIPGNOSIS
P 1969
STUDIO ALBUM
Side Three
1. RICHARD WRIGHT—SYSYPHUS—Parts 1 - 4 (Wright)
2. ROGER WATERS—
1. GRANTCHESTER MEADOWS (Waters)
2. SEVERAL SPECIES OF SMALL FURRY ANIMALS GATHERED TOGETHER IN A CAVE AND GROOVING WITH A PICT (Waters)
Side Four
1. DAVID GILMOUR —THE NARROW WAY—Part 1-3 (Gilmour)
2. NICK MASON —THE GRAND VIZIER'S GARDEN PARTY
Part 1—ENTRANCE
Part 2—ENTERTAINMENT
Part 3—EXIT
Engineer: PETER MEW
Produced by NORMAN SMITH
PATHE MARCONI

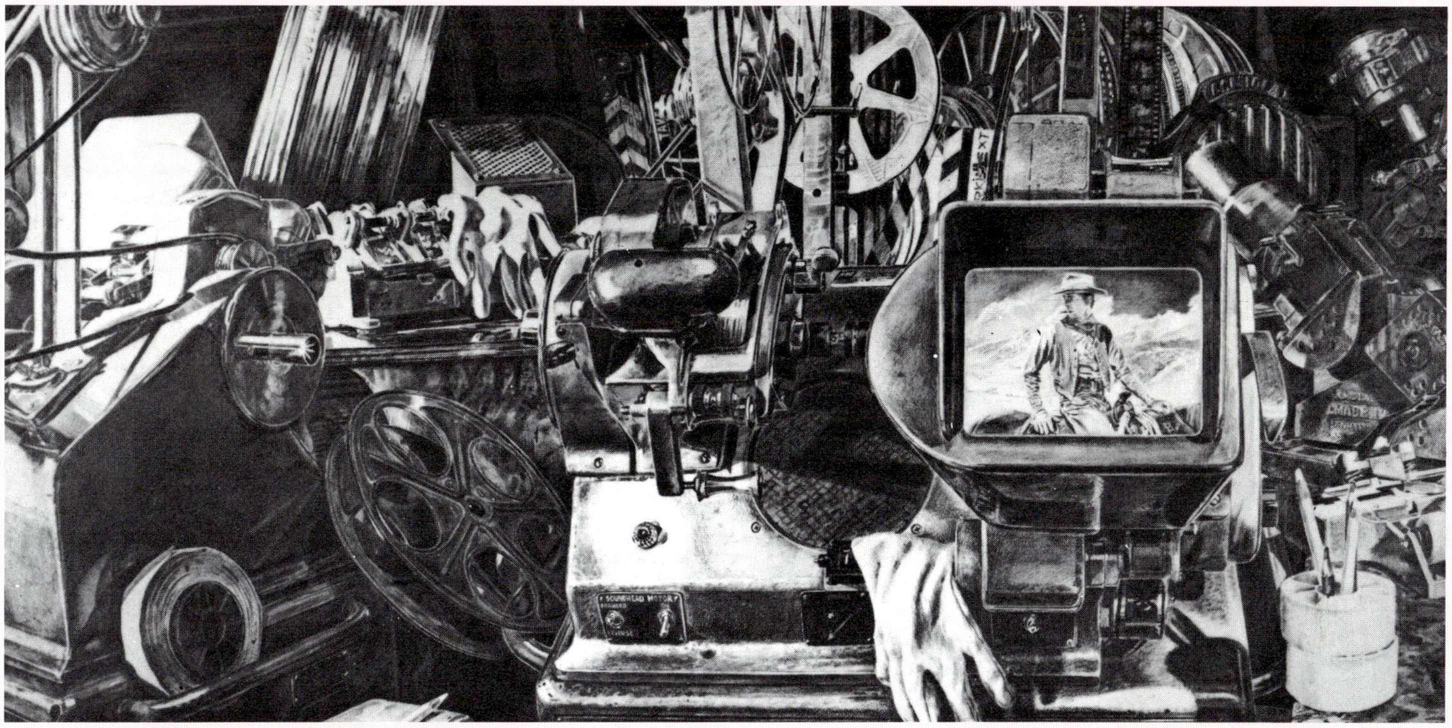

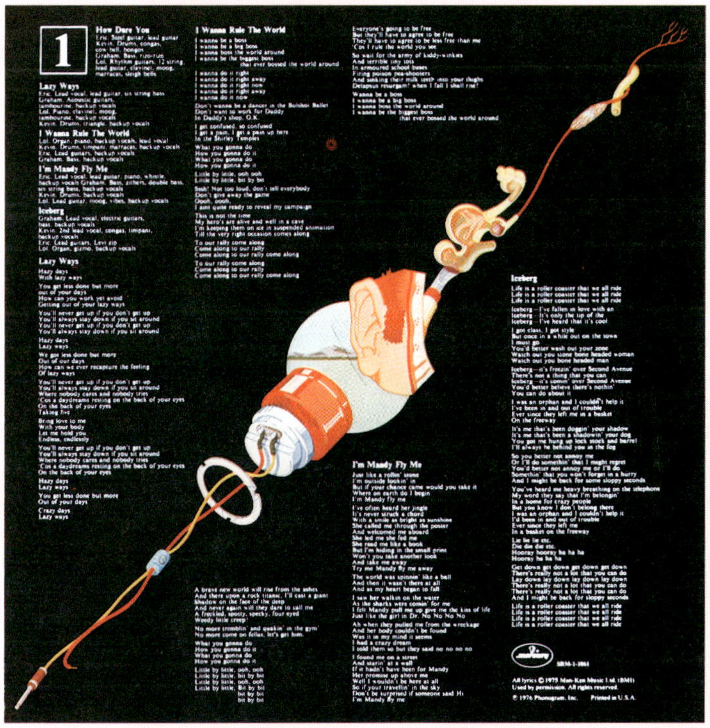

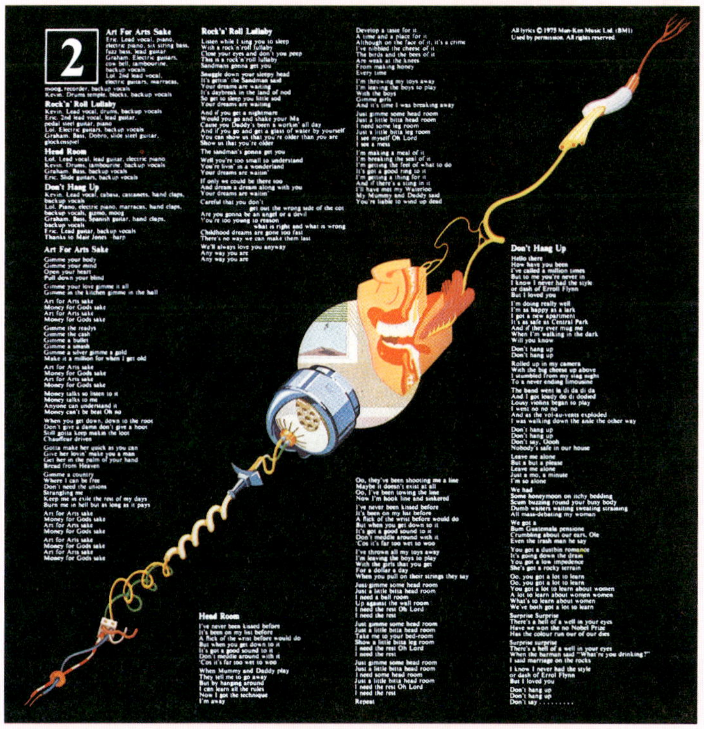

10CC 'ORIGINAL SOUNDTRACK' 10 CC 'HOW DARE YOU' ILLUSTRATIONS HUMPHREY OCEAN/GEORGE HARDIE

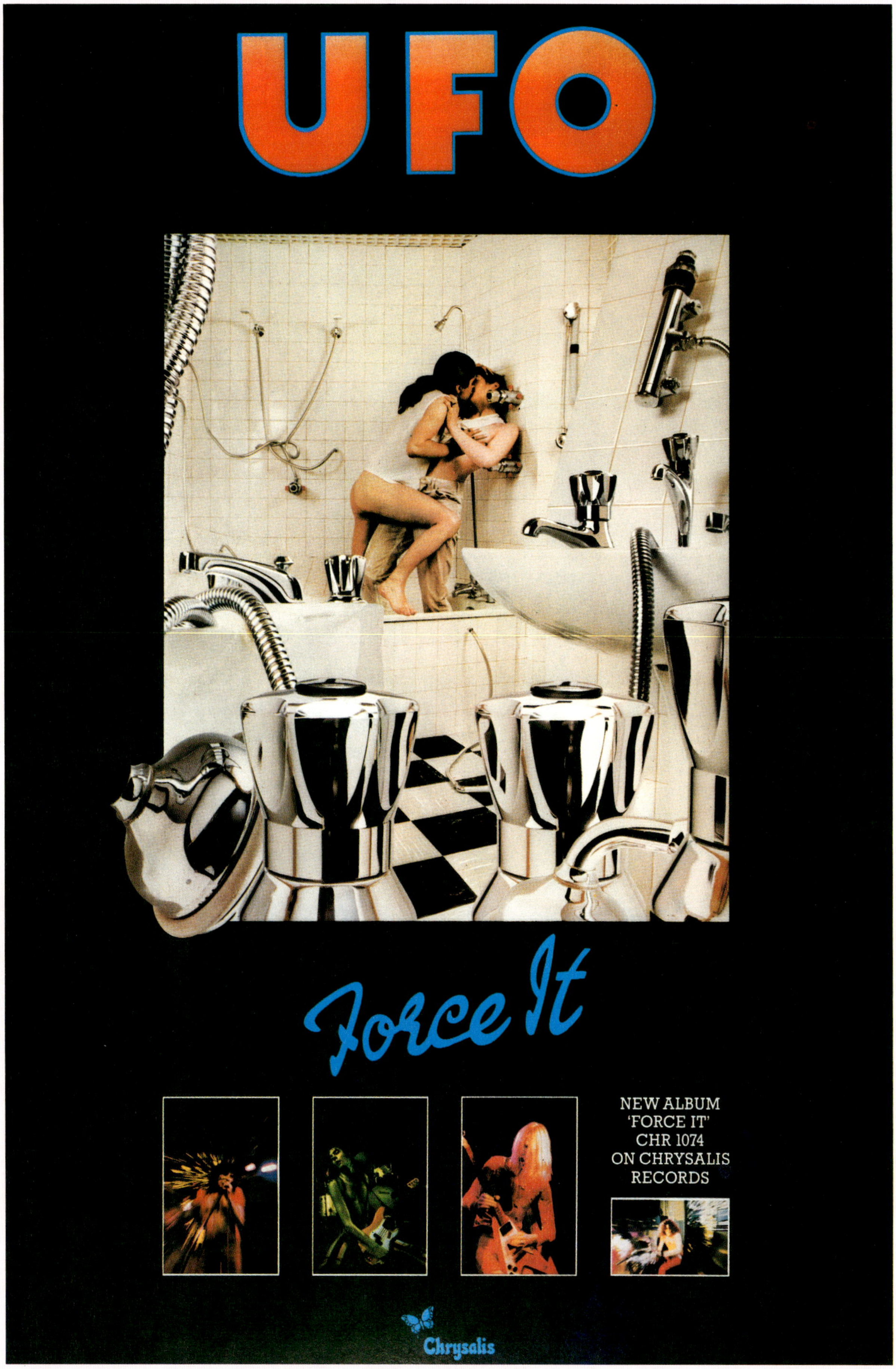

1975 | UFO 'FORCE IT' | POSTER

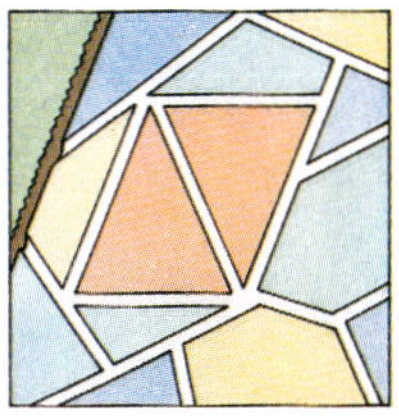

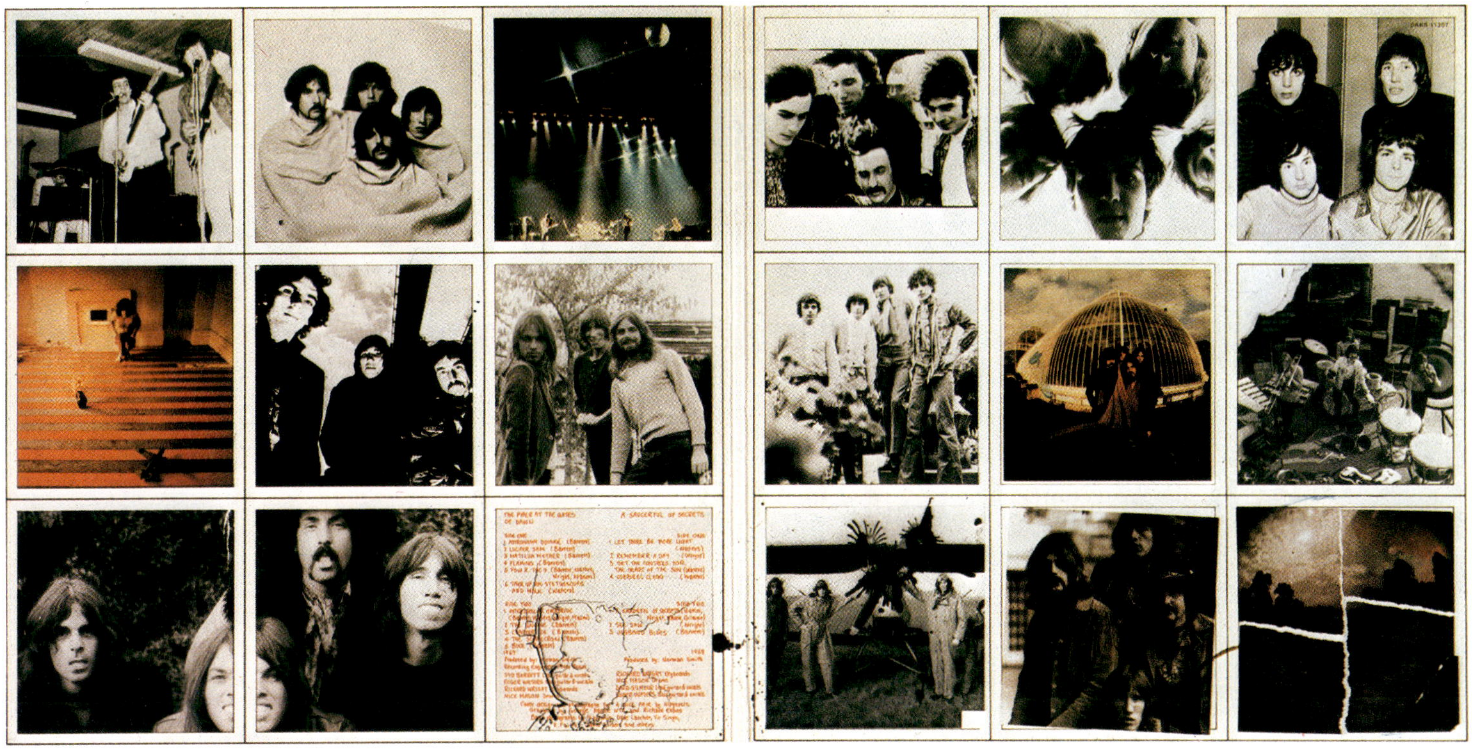

At first we couldn't think of anything for this cover. Slowly we amassed a collection of notes and pencil roughs. But they were mostly silly jokes and didn't feel sufficiently strong to work on their own. In the end we got so attached to them that we decided to use them all. Nice Pair is, essentially, eighteen individual sleeve designs and it took, therefore, a very long time to do. The inner spread above comprises numerous Floyd photos from the archives and shows how the rigid layout began to bore the pants off the designer — his concentration flagged and he simply made a mess of it at the end.

The Floyd have a good sense of humour so many of the ideas were jokes, pictures of puns or aphorisms like 'laughing all the way to the bank' (Bob Lawrie), 'nip in the air' (Colin Elgie), 'fork in the road' and a 'frog in the throat'. Other pictures are just ones we like, for instance, the cinema foyer (one of our favourite locations, see 10cc 'Sheet Music'). Some are a bit wry like the paranoid peephole in the door for a family called Fear, and the spectacles out of focus. The latter belong to the photographer taking the picture. When he took them off to shoot them he couldn't see too well, and so was unable to focus correctly. The completely stoned freak with his kaftan and psychedelic goggles is a reference to the Floyd's psychedelic past. The one of Po and I in our studio is about discussing this Floyd sleeve ('Dark Side' has gone, or is disappearing). We are in the process of rejecting an all pink cover as a solution. We're no fools. The Floyd's own football team, PFFC, is an oddity. In fact, it's a replacement for a photo of Floyd Patterson, the boxer, painted pink all over. But he wanted five grand for the privilege so it was quickly forgotten. You'd think he'd pay to be on a Floyd sleeve.

1973 PINK FLOYD 'NICE PAIR' INNER SPREAD

PINK FLOYD 'NICE PAIR' FRONT COVER ▷

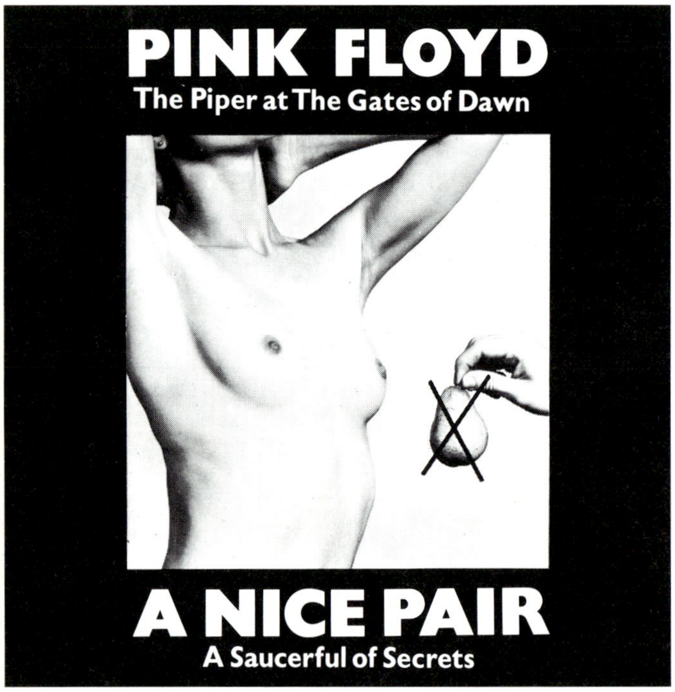
PINK FLOYD
The Piper at The Gates of Dawn
A NICE PAIR
A Saucerful of Secrets

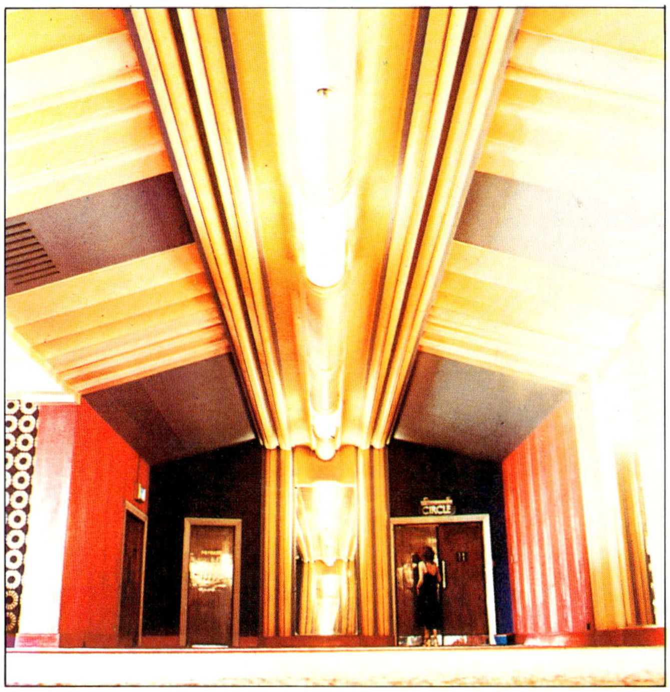

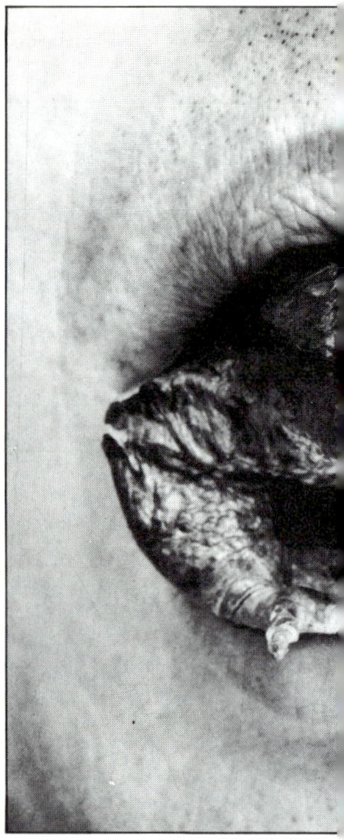

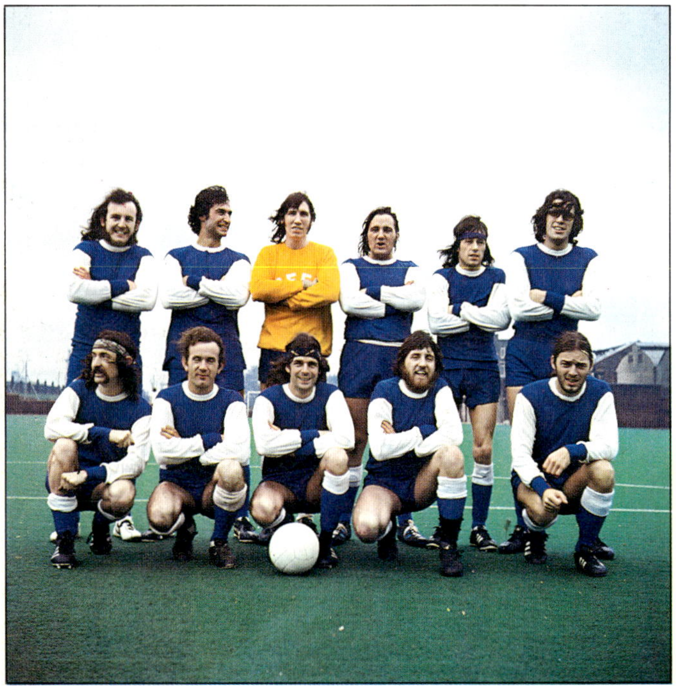

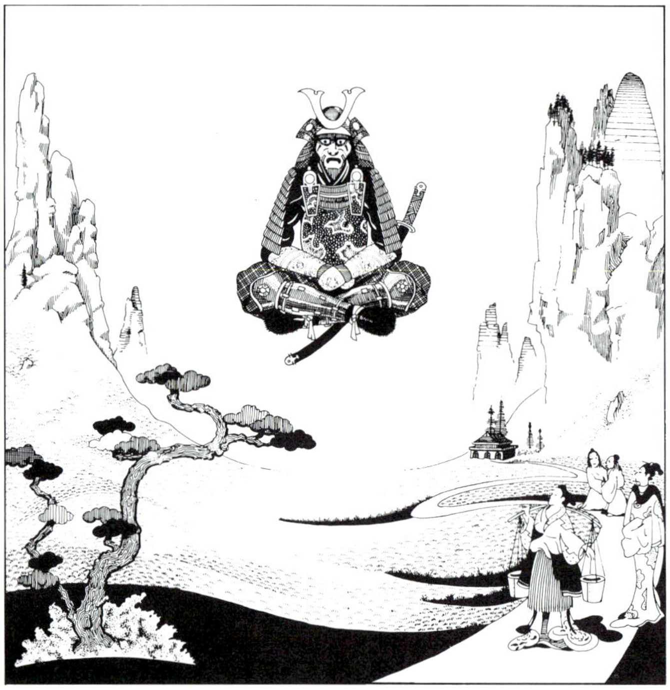

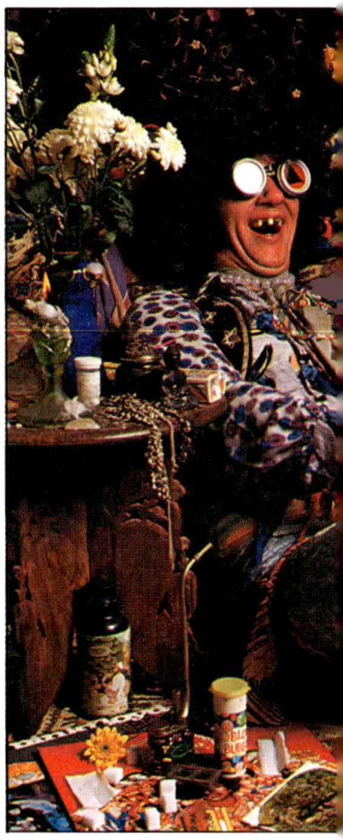

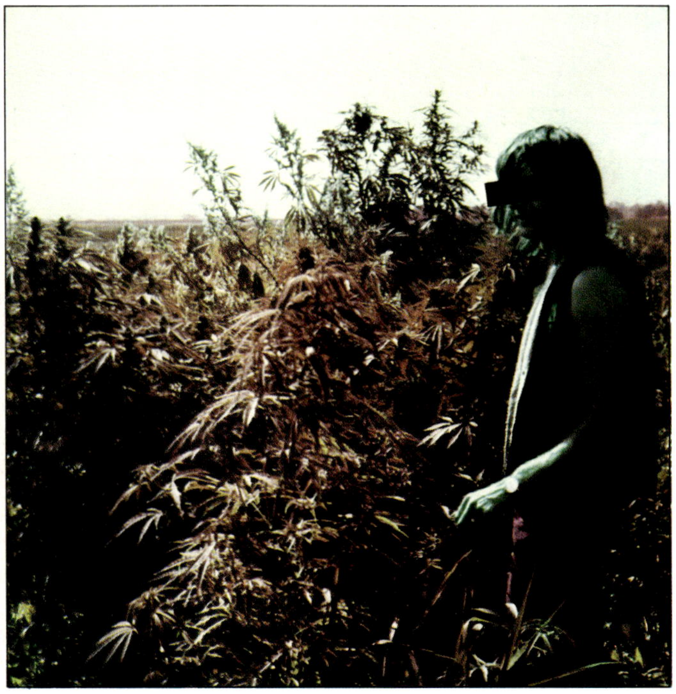

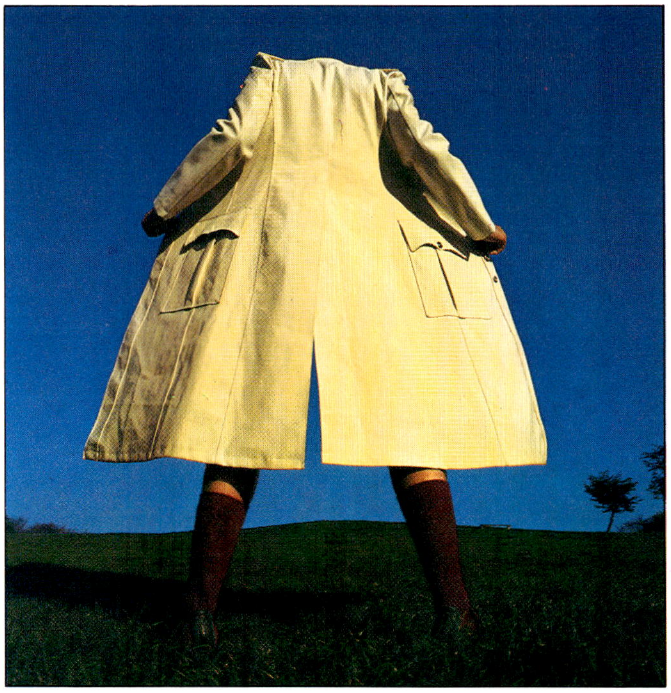

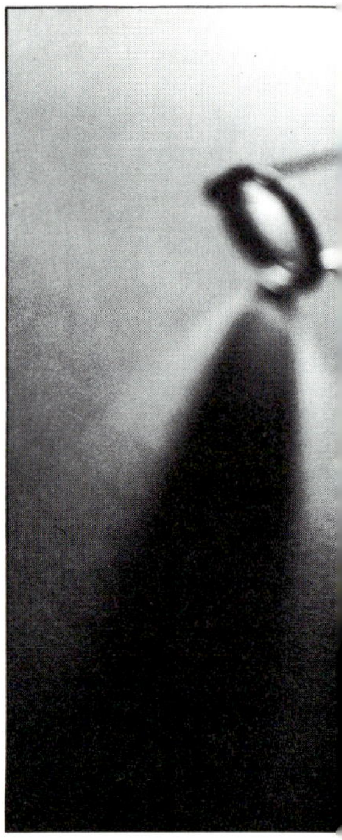

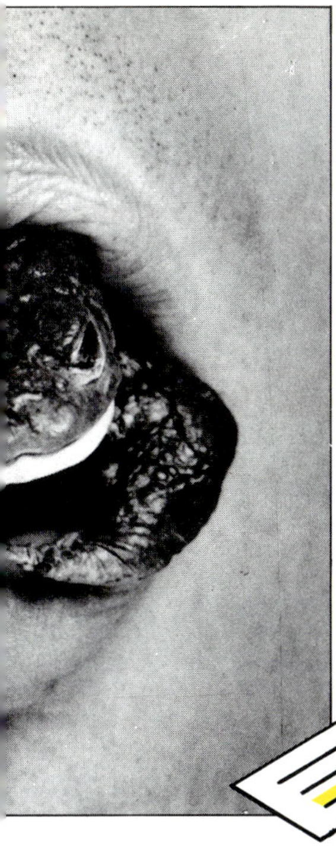
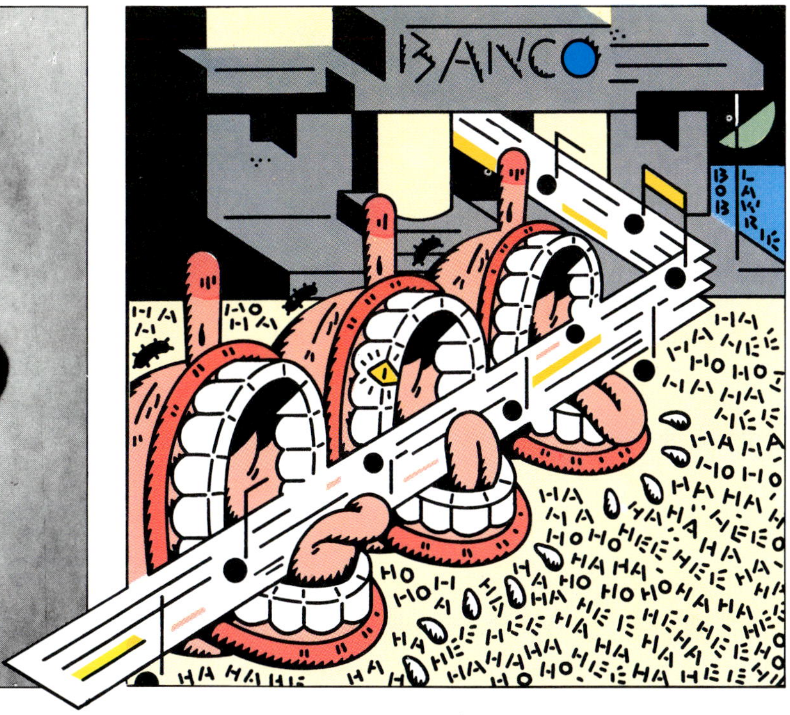
BANCO
BOB LAWRIE
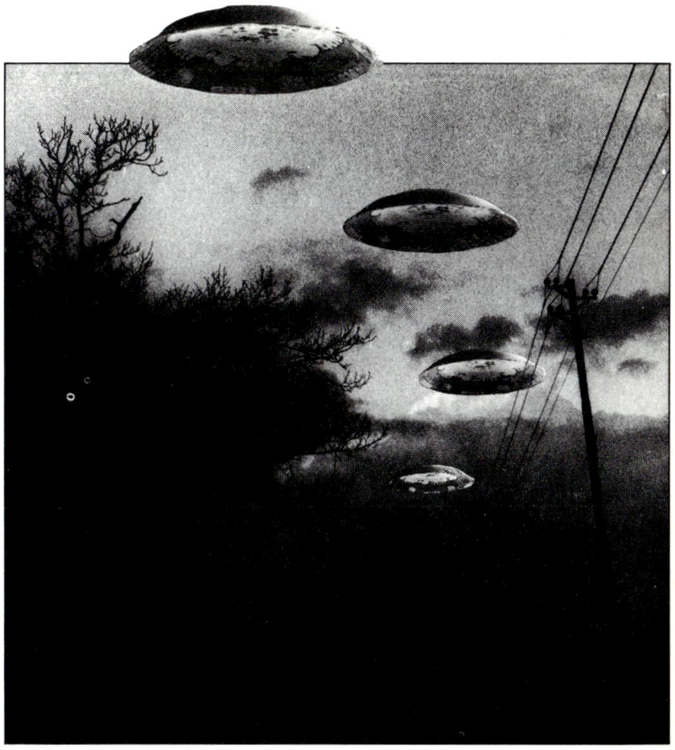
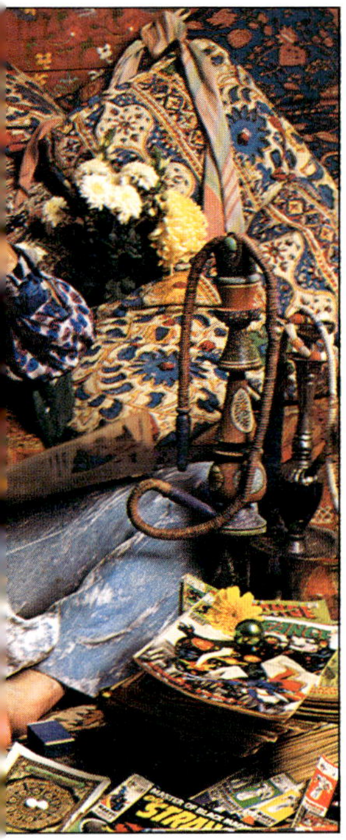
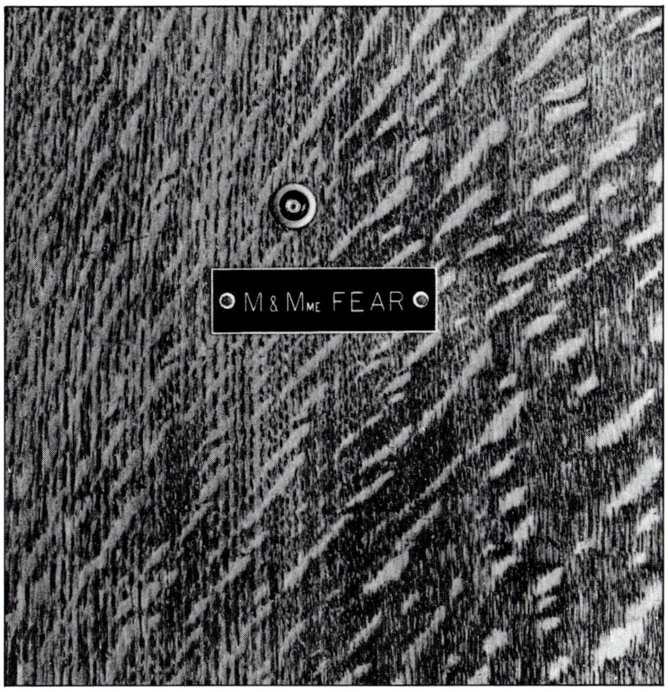
M & Mme FEAR
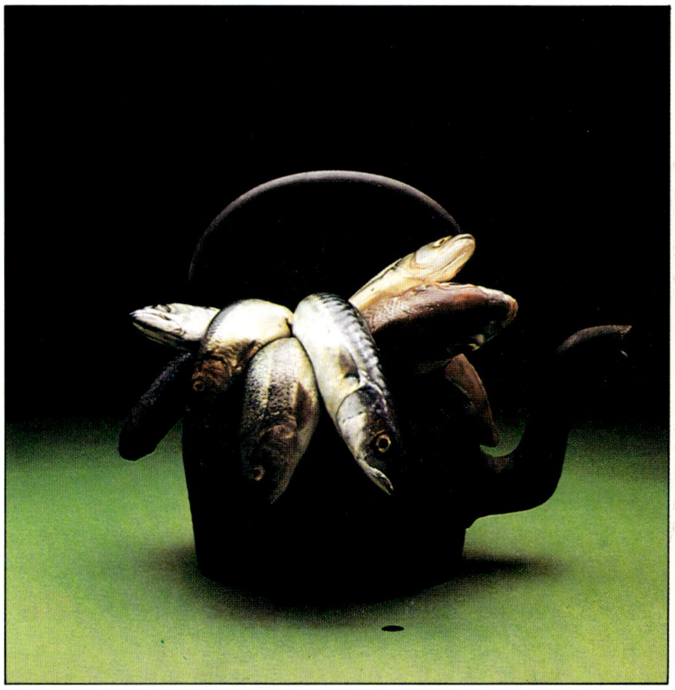
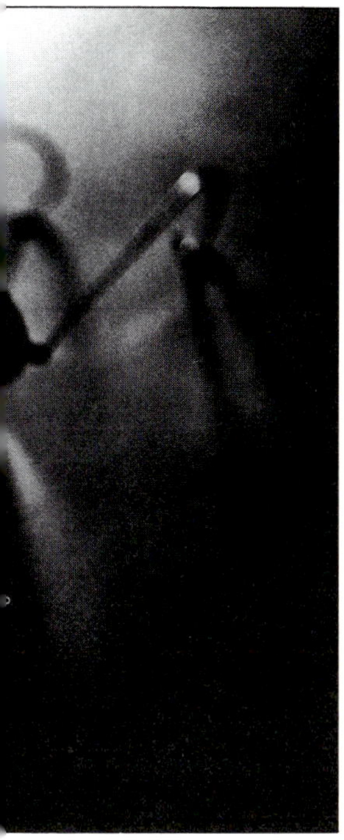
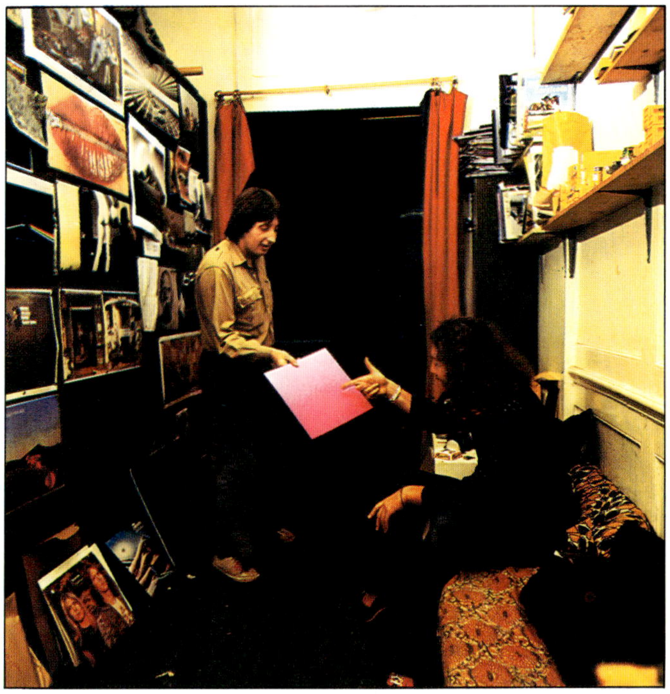
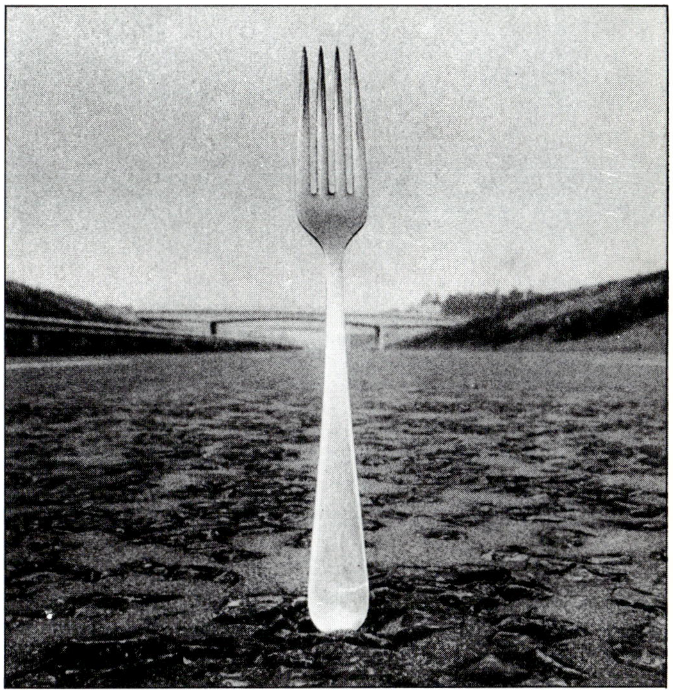

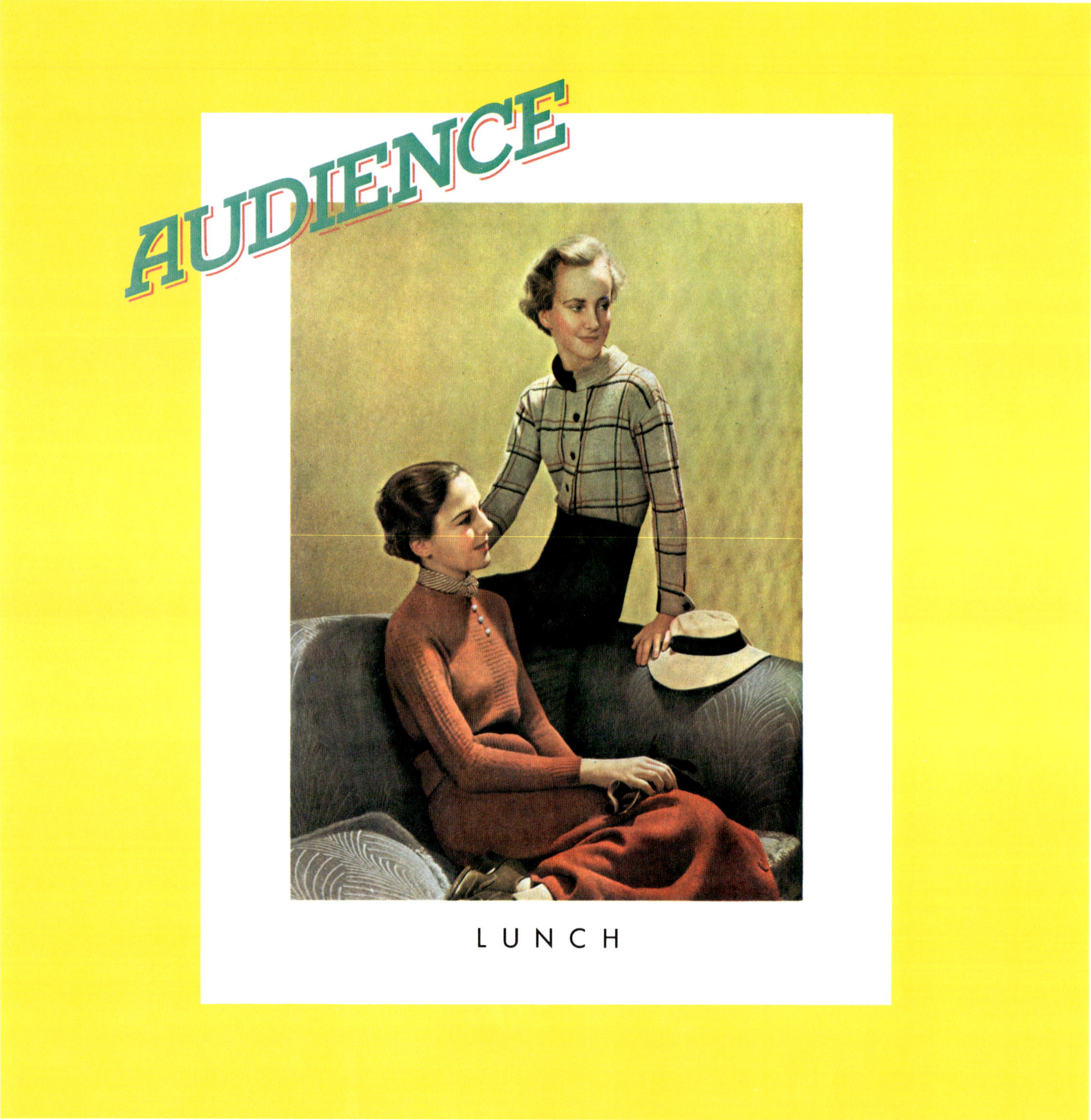

1972	AUDIENCE 'LUNCH'	FRONT COVER

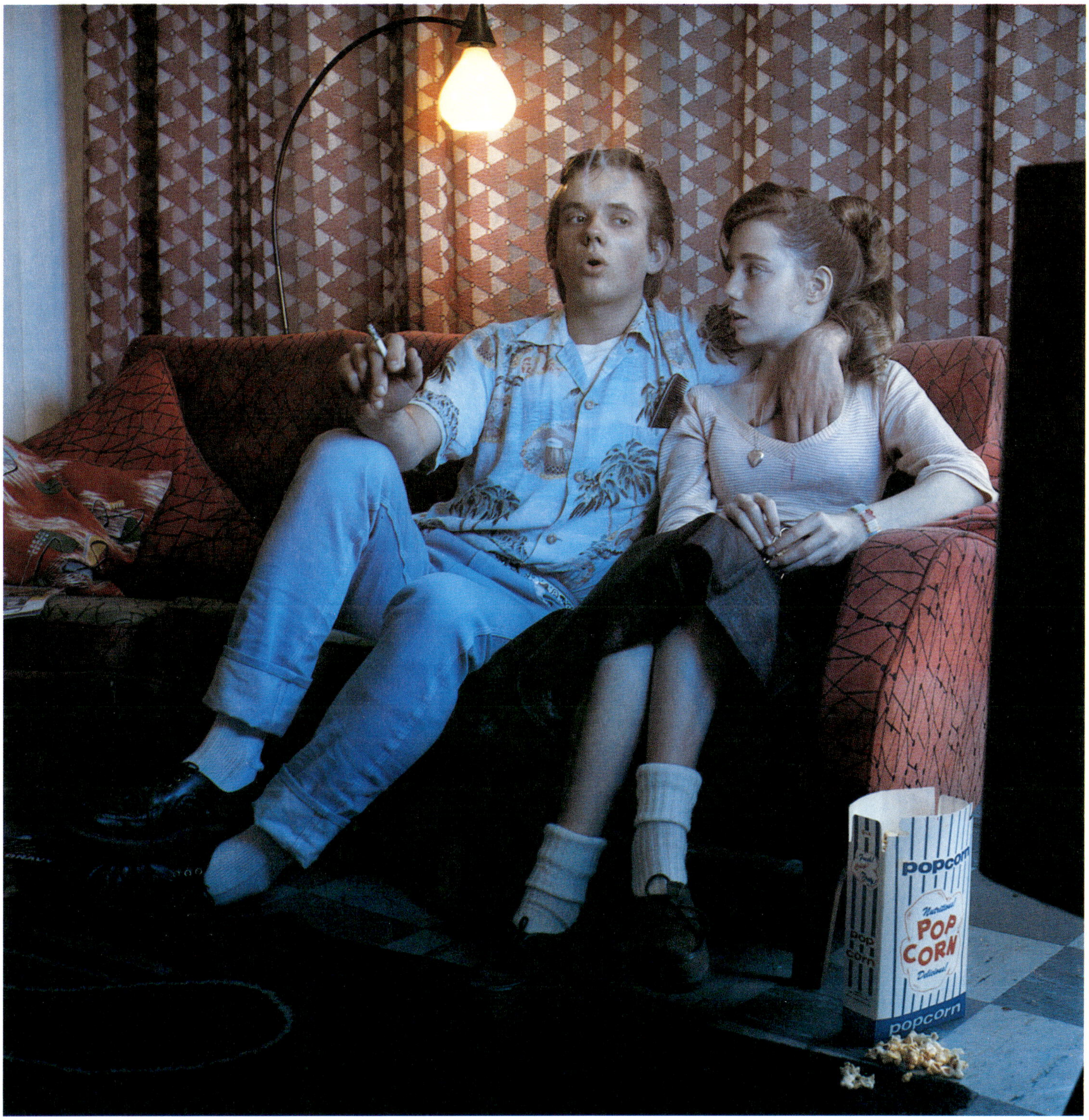

1972 FUMBLE FRONT COVER

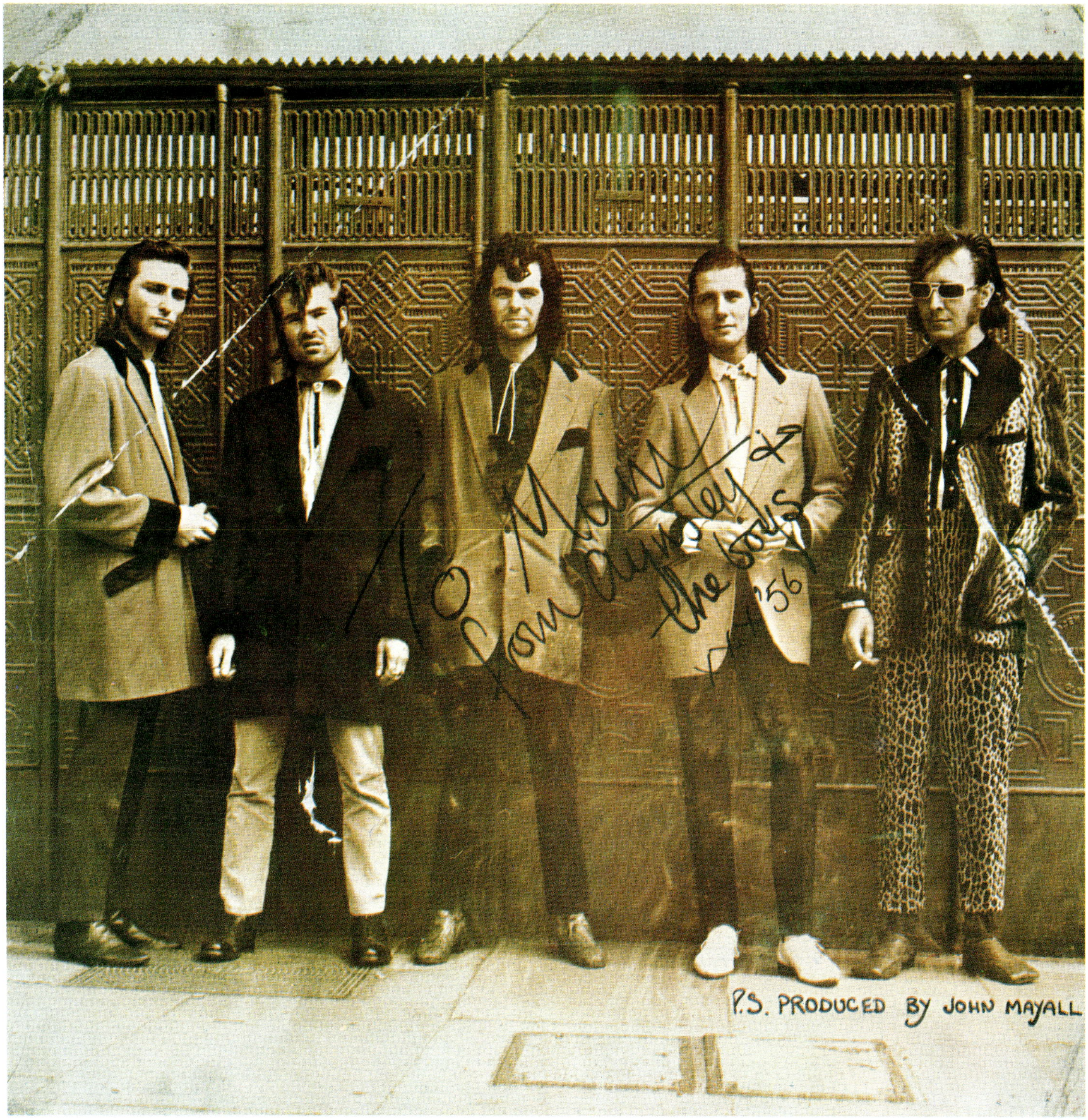

AYNSLEY DUNBAR 'TO MUM WITH LOVE' FRONT COVER

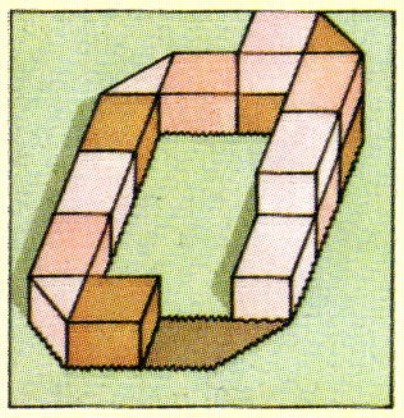

Five Articles of Faith

In the early summer of 1968 in a small bistro in Chelsea, I had dinner with a beautiful, but remote, lady called Victoria. Also present was her book publisher, for Victoria had just written her first children's story. We were celebrating in the English way by getting very lushed. It seemed that this publisher chappie was responsible for book covers. Since I was looking for pocket money I asked, through a drunken haze, if he would give me some work. I'd not done anything like a book cover in my life before but he was an inebriated as I and didn't bat an eyelid. "Sure," he replied, "Why not?" Two weeks later we photographed four paperback book covers. And that's when we began. Lucky Circumstances and Alcohol — the first two Articles of Faith.

I was living in a flat in South Kensington with a bunch of old friends. We were fired with youthful desires to change the modality of normal thinking, besides being rather stoned, and decided to call ourselves . . . 'Consciousness Incorporated'. (At the time we thought that was pretty cute.) Armed with a battered Pentax we headed out for Richmond Park with hired guns and cowboy gear. We horsed around playing cowboys and . . . er . . . cowboys, photographed four western book covers at £50 a throw and returned to our ranch, exhausted but satisfied. We had prints made and delivered to the book company. Our first job was completed.

That summer our flat split up and 'Consciousness Incorporated' died rapidly. Dreams of photographic assignments in romantic places evaporated in the wake of severe personality clashes. One result of this was that I went to a therapist, and at a fiver a session there simply weren't enough funds from my college grant to survive. Extra scratch was urgently needed. I visited the book publisher again and asked him for still more work. He wasn't overjoyed at the idea since our book covers had not been a resounding success. But I hustled, and I grovelled, and he relented — maybe he just wanted me out of his office. Economic Pressure — the need to earn bread — is then the third Article of Faith.

Po was the only other party I knew interested in continuing 'Consciousness Incorporated'. Fortunately, the name had to be dropped, since the word 'incorporated', like 'limited' is for general usage and cannot be adopted for the specific naming of a company. We called ourselves 'Hipgnosis' after we'd discovered the word scrawled by some ingenious dope freak on the door of our flat. It was chosen because it sounded, of course, like ordinary hypnosis, and if we could design hypnotic visuals then that would be absolutely great. In addition, the misspelling possessed a nice sense of contradiction, of an impossible co-existence, from Hip = new and groovy, and Gnostic relating to ancient learning. The old and the new, cohabiting a word that implied bewitchment. Thus the first business card was a picture of contrariness, of things not normally living together (the cat and mouse).

We were still at college — the London School of Film Technique and the Royal College of Art. We wormed our way into the photo department of the RCA, borrowed darkroom facilities and picked the brains of the current technicians (gratitude forever owed to Frank Thurston, Dave B., and Charlie). We had been friends with half of Pink Floyd since our school days and in November '68 they underwent a change of personnel. Founder member and main creative drive Syd Barrett began to travel his very own pathway to the extent of playing literally a different tune from the others on stage. His behaviour was experienced by them as 'erratic', to say the least, and feelings were pretty uncomfortable. The other three wanted out, or wanted him out. In the midst of all this, we got involved, trying in some measure to act as intermediaries. The Floyd asked if anyone in our flat was interested in doing a cover for them. We leapt at the chance and commenced 'Saucerful of Secrets'. Hence the fourth Article of Faith — Who Do You Know?

The outcome of the Floyd's internal disagreements, about which we were, in fact, little concerned, was the departure of Syd and the appearance of Dave Gilmour in the line-up. We were introduced to the Floyd's agent Bryan Morrison who gave us other work, and to the record company who did likewise. Alexis Korner's 'New Generation of Blues' was actually the first finished cover, since 'Saucerful' was rather complex and involved thirteen different colour print superimpositions. We then did some publicity shots of an emergent band called Free and some sleeves for EMI, namely Toe Fat, Panama Jug Band and the Gods. We continued to purloin the facilities of the Royal College of Art until we both finished school in the summer of 1969. We decided to continue Hipgnosis. The idea of no spending money, and even more disastrously no rent money, was more than the mind could bear.

For a further six months we worked from Po's bathroom which measured no more than 10ft x 6ft. We used a dilapidated enlarger bought second hand and developed prints in a tray on the floor; we washed them in the bath and dried them on a pre-war print dryer. Gosh, those were the days! Impoverished, beset by terrible conditions, no capital and no idea of the future. We didn't care where we worked so long as there was work to do. But it couldn't last. After three months we knew we had to get our own studio. We scoured the newspapers day after day and eventually Po saw an ad for Denmark Street. We took it even though it looked grim and spooky. We cleared the place out, built our own darkroom and started to work February 1970. This operation obviously required money but we didn't have any. The great white Mother came to the rescue and lent us a grand. Hence the fifth Article of Faith — A Doting Mum.

We looked hard for work. We did 'Ummagumma' and 'Meddle' sleeves for the Floyd, publicity shots and odd bits and pieces. They were one of our main sources of business. Slowly our name got around and other people and record companies started to employ us.

For five years we earned very little but did progressively more and more work. We lived off our girlfriends and gradually obtained equipment, made contacts, learned the mechanical side of doing prints and artworks, and improved our own abilities. We are self-taught photographers and designers and fundamentally what we do is to dream up pictures that we have to go out and shoot. Since we'd both been at film school we had already learnt some of the basics of cameras and photography before we started Hipgnosis. This background helps by lending some of our designs a film-like quality wherein they may seem to be about something or to tell a story and are not just a pretty picture or commercial image.

Peter Christopherson joined us in '74 as an assistant but is now a full partner. George Hardie and Colin Elgie work with us a lot although they are freelance illustrators and designers in their own right. Frequently we each individually think of suggestions for the beginnings of ideas, or design entire pieces by ourselves. Alternatively we sit about in a group, listen to the music and word associate with a title or phrase from the client's brief. Thus by working separately or together in various combinations we can produce material which exhibits different but related styles. This in turn encompasses a wide range of clients and music as well as allowing for some personal freedom of expression within Hipgnosis itself. When designing together we basically play with ideas that turn into pictures that inspire further ideas and so on, until in the end an idea that appeals comes to light. And it can appeal just because it's odd, cute, romantic, bizarre, appropriate or striking, and so on. By a further process of analysis we quite often find that this idea is nowhere near as difficult to do as it had at first seemed. So then we tell the client and if he agrees, we go out and do it.

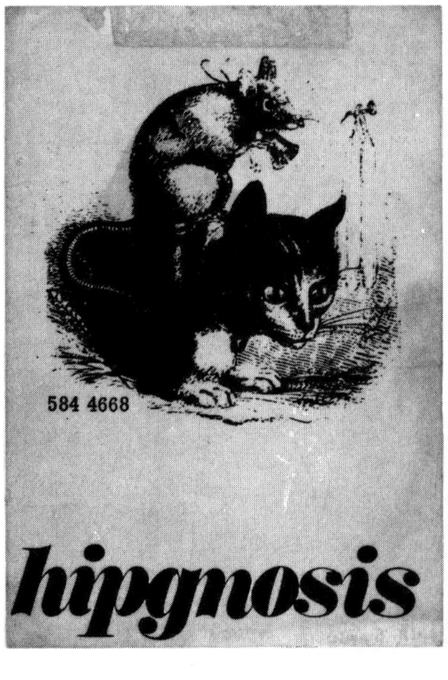

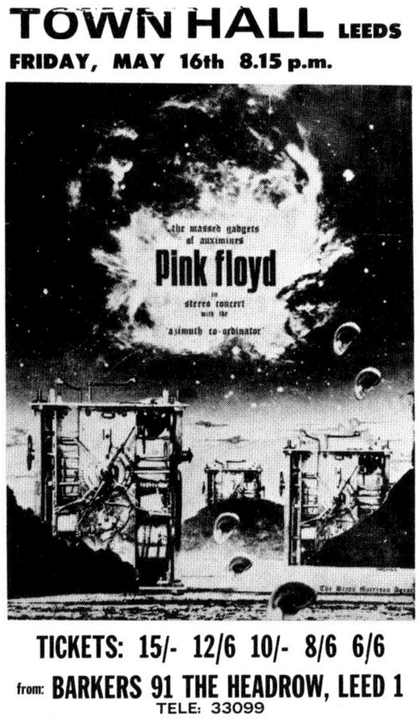

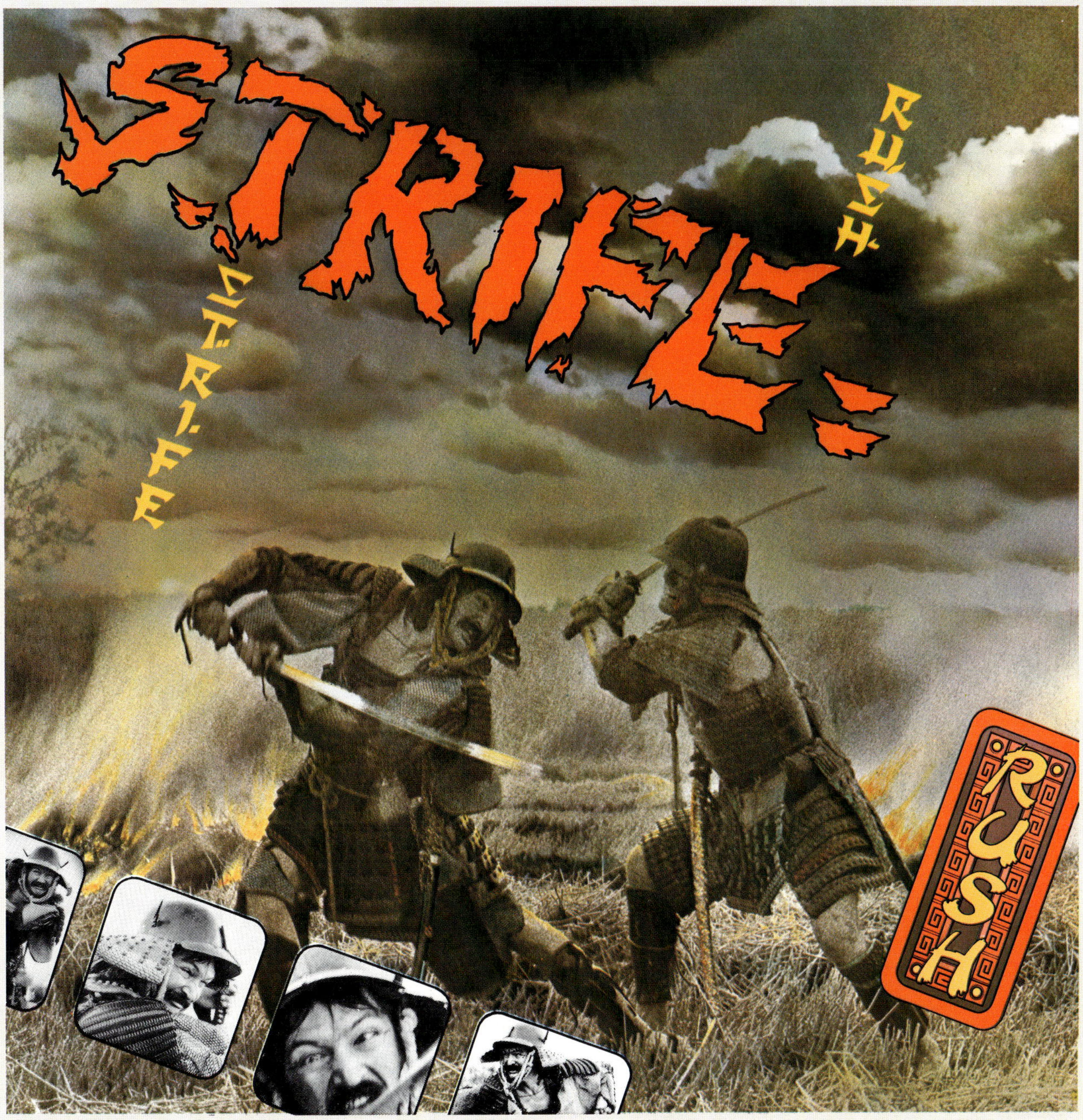

1975 | STRIFE 'RUSH' | FRONT COVER

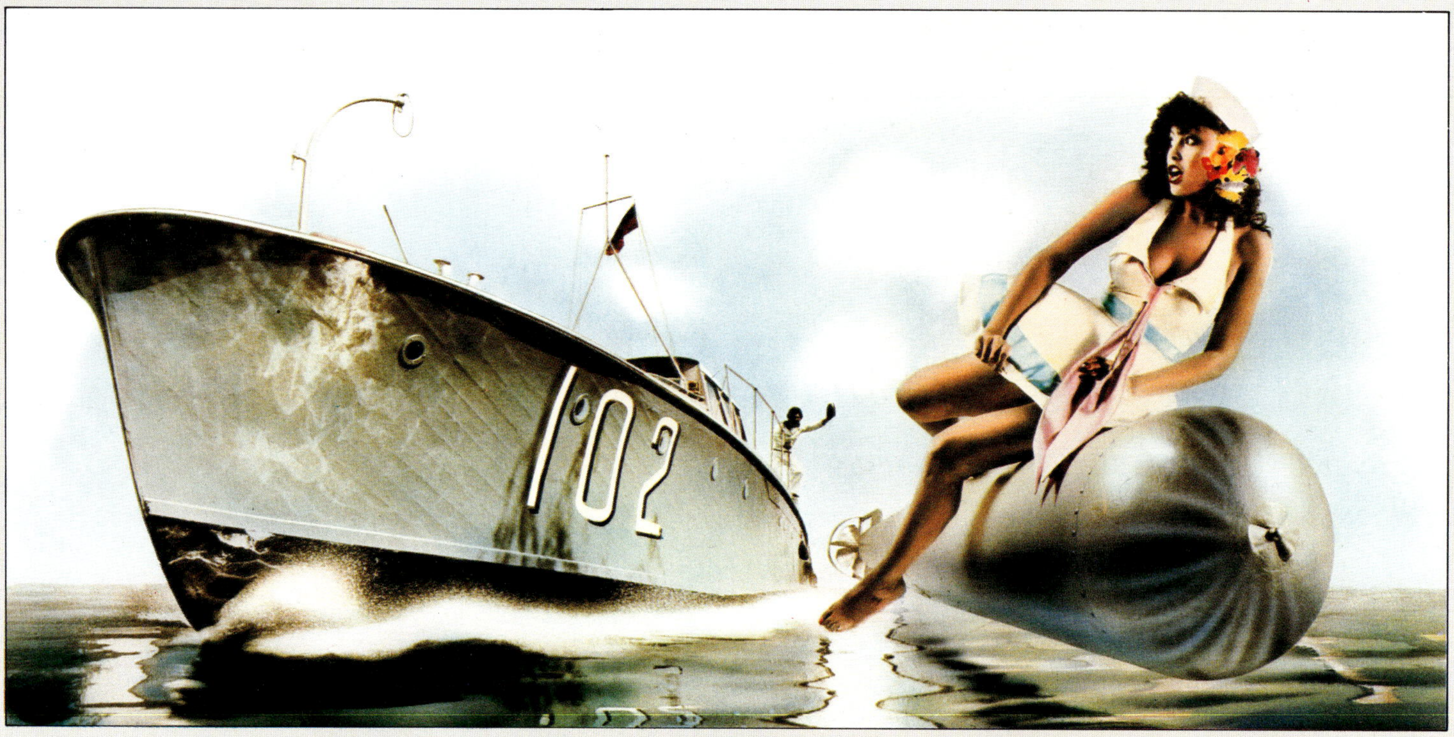

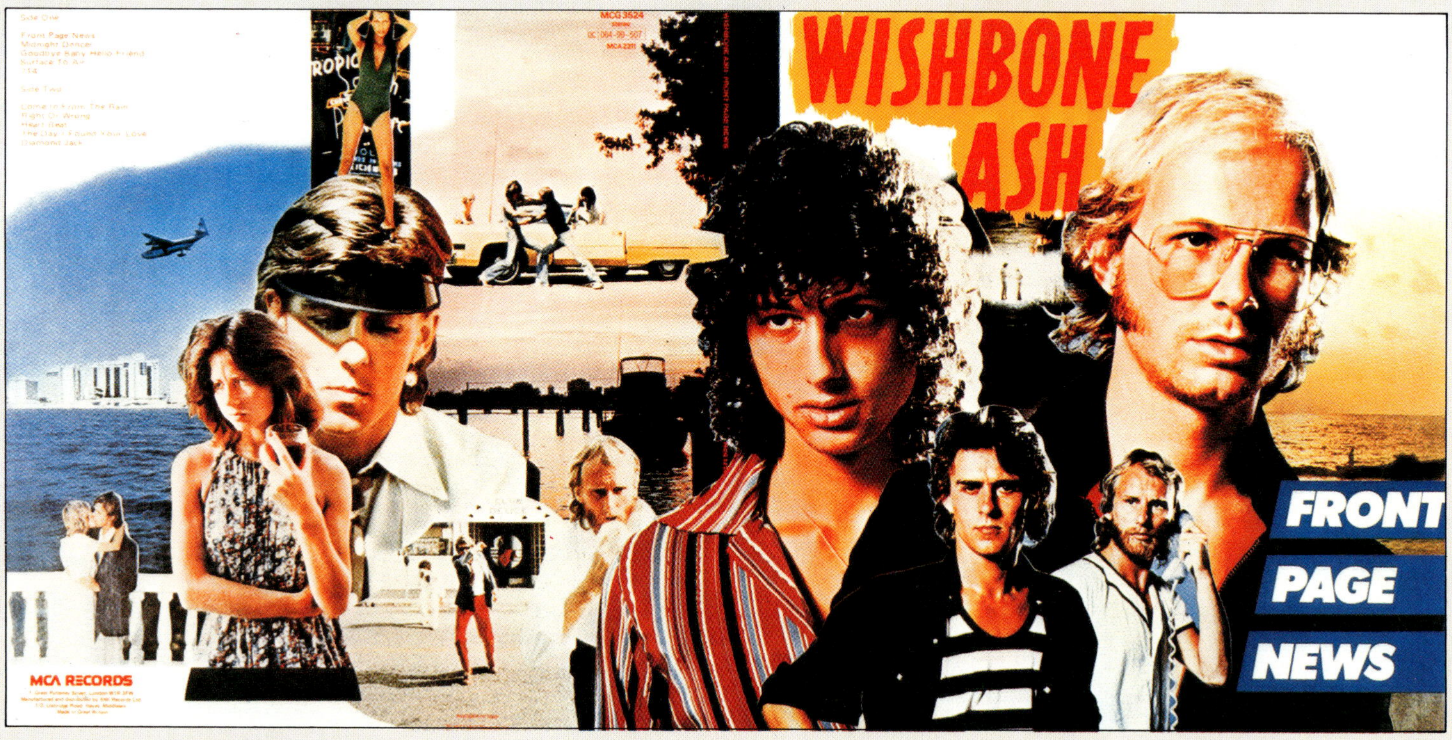

PRETTY THINGS 'SILK TORPEDO'   WISHBONE ASH 'FRONT PAGE NEWS'

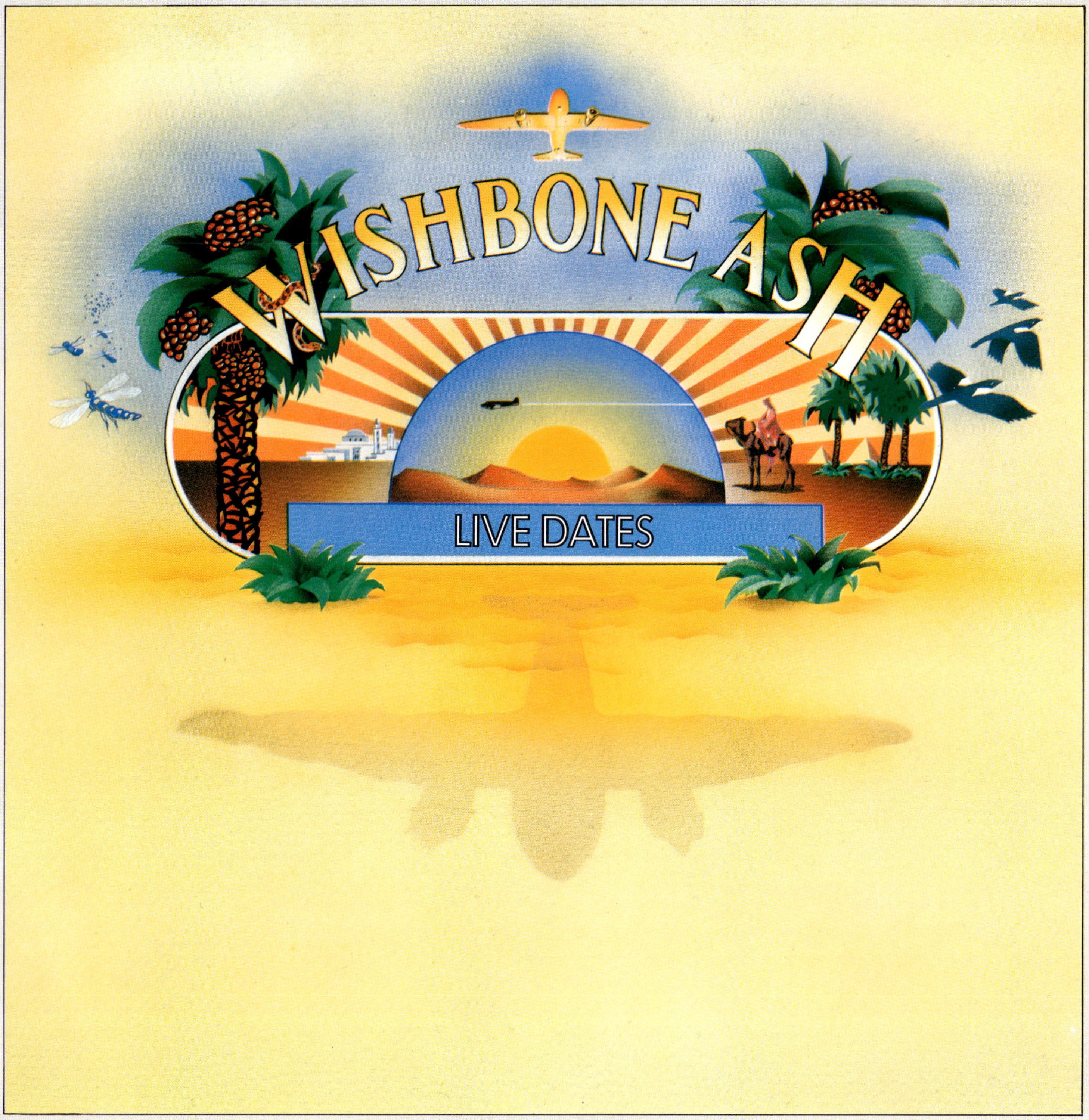

1973 WISHBONE ASH 'LIVE DATES' ILLUSTRATION COLIN ELGIE FRONT COVER

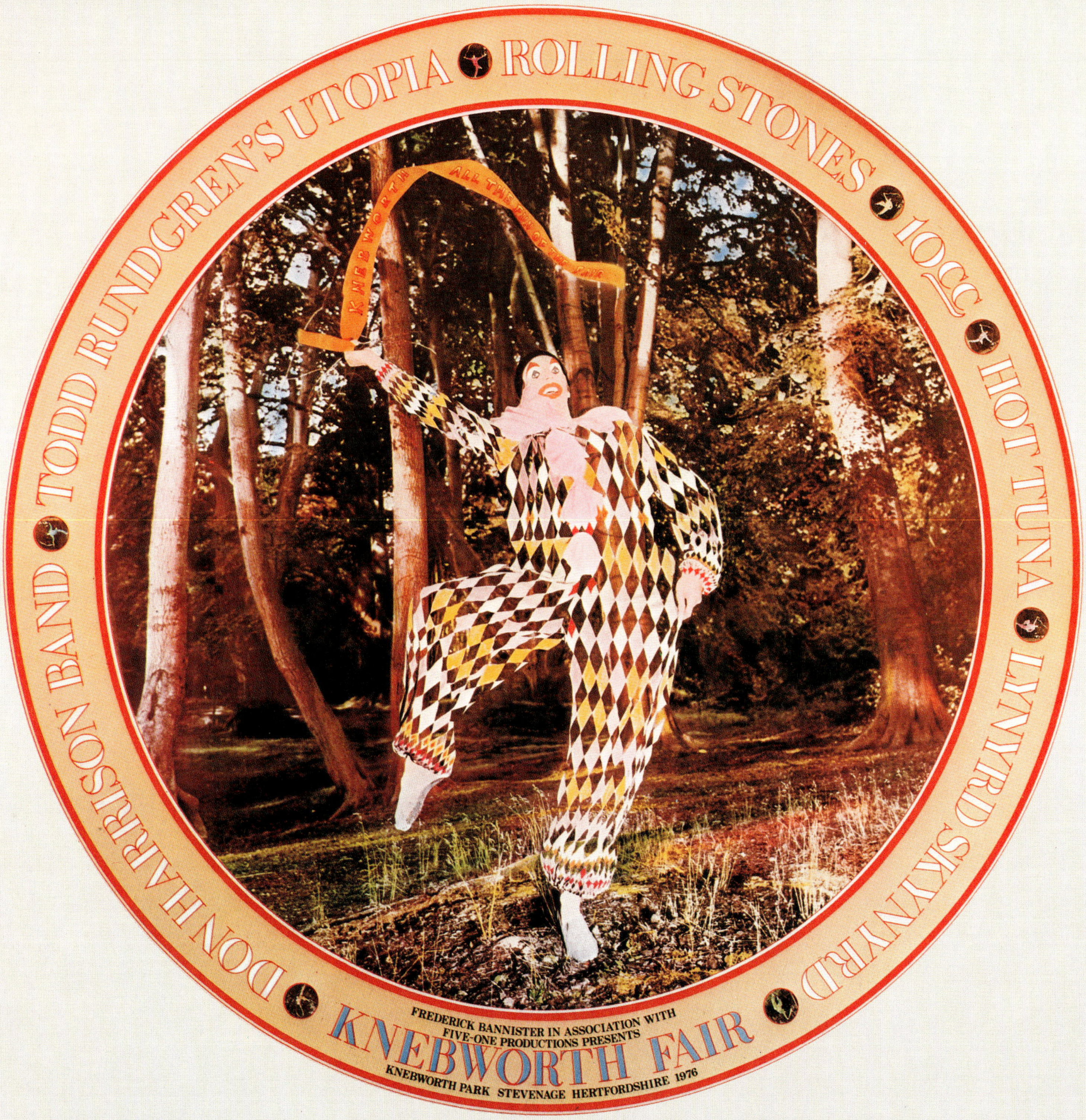

1976 | KNEBWORTH ROLLING STONES | POSTER

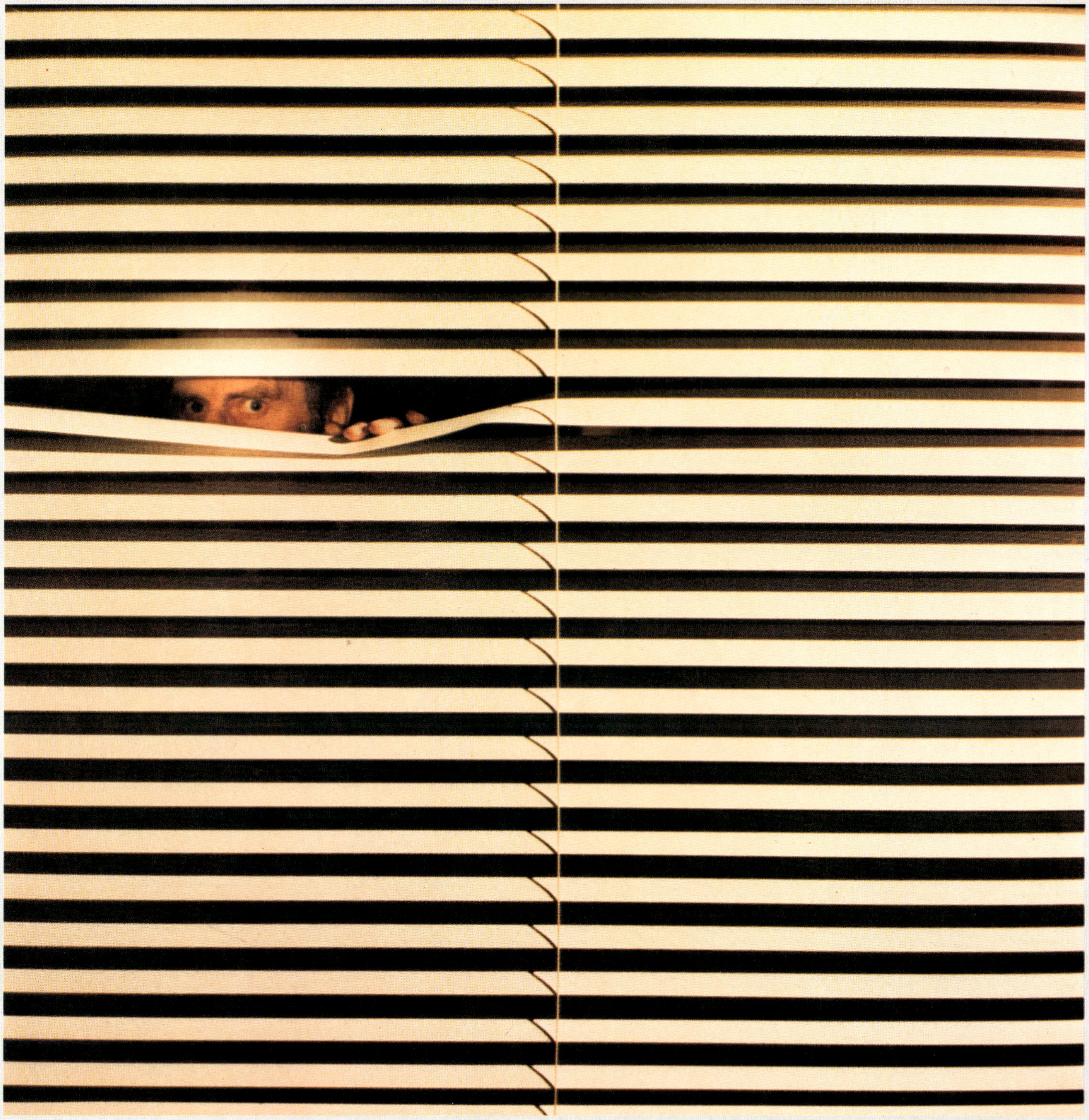

1976 BRAND X 'UNORTHODOX BEHAVIOR' FRONT COVER

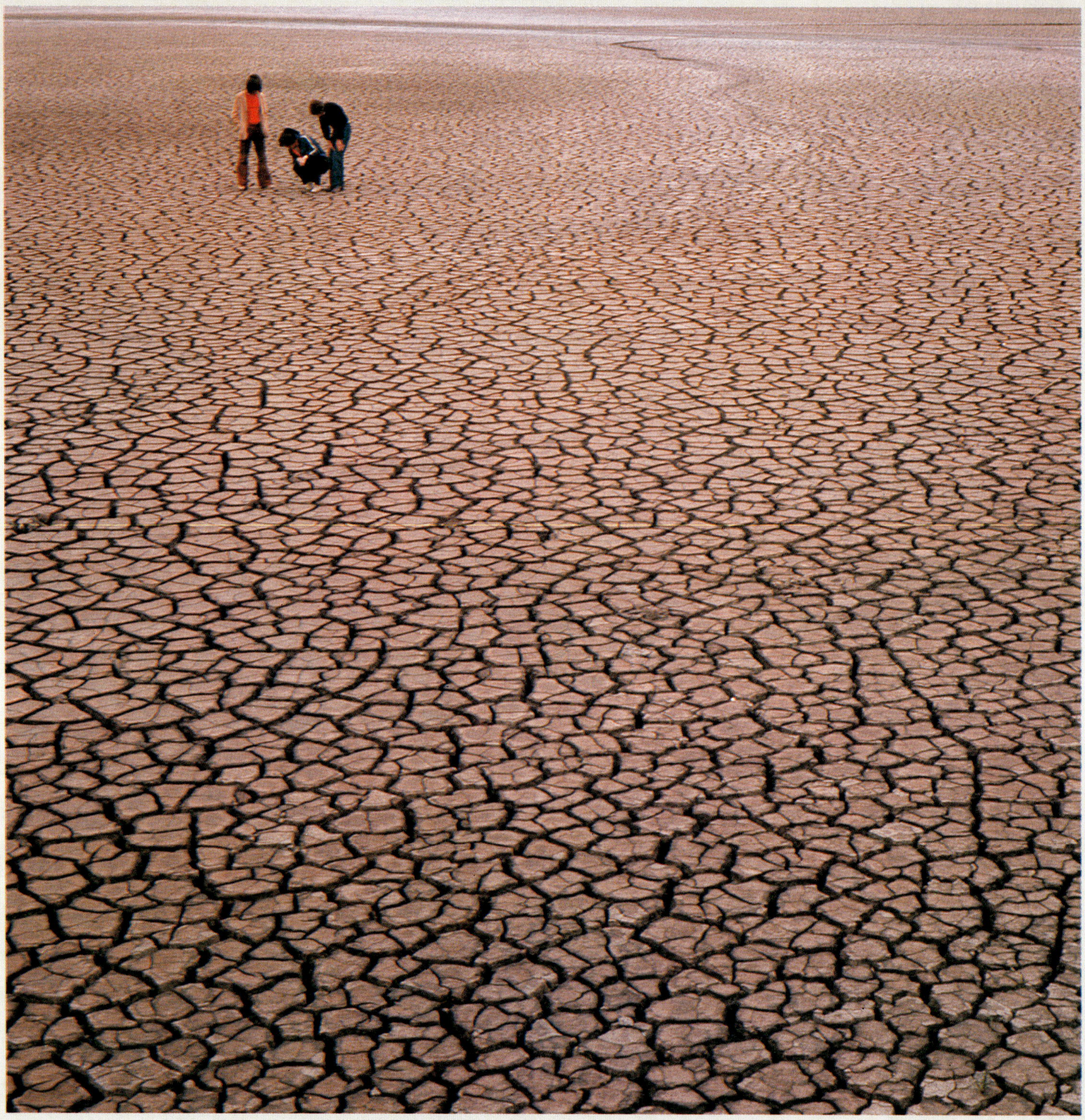

1971	MARVIN, WELCH & FARRAR 'SECOND OPINION'	FRONT COVER

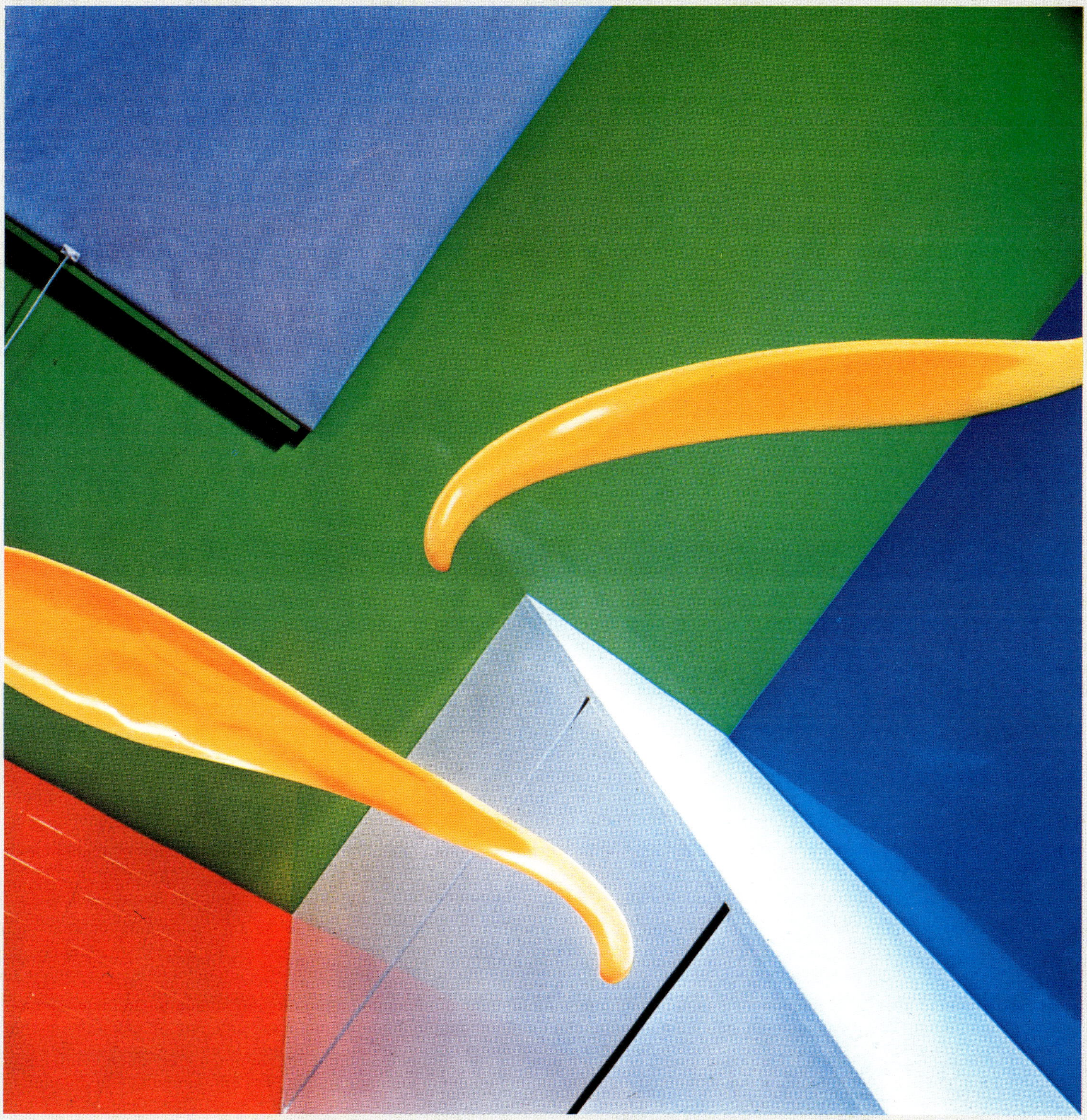

1978 | BE BOP DELUXE 'DRASTIC PLASTIC' | FRONT COVER

We don't particularly feel that portraiture is a forte of ours but we have tried several different approaches that can be seen in this section. Though we may personally and selfishly view portraits as a restraint — we don't encourage people to ask us to do them — a photo of the performing artiste is often what that artiste wants. For us it constitutes a change and can be an intriguing challenge against our own inclinations. The options left open to us are basically as follows.

Firstly we can choose an interesting setting. The sleeve for Syd Barrett's solo album 'The Madcap Laughs' (pg. 103) is simply a picture of Syd in his room. The photograph is potentially a straightforward affair except that he painted his floorboards in red and blue stripes just for the session. Sammy Hagar's favourite colour was red so we adapted an earlier idea about a room populated with objects and furniture all of the same colour and transferred it out into the street. All the people and props have been arranged by us. The idea is that these red things have converged on this spot at one very unlikely point in time. It's an all red coincidence.

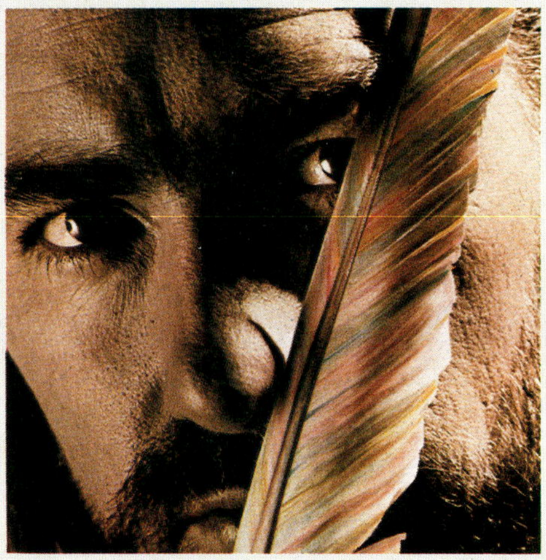

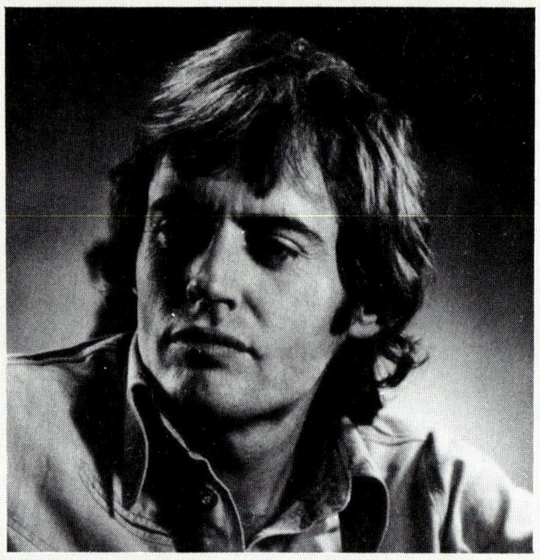

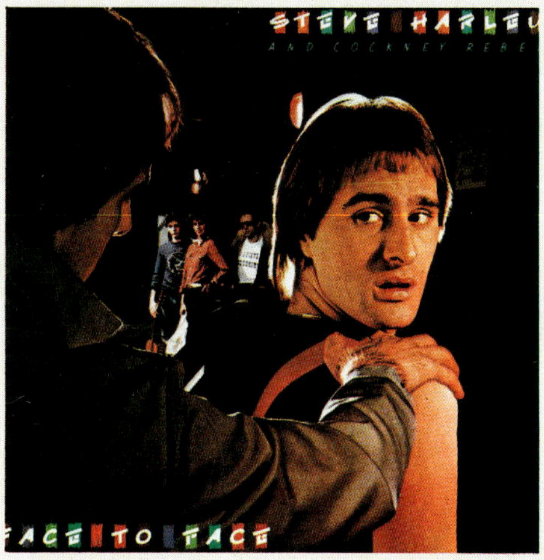

Secondly we have tried to involve the artiste in some kind of action or event. If he agrees then it adds something apart from the purely visual aspect, but it is not often that he just happens to be the right person or is even prepared to do it in the first place. Peter Frampton and his band braved many buckets of water hurled without remorse at their heads (pg. 146). Roy Harper, though possessed of many talents, can't, as far as I know, walk on water (pg. 96). As a consequence the photo for 'HQ' is a montage. Steve Harley's live album 'Face to Face' shows a situation in which he has been apprehended just before going on stage. He is none too happy about it so his expression is aggressive. He is also alarmed, for he is being apprehended, in fact, by himself.

'Ummagumma' is a visual play on the impossible where the receding perspective is theoretically infinite yet practically finite. The photos of the whole scene plus an empty picture frame are printed progressively smaller and montaged into place. The positions of the band members have been rotated for fun. We were also interested in the comparison of mental perspective (the picture on the wall) with physical perspective (the people in the garden). One source for this picture was a line drawing in a psychological text book which showed a similar infinite regression — we just wanted to try it photographically since it would then be more real and more incongruous. It was designed in conjunction with Libby January. 10cc is a further attempt at exploring the impossible but this time by trying to suspend disbelief. If the outer edge of the picture could really be pulled into the central area then the latter must be physically behind the former. This is, of course, not the case because the whole image is two dimensional, isn't it? Sharks' LP cover is simply a mild joke about Oedipus and barbiturates (??). The subjects have closed their own eyes and we have drawn fake eyes on their lids with body paint. At least they didn't blink when the flash went off. 'King Brilliant' is an attempt at photographic cubism and Howard Werth is rumoured to be in there somewhere.

The sleeve for Sassafras is based on the visual dynamics of a simple diagonal. It is noticeably more graphic than our usual approach. George Hardie cut strips of pretty coloured paper for the artwork and Bruce Atkins supplied us with a bromoil print of the band. Bob Sargeant's 'First Starring Role' is another of our rare attempts at a graphic treatment. He asked for a 30's movie image and so we built a set in our studio that we thought was appropriate. We then lit it with tungsten lights as they would have done back in those halcyon days. The graphics are by Colin Elgie.

One can make a portrait picture interesting by lighting alone. A good proportion of our pictures are taken using

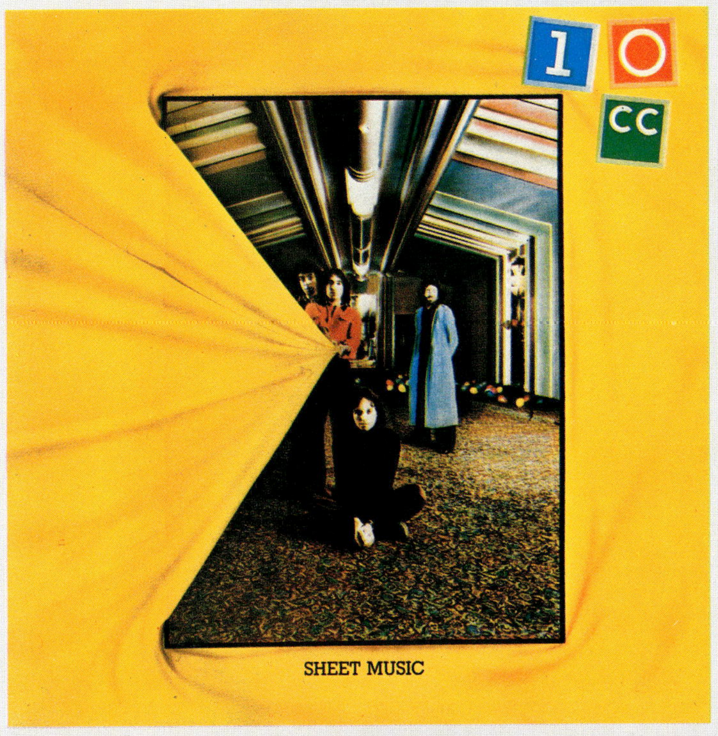

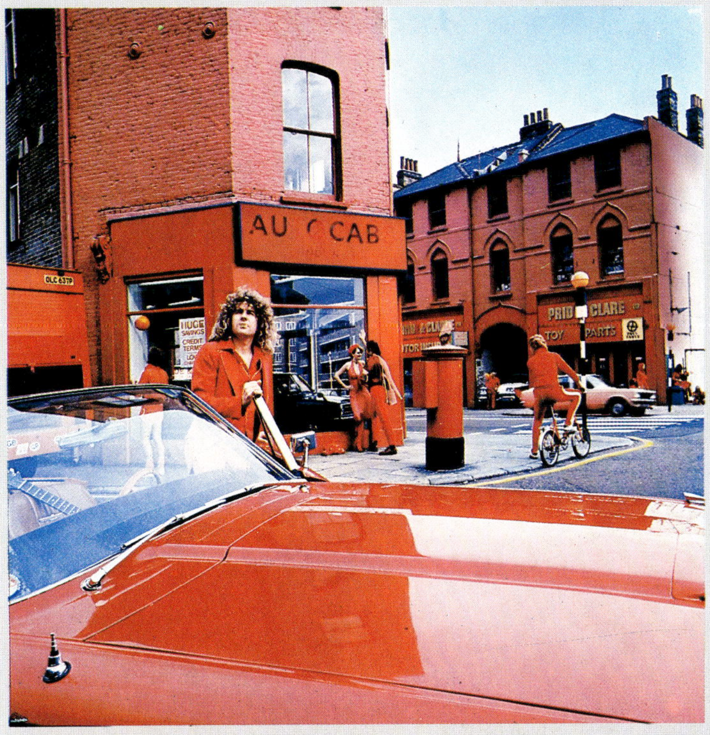

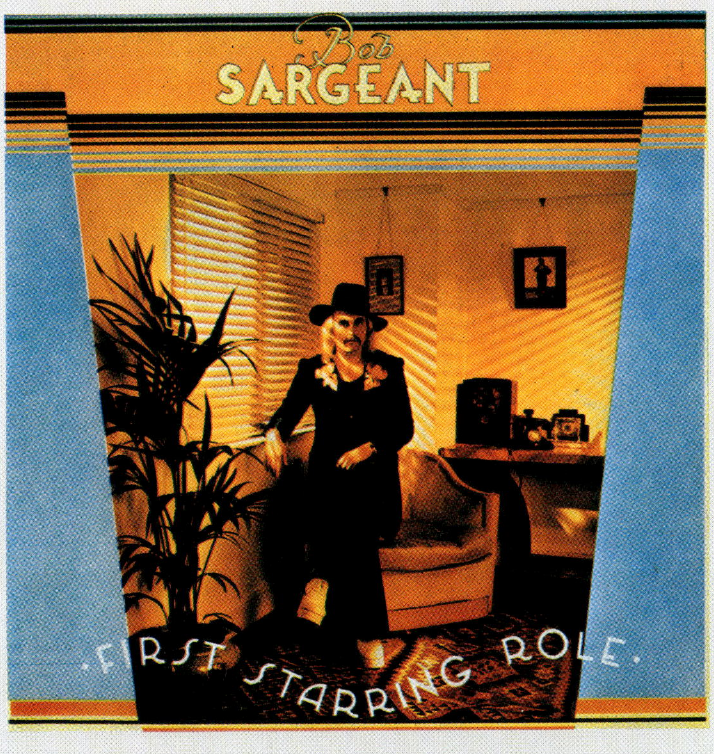

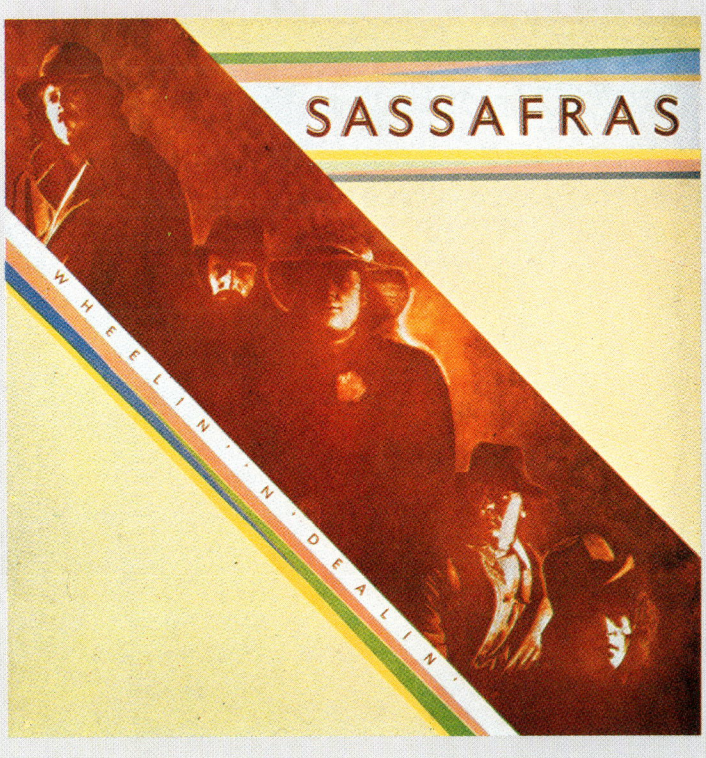

10CC SAMMY HAGAR BOB SARGEANT SASSAFRAS

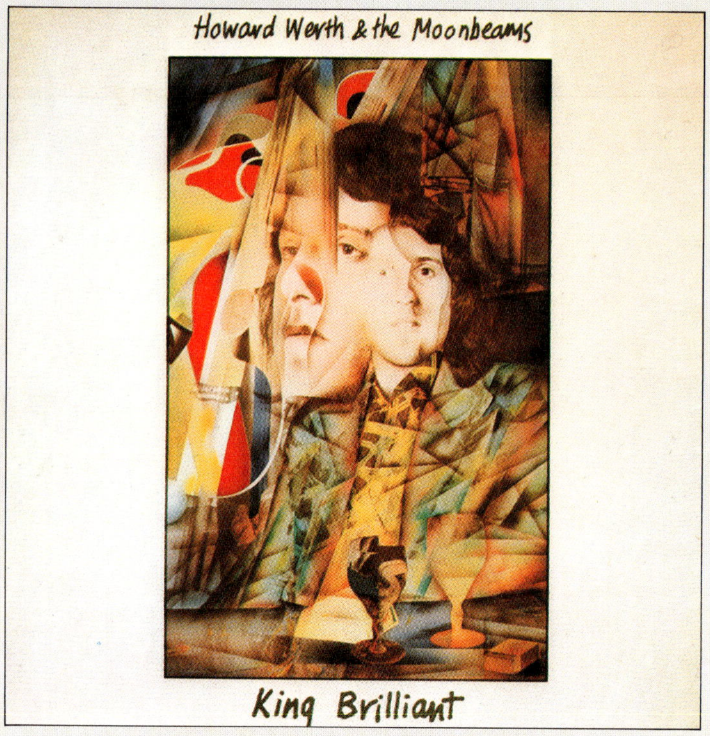

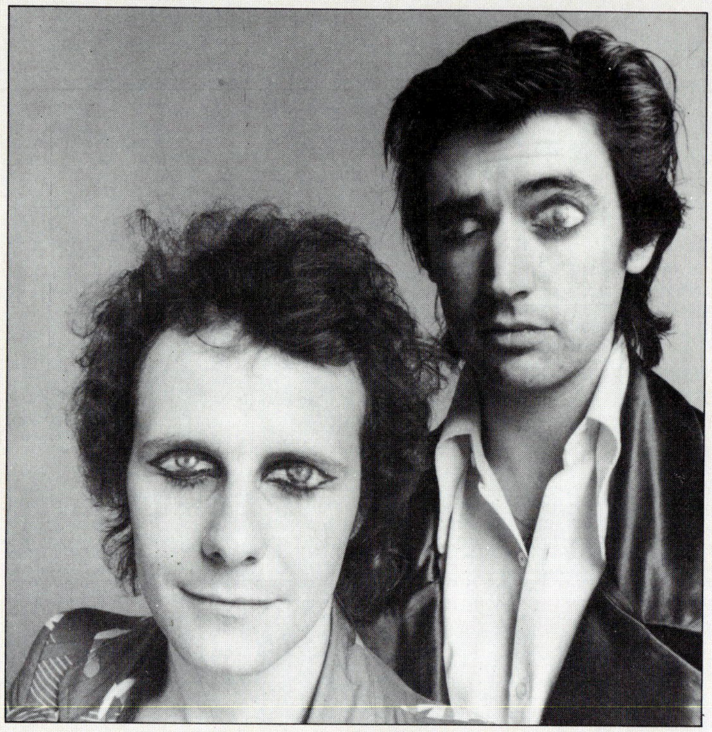

natural 'available' light — sun, clouds, streetlights etc. and depending on where you are and what time of day you shoot this can be utterly amazing. (It can also, at midday on a dismal overcast day in the city, be thoroughly rotten.) In general, for portraits that are about the faces of the artiste, we would shoot in the studio using photographic lights. Studio lights come in two main families, tungsten and flash, and the basic difference between the two is that tungsten lights have an old fashioned Hollywood-type feeling and flash has a clean, modern, slightly antiseptic feeling.

The picture of Gary Shearston is one of our better examples of the traditional tungsten technique. In this case the light sources are spotlights very like the ones used in theatres and on movie sets. Each of the lights can be focused down to a very small area or flooded out wide to cover a larger one. The final picture is made up of three or four different lights shining directly, or reflecting indirectly, onto different areas of the subject at various levels of intensity. Specific areas of the face can be highlighted whilst others can be cast into shadow or lit only dimly. Tungsten lighting is actually a craft all of its own and whilst it often tends to give a somewhat dated feeling it is extremely controllable. It is by no means always flattering but it can certainly be very moody.

As a footnote to talking about tungsten, 'Bull in a Ming Vase' was actually taken with flash but it's done so that it has some of the appearance of tungsten. As far as I remember the reason we did this was to overcome the one main disadvantage of tungsten light which is the low light level — although they seem alright in a darkened hall spotlights are not at all strong by comparison with daylight and consequently one doesn't have much by way of depth of field (range of distance from the camera at which things are in focus).

Wishbone 4 is a good example of a typical flash-lit portrait. The light sources here are two flash heads shone through a large sheet of white perspex positioned about seven feet in front of the band, slightly to one side and above them. This perspex softens the light and is our improvised imitation of expensive strobe units ('fishfryers' and 'Swimming pools') that ritzy professionals get to buy

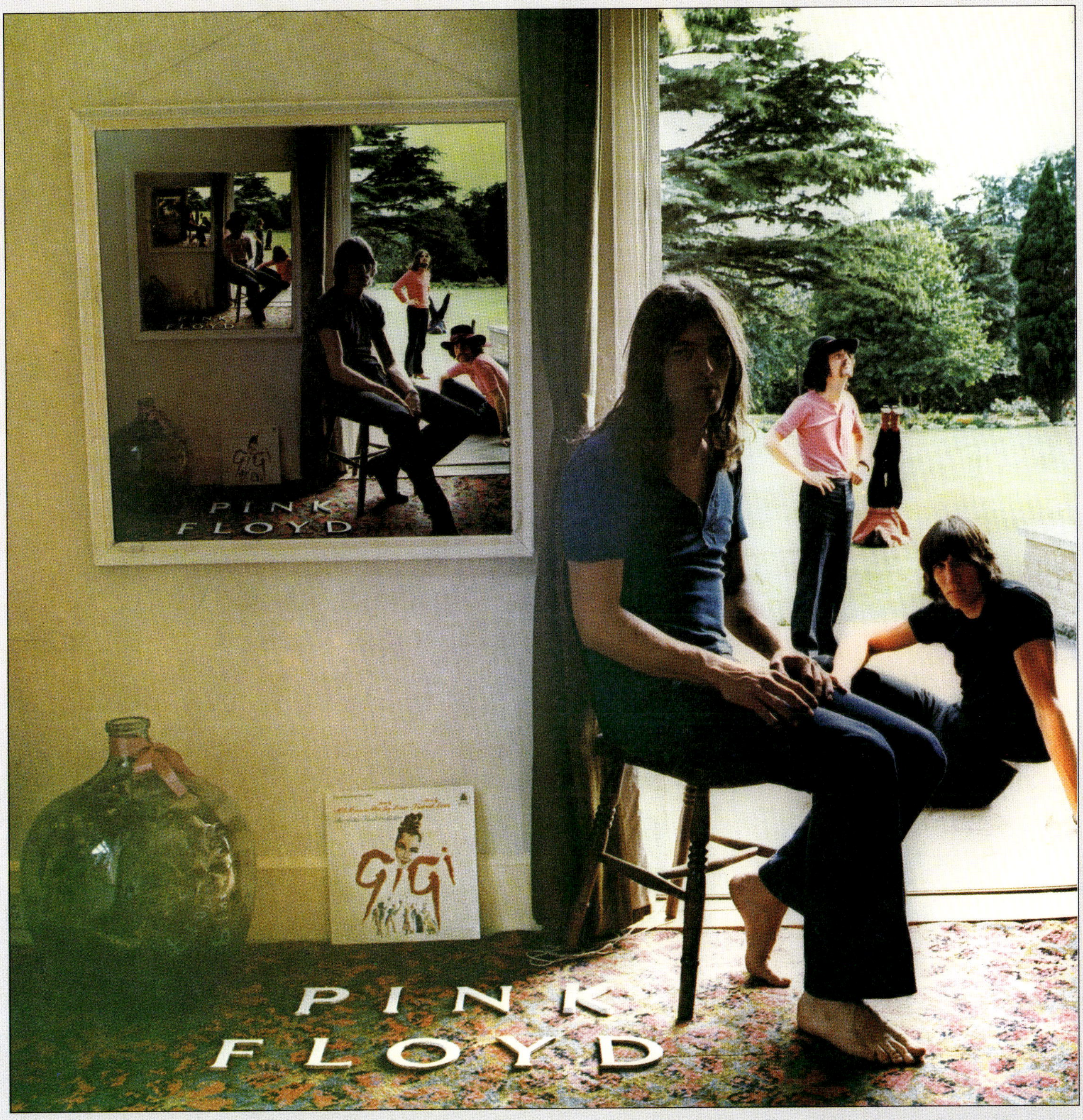

1969 PINK FLOYD 'UMMAGUMMA' FRONT COVER

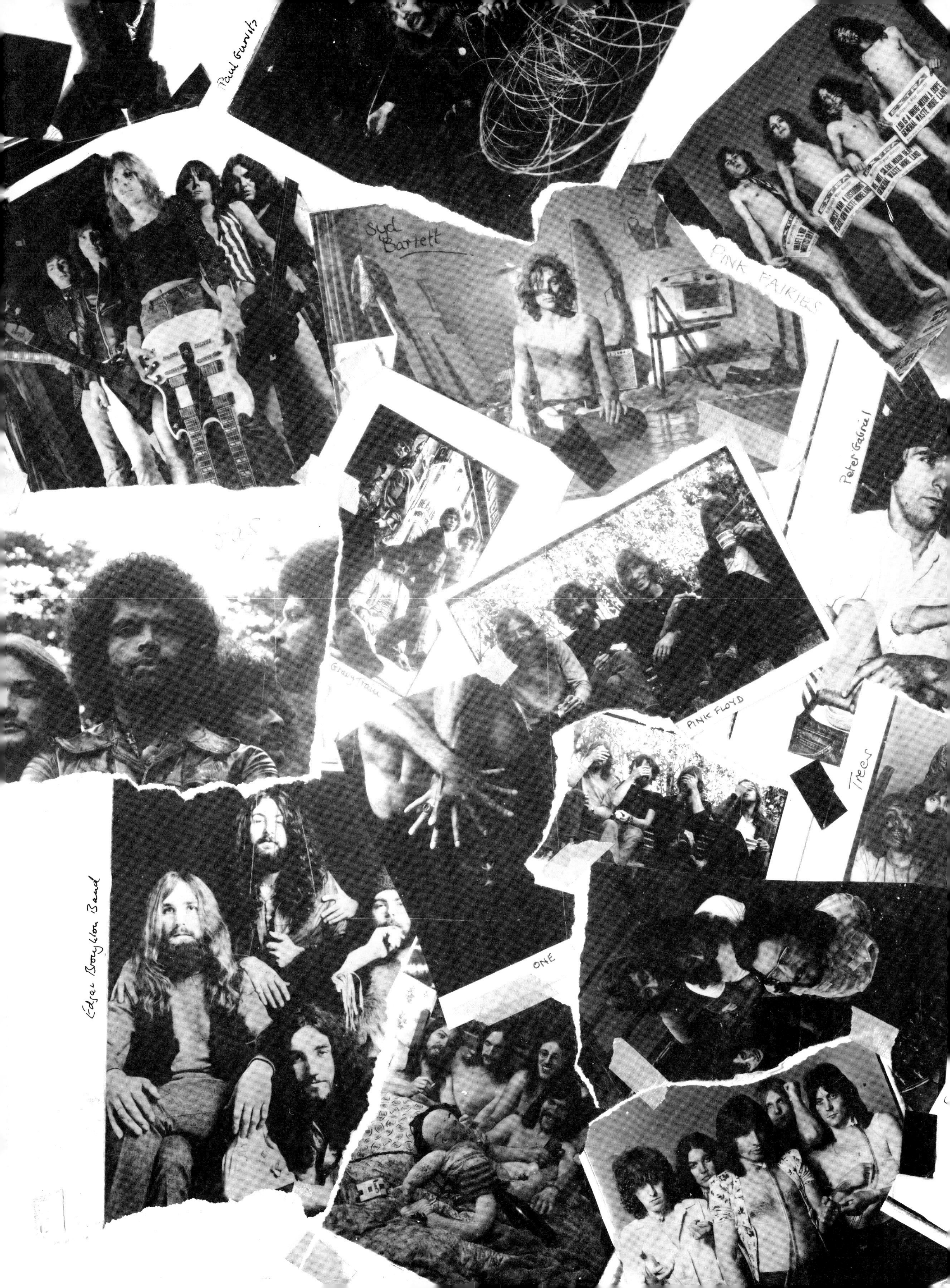
Paul Gurvitz
Syd Barrett
PINK FAIRIES
Peter Gabriel
Gravy Train
PINK FLOYD
Trees
Edgar Broughton Band
ONE

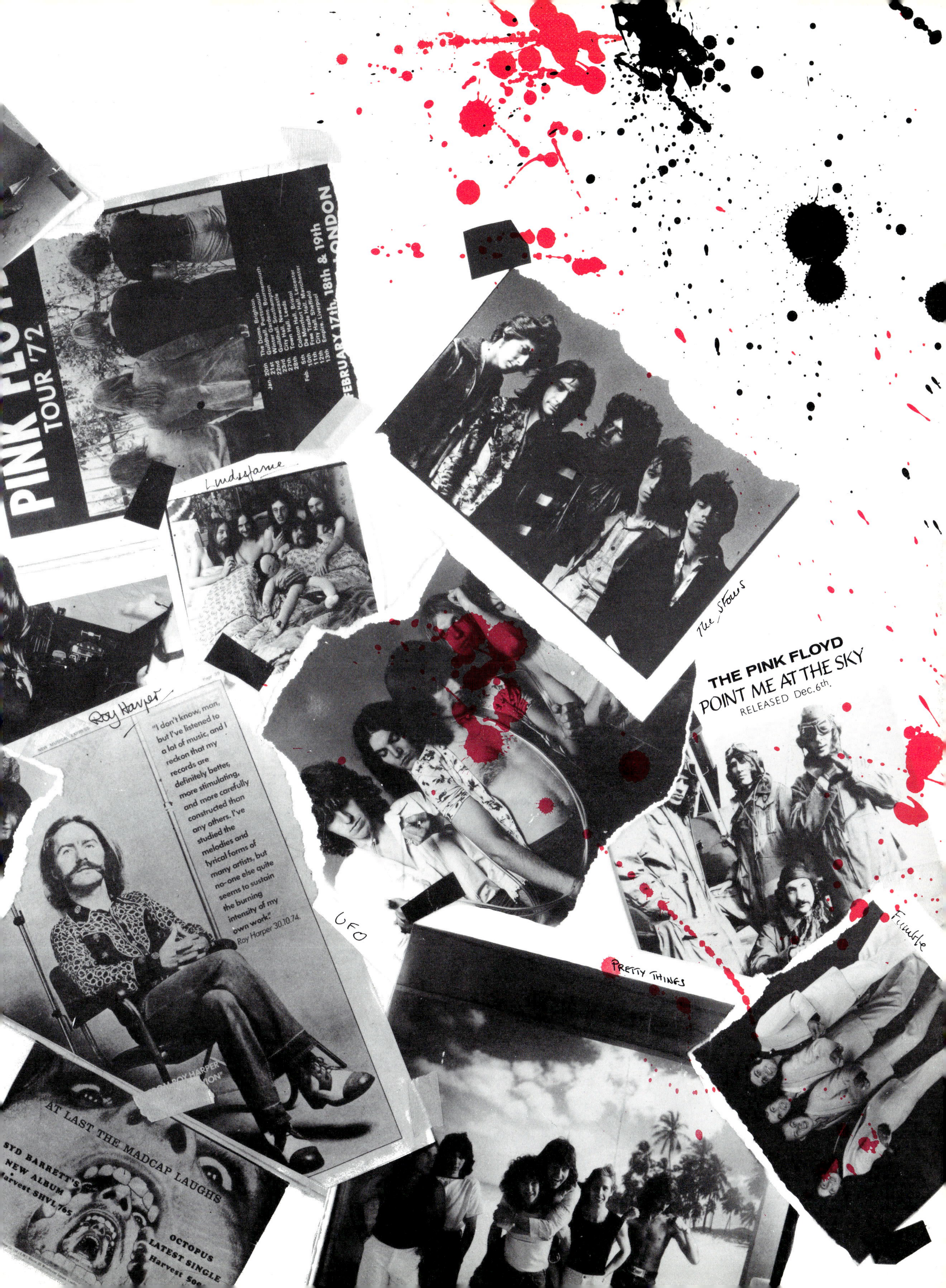

PINK FLOY
TOUR '72
Jan. 20th The Dome, Brighton
21st Guildhall, Portsmouth
22nd Winter Gardens, Bournemouth
23rd Guildhall, Southampton
27th City Hall, Newcastle
28th City Hall, Leeds
Town Hall,
Feb. 5th Colston Hall, Bristol
10th De Montfort Hall, Leicester
11th Free Trade Hall, Manchester
12th City Hall, Sheffield
13th Empire, Liverpool
EBRUARY 17th, 18th & 19th LONDON
Lindisfarne
The Stones
Roy Harper
NEW MUSICAL EXPRESS
"I don't know, man, but I've listened to a lot of music, and I reckon that my records are definitely better, more stimulating, and more carefully constructed than any others. I've studied the melodies and lyrical forms of many artists, but no-one else quite seems to sustain the burning intensity of my own work."
Roy Harper 30.10.74.
THE PINK FLOYD
POINT ME AT THE SKY
RELEASED Dec. 6th.
UFO
PRETTY THINGS
Fumble
AT LAST THE MADCAP LAUGHS
SYD BARRETT'S
NEW ALBUM
Harvest SHVL 765
OCTOPUS
LATEST SINGLE

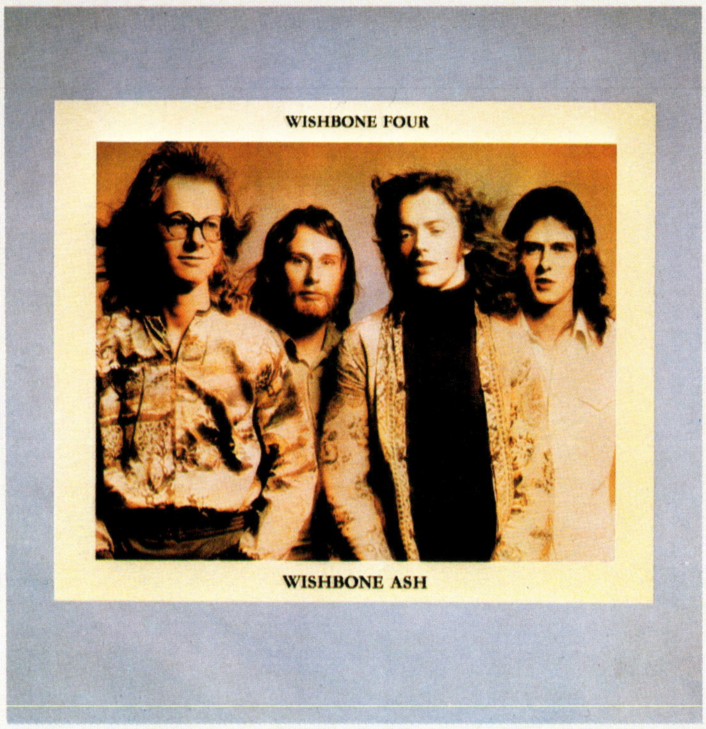

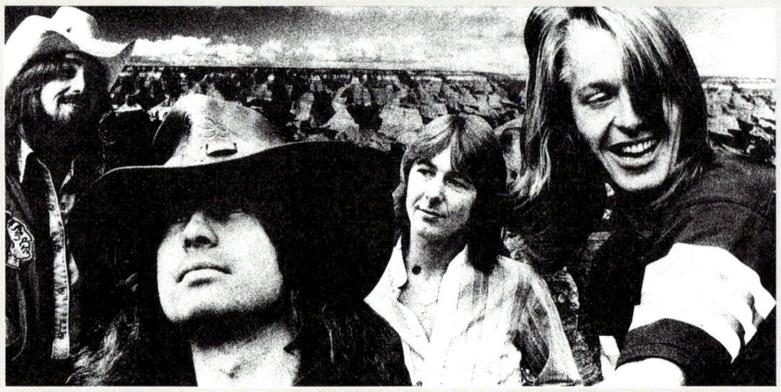

for themselves — we neither have the money nor the room. A wind machine gently blowing Wishbone's hair and a 'softar' filter on the camera lens enhance the voguish effect once popular in fashion magazines and chic advertisements.

There are a few other things that can make a portrait interesting. One that we quite like is grain, such as Syd Barrett or 'Olivia'. If you underexpose your negative and then give it more time in the developer to compensate for the lack of light, the grains of silver (or dye in colour film) have a tendency to clump together and produce an almost pointilliste appearance. In a similar vein (though a totally different way) it is possible to convert one's picture photographically into a line screen which gives a representation in lots of areas of solid ink of the image without a continuous range of tones as in a normal photo, such as Bad Company. However, it should not be forgotten that it is frequently the subject rather than the photographer who is responsible for a good portrait. An expressive face and a projective presence can often make the photo come alive whatever the particular merits of the photographer. On the other hand, a dull, listless subject can make it all very hard work, but we won't go into that.

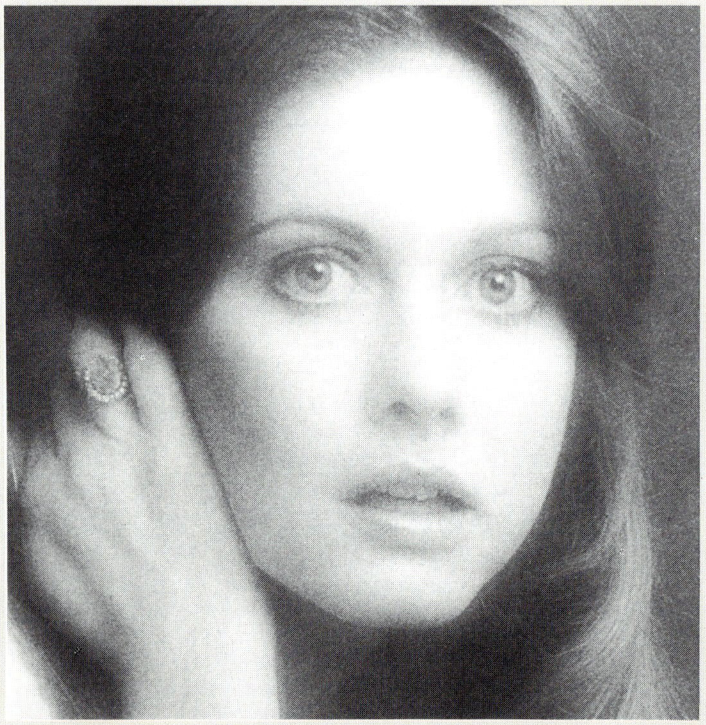

OLIVIA NEWTON-JOHN 'OLIVIA'   WISHBONE ASH '4'   BAD COMPANY

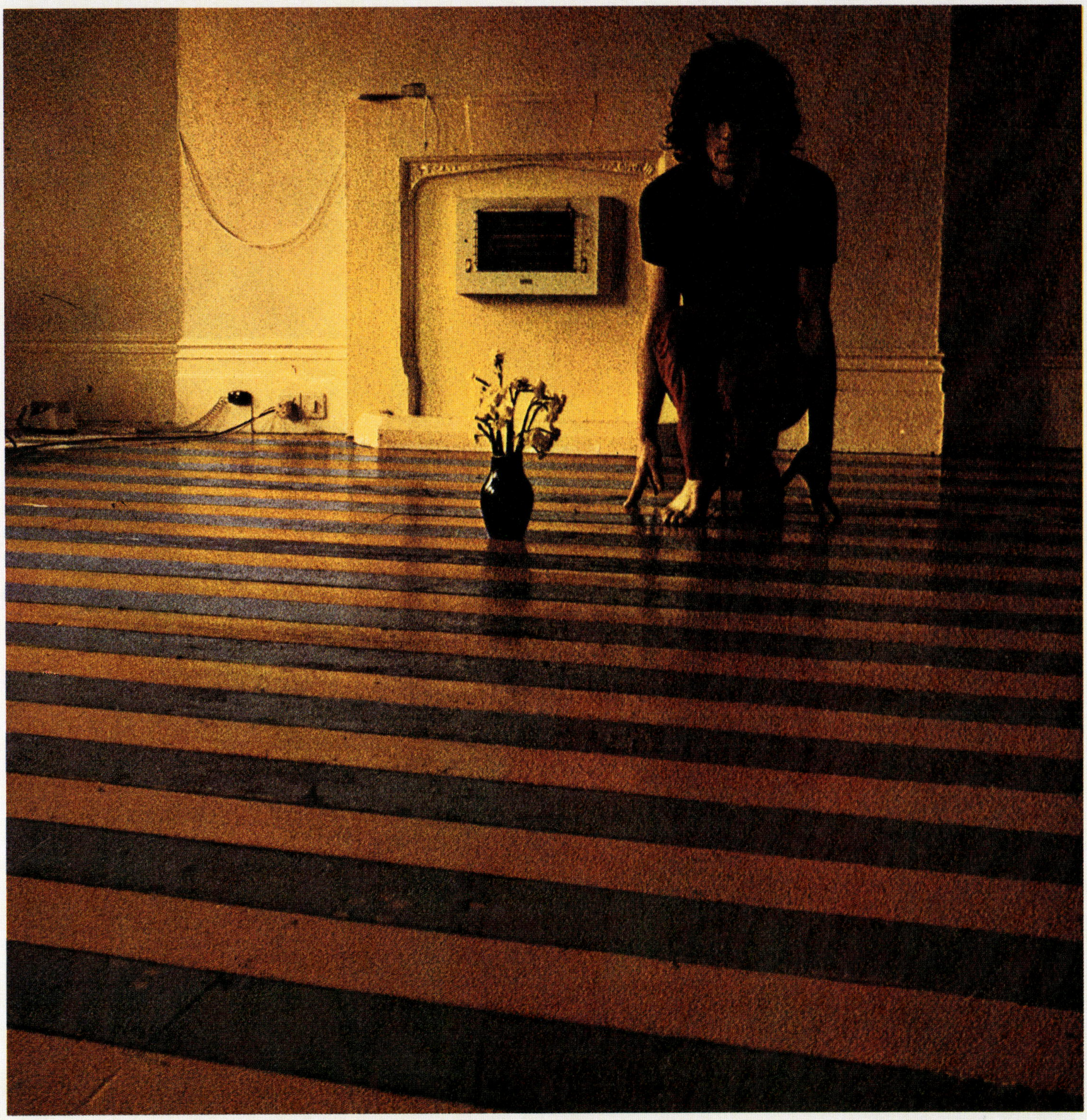

1970 SYD BARRETT 'MADCAP LAUGHS' FRONT COVER

I'm going to take a couple of examples of our work ('Presence' and 'Wish You Were Here') and try to explain how they came about and how we imagined they might affect the viewer. Not so much in terms of the mechanics of the job (see H) but more in terms of what they mean. If you don't like or believe in explanations of designs then read no further. I find it pompous and silly when designers repeatedly refuse or claim it impossible to explain their work in words, although I grant that in some cases it may be pretty difficult, when the inspiration is very spontaneous and the source very subconscious. Mind you, I find it equally annoying if artists always feel a driving necessity to explain their efforts verbally. Explaining a piece of work is an attempt to illuminate it, not to validate it. If a client asks us "Why?", we do try to answer him but it sometimes gets to be a habit with clients and is not to be recommended or particularly supported. If we kept having to say why a line goes here or there, or this exposure is better than that one, we'd go daffy.

The idea for 'Presence' was generated in a group meeting between Po, Peter, George and myself. It occurred on a very hot night because we thought up and designed two others besides ('Year of the Cat' and Golden Earring). There were two original strands to the idea — anachronism and obsession. The first one simply concerned placing an item from one time or age into a surrounding from another time. It seemed easier to put an object from the future into a setting from the past. The object could be anything from a utilitarian thing to a person. In order to do this we would have to use old pictures and this provided for another idea — the deliberate and playful defacing of nostalgia. The use of old pics, styles and motifs on record covers is fairly common. One often sees designs executed in the art nouveau or art deco idiom. 'Lunch' for Audience is a 30's piece which I found in an old box of knitting patterns. Generally, however, we're not that in favour of imitating obvious styles (if we can help it, that is) and we were beginning to think unfavourably towards any such trend. The aphorism 'nostalgia isn't what it used to be' came to mind whilst we were talking of taking an old picture from the 40's or 50's and then dislocating it in some way with an anachronistic addition. This foreign intrusion, both out of style and out of time, would allow us to use nostalgic pictures that we liked anyway and would also permit us to poke fun at ourselves (and others) by purposely disturbing them.

At the same time we were also talking about obsessional objects — either that a person has many such objects, or variations of this object (see 'Year of the Cat' in Animals), or everyone has one of the same. It could be an ordinary domestic thing or a household pet, even a non-peculiar object such as a chess board. The circumstances could be equally 'ordinary'. Imagine a family scene in the living room and everyone is clutching say, a saucepan, or a cat.

The situation required a further ingredient and a slight change of emphasis somewhere. These things often emerge through interaction. One party picks up on a train of thought of another and then someone else chips in a fresh notion. Yet again, they quite often don't. However, this night most parties were paying attention, except Po who was a little drowsy. (This was to come in very useful later.) We'd been interested in 'holes' in pictures or frame breaks. Any device that might temporarily throw a picture 'out' or suspend disbelief for a moment and cause a picture to appear fractionally as though it were indeed three dimensional, that it stretched away from the viewer. It was felt appropriate that the disturbing presence in the anachronistic picture should be a 'hole', a blackness, a non-dimensional thing (no depth cues), although it could have a shape — a hole can have shape. Then someone suggested that the obsessional object which everyone needs is not just a self-obsession but, in fact, inflicts itself upon people from outside. It is a power source which people cannot do without. It is true that objects of obsession are also things that people cannot do without, but the change of emphasis was to consider the object as deliberately sent from another time or insidiously employed by some secret society to subjugate people. The object had a function, a causal reason for being there, as well as constituting a pictorial metaphor for obsession. It was 'sent', in effect, to contaminate the nostalgia of the picture as well as the people themselves in the picture. It controlled people, fed them, gave them all that they required — that's why everyone had one. The object was telepathic, a mechanical religion, a mini version of 2001; it was and is all things to all people — one needs no more than to sit down and bask in its glow.

The two strands of obsession and anachronism were put together in a rough. George chose pictures from the 40's and 50's by painstakingly searching through old magazines. They were composed of people in ordinary situations. He then contaminated the pictures with the black obsessional object, to which many, if not all, the persons in the picture related or were looking. Apart from the irony of paying homage to these nice old pictures by including them in the first place and then defacing them, there was the irony that the object upon which everyone was dependent was, in fact, a 'hole', an absence, rather than a presence. That Po had been a bit drowsy during the original meeting meant that when he came to explain it to Zeppelin he didn't entirely remember or understand what it was. He'd had the great idea of making up a real black object which he took along. The mysteriousness of it was transmitted to the band, in part by Po's slight uncertainty. But that was fine. As Robert Plant was reported to

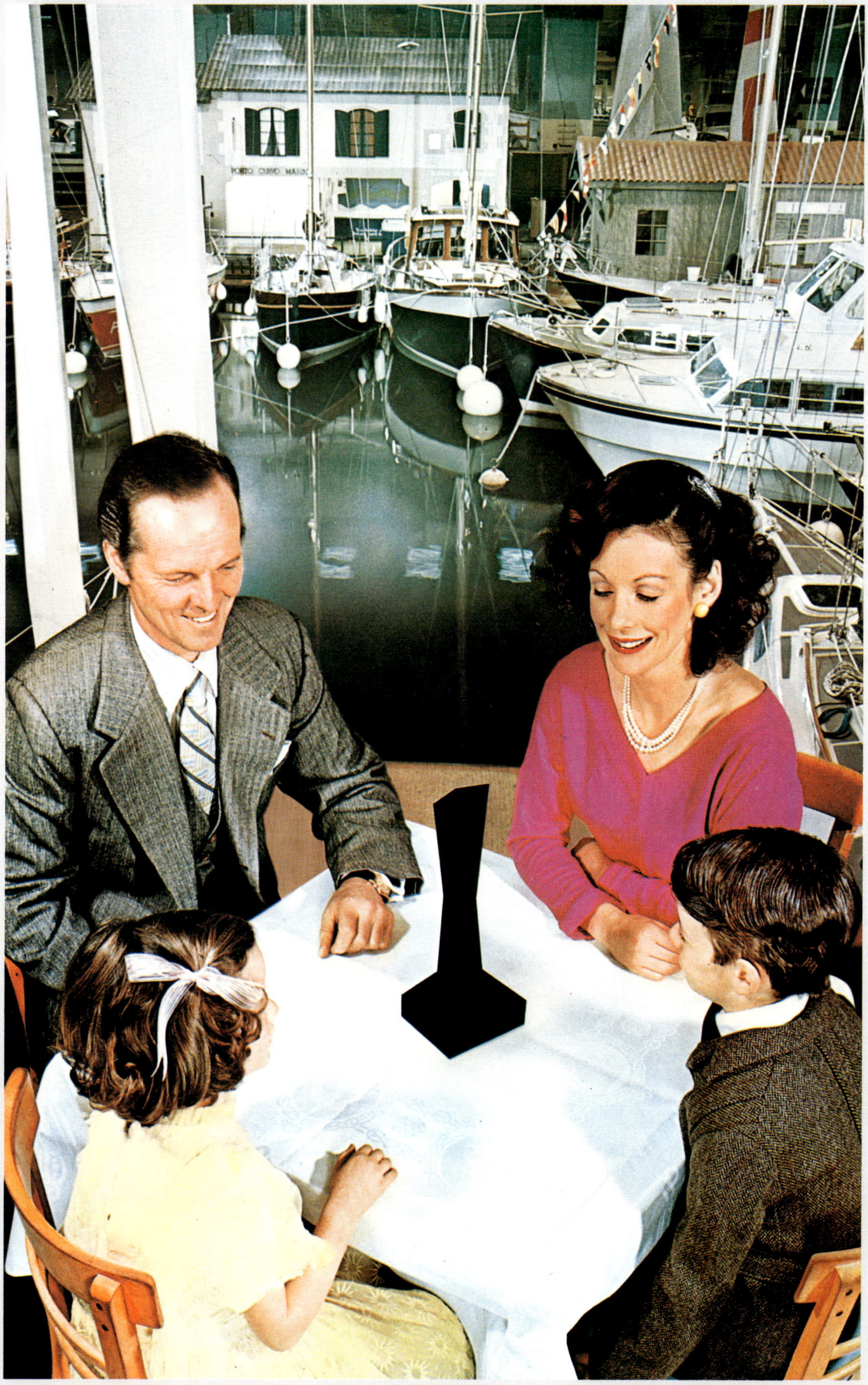

1976 LED ZEPPELIN 'PRESENCE' CO-DESIGN GEORGE HARDIE FRONT COVER have said later, 'Who the hell needs to understand everything anyway?' Who understands the power (and success) of Zeppelin? The black object is as powerful as one's imagination cares it to be, and Zeppelin could, rightfully perhaps, feel the same about themselves in the world of rock music.

When they saw it there were also roughs of the back and inside. Pictures from all walks of life, showing all kinds of people and illustrating just how widespread was the 'presence'. The object was essential to all parts of society, whether it be lovers by a pool or workers in a factory, whether it be leisure or serious scientific investigation. You see, they were still trying to discover what the object was, what it was made of, and where it came from. It was important, also, to introduce it to young infants to help them grow properly, and in education to teach them that of all things in life the 'presence', the nameless, unknown and undefined black object, was of paramount significance. I particularly like little details of the whole design, like the record player (the Dansette) and the sandals in the young groovers picture. Or the lady by herself. What a trite and sentimental picture! Yet it was completely altered when we painted out the daffodils in her arms and replaced them with the object. Or the citizens carefully storing away the official council object in the vault for safe keeping.

The front and back pictures were photographed by us, but based on pictures we'd seen. All the inner spread photos are genuine nostalgia. The object was painted in by Richard Manning on all pictures, although we used an actual one for the front and back as a guide. Zeppelin had real ones made up, one of which we photographed for the inner bag. The layout was as simple as could be, as it is on 'Wish You Were Here', or 'Lunch' or 'Peter Frampton', in order to let the picture be seen as clearly as possible. Jimmy Page did ask us to change the original shape of the object, so George redesigned it. This was the only alteration in design asked for and on reflection, may well be for the better. The title is also theirs.

I consider 'Presence' to be one of our best pieces, and also one of the most appropriate — Zeppelin are a very powerful band both musically and socially and the black object is a definitive thing of power. I think, as well, that its pervasive presence and its mystery appealed very strongly to them. One of the stranger elements of the whole puzzle is the notion that whatever it was, this black presence, it came and went. It used to be around but now it isn't. It was an experiment conducted back in the 40's by either alien visitors or political suppressors of some secret society. Not only was it universally successful (and we still do not know how we were affected), it was also so powerful that it even erased its own physical memory from our recall. Hipgnosis was lucky enough to 'find' these pictures which reveal this amazing visitation, or horrendous piece of social brainwashing. You don't remember it, even your parents don't remember it, and hence, what it did to them. I like also the feeling it gives me of a metaphor of middle class taste, of repression and safety. Now, if everybody had one of these we'd all be OK. The black hole, the nothingness, the bastion of safe and comforting morality. The family on the front, all proper and correct, smiling safely in the narrowness of their middle class existence.

'Sounds' ran a little competition amongst its readers to submit interpretations of 'Presence'. With many thanks we include the following letters:—

"The object is a window which we can either look at or through thus creating a totally illusory image floating in a material world. Its implacable depths are the fast flowing rivers of the tunnel of life at the end of which the searchers' souls will be joined as one. At the same time the proximity produces the Karma necessary if we are to search for our own ethereal esotericism in the pure white light of the soul.

"Just as the Sun creates external constancy so the Obelisk represents the unchanging elements in the changing mind of man." — Xenopus Toad, Wolverhampton. 28.25 February, 2234

"'The Object' was a Telepathic Wave Receiver and Transmitter (TWRT). In the year 2108, the specific static factor of telepathic linkage was finally defined. It was electronically synthesized, made infinitely turnable and incorporated in the TWRT.

"Some TWRTs were projected into the mid-20th century as an experiment in four dimensional communication. Messages could not be received though, until their use

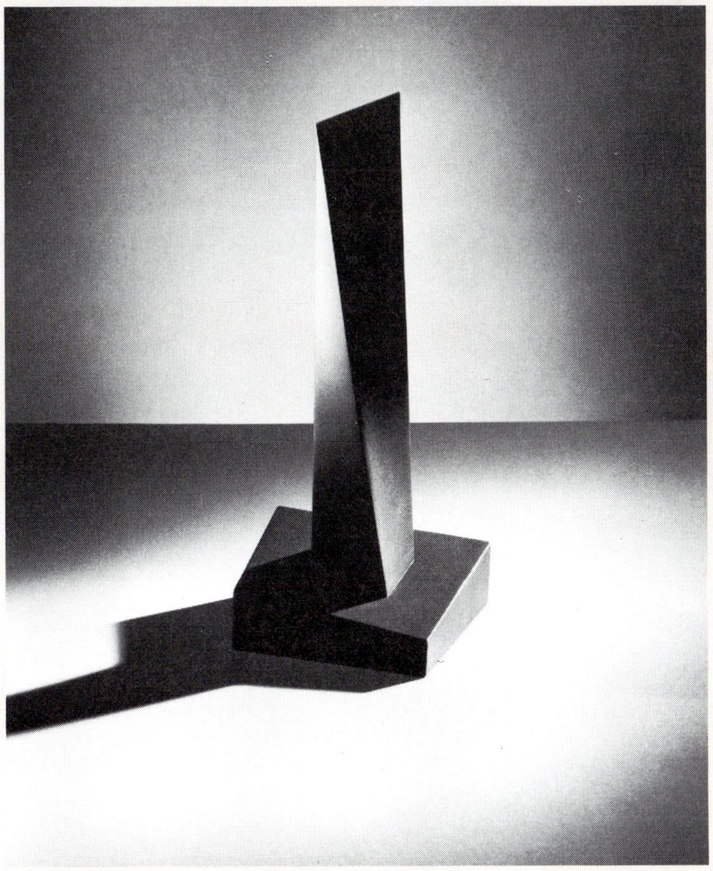

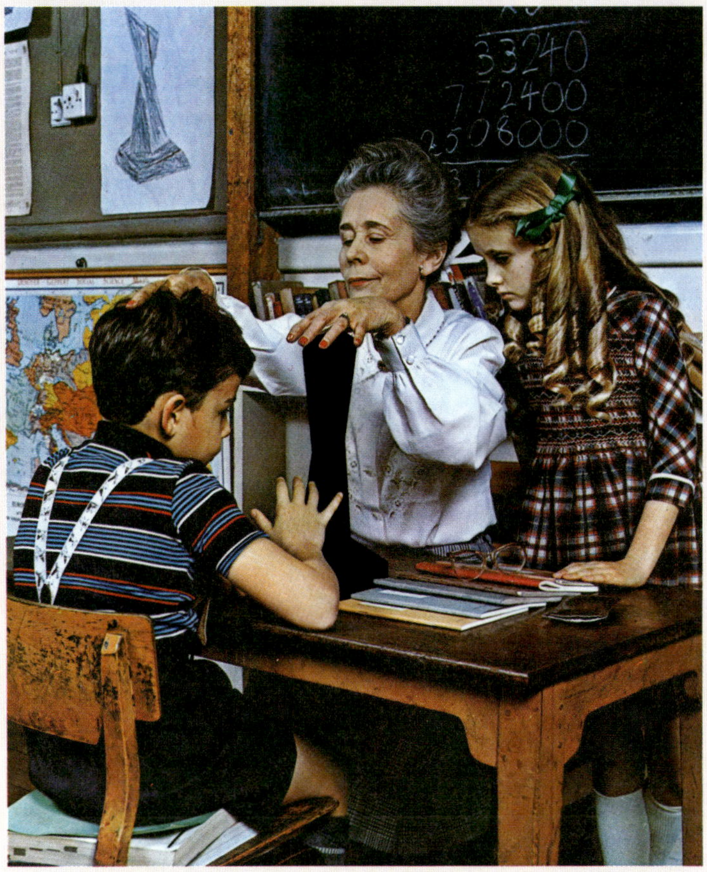

could be explained. This occurred in about 1976, when a telepathic recipient attempted a diagnosis of the TWRT in a music publication. He was largely ignored and disappeared without a trace. The TWRT remained unexplained evermore.'' Steve Colley, Leeds.

''To devotees of the American Way of Life, the 'mysterious' object in question is a familiar artefact encountered in Middle-Of-Road locales, hence its nickname, the MORphy. MORphys are to be found wherever MOR philosophy holds sway, and are much valued possessions.

''There are those who claim that MORism began with the discovery of the first MORphy among excavations at Disneyland, but whatever its origins, this comforting device is now a firmly established facet of the All-American scene. Its precise function is still obscure, but scientists have noted that it induces trancelike (MORphine) automatism in its faithful adherents.'' Jack Hart, Paisley, Renfrewshire.

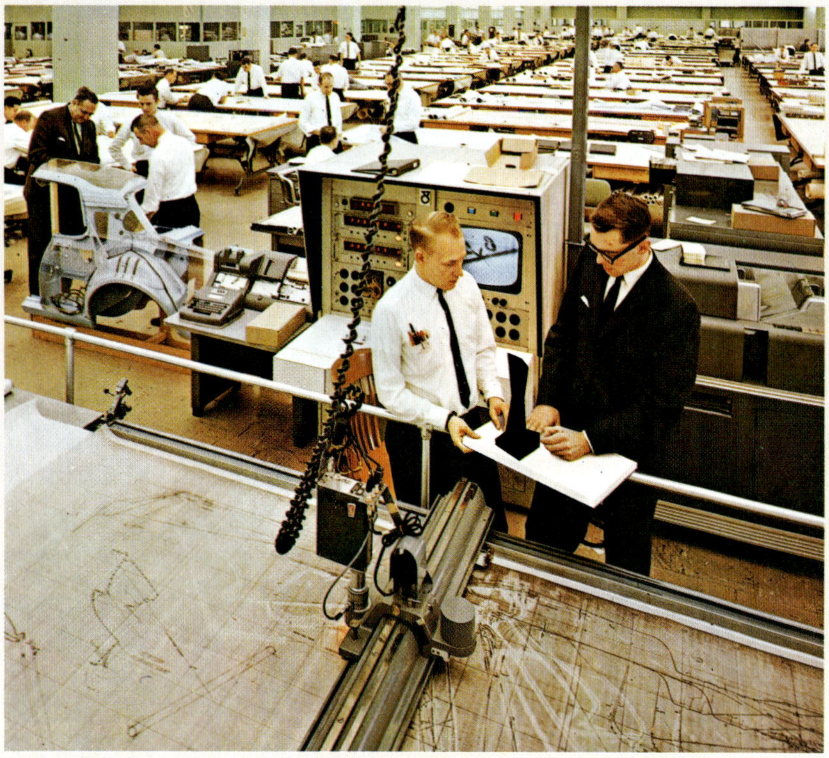

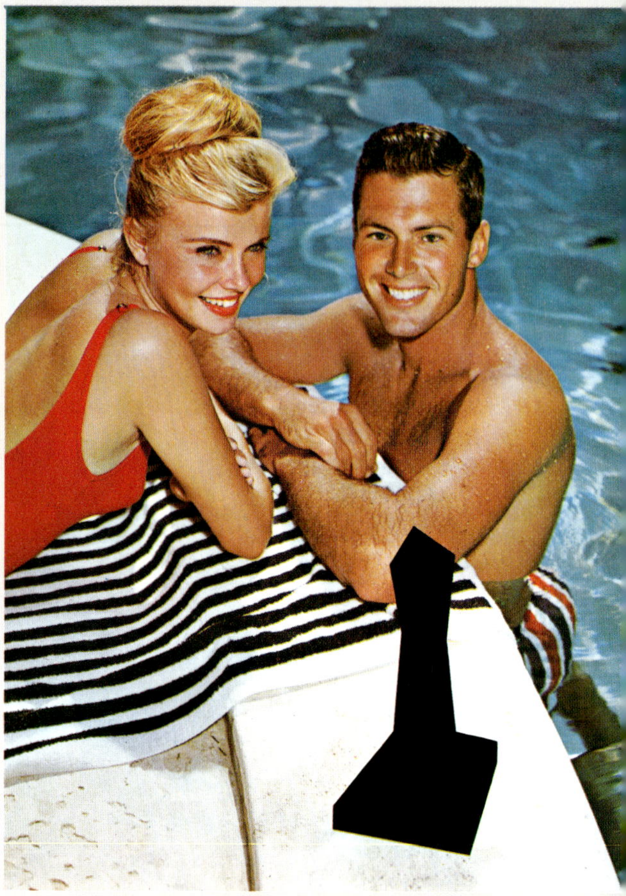

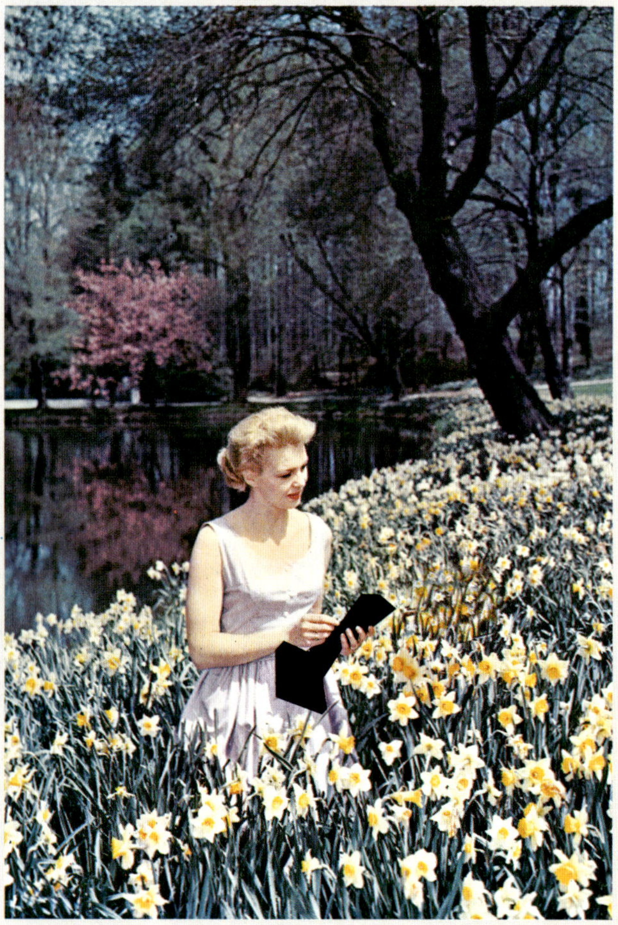

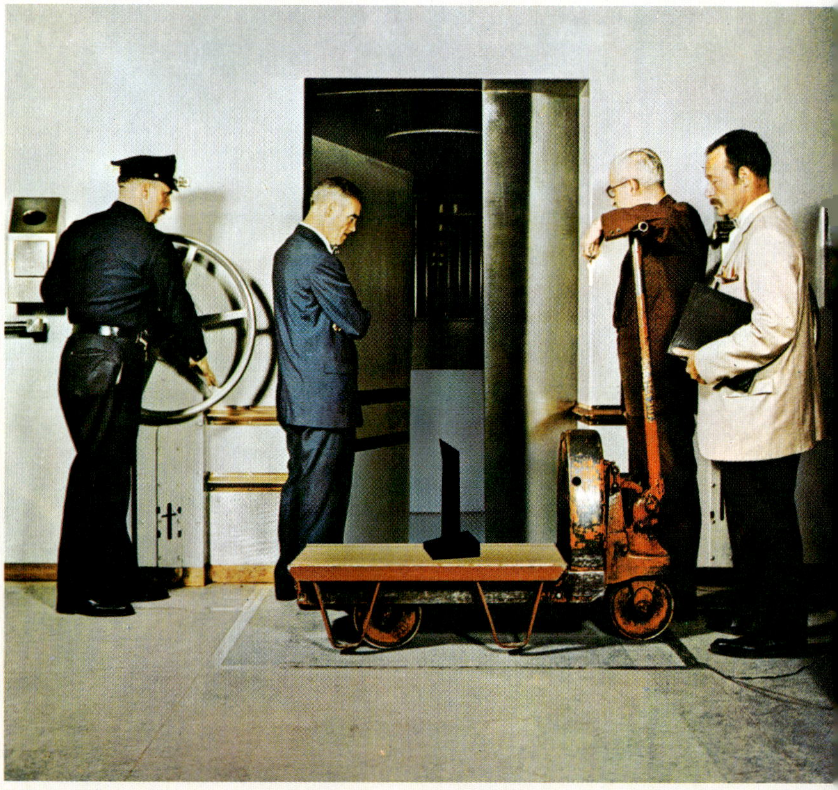

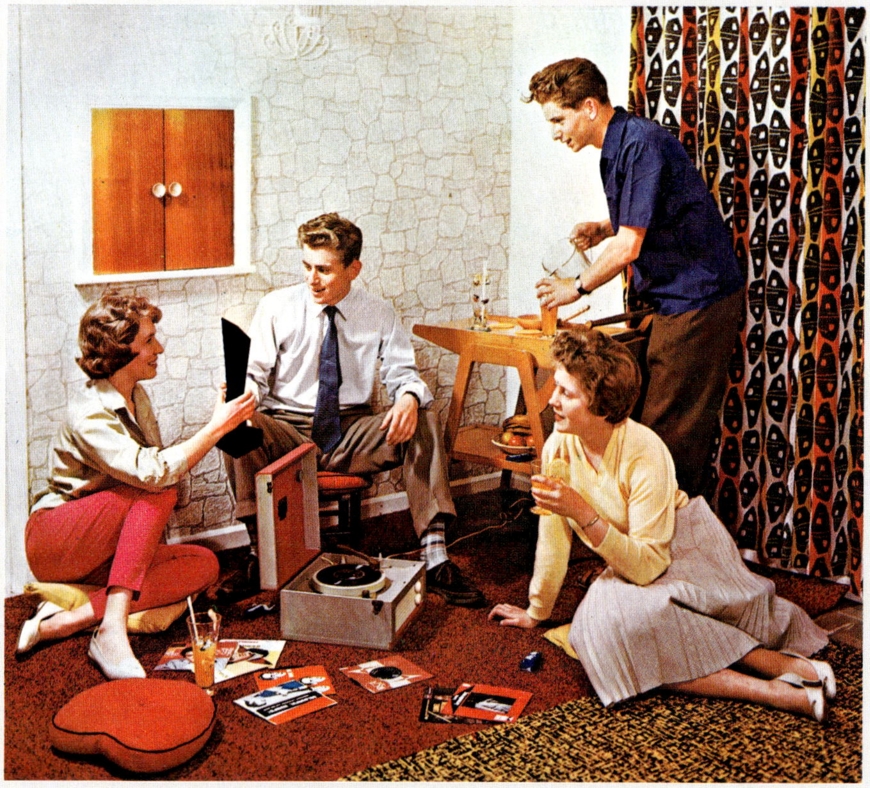
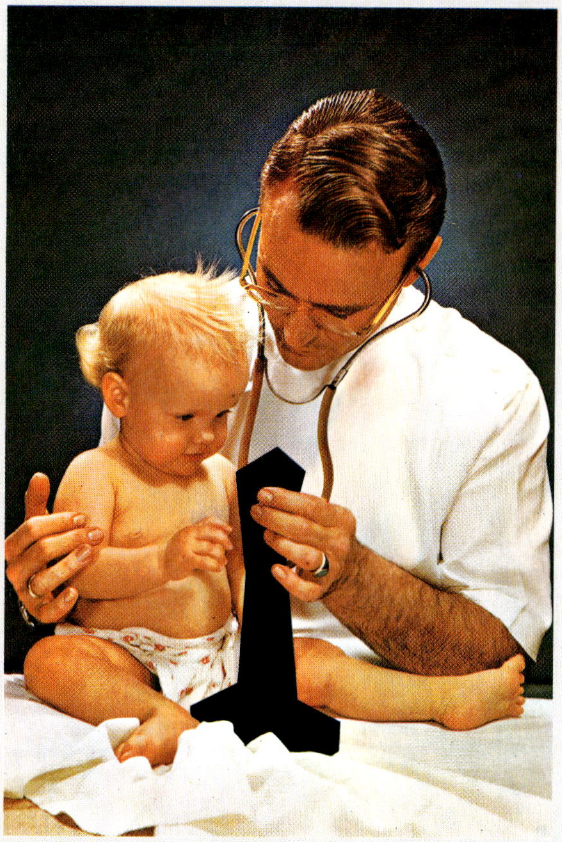
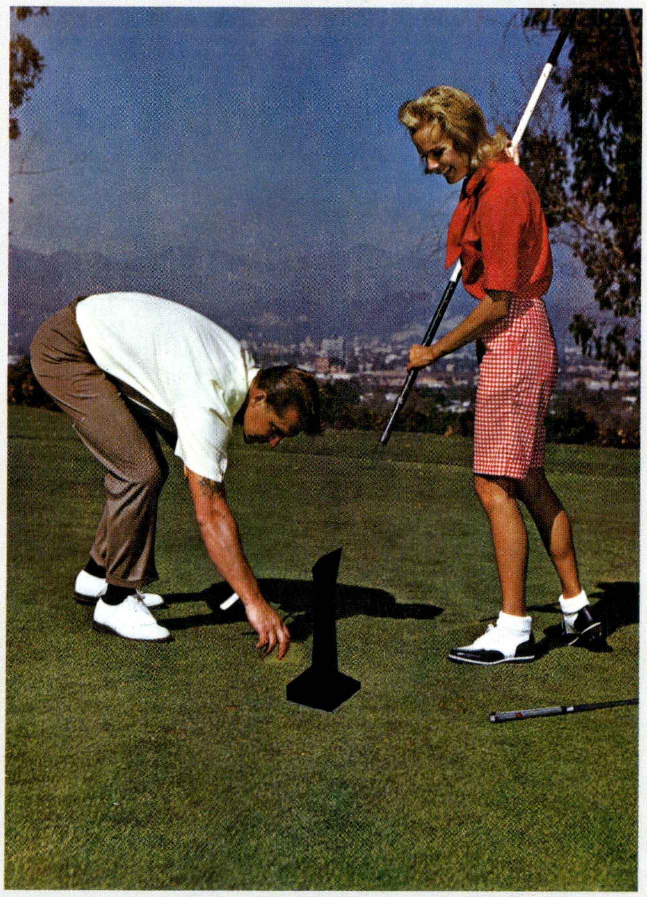
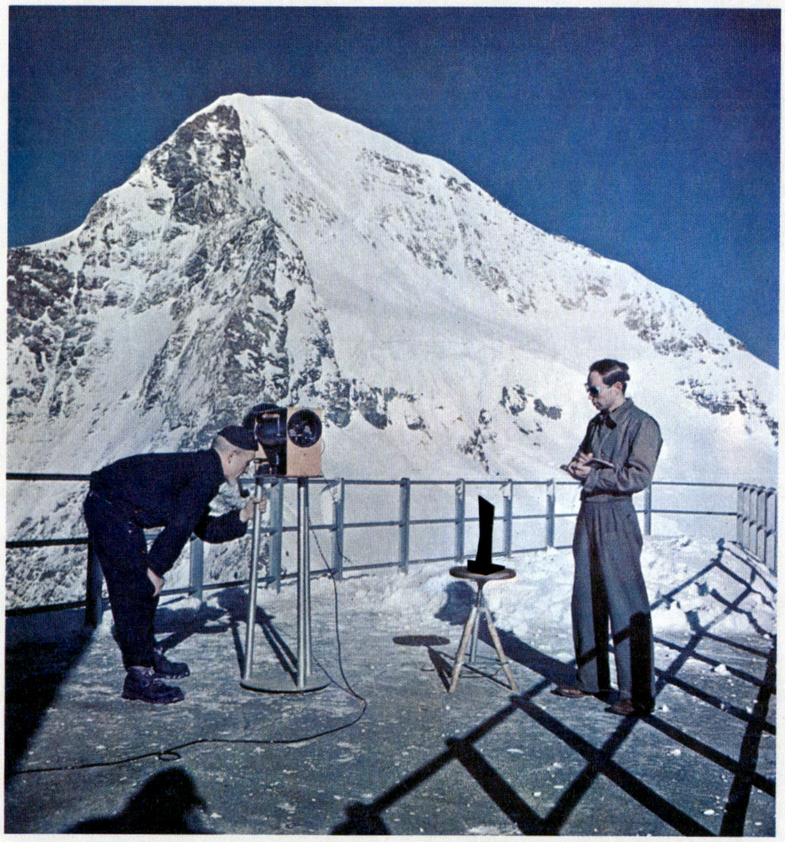

Nick Mason is the drummer for Pink Floyd. He suggested doing a parody of comics like Tiger, Eagle, Lion and Hotspur (you oldies out there may remember them) as the basis of a concert programme for a Floyd tour. The band were disenchanted with concert programmes in general — how pricey, full of boring adverts and biographical drivel they were. Since a comic is often composed of black and white material and can be printed on loo paper, the printing costs were kept low enough to retail the finished item at only 15p. What a bargain! And no ads. We threw in a braintwisting quiz and some absurd lifelines on the band plus an original Scarfe cartoon. The stories featured the four members of the band in four escapades that rather vaguely refer to their alter images or daft fantasies of themselves. Rich Wright is so unlike comic heroes that we had to stretch the medium a bit and do a touch of Playboy's Little Annie Fannie. It was good fun and something very different, but because it is a pastische and not very original (or even pretending to be) we've not given it much space here.

'Hands Across The Water' is a photographic book about a rock and roll tour — Paul McCartney and Wings 1976 Tour across U.S.A. The idea stemmed from a detailed book about Pink Floyd, written in conjunction with Nick Sedgewick, which has not, unfortunately, seen the light of day. We printed up many of the pictures I'd taken of a West coast tour and arranged them in groups corresponding to each town visited, and suggested producing them as a small book on their own, without words, but the band turned this down. When it came to 'Hands Across The Water' we knew pretty well what a tour involved — the events and people that would need to be photographed. Instead of venues as a means of ordering the contents we chose times of the day. Po went to America with McCartney for two months and photographed on or near the hour. He travelled with the band, and then with the road crew; he explored places on his own and hung about the halls and hotels. The aim was to provide an impressionistic picture of life on the road with Wings. The hours span a whole day. It is a 'typical' day in so much as it's made up of fragments of all the days. No *one* person on the tour could do what is shown in a single day, but many different people could. We decided to photograph in black and white because of the grinding reality of slogging two months across America. You can see a sampling of the kind of stuff included in the book but it is, in fact, a sequence of pictures designed to be viewed not singly but as a whole, as a collection.

The project for Thames TV was a curious thing because it was internal and not public. Thames were proposing to do a thirteen part serial documentary on the Beatles, at the meagre cost of a million quid. When they attempt such a long series they send out a piece of private promotional material firstly to inform all the people whom they hope will co-operate in the series, and secondly to help sell the finished product around the world. Even though they had permission to use Beatles music and could go ahead anyway, the whole project would be much better off with participation by the Fab Four themselves. The publicity we were to do was directed personally at the Beatles. Two guys, one from Thames and one freelance, asked us to devise this piece of publicity. It could be anything, like a box, a book or an album sleeve — and we could design whatever pictorial matter we felt appropriate. The necessary text would be supplied by them. A simple book with reportage photos and a story that the Beatles would already know seemed inappropriate, if not stupid. We felt it had to comprise original pictures but not in any ostentatious way. But it was very unlikely that four different guys would all like the same pictures. They might like some and not others, so it seemed best to keep the pictures separate and, therefore, potentially disposable.

Working in collaboration with George Hardie, we suggested a folio of original designs to illustrate approximately the thirteen different programmes. The full thirteen are shown but two of them are repeated large.

'Beatlemania' is fairly clear — the numbers indicate the possible stages of developing mania where each girl represents a different stage that would occur in only one person. The bus queue is being passed by a car carrying the four lads (the camera position). The girl at the left hand end hasn't even noticed them, whilst the girl at the right hand end has exhausted herself in manic delight and is drenched in her own sweat. The other picture, referring to the time of the Maharishi, is about finding the path, about seeing the 'light' and discovering a mystical and philosophical route to internal peace. The 'light' path is not sprayed on but is done mechanically in the printing by leaving out one or two of the primary printing colours in a prescribed area which was indicated by a simple overlay (see also Sammy Hagar under 'Balls'). The printing of sleeves, magazines and books involves the use of four primary inks — red (magenta), blue (cyan), yellow and black. Combinations of these four colours will give the majority of most other colours. In this picture the blue and black have been left out of the 'band' so that only the red and yellow, either separately or together, will show. Yet there is still enough detail to give the impression of translucence, as though the band of light was passing in front of the background.

In an attempt to elevate cover design in general, we devised and edited a book on record sleeves, in conjunction with Roger Dean. Four years ago I had taken a synopsis of a similar project to Penguin who turned it down flat. We forgot about it until Roger spoke to us of his

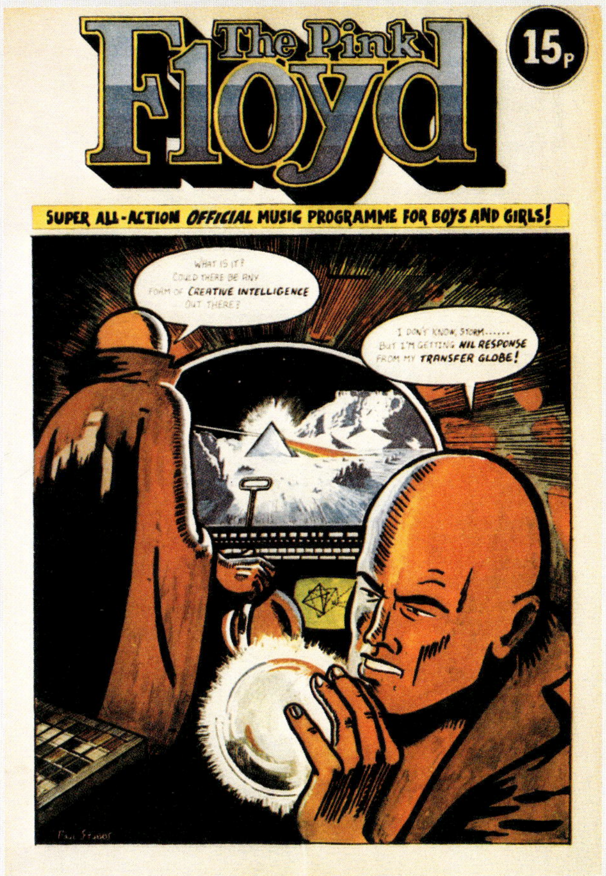
The Pink Floyd
15p
SUPER ALL-ACTION OFFICIAL MUSIC PROGRAMME FOR BOYS AND GIRLS!
WHAT IS IT? COULD THERE BE ANY FORM OF CREATIVE INTELLIGENCE OUT THERE?
I DON'T KNOW, STORM...... BUT I'M GETTING NIL RESPONSE FROM MY TRANSFER GLOBE!

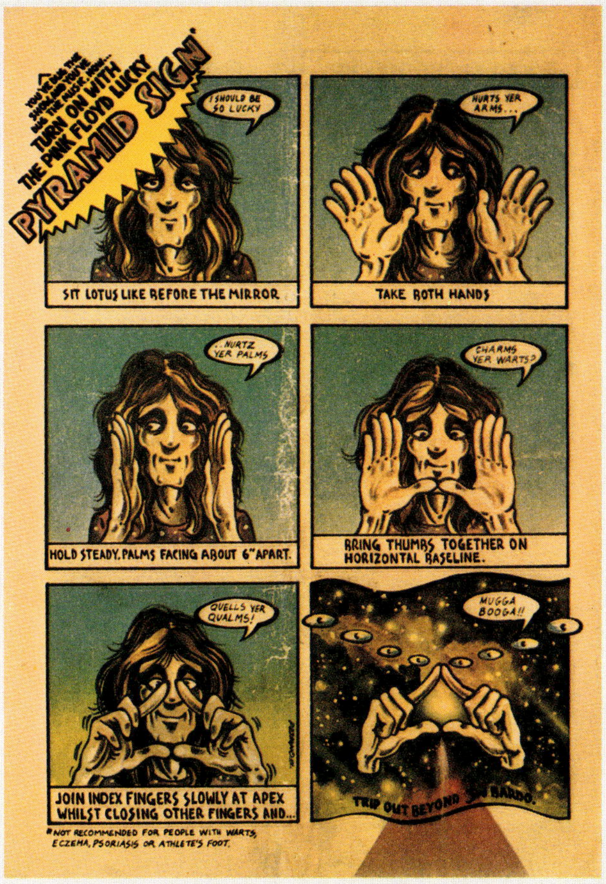
TURN ON WITH THE PINK FLOYD LUCKY PYRAMID SIGN*
I SHOULD BE SO LUCKY
SIT LOTUS LIKE BEFORE THE MIRROR
HURTS YER ARMS...
TAKE BOTH HANDS
...NURTZ YER PALMS
HOLD STEADY, PALMS FACING ABOUT 6" APART.
CHARMS YER WARTS?
BRING THUMBS TOGETHER ON HORIZONTAL BASELINE.
QUELLS YER QUALMS!
JOIN INDEX FINGERS SLOWLY AT APEX WHILST CLOSING OTHER FINGERS AND...
MUGGA BOOGA!!
TRIP OUT BEYOND [illegible] BARDO.
*NOT RECOMMENDED FOR PEOPLE WITH WARTS, ECZEMA, PSORIASIS OR ATHLETE'S FOOT.

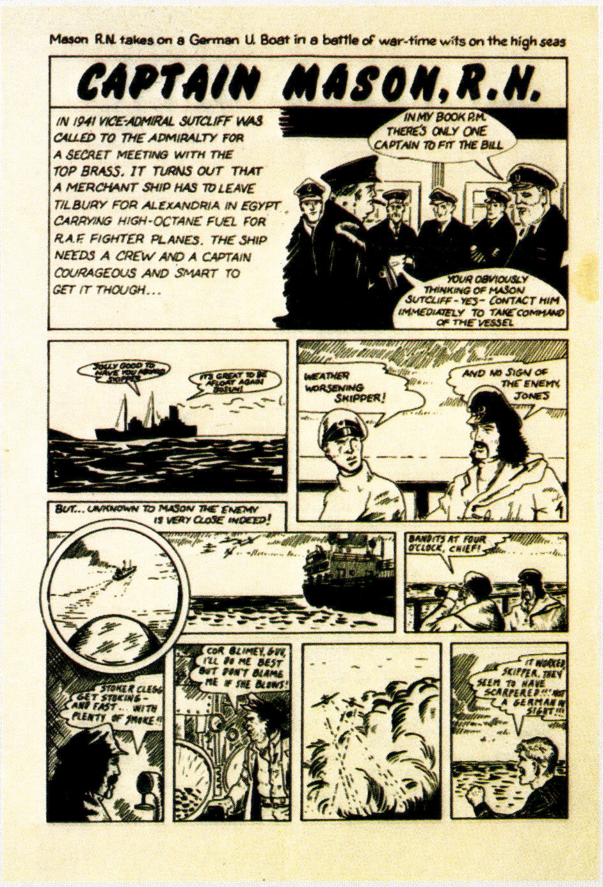
Mason R.N. takes on a German U. Boat in a battle of war-time wits on the high seas
CAPTAIN MASON, R.N.
IN 1941 VICE-ADMIRAL SUTCLIFF WAS CALLED TO THE ADMIRALTY FOR A SECRET MEETING WITH THE TOP BRASS. IT TURNS OUT THAT A MERCHANT SHIP HAS TO LEAVE TILBURY FOR ALEXANDRIA IN EGYPT CARRYING HIGH-OCTANE FUEL FOR R.A.F. FIGHTER PLANES. THE SHIP NEEDS A CREW AND A CAPTAIN COURAGEOUS AND SMART TO GET IT THOUGH...
IN MY BOOK P.M. THERE'S ONLY ONE CAPTAIN TO FIT THE BILL
YOUR OBVIOUSLY THINKING OF MASON SUTCLIFF - YES - CONTACT HIM IMMEDIATELY TO TAKE COMMAND OF THE VESSEL
WEATHER WORSENING SKIPPER!
AND NO SIGN OF THE ENEMY, JONES
BUT... UNKNOWN TO MASON THE ENEMY IS VERY CLOSE INDEED!
BANDITS AT FOUR O'CLOCK, CHIEF!
STOKER CLEGG GET STOKING - AND FAST... WITH PLENTY OF SMOKE!!
COR BLIMEY, GUV, I'LL DO ME BEST BUT DON'T BLAME ME IF SHE BLOWS!
IT WORKED SKIPPER. THEY SEEM TO HAVE SCARPERED!!! NOT A GERMAN IN SIGHT!!!

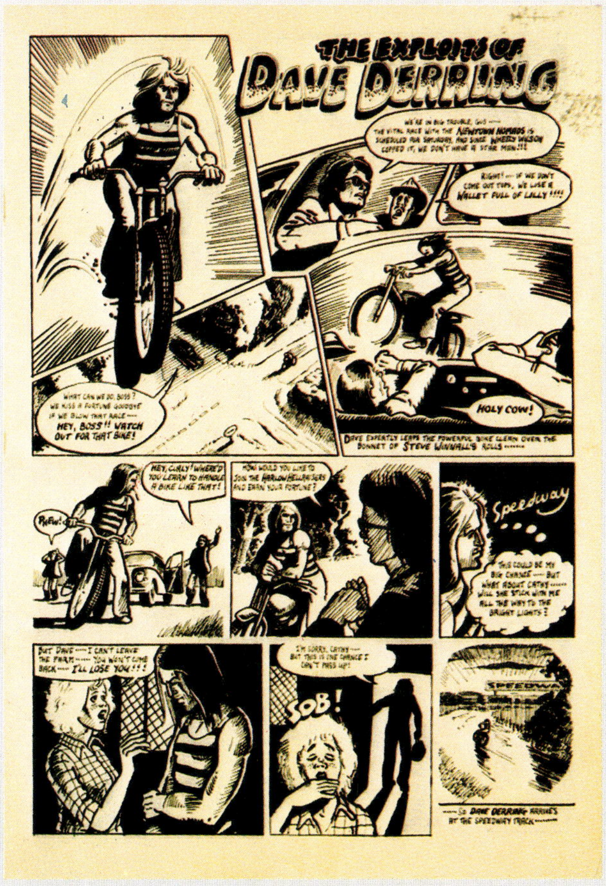
THE EXPLOITS OF DAVE DERRING
WE'RE IN BIG TROUBLE, GUS — THE VITAL RACE WITH THE NEWTOWN NOMADS IS SCHEDULED FOR SATURDAY, AND SINCE WHEELY WILSON COPPED IT, WE DON'T HAVE A STAR MAN!!!
RIGHT! — IF WE DON'T COME OUT TOPS, WE LOSE A WALLET FULL OF LOLLY!!!!
WHAT CAN WE DO, BOSS? WE KISS A FORTUNE GOODBYE IF WE BLOW THAT RACE — HEY, BOSS!! WATCH OUT FOR THAT BIKE!
HOLY COW!
DAVE EXPERTLY LEAPS THE POWERFUL BIKE CLEAN OVER THE BONNET OF STEVE WINNALL'S ROLLS......
PHEW!
HEY, CURLY! WHERE'D YOU LEARN TO HANDLE A BIKE LIKE THAT!
HOW WOULD YOU LIKE TO JOIN THE HARLOW HELLRAISERS AND EARN YOUR FORTUNE?
Speedway
THIS COULD BE MY BIG CHANCE — BUT WHAT ABOUT CATHY...... WILL SHE STICK WITH ME ALL THE WAY TO THE BRIGHT LIGHTS?
BUT DAVE — I CAN'T LEAVE THE FARM...... YOU WON'T COME BACK — I'LL LOSE YOU!!!
I'M SORRY, CATHY — BUT THIS IS ONE CHANCE I CAN'T PASS UP!
SOB!
— SO DAVE DERRING ARRIVES AT THE SPEEDWAY TRACK —

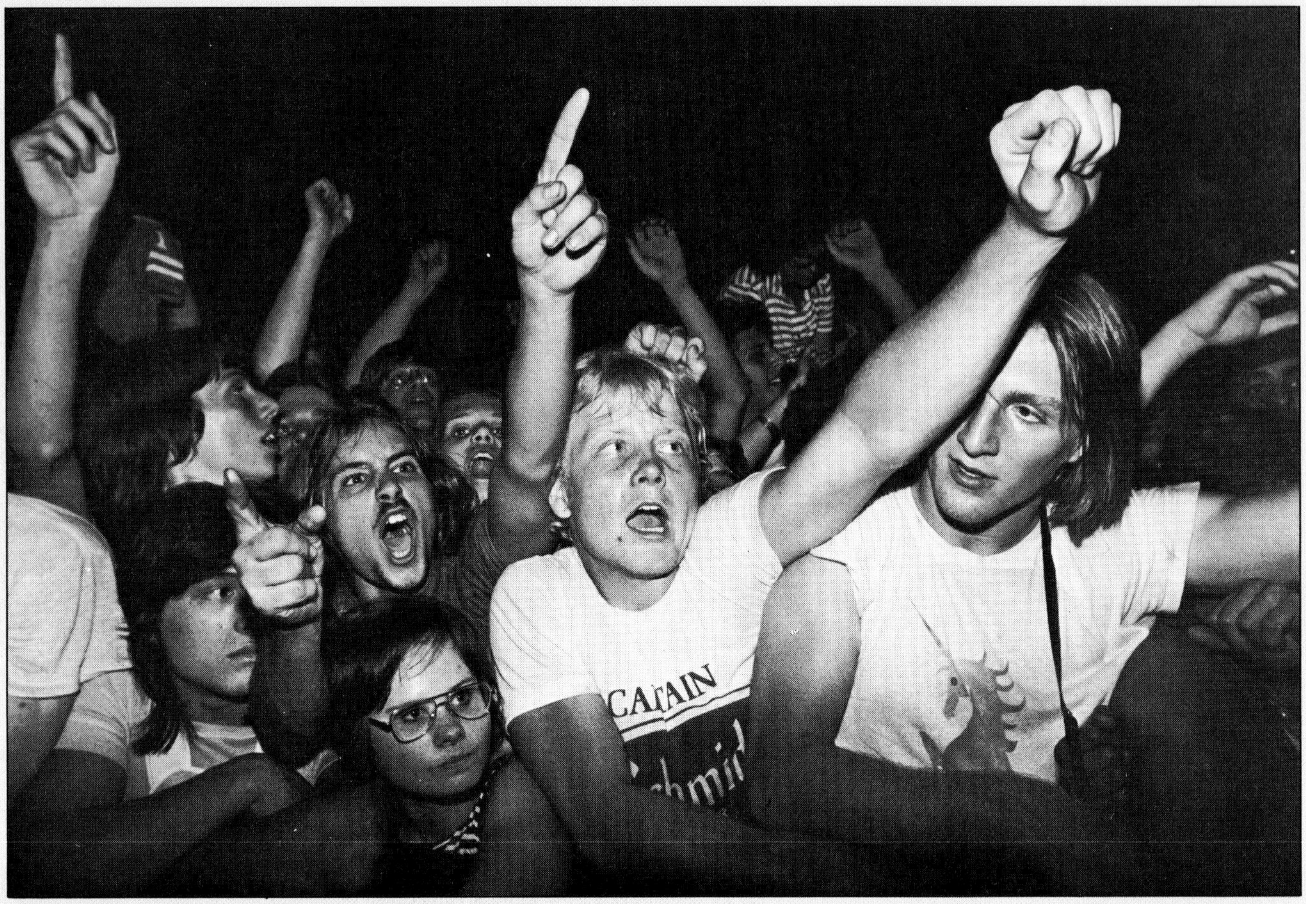

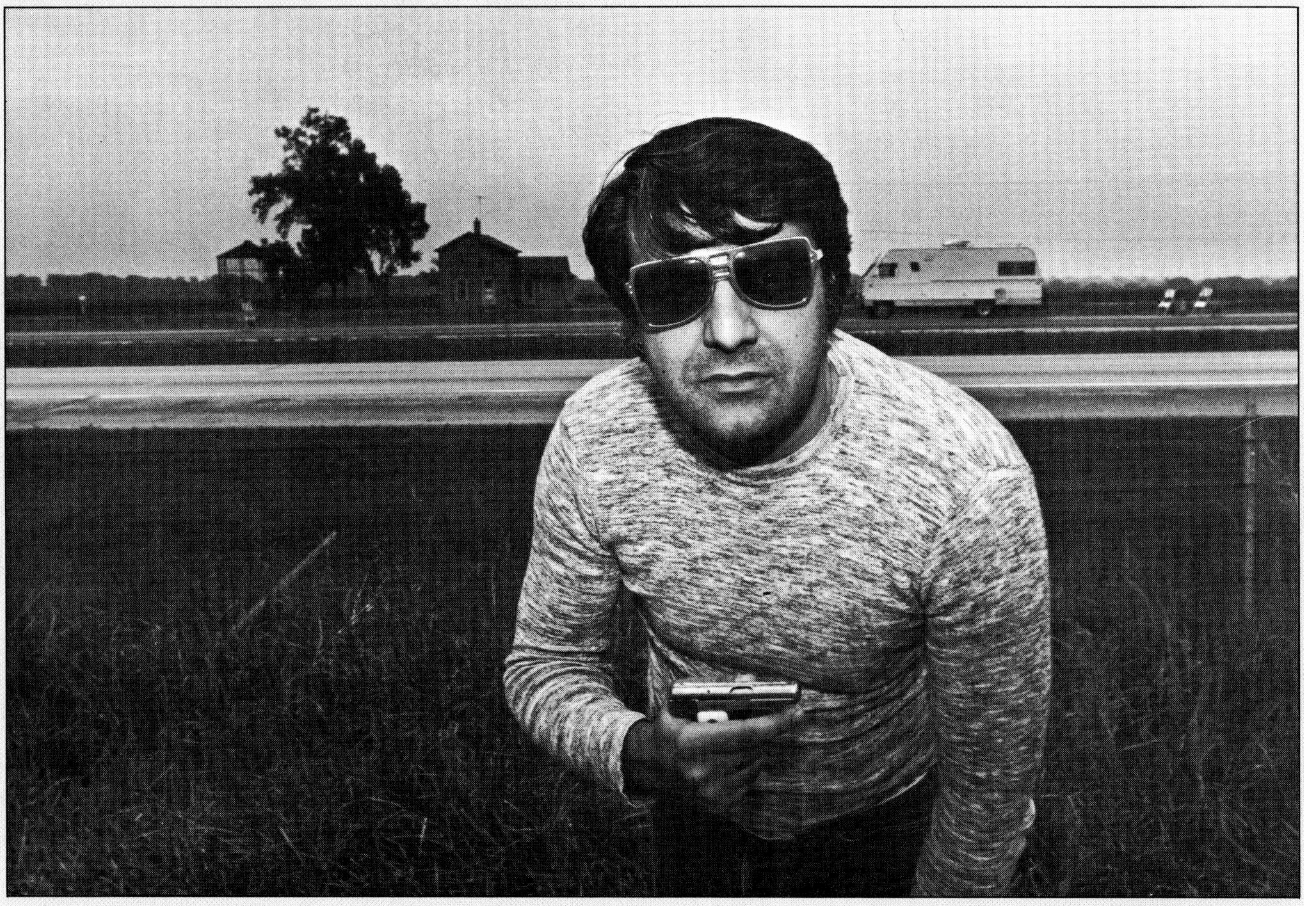

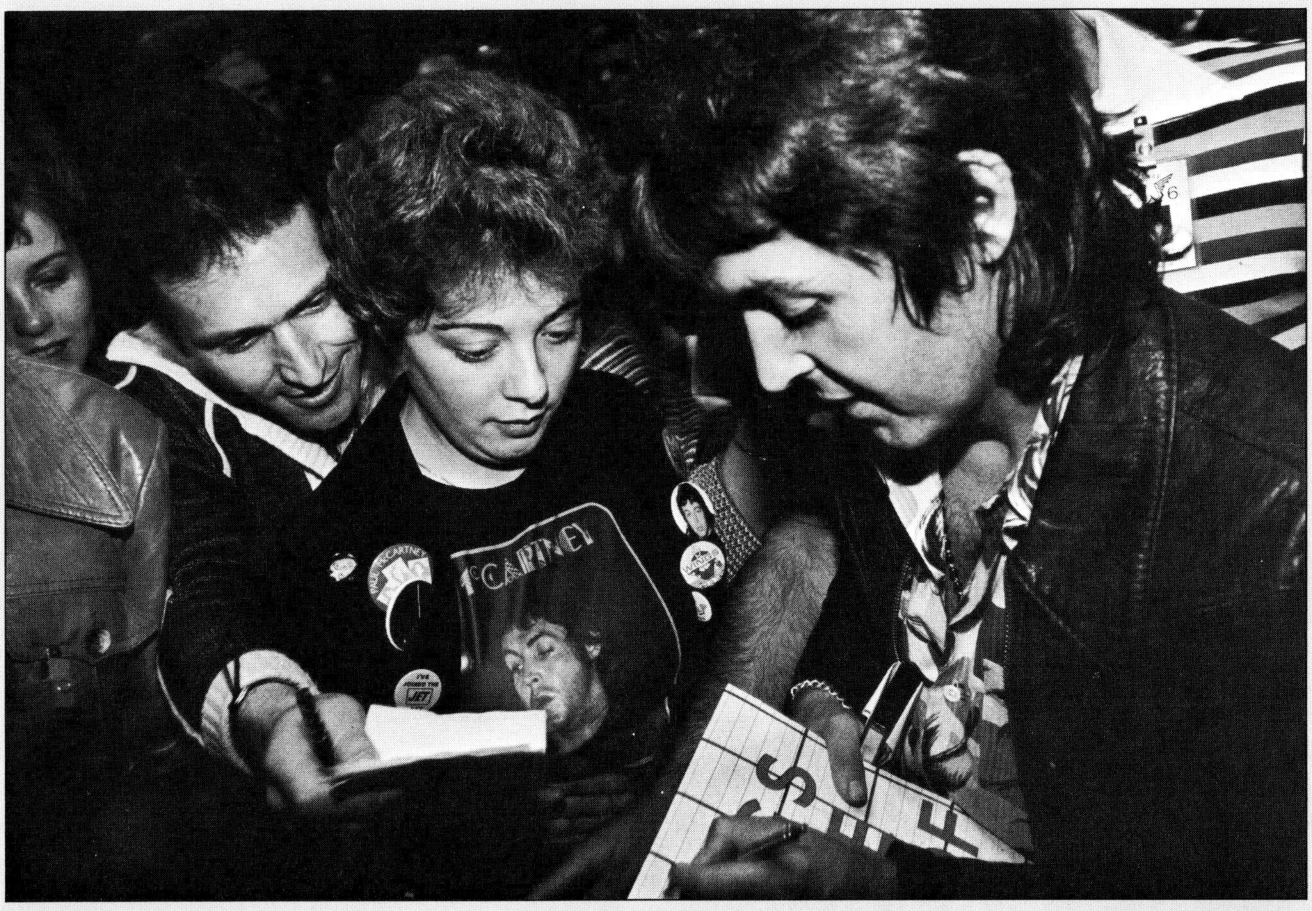
McCARTNEY
JET

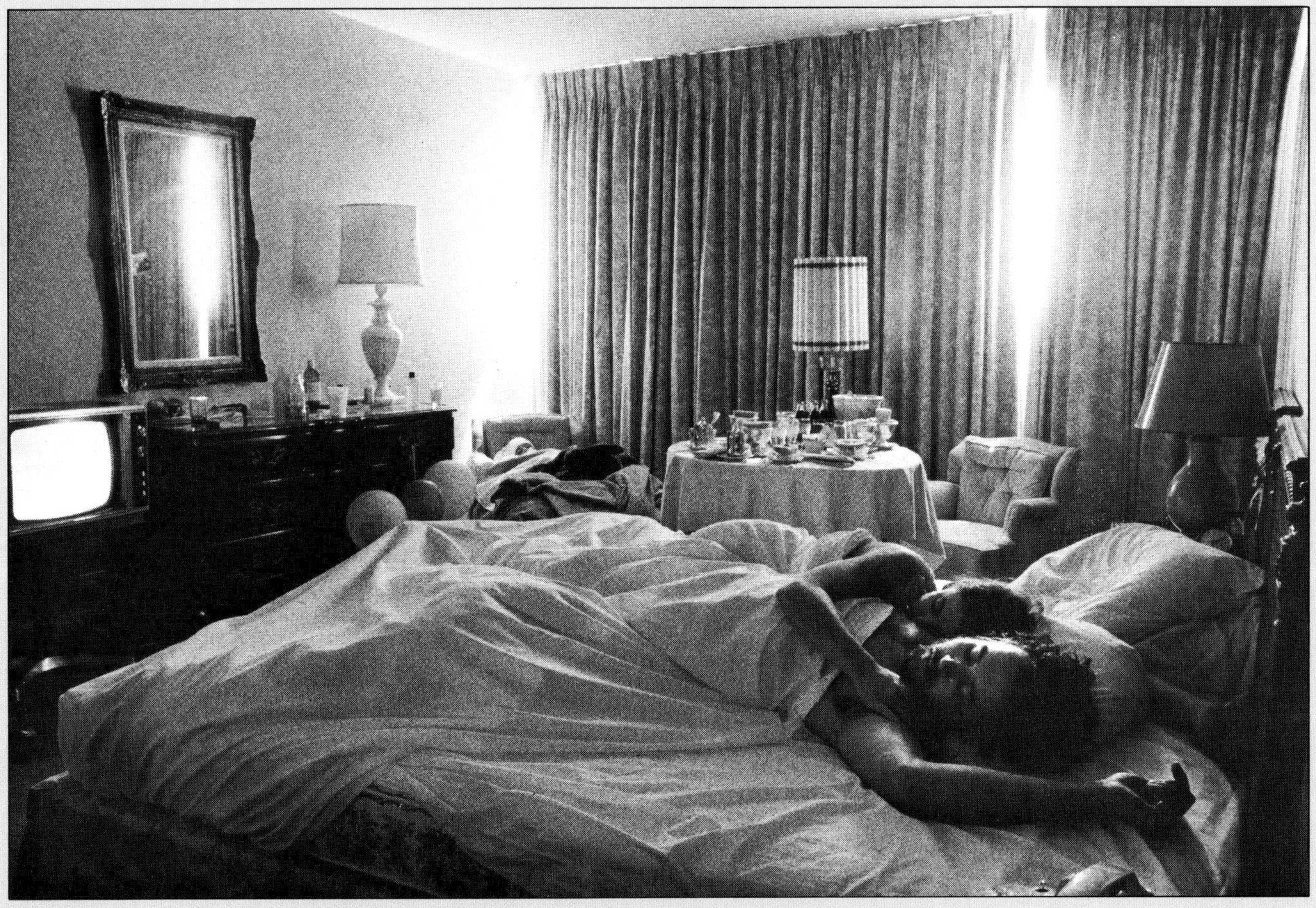

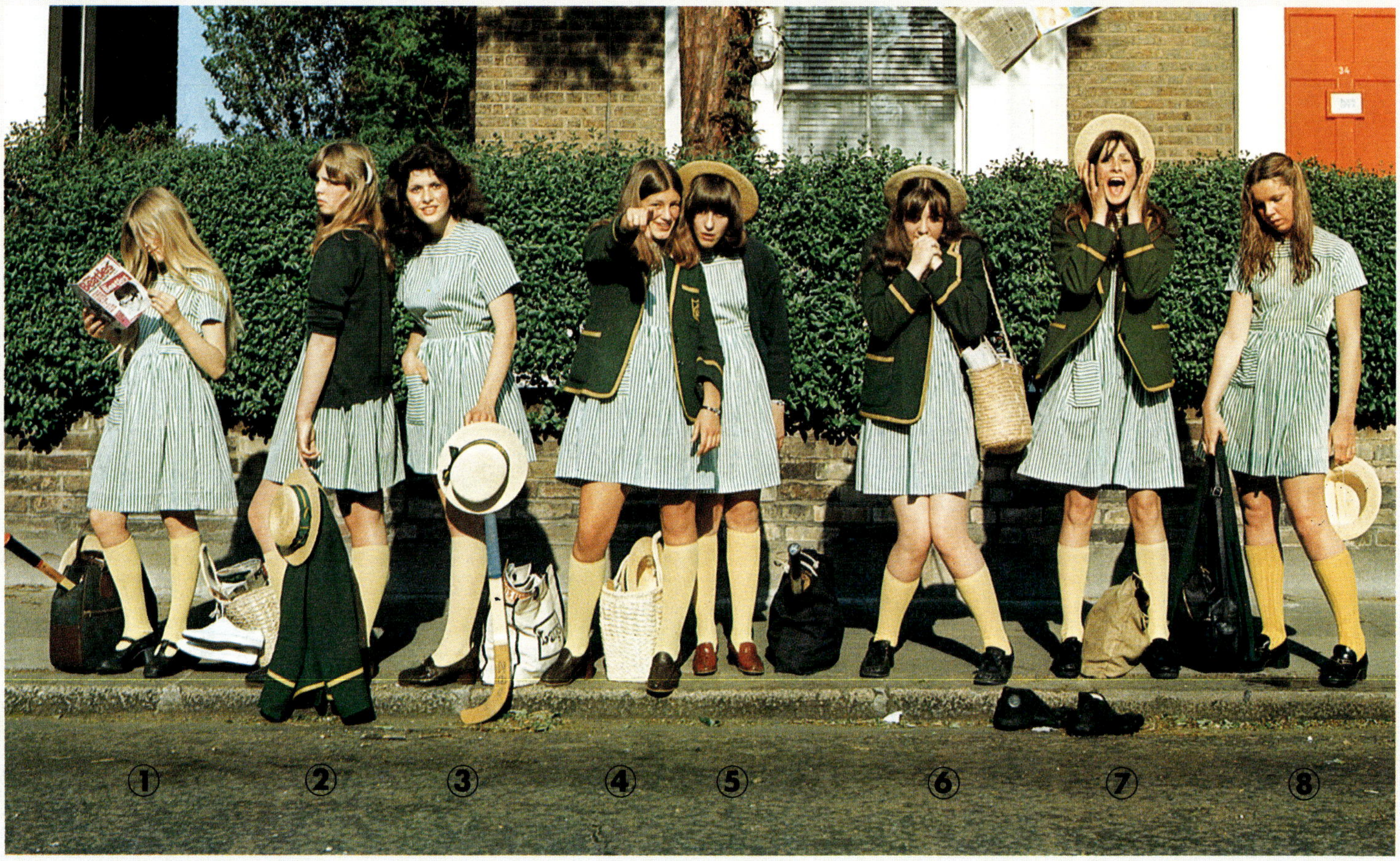

B E A T L E M A N I A

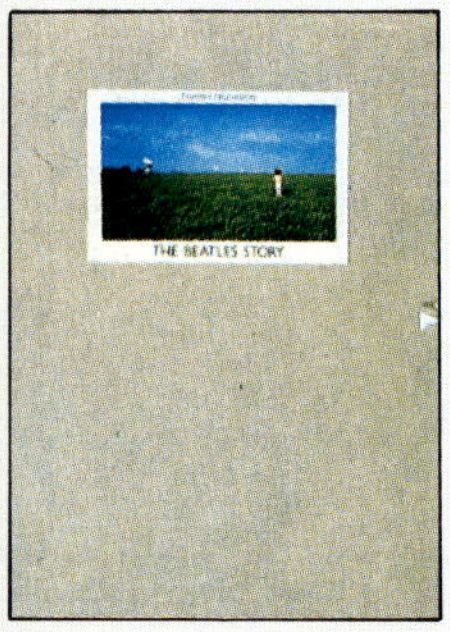
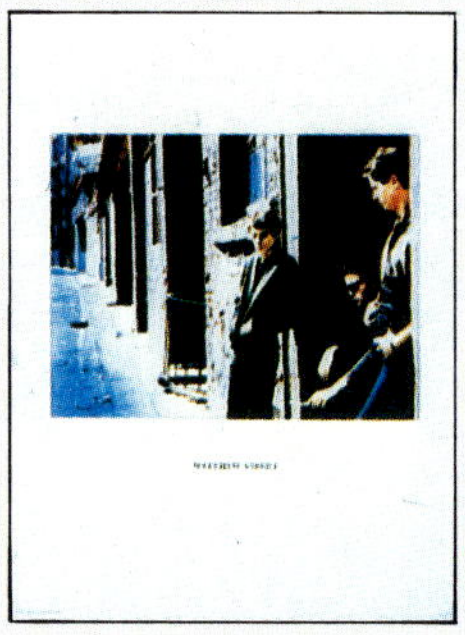
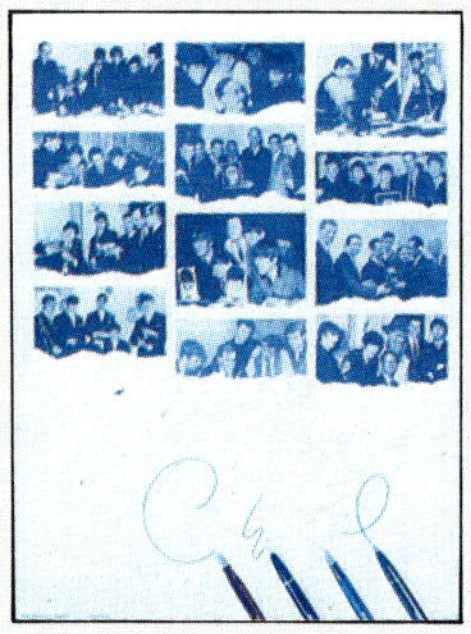
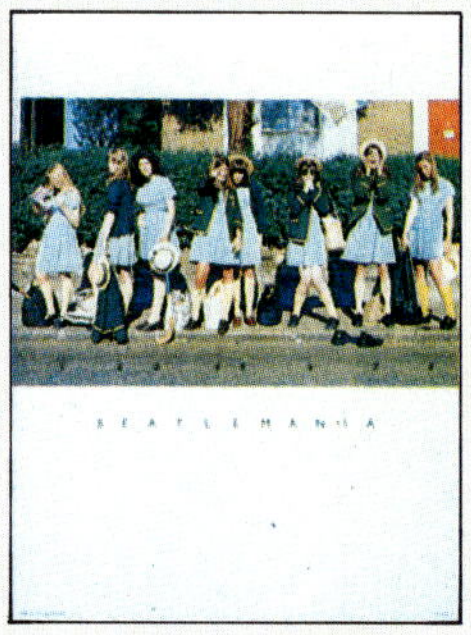
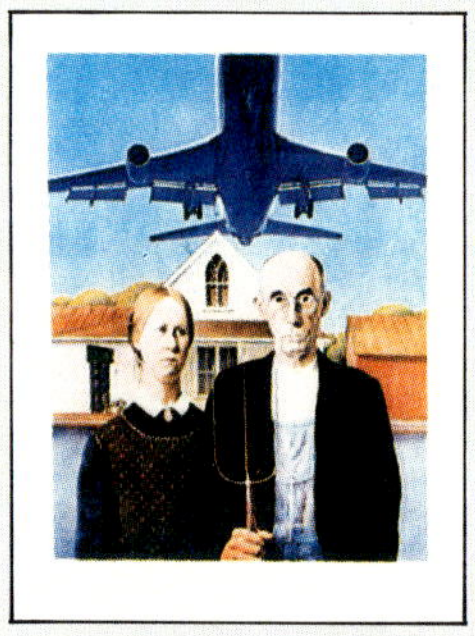
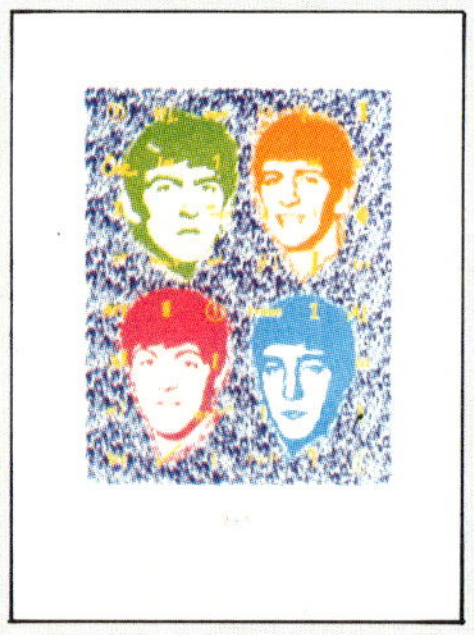
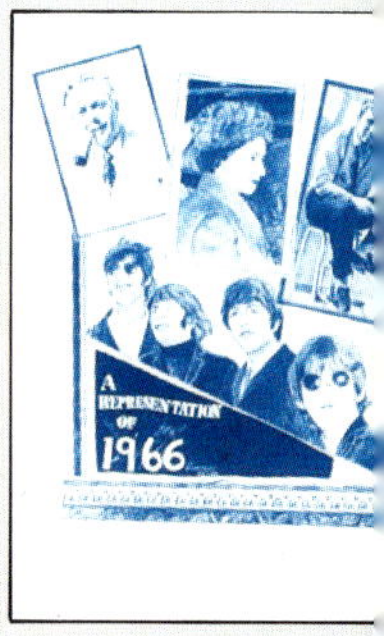

1977 BEATLES THAMES TV 'BEATLEMANIA' CO-DESIGN GEORGE HARDIE FOLIO

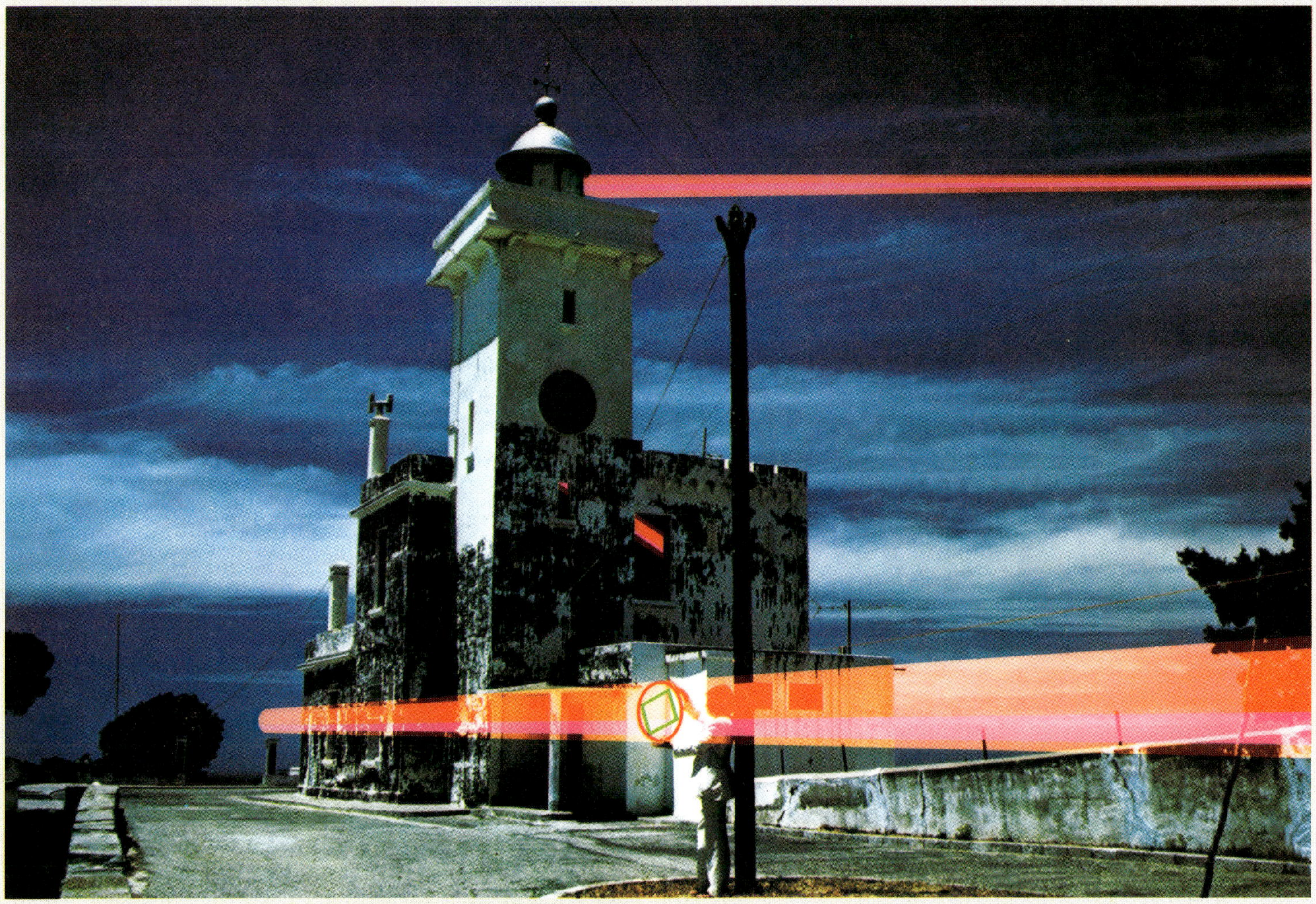

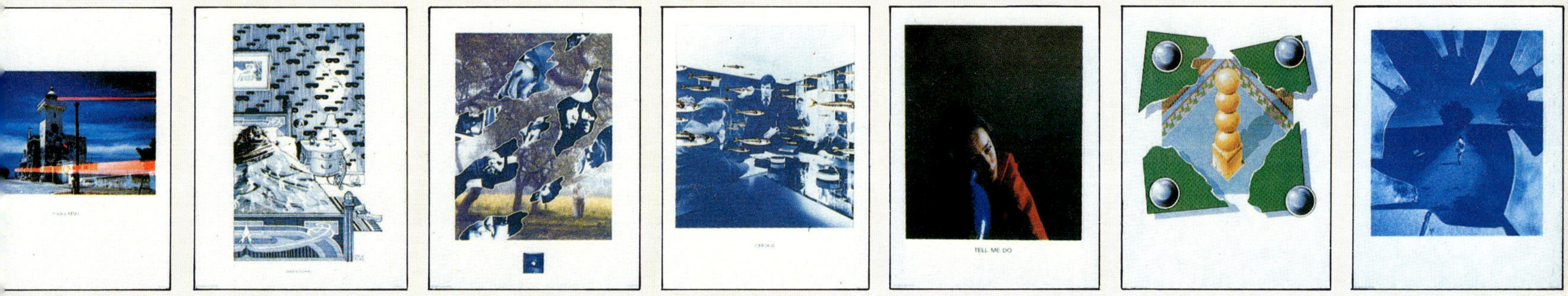

1977 BEATLES THAMES TV 'FINDING A PATH' CO-DESIGN GEORGE HARDIE FOLIO parallel ideas on the subject. The success of his book 'Views' had, in part, laid promising foundations for his own publishing company. The nature of our book, The Album Cover Album, was based on the following decisions:—

All colour, because sleeves were usually in colour; as close to full size as possible, since covers are all $12\frac{1}{4}''$ square or thereabouts; broad based rather than specialist — instead of the best fifty or sixty sleeves ever, it would contain many more different sleeves, reproduced in varying sizes; an attempt at a definitive book which would, therefore, include an historical survey, appendices on printing, the process of sleeve design and art direction, and, most importantly, a set of chapters referring to different areas, types and themes; lastly an unfussy layout which would let those designs chosen appear clearly as themselves.

All that remained was the onerous task of selection. We asked record companies to send us their own suggestions and in addition, Peter wandered round the States for a month collecting material, whilst the rest of us collected at home. The criterion of the choice was basically what Roger and I liked. A secondary consideration was the chapter headings we had arranged and thirdly, some material was selected because of its reputation, though one of us had to respect it as well. The book transpired to be a much harder task than we'd imagined and to involve more people than anticipated. Dominy Hamilton wrote the introduction after arduous research, whilst Diana Korchien spent painful months endeavouring to contact all the designers, photographers and companies to get clearance. James Slattery was the text editor and David Howells did invaluable research into the jazz field. It took one year to complete 'The Album Cover Album'.

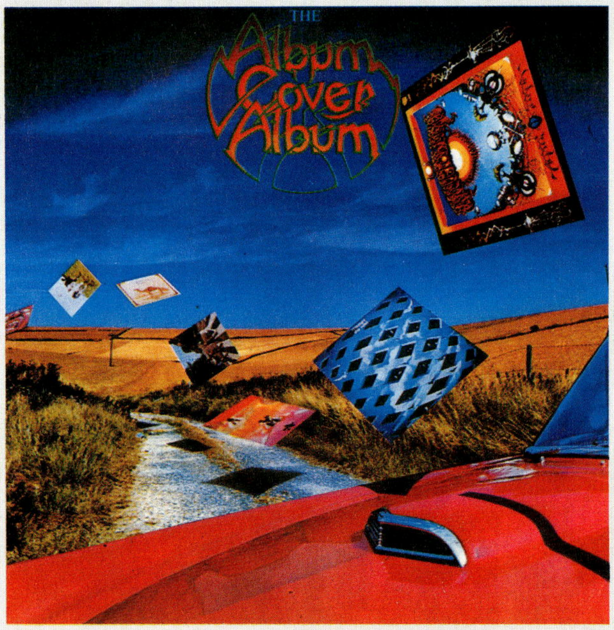

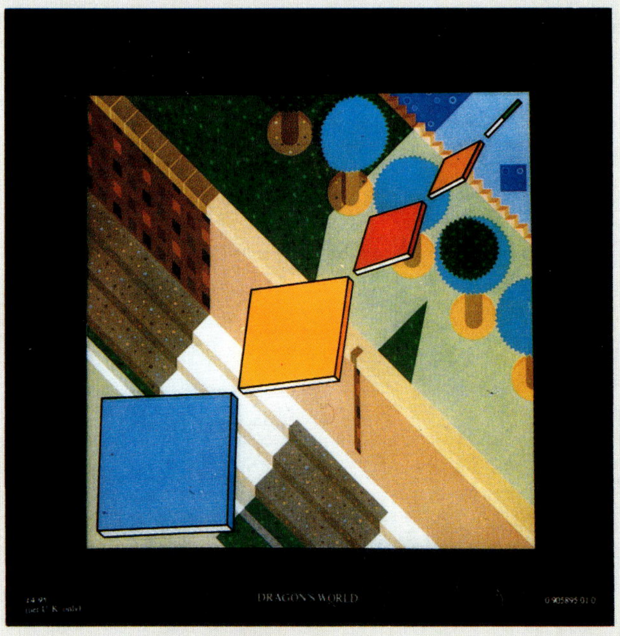

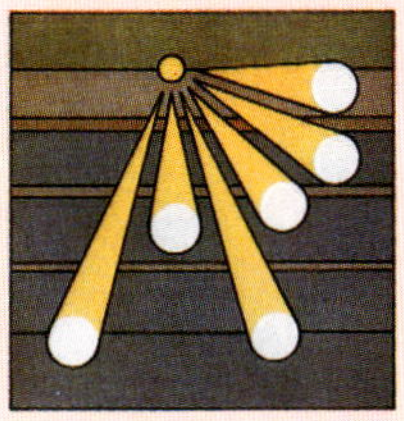

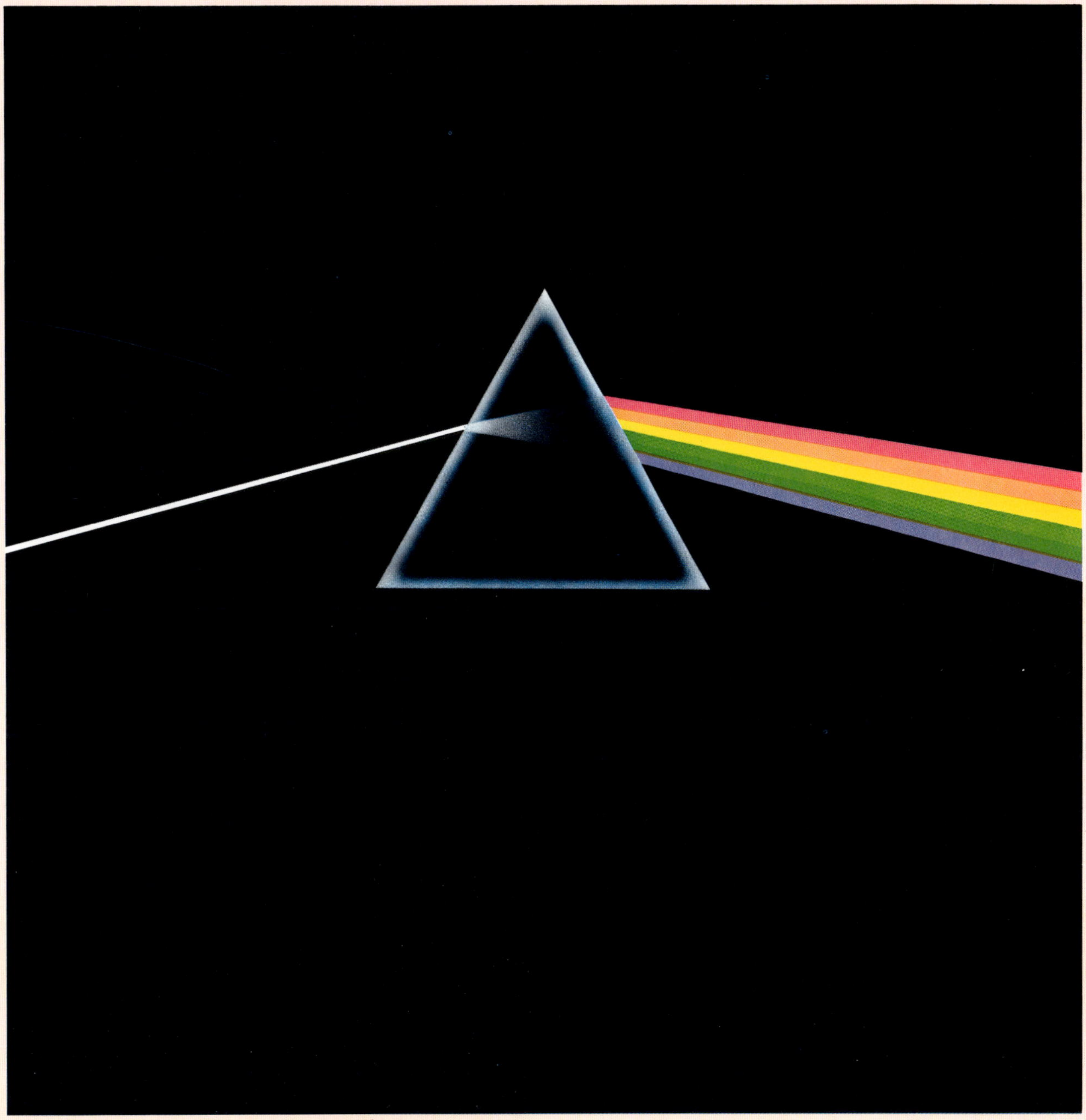

1973 PINK FLOYD 'DARK SIDE OF THE MOON' FRONT COVER

We borrowed the idea for Unicorn from Malcolm Harrison of NTA Studios. He had drawn a picture of a wood pierced by the sun's rays. These rays looked solid rather than translucent. The photograph we took is of a sculpture, long cardboard cylinders wrapped in silver card, carried into a wood and positioned against the trees. They were placed slanted and parallel so as to resemble real beams of sunlight. In nature sometimes these real beams may be so bright and definite that you can barely make out the background behind, especially if you come upon them suddenly and the eyes are not 'adjusted'. The pale border is a continuation of the picture which has been exposed for only five seconds in the printing whereas the rest has been given forty-five seconds.

'Dark Side of the Moon' is one of seven or eight suggestions we submitted to Pink Floyd. It relates to the Floyd's concerts and their use of light shows. Specifically it was sparked off by Rick Wright who wanted something very simple, clinical and precise. It's not a particularly original design but I do feel that it is very appropriate and highly effective. The artwork was mainly mechanical — the spectrum was drawn up in black line and the colours indicated. The prism was airbrushed, black on white, and the separator reversed it out of a mechanical (printer's) black background. We purposely omitted one colour, purple, since we thought it would not 'read' clearly. The continuation of the light onto the back of the sleeve involves an impossible diminishing of the spectrum when it enters the second (inverted) prism so as to form a thin white beam again which then enters the first prism on the front sleeve. The inside spread has been designed to join up with either end of the outer spread. Thus when the sleeves are opened out and placed next to each other they form a continuous pattern (see Mandalas pg. 73). Roger Waters of Pink Floyd helped us design this inner spread.

The rays of light for Al Stewart are the sun's own reflections. The cloaked magician is again a sort of Dr. Strange figure as it was on 'Past, Present and Future', Al's previous album. This figure is simply holding a mirror to his stomach. It's supposed to remind you of Castaneda and the energy bands that emerged from don Genaro's stomach as Carlos watched him scale the waterfall in 'A Separate Reality'.

Whereas the rays in Al Stewart are natural, those for Unicorn are unnatural but real; those for 'Dark Side' are mechanical and those for Wings are drawn. Or rather they are airbrushed. We photographed the fuselage of an actual plane plus a number of reference shots that showed reflections and arbitrary patterns of light and shade on metal. Richard Manning then copied the photograph and painted it in a photo-realist manner by using the dyes and methods he uses in general retouching, as opposed to oil or acrylic paint. We hoped that this would give the finished piece a greater photographic quality — a sense of exaggeration that would be more stimulating than a simple photo of the same thing.

Richard drew out the shapes, inserting windows, lights and panel markings where we thought they'd look better. The design is made up of copies but is in no way a tracing or an exact replica. This method also allowed us to alter the design to fit the actual proportions of the sleeve. The drawn shapes were then photocopied. We experimented several times on big prints, adding tones with airbrush and then painting in highlights, light and dark patches,

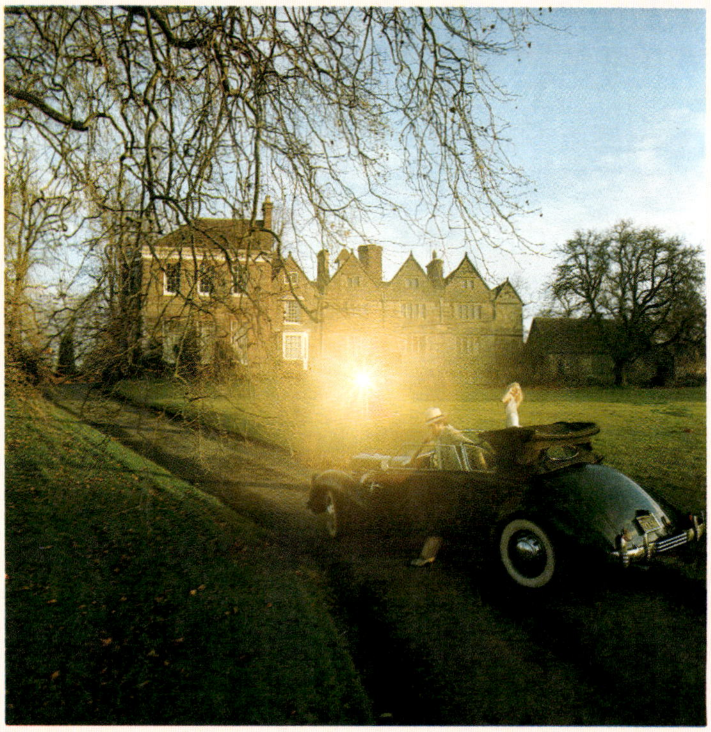

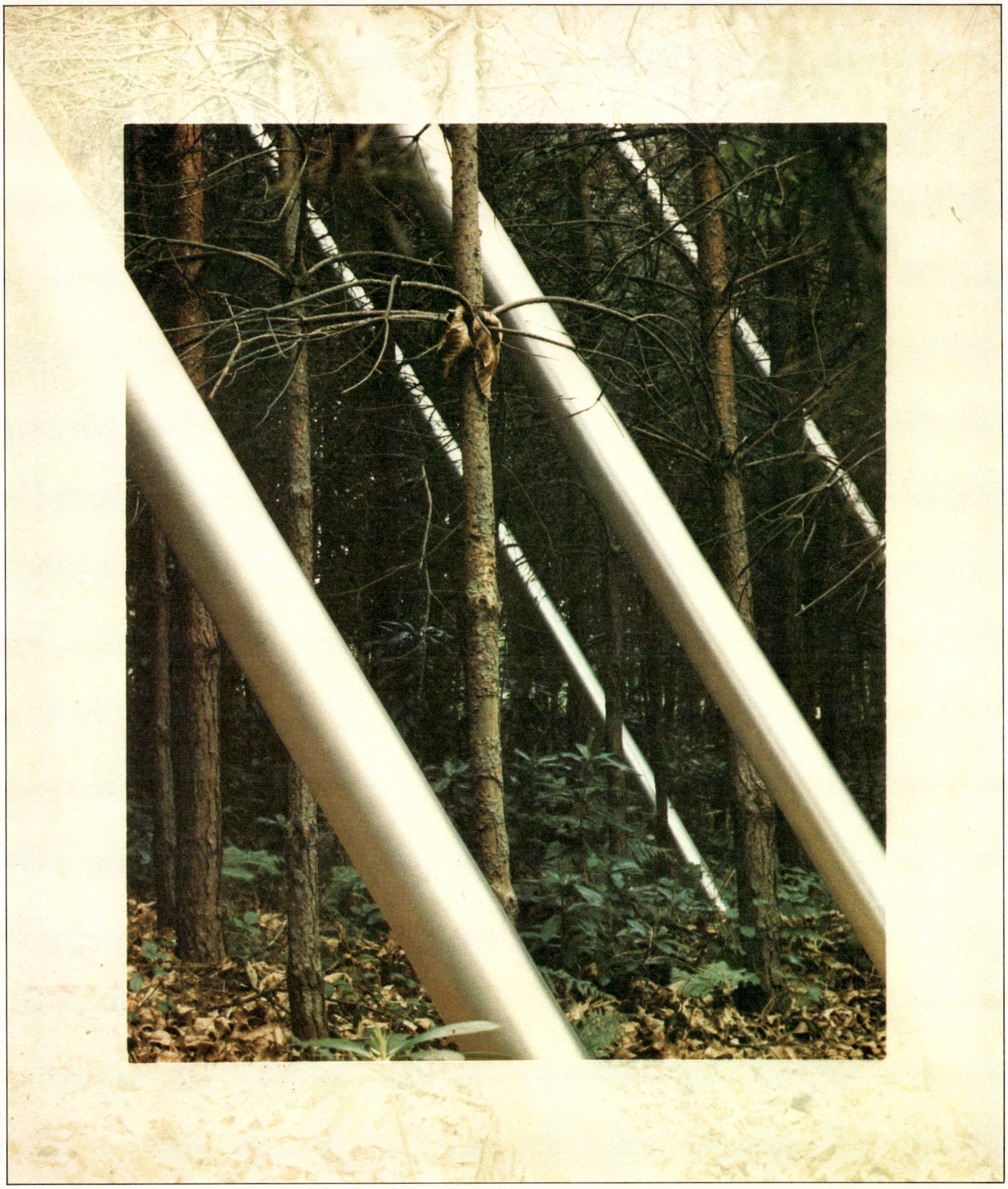

1974	UNICORN 'BLUE PINE TREES'	FRONT COVER

ribbons of colour and a thousand rivets with a small brush! And each time we added or took away anything we would look at it and then try some more, until arriving at what you now see.

The idea is about Paul arriving in America with Wings after ten long years and opening the airplane door, symbolically the raising of the curtain at a concert. As the door opens (the curtain rising) the light streams out. This light coming from the door is a metaphor for music. The idea is also related to a movie called 'Kiss Me Deadly' in which a box of nuclear material is stolen from the authorities. The thieves are warned never to open it, but Ida Lupino, one of the gangster molls, is too curious and greedy. She opens it and is blasted into nothingness by the energy of the emerging light beam. There is nothing in the heavily fortified box but light — the mysterious energy, the unknown source.

The painting or retouching on Wings is the same process as we use on all designs. Wings is totally retouched, whereas Black Sabbath (pg. 48) for example, is half retouched. In most other instances however, the retouching is used to tidy up a picture, to remove unwanted bits and to add other little alterations that we think will improve the final result. The idea is to literally re-touch, and to do it in a fashion that cannot be detected, so that it looks like part of the original photo. If you can see it (apart from when you're intended to) then it can be deemed as poor retouching and can interfere with the 'looking' at a picture. We used to think of retouching as a kind of cheating — why couldn't one take the picture the way one wanted it in the first place? But it is virtually impossible to print without some little impediment, some hair or speck of dust, settling on the print surface which obstructs light in the exposing and leaves a white mark (an area receiving no exposure). The removal of these irksome things is called 'spotting' and is done with a small brush, using dye (which merges) or paint, which is opaque. The dye has an advantage by virtue of its translucence for it can be diluted with water and worked into the print until it is unnoticeable.

It is not a big step to add or remove larger areas. In 'Lamb Lies Down' (page. 126) the white hole where Rael was before he 'stepped out' to look at himself is bleached out. A piece of adhesive cellophane (frisk film) is pressed firmly onto the print. Because it is transparent one can see the image beneath. The area that Rael occupied is scored with a scalpel, so as not to cut the print, and is then peeled away. A chemical bleach is then applied to the bromide and the photo image is slowly dissolved away. When it has gone the print is washed again with water and dried and then the rest of the frisk film is removed. All this is done whilst the print is mounted down on card. In the same design Rael's mouth is removed by bleach, as is the timegate in Al Stewart (pg. 37). Since the bleach can be diluted and applied progressively with cotton wool, it therefore becomes possible partially to remove an image, or ghost it, or vignette an edge — blurring it gradually into white. (The basic nature of printing paper is white, or off-white.)

If, however, one wishes to reduce an image with a sense of mistiness one can airbrush white paint over it. By altering the nozzle of the airbrush one can control the dispersion of the paint granules — a fine or wide spray, small or large grains. Paint has the advantage of being easy to remove (just washes off) although it is detectable — one can often see how it is applied. In the same way one can spray on darker tones (grey or black) with either paint or dye. The effect then is to deepen shadows. On Wings we had a lot of trouble with darkening the tones of the fuselage. Since it is night-time the light from the door will be clearly contrasted against the plane, but if the plane had been painted jet black then although the light would have been clearer the plane would have been very dull. Conversely, if we made the plane interesting but too pale the light from the door would not have showed up so much.

In 'Lamb Lies Down' Rael's mouth has been bleached away and then some tone has been sprayed back on to give the face a skin feeling, whilst all the figures behind are airbrushed over with black to knock them back — they're only in Rael's imagination. Thus by bleaching, or by spraying in white or black, one can alter and perhaps improve many a black and white print. With montage (see Buildings) it becomes very important because it is quite common for prints not to 'marry' properly and then they require alterations, which can only be determined when they are laid alongside each other. Varying the exposure,

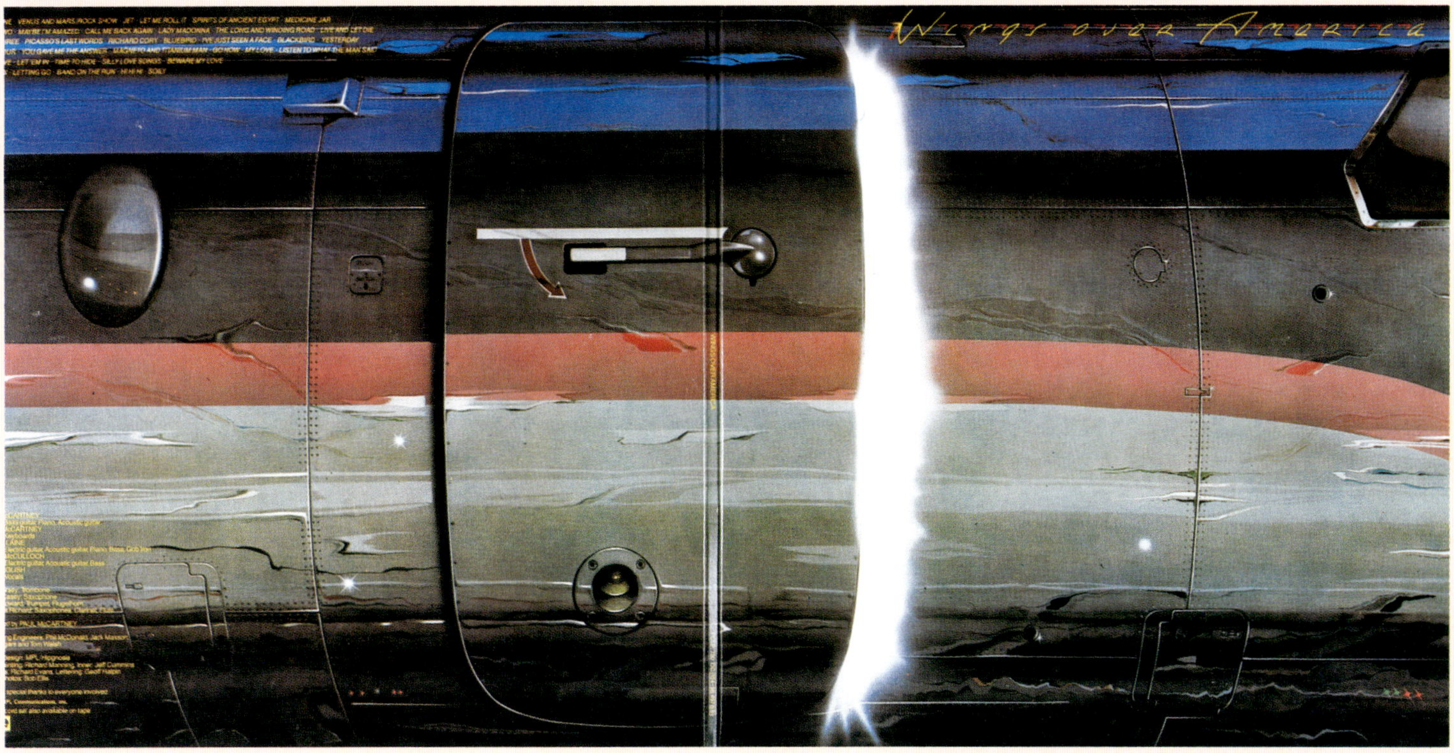

shielding and vignetting whilst exposing the print in the enlarger will give similar control over image density, but it is simply not accurate and it takes far longer.

Colour retouching involves the same technique except obviously that it is colour and the whole thing becomes more complex. The darkening and lightening of colours requires a greater dedication — one darkens by adding more colour and then maybe adding a darker shade. In black and white it's quantity, in colour it's both quantity and quality. But retouching is a fine skill and therefore quite expensive. Apart from money all you need are good prints (uncontaminated by traces of foreign chemicals like left-over fixative) and a good retoucher.

1976 WINGS 'WINGS OVER AMERICA' FRONT COVER

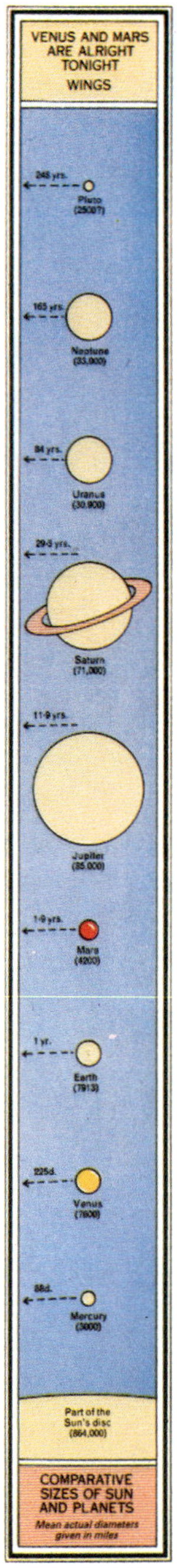
VENUS AND MARS ARE ALRIGHT TONIGHT
WINGS
248 yrs.
Pluto (2500?)
165 yrs.
Neptune (33,000)
84 yrs.
Uranus (30,900)
29·5 yrs.
Saturn (71,000)
11·9 yrs.
Jupiter (85,000)
1·9 yrs.
Mars (4200)
1 yr.
Earth (7913)
225d.
Venus (7600)
88d.
Mercury (3000)
Part of the Sun's disc (864,000)
COMPARATIVE SIZES OF SUN AND PLANETS
Mean actual diameters given in miles

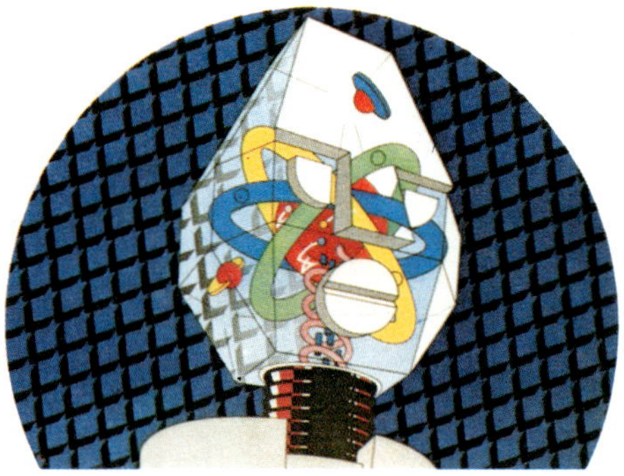

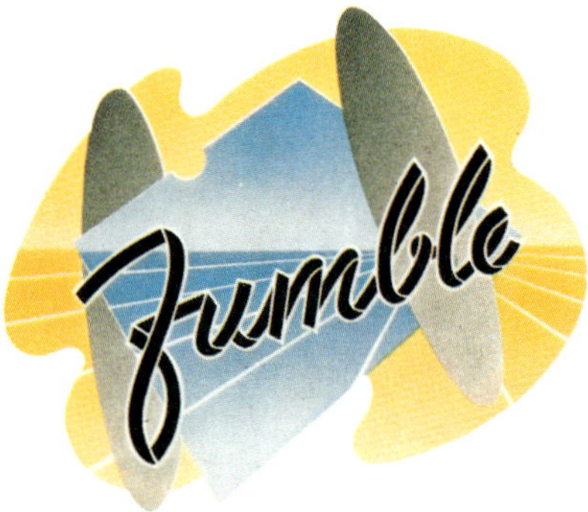
Jumble

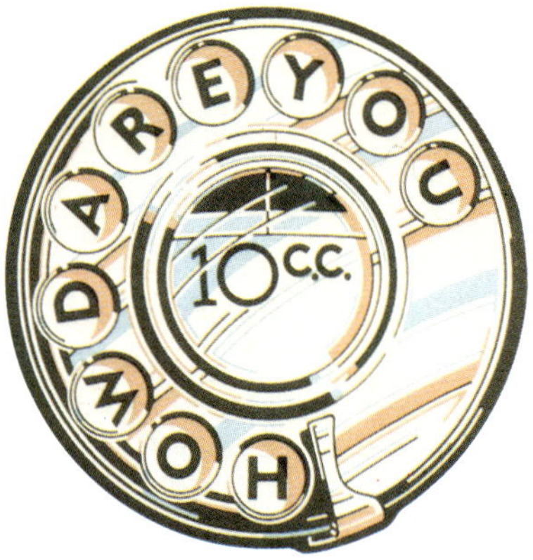
HOW DARE YOU
10 C.C.

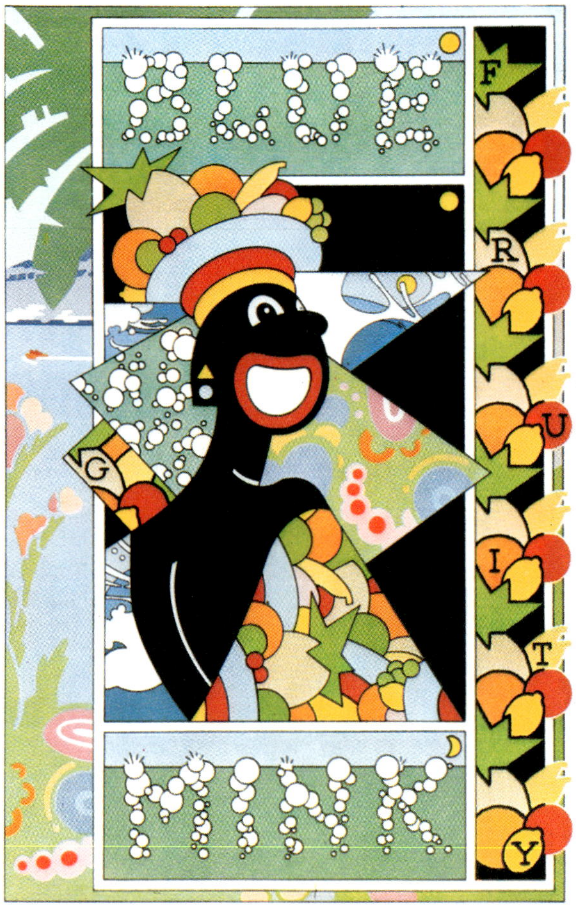
BLUE
MINK
FRUITY
G

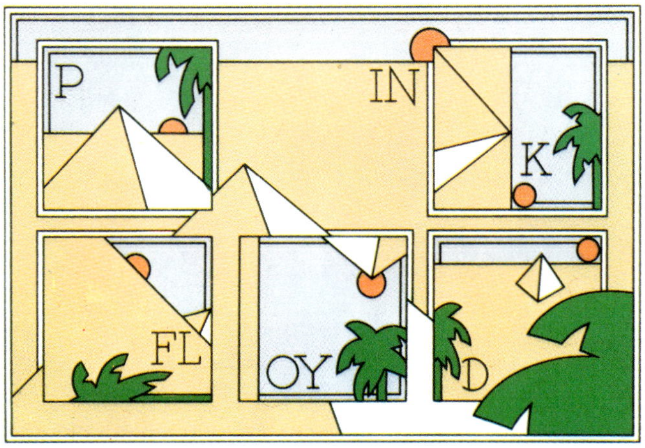
P
IN
K
FL
OY
D

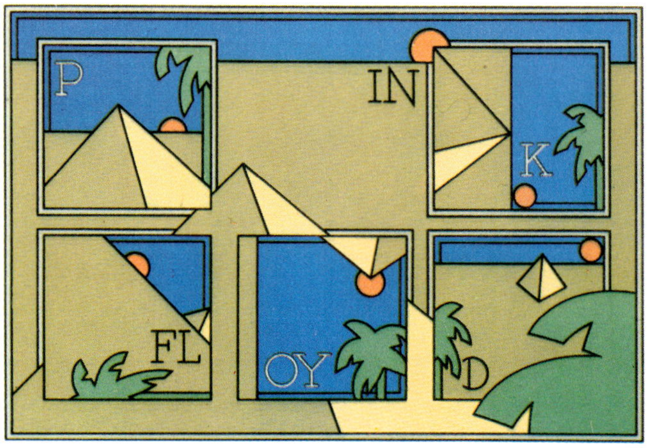
P
IN
K
FL
OY
D

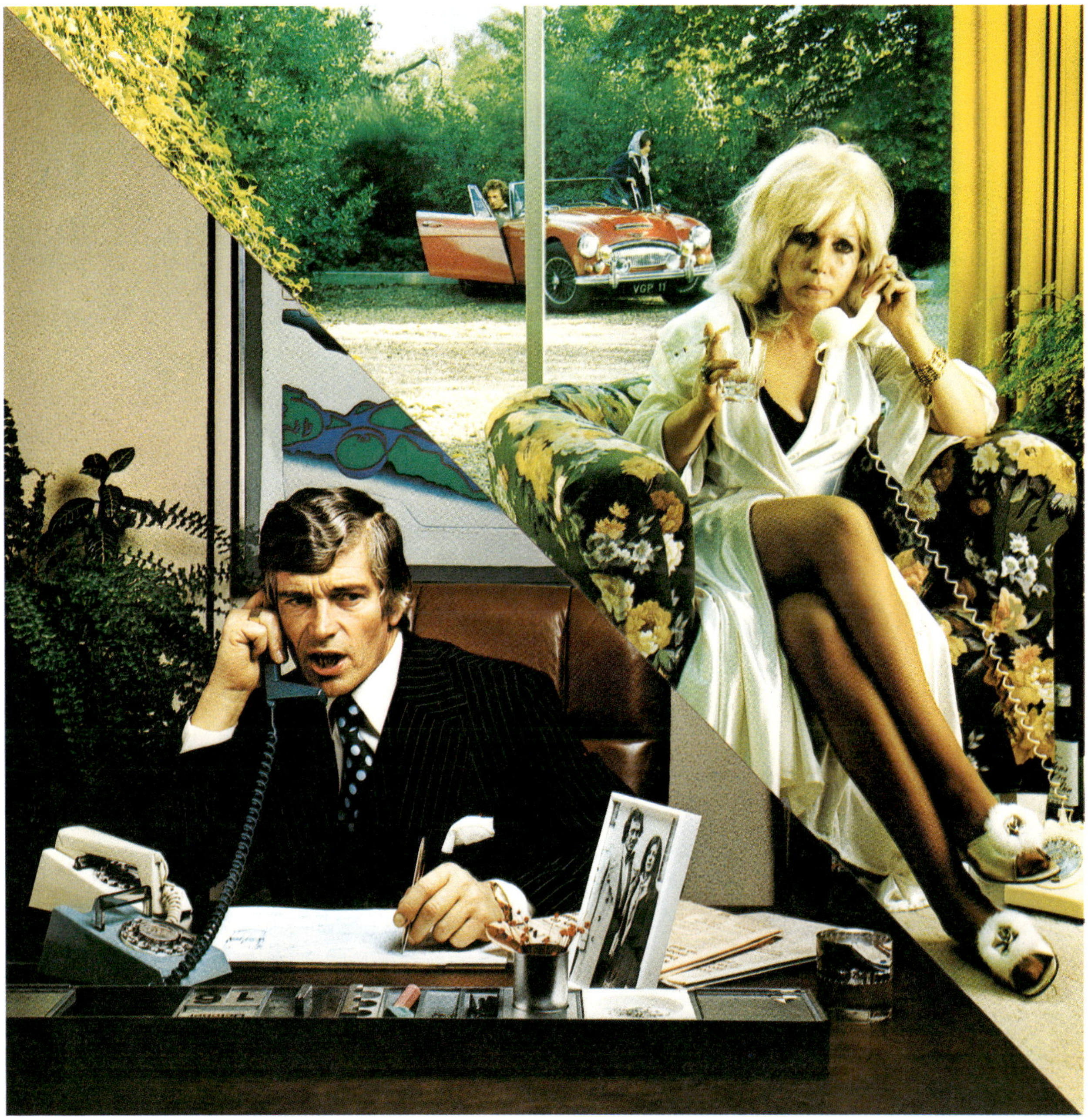

1975 10CC 'HOW DARE YOU' FRONT COVER

This bunch of pictures shows the narrative or filmic side of our work in which we invent or are given stories to unfold, usually in a single picture. I'll tell you how these particular pieces refer to their briefs. 'House on the Hill' was designed in direct collaboration with Howard Werth of Audience. The album title suggested a 30's film. The title song itself related this tale of a scheming femme fatale who lured would-be suitors to her mansion and then disposed of them unceremoniously. Not surprisingly, the guy in the picture looks a little apprehensive. We staged the scene like a movie using models to play the appropriate roles. We then decided to hand paint the final print as though it were an actual movie still, perhaps even on display outside the cinema.

Like Pink Floyd and Wishbone Ash, 10cc are a band we've worked with for some time. One advantage of this is that we get to know them and their music fairly well. We don't have to have a specific brief because we can work from the general vibe, from the group's ambience. It took a whole month before I was able to reduce 10cc's 'How Dare You' to some workable bottom line. In this case it was that there were a lot of connections in the lyrics involving puns and unlikely word associations. As soon as I said that to Peter he suggested telephones (because they connect, of course) and we both immediately thought of that old film thing of split-screen phone conversations. The band rejected the filmic side of the idea, but liked the telephones because, unbeknown to us, they already had a phone song on the record ('Don't Hang Up'). What a connection indeed! They wanted something modern and sophisticated so we did a style piece, a parody of Sanderson ads, full of tastefully furnished rooms occupied by very tasteful people; 'very Sanderson, very 10cc'. We chose characters and situations from the songs and then added a sub-plot involving the couple that appear in every shot, in the desk photo or behind the blonde lady where we see them getting out of the car. This sad lady in the foreground is a gin soaked housewife, wasting away in rich suburbia, whilst her smooth businessman husband works too hard and consequently neglects her. Hipgnosis goes socially conscious. He is furious at being interrupted at work, again. How dare she!

If a band is called UFO how do you avoid pictures of flying saucers? I mean, walking down a country lane with one's mate and coming upon a real one suddenly would be pretty remarkable. I think even the most sceptical of people would react to that. But pictures of flying saucers are something else. Such photos are invariably of dubious quality. They tend to make people disbelieve rather than believe in alien phenomena. So instead of doing a flying saucer straight, we imagined how people would perpetrate pictures of one, you know, like those in books on UFOs, all out of focus, seen just going over roof tops or out of lorry windows. Again the scene is suburban, as though these things go on with very normal people. What

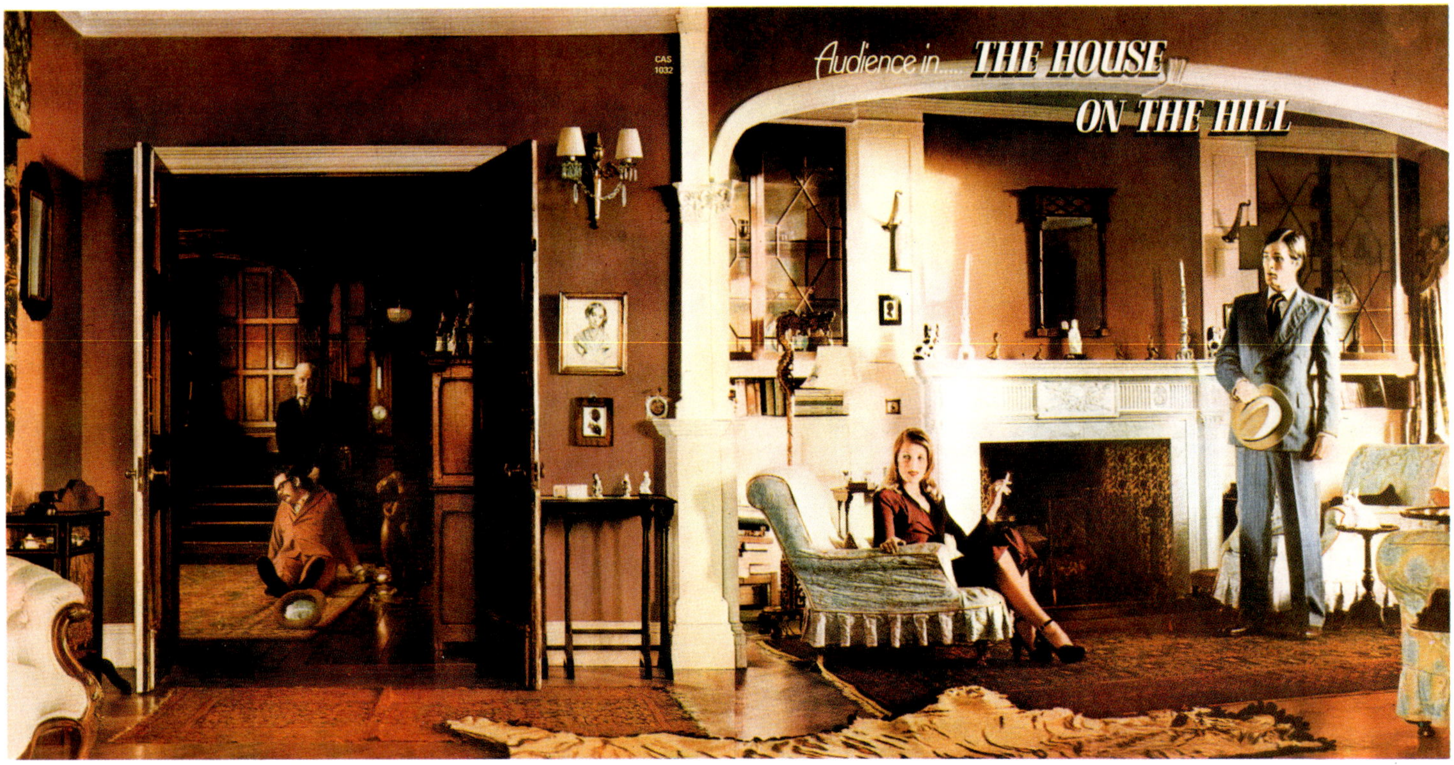

1971 AUDIENCE 'HOUSE ON THE HILL' CO-DESIGN HOWERD WERTH FRONT COVER

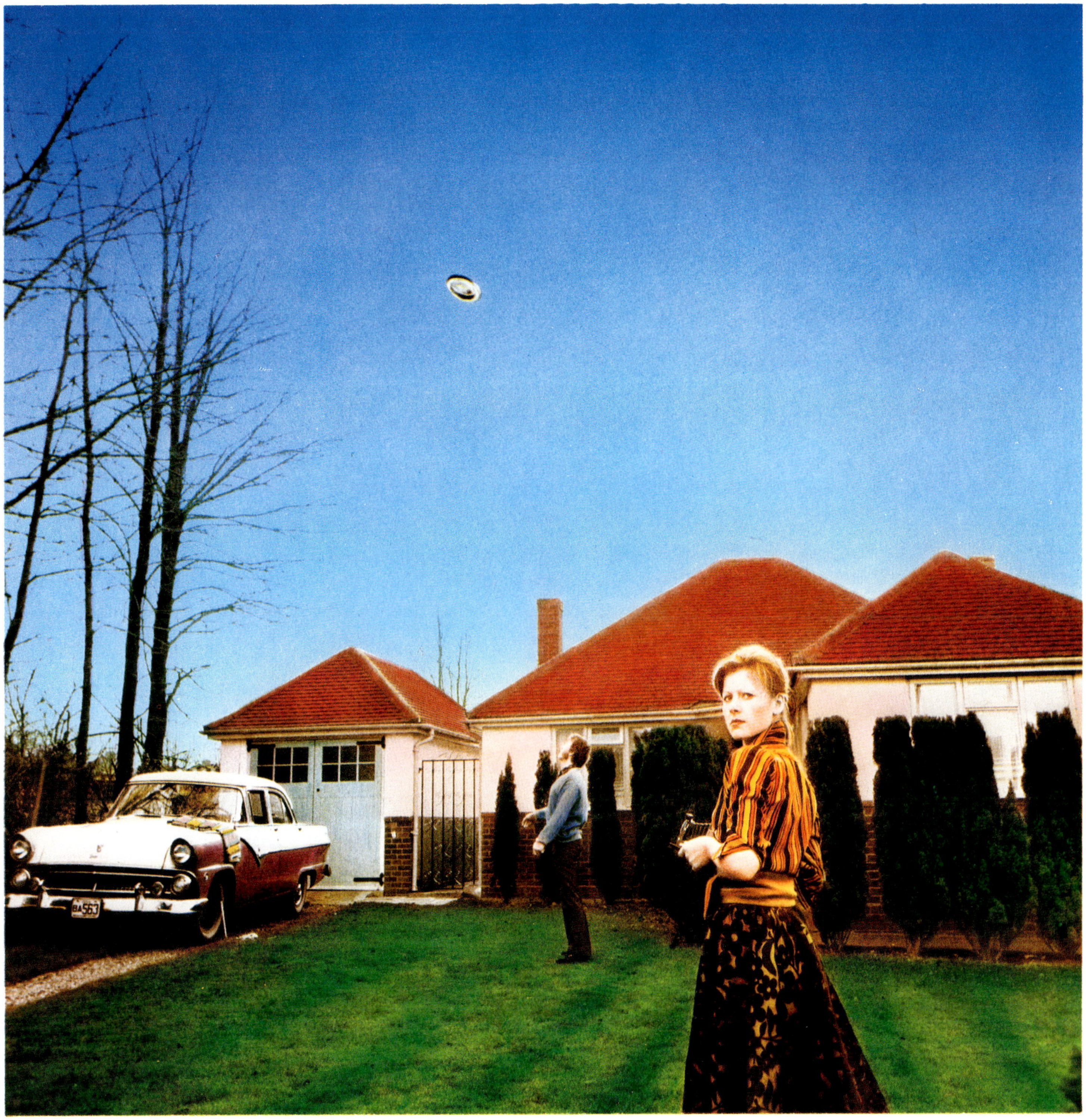

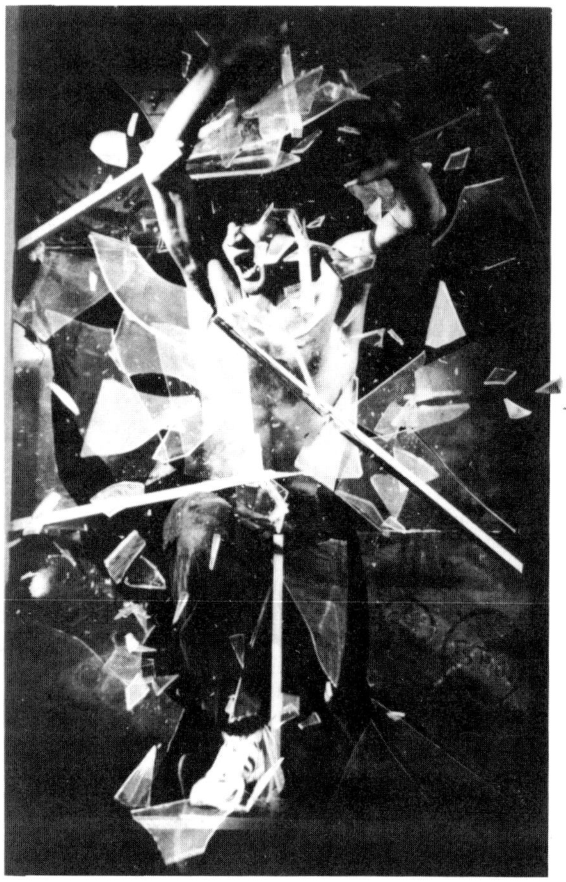

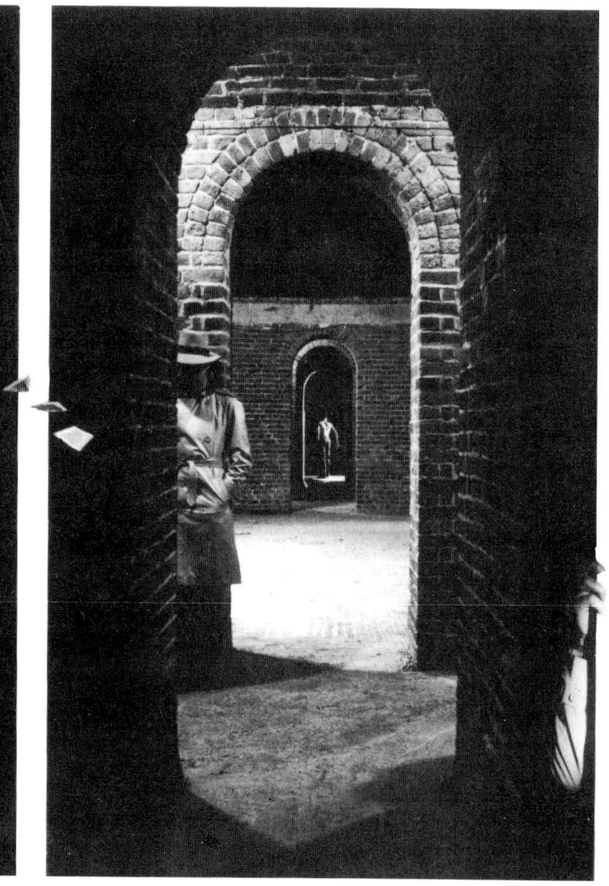

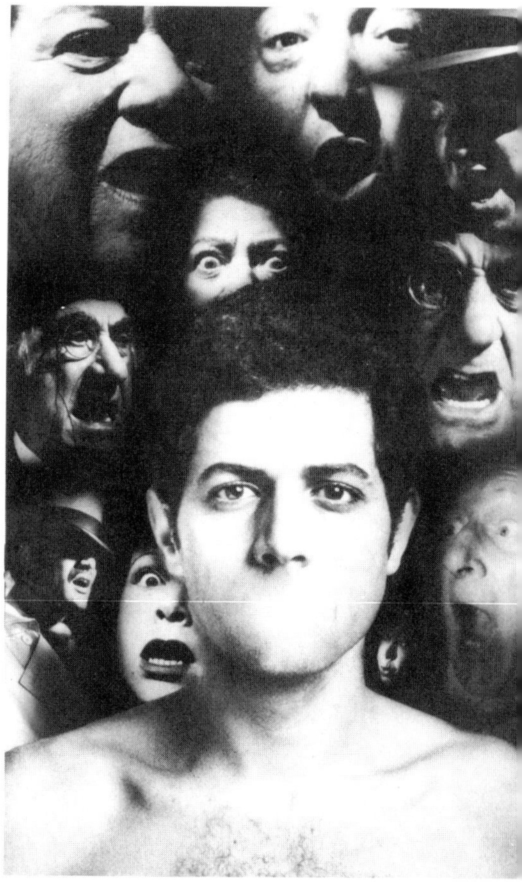

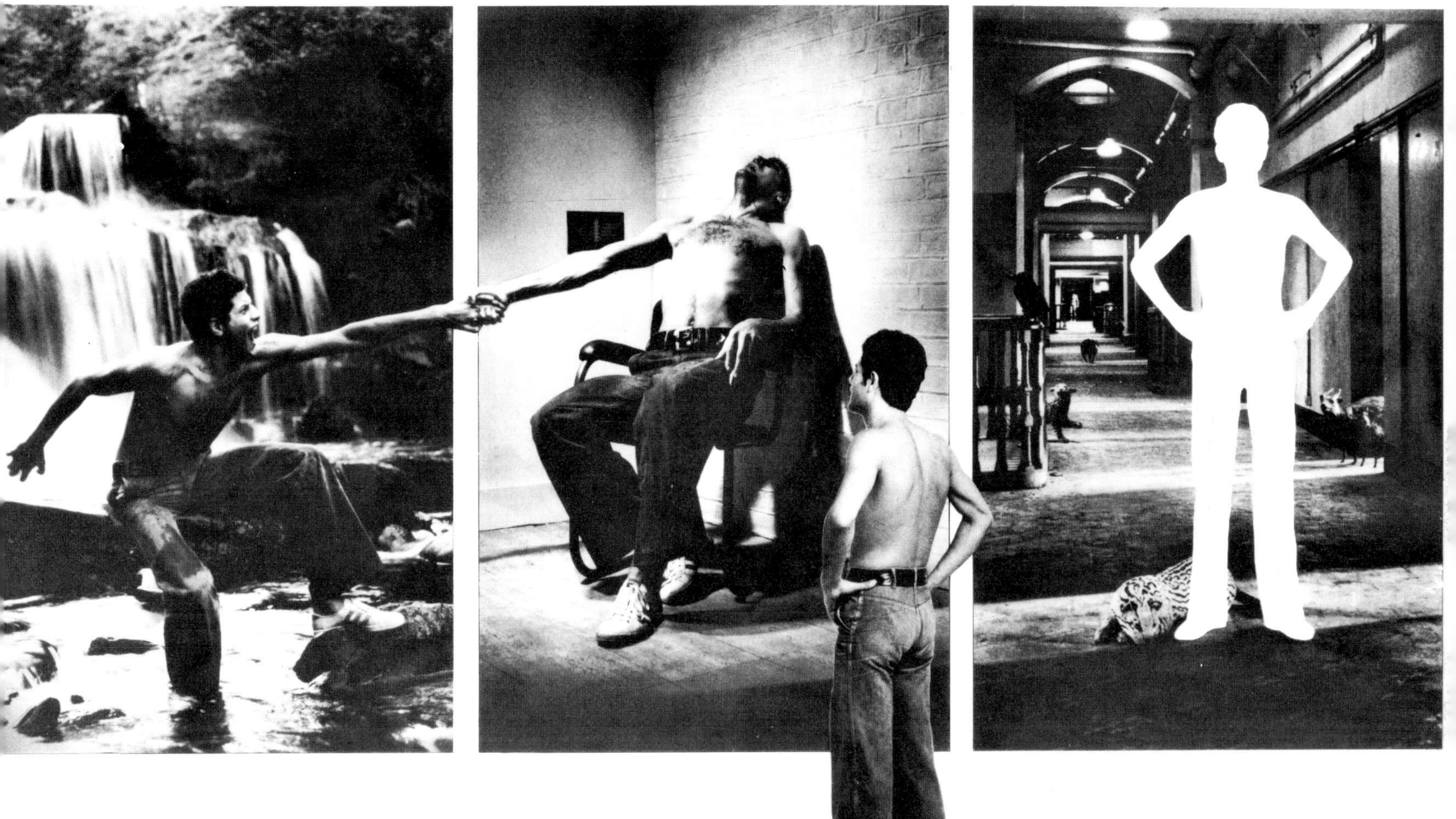

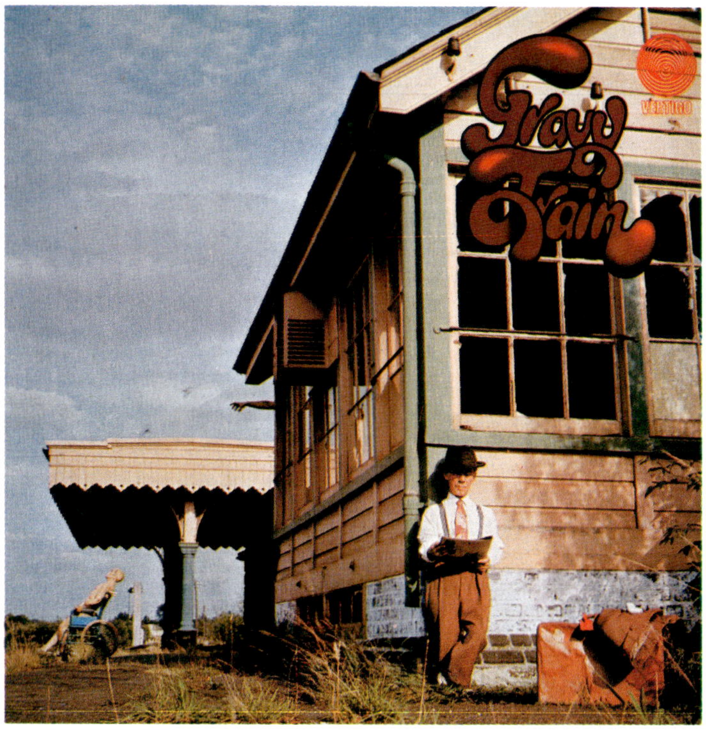

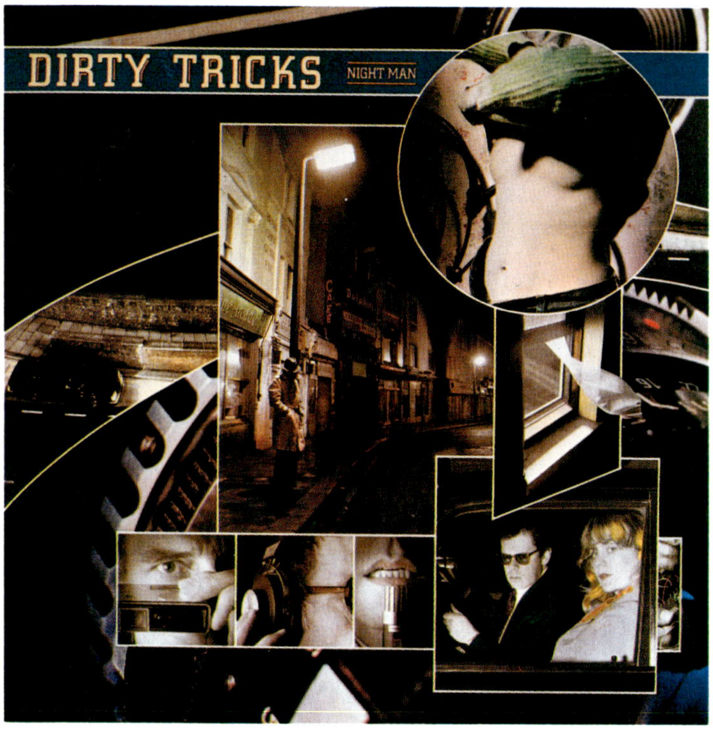

we see is a picture of people about to take a UFO photo. The UFO is a car hub which the man has launched into the air. And the girl is very cross because we, the photographers and viewers, have just interrupted her about to photograph it. The cover design is a real picture of someone faking a picture they will later purport to be real.

Genesis had written their own story for 'Lamb Lies Down on Broadway'. The central character Rael gets involved in adventures of a real, yet dreamlike nature. What we simply did was to take some scenes from the story and illustrate them photographically, and then arrange them like a comic strip. They're not in chronological order. The frame breaks are reminiscent of what comic illustrators do anyway, whilst the figure of Rael looking at himself in his dream was an idea snitched from an art nouveau illustration. The man jumping through the glass was one of the most exciting things we have ever photographed — five cameras and only one shot to take. Synchronization by eye and brain alone!

Dirty Tricks' 'Nightman' and Gravy Train are both derived from the album titles. 'Nightman' is about a voyeur and his equipment and some of the goings on he might see, perhaps to use later in a divorce or blackmailing situation. Gravy Train is simple fare and a bit weird, man, as the dwarf waits endlessly at the deserted station for the train that never comes. The Gravy Train.

Golden Earring's 'To The Hilt' is an idea of George's about a colonial type detective who continually gets into some pretty close scrapes. However, he always manages to extricate himself, only to become immediately caught in another one. The whole sequence is purposeful cliché, our hero ensnared in some dreadful dilemma, his demeanour never faltering. Unmoved by dastardly Chinese or man-eating sharks, he may be up 'to the hilt' at any time, but you can be sure that he will survive to fight another battle.

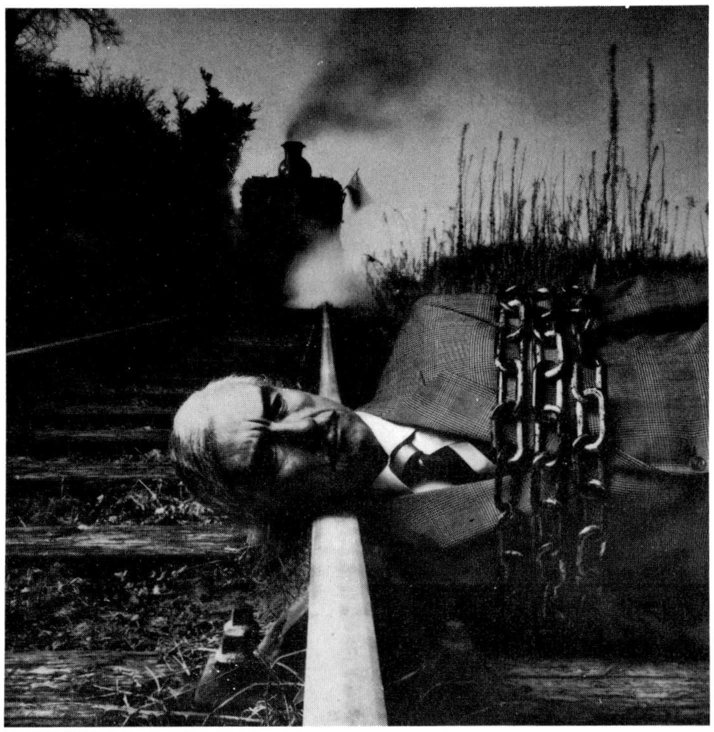

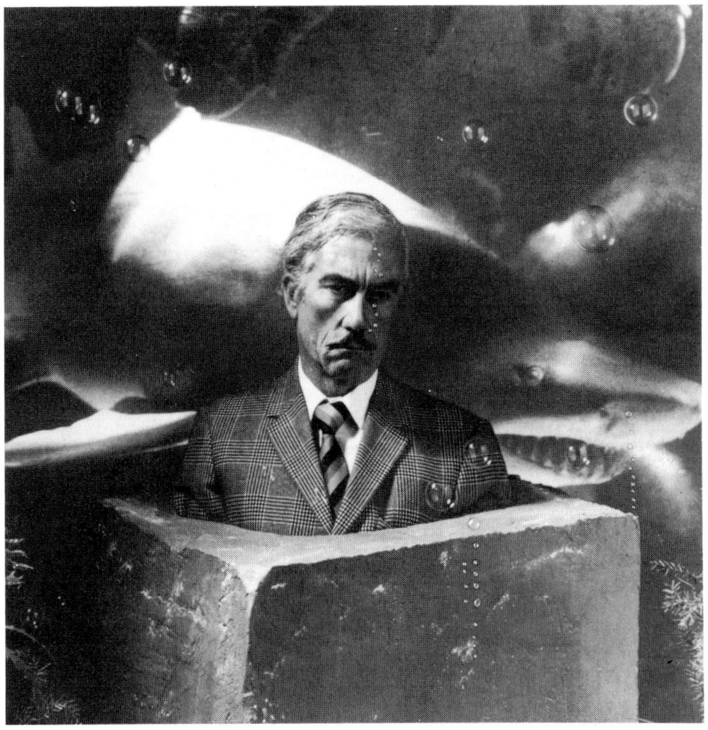

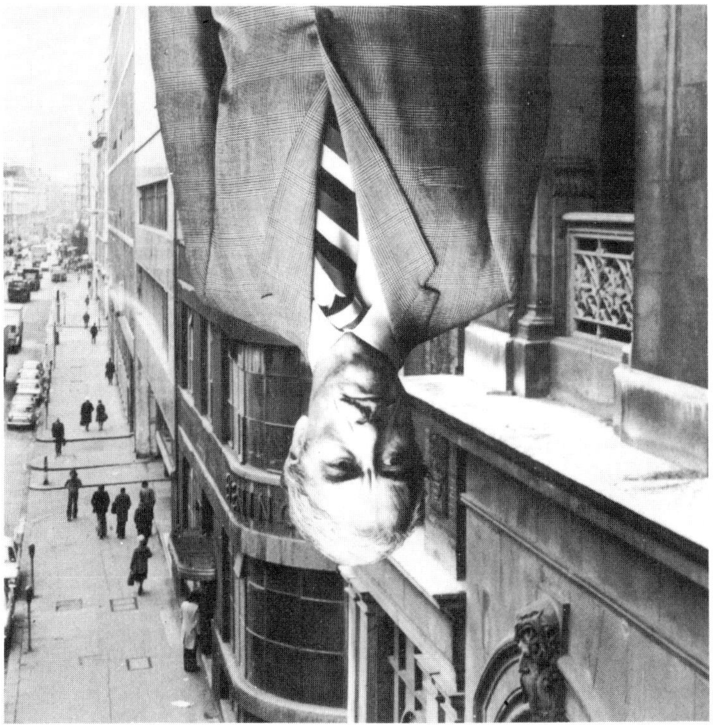

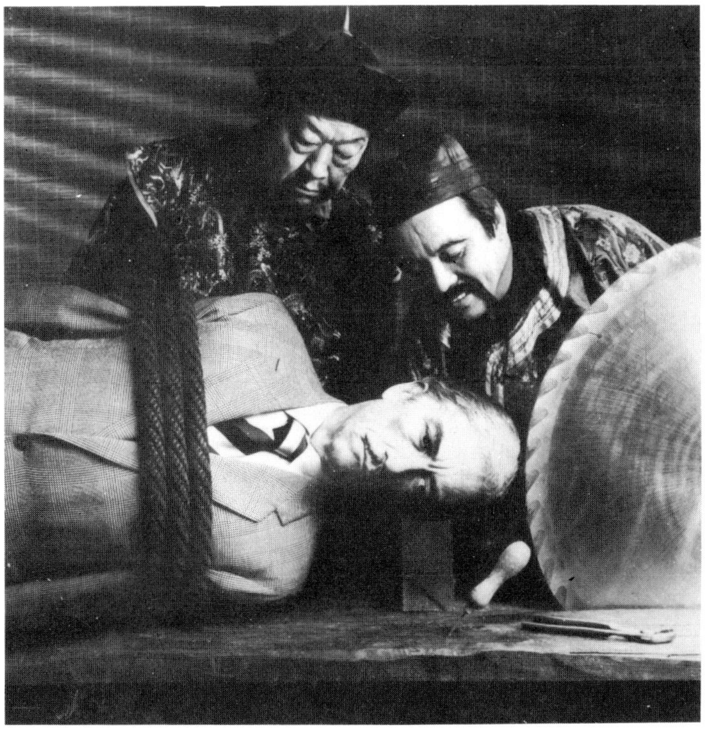

1975 GOLDEN EARRING 'TO THE HILT' FRONT & INSIDE COVER

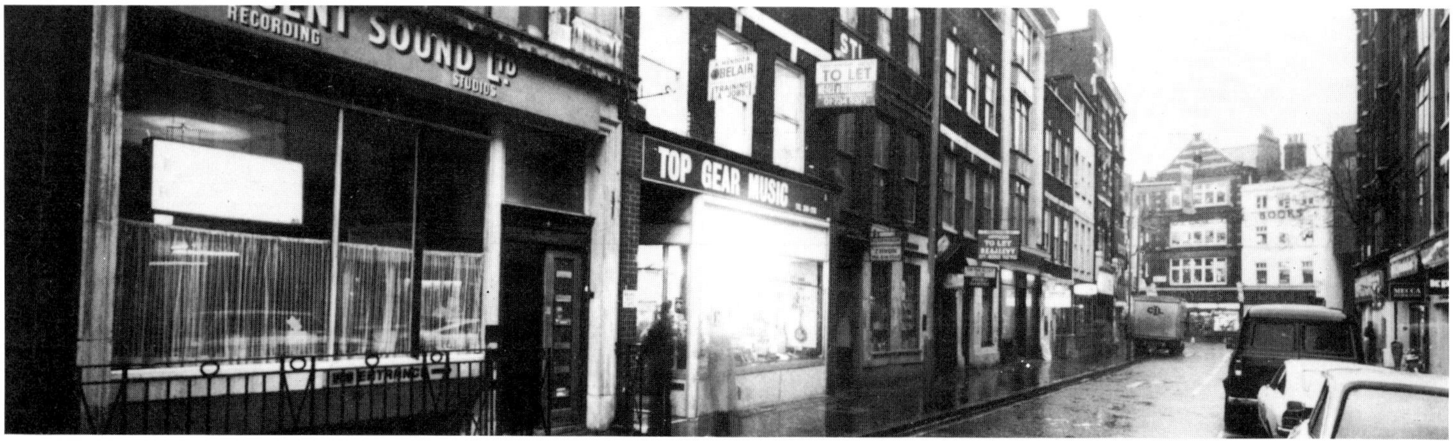

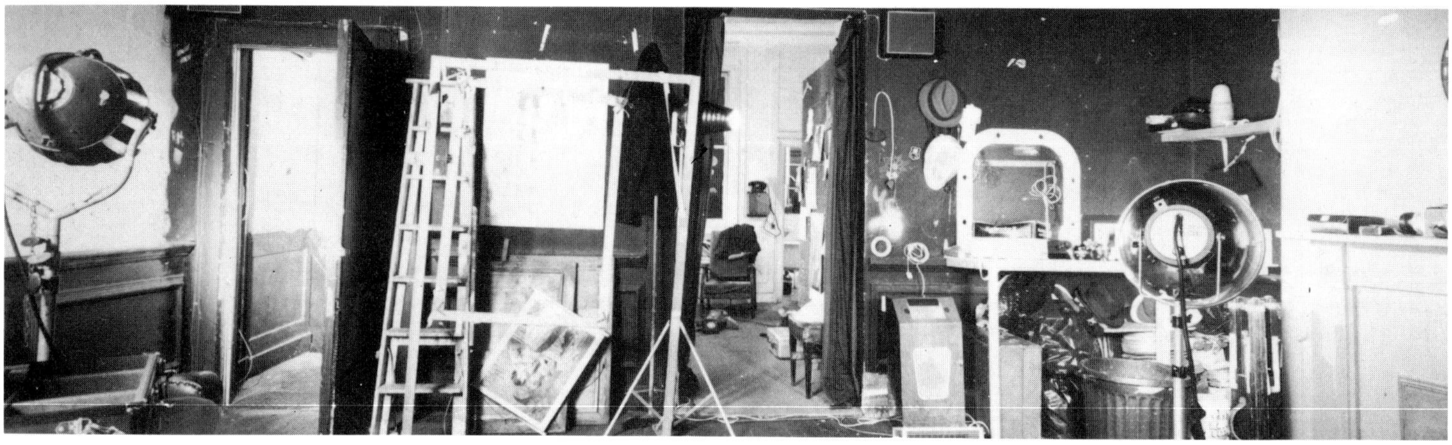

The office and studio are located in Denmark Street off Charing Cross Road in the West End of London. We have two floors and on the first is a rectangular room approximately 180 sq.ft., which is where we shoot. It's not very big but having moved from Po's bathroom it seemed like an aircraft hangar. A widened doorway leads off one side to another room which used to be the office, darkroom, reception and changing rooms etc. when we first moved in. It is now just the darkroom, home-made and very cramped, with space on one side that allows us to shoot into the studio and to get some distance back from the subject. At the rear is a small kitchen where prints are washed and dried. The studio is painted black and the darkroom is white inside.

Upstairs is our artwork room, office and reception room. For some reason the reception room has nowhere to sit down. The artwork room has a work bench round half of it, whilst round the rest of it stand a Grant enlarger, a drawing desk and shelves for storing job files, roughs and odds and sods. A plan-chest which lives in the office/reception area and probably accounts for why there's no seating there, contains cover paper, tracing material, posters and proofs. Strung about the artwork room in profusion are old jars full of blunt pencils, assorted rulers and chipped triangles, T-squares etc. and all sorts of artwork, in all kinds of stages of completion. It looks jolly good after a springclean.

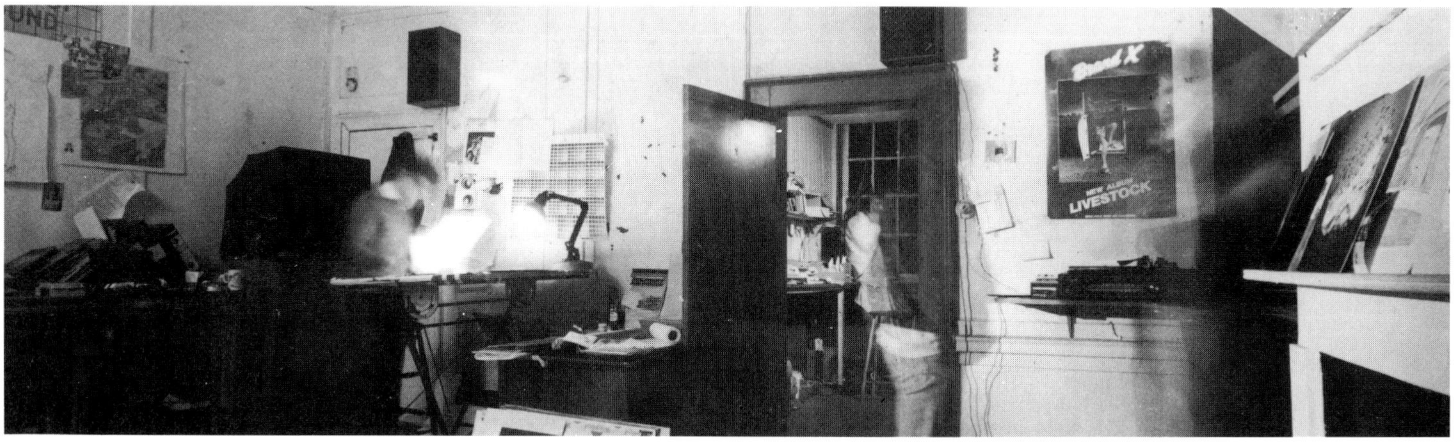

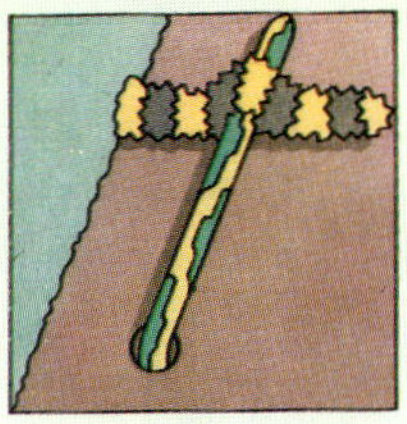

Eric Woolfson and Alan Parsons concocted a thematic record loosely based on the works of Edgar Allen Poe. The music was a mixture of classical and rock. Alan Parsons is a producer of other artistes' music but this record was his own — the beginning of a sequence of producer's recordings in which no band or vocalist was particularly featured nor was the music ever intended for stage performance. The music is carefully arranged and excellently produced. They wished, therefore, for what they called a 'classy' sleeve design. In addition, the package would include a booklet of lyrics, lengthy credits and a chronology of Poe's life.

Poe was preoccupied with entombment. Many of his characters have been incarcerated in some form or other — in coffins, brick walls or under floorboards. We came up with the 'taped' man — a mummy-like figure who is wrapped, not in bandages, but in 2″ recording tape. This motif is partially horror-like, as well as being 'entombed', and the 2″ tape appropriately suggests that the album is done by a producer in a studio, as opposed to a band recording material they will play on stage. Although the clients were intrigued by this idea they did not desire a pictorial cover but preferred instead a precise graphic representation. This narrow strip of illustration from George shows a long shadow of the taped man.

The booklet (attached to the inside of the cover) is composed of photos related to the songs, and line drawings which explore the taped man as he thrashes about in his restricted world and strives to unravel himself. The illustrated capital letters continue the idea. The layout and drawings are by Colin Elgie. The sleeve is one of our better attempts at combining photographs and illustration.

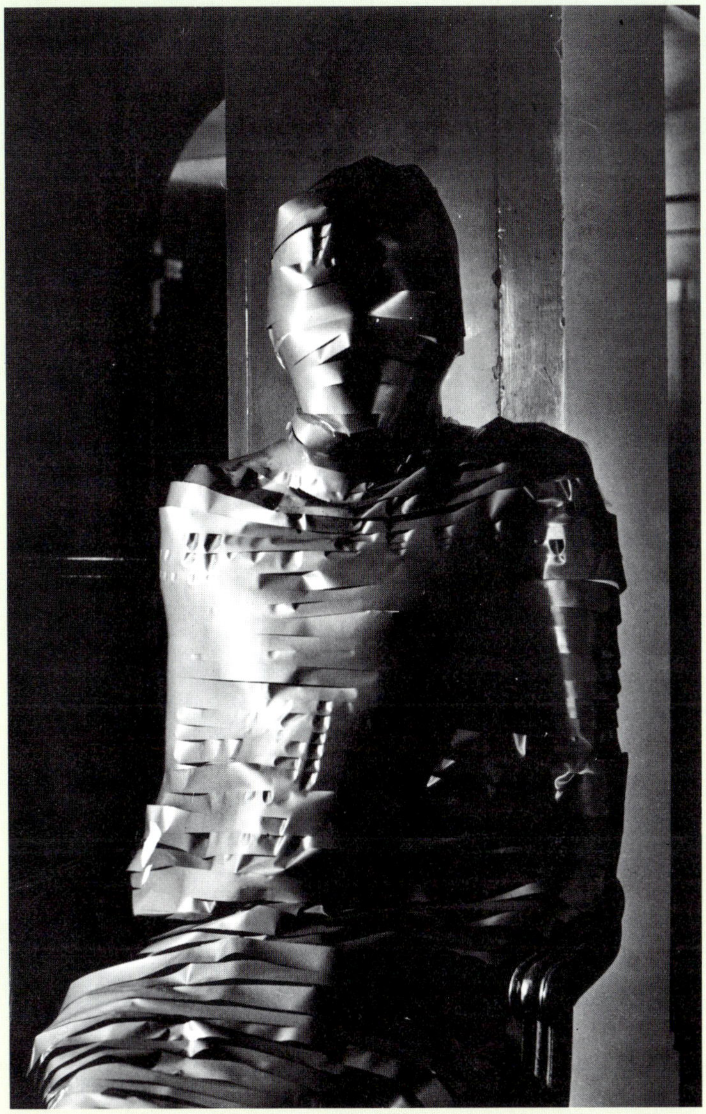

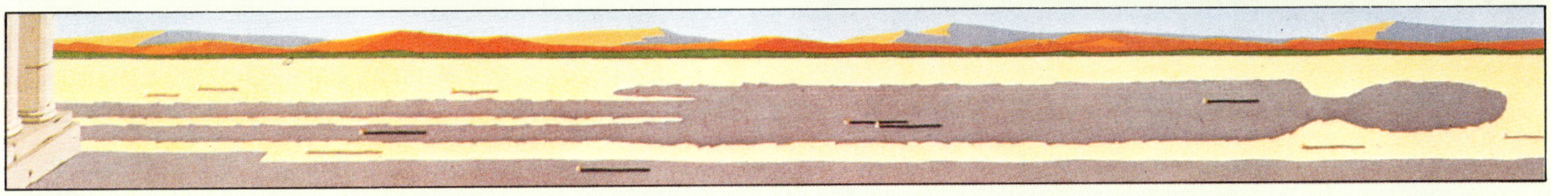

1976 ALAN PARSONS 'TALES OF MYSTERY AND IMAGINATION' ILLUSTRATION COLIN ELGIE ▷

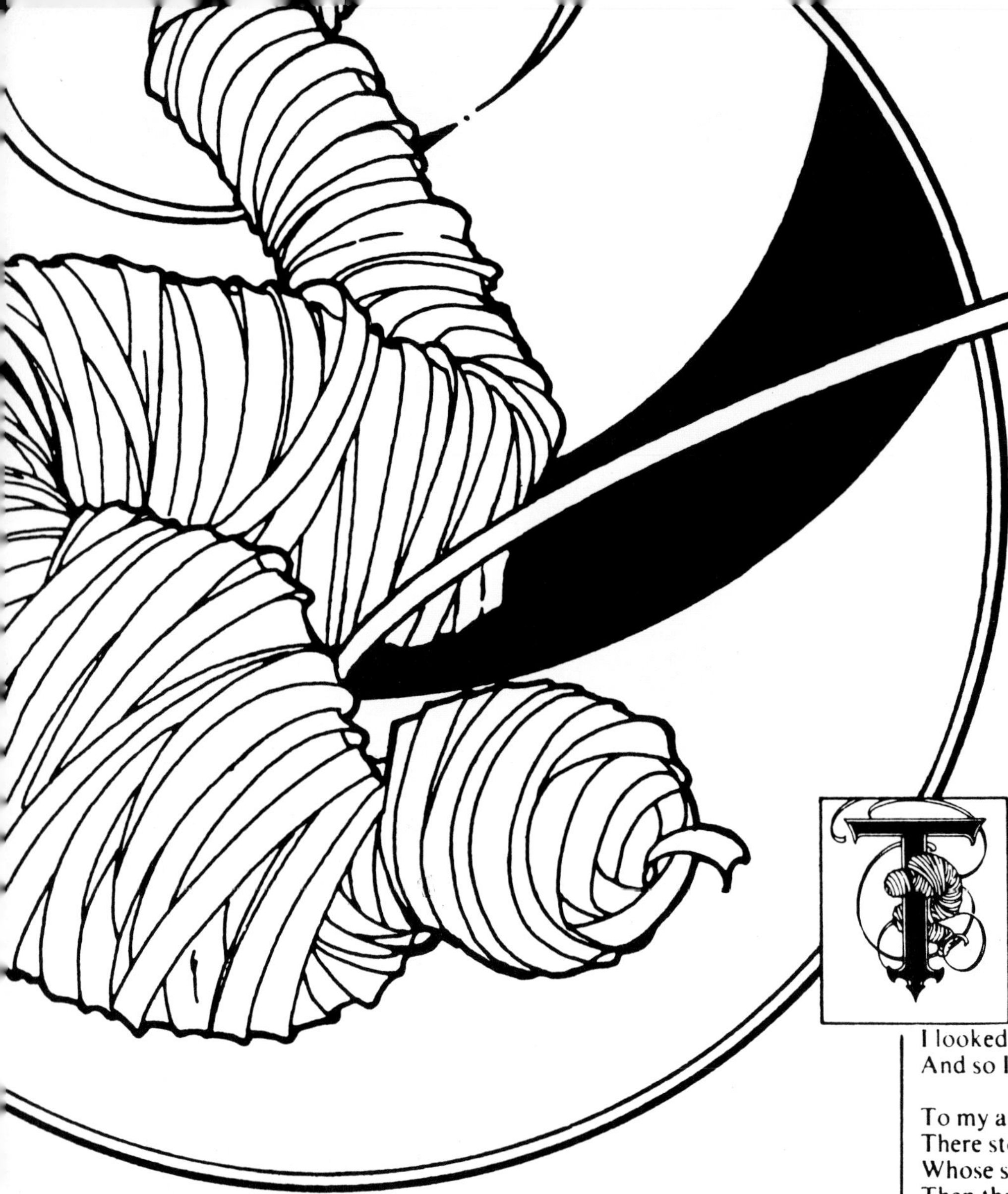

THE clock struck midnight
And through my sleeping
I heard a tapping at my door
I looked but nothing lay in the darkness
And so I turned inside once more

To my amazement
There stood a raven
Whose shadow hung above my door
Then through the silence
It spoke the one word
That I shall hear for evermore

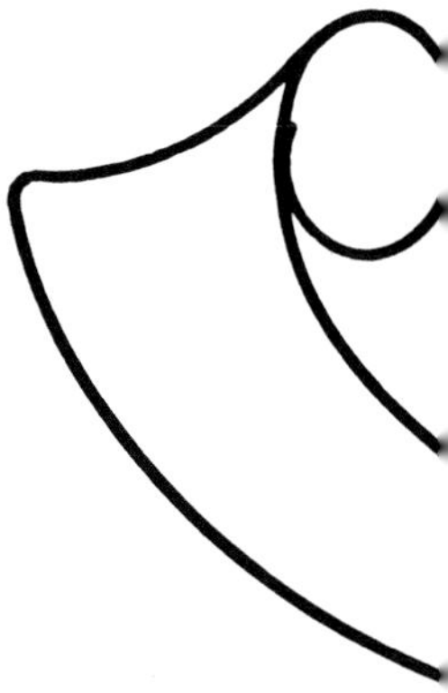

Nevermore
Thus quoth the raven, nevermore

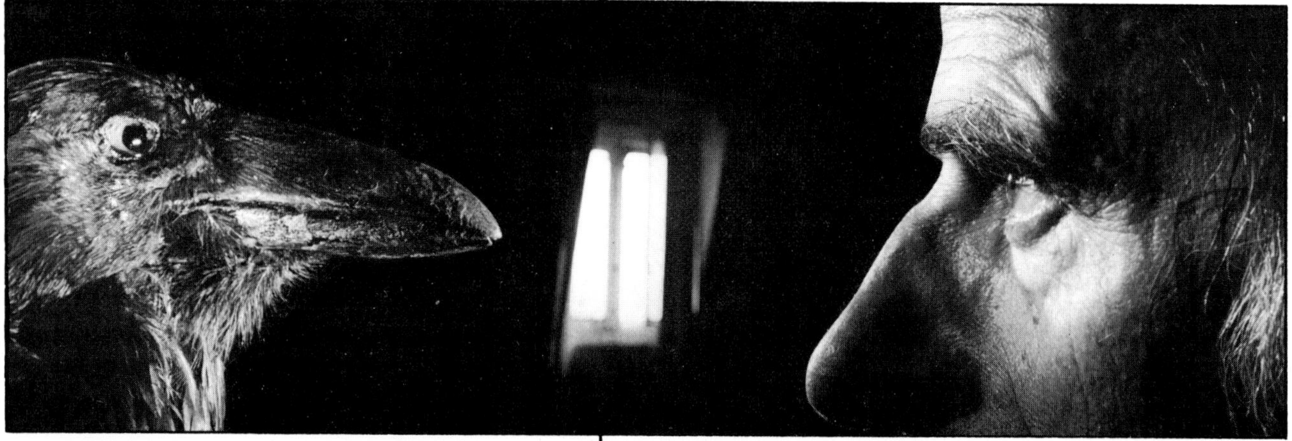

And still the raven remains in my room
No matter how much I implore
No words can soothe him
No prayer remove him
And I must hear for evermore

Quoth the raven, nevermore
Thus quoth the raven
Nevermore

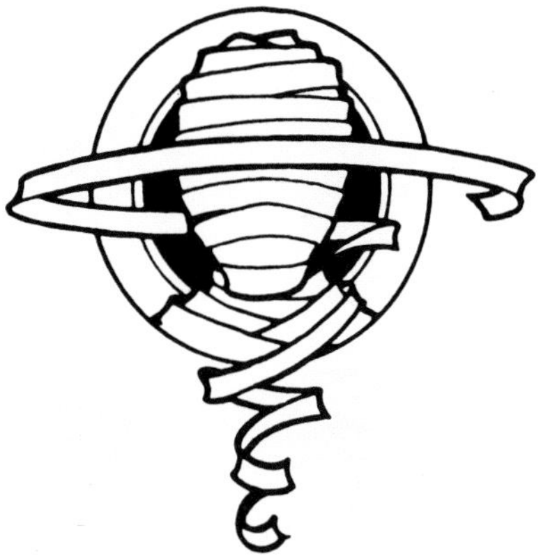

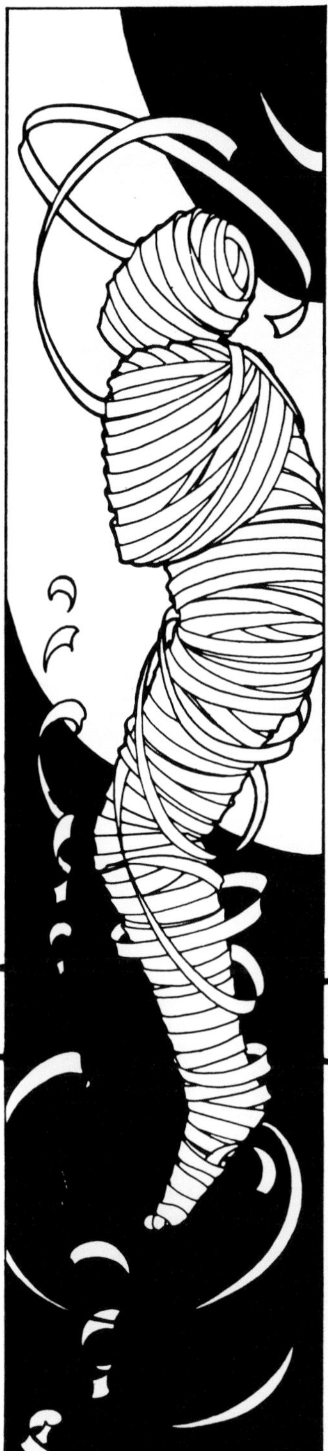

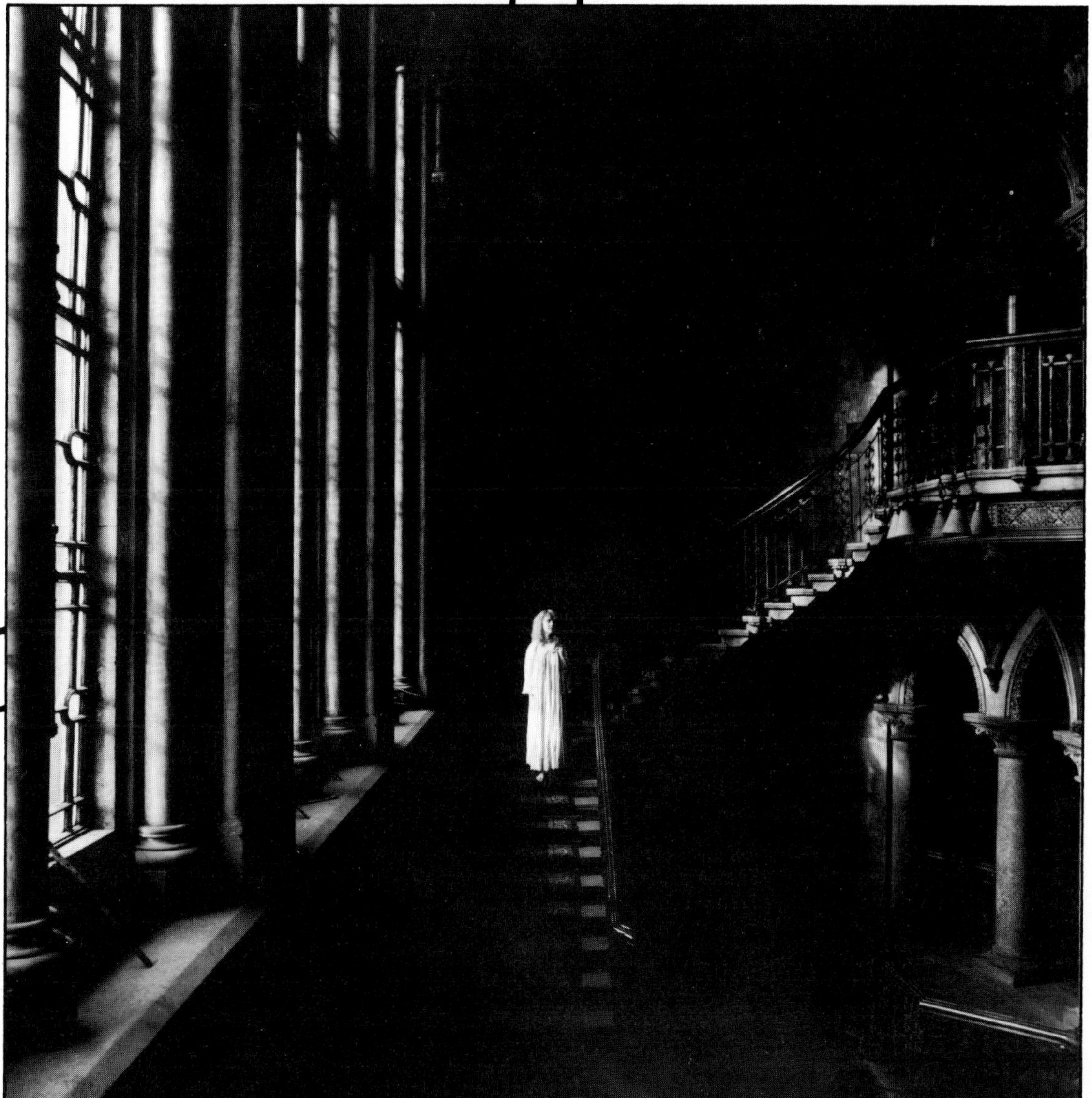

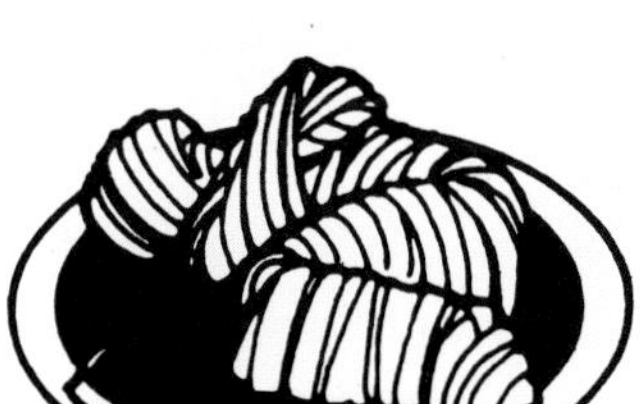

We don't really know what a good album cover design is. We can, perhaps, say that such and such is a nice picture and may well be a good cover design — but then again, it may not. In a sense it's not even that interesting a question because as often as not a good sleeve is not a good design and even less a good picture. Clearly this word 'good' that I'm using so freely means something quite different to different parties.

I'm guessing but I suspect that a good cover for the artiste is one which appropriately represents his music, helps promote his image and sell his albums. The record company may well feel the same things though in a different order. For a member of the public a good album cover is one that turns him on by showing a picture of his favourite artiste or providing written information or simply delighting him with its design — the more ways the better. And a good cover for the designer is one that represents the music and satisfies the artiste, but which also 'works' for him artistically.

I think what works for a designer is something that he feels realises his intentions, that both he and the viewer enjoy looking at in the fashion intended as well as in any other way. We personally like to share a 'good look' — something we ourselves have enjoyed looking at and enjoyed inventing to be looked at. This enjoyment may well relate to other feelings and ideas that the design conjures in the viewer. It may even re-enthuse the viewer in the general art of looking, reminding him to look better and that to look, like to taste or touch, can be pretty rewarding in itself.

I'm a lot less clear about how a cover works for a record company because it's not the cover that people are buying. Common sense suggests that if a design is moving in some way then D.J.s might mention it (more air time), reviewers might refer to it (more column space), retailers could enjoy it (more display space), and people who saw it might tell their mates about it — all as a bonus to the music on the actual album. Perhaps a design can be a visual mnemonic like a catchy tune and therefore promote the album by being easily remembered. In the end it may just be a matter of personal choice by the artiste — it's not a proven economic necessity to have any particular kind of cover design — and perhaps it's simply better news to have an evocative picture, whether portrait or abstract, rather than a boring piece of shit. Yet these possibilities are unknown and in terms of the money laid out, it's the music that matters — anyone who buys a record for its cover has got to be a little crazy, or very rich.

However, cover design has been a very conscious matter for many years now, which is fine when good designs are forthcoming but depressing when they are pretentious or over serious. The cover is, after all, what one usually sees first and record companies are concerned with it in terms of what is commercial or saleable. They are not sure of the connection between commercial design and improved sales, but they think there is one. Simon and Garfunkel sell millions with a pleasant but unmoving portrait whereas Zandor and the Brown Warts may have a stupendous eye-popping cover design yet cannot sell a bean. It is a difficult problem to elucidate. I visualize marketing men going bananas trying to anticipate what could possibly help them. For better or worse they and their art directors seem on the whole to incline towards clear, striking and impactful imagery, bold lettering and up-front portraiture, or design that is dynamic, weird and contemporary but not too risqué, and is above all tasteful and appropriate with regard to the market at which the album is aimed.

As often as not the commercial outlook actually comprises a misconception of what is saleable, an attitude which forever believes that the public are intrinsically a bunch of sheep and will continue to like the same thing over and over again. The subtle and esoteric approaches, for example, are prohibited unless the band is large enough to demand what they like and would sell even in a cover designed like a serviette. Rock and roll is by nature changing all the time; what is fashionable varies yearly and hence what's commercially viable, whether in terms of the music or cover design, varies accordingly. In the mid-sixties psychedelia was predominant; in the mid-seventies Punk rock, at least in London, has a similarly idiosyncratic and pervasive style. I lament only that record companies generally retreat into tastefulness and predictability in the face of this dilemma. This is the crux of the matter, for if tastefulness and predictability become synonymous with banality and boredom (which they usually do), then we want no part of it.

Of course, what may work for us may not work for the record company and this can develop into a serious disagreement. It comes to a head over schedules which the record company need to maintain for manufacturing or promotional reasons when the criteria, say, for assessing the need to do extra work are not mutually agreed upon. They may think us fussy for being concerned with details that couldn't affect sales and which most people 'would never notice'. Apart from the possibility that this attitude belittles the public, which is unnecessary and probably untrue, we are working to criteria connected to the artistic goodness of the design and not to supposed commercial viability. At these times I wish in my heart that they would strive for good records and good designs and let schedules go to the wind. But we do work for musicians; it's their record and their cover too so when we wage battle we try to do it for them as well. To get the design right for us is hopefully to get it right for the artiste. That's the intention anyway. Ideally we wish to do a pic-

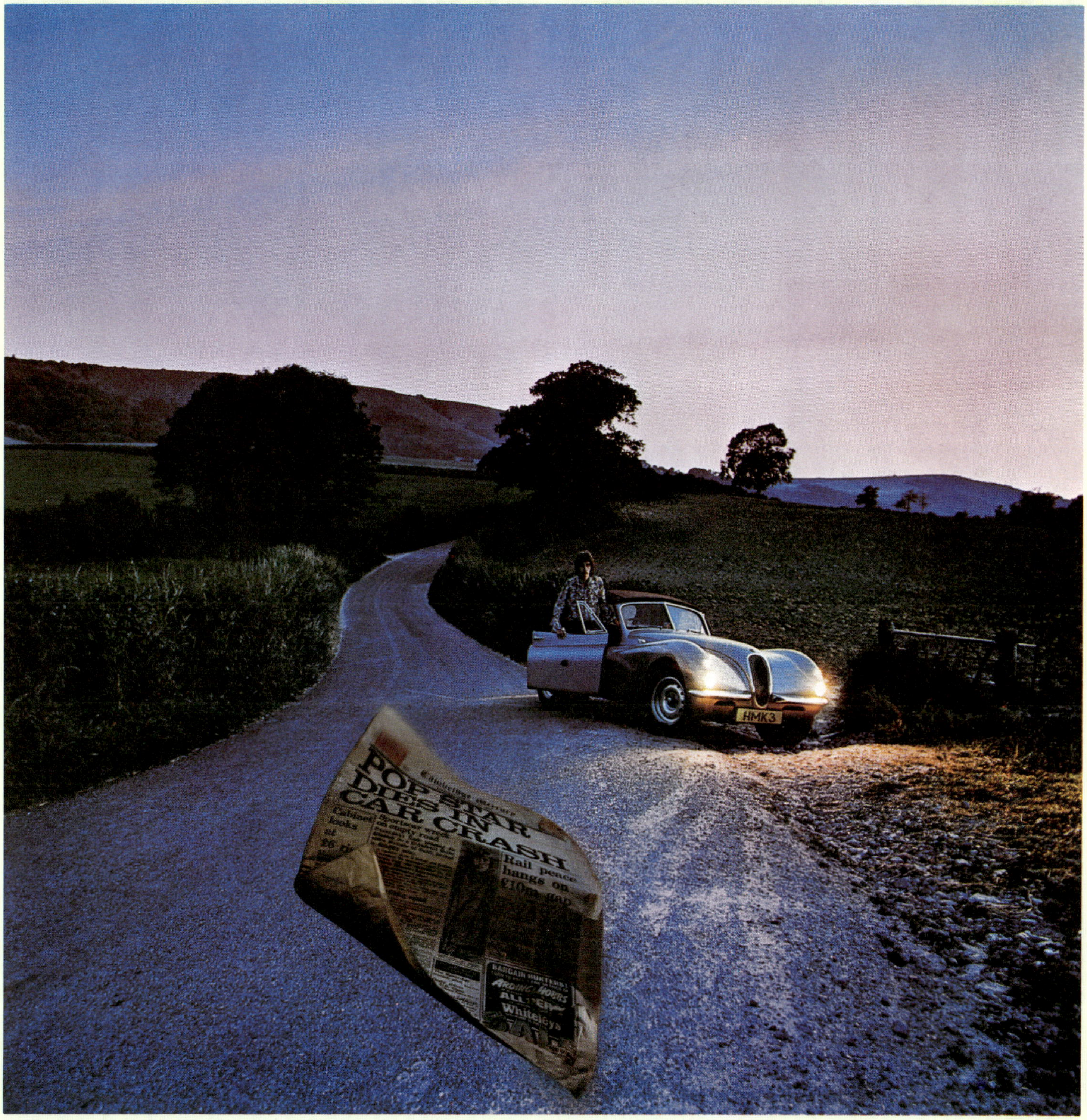

HEAVY METAL KIDS 'KITSCH' FRONT COVER

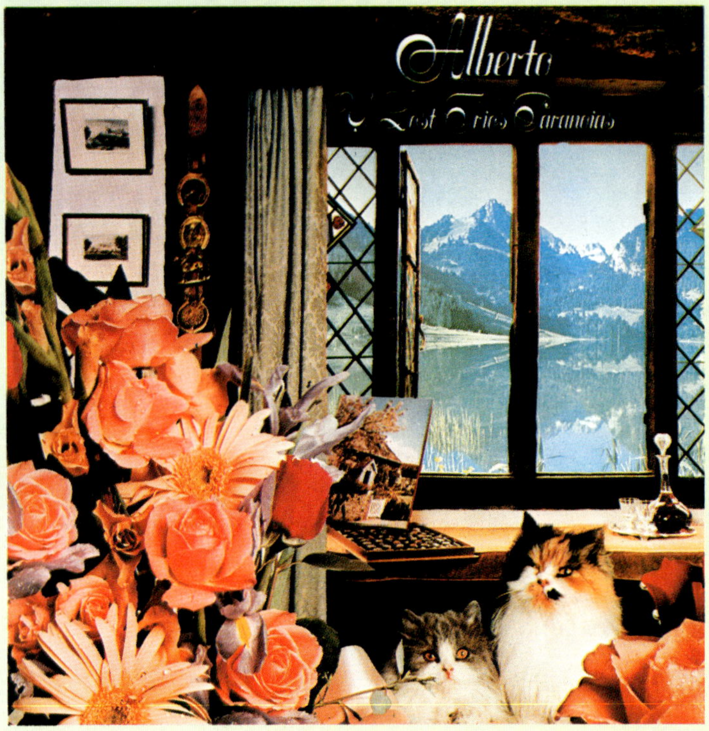

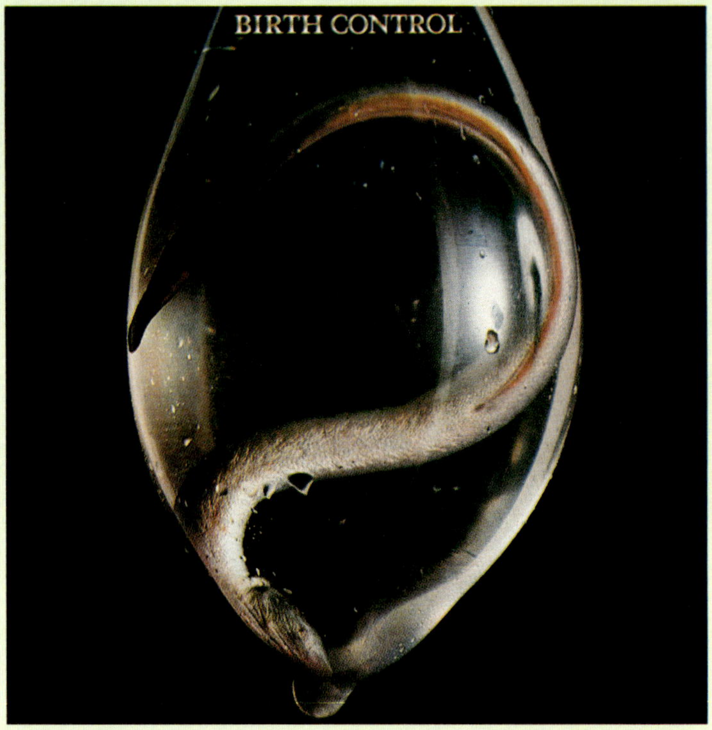

ture that moves the viewer at first and then later, and doesn't simply evaporate after the initial impact.

But enough of this, back to the matter in hand. This section is composed of pieces that are a little tasteless in some way (though not necessarily in contradiction to the tastefulness which may be envisaged by record companies).

'Kitsch' for the Heavy Metal Kids is interesting because we used a piece of our own that we'd done a year previously for Pink Floyd. It had been rejected on the grounds of intellectual simplicity. Kitsch implies, I would think, a serious intention to be good and meaningful but fails because of its naivety and gawdiness. Kitsch is both loved and reviled for the same reasons. Somehow its attractiveness lies in its tastelessness. Since it was the album title we thought up several kitsch situations, mostly sentimental or irreligious, but because we actually liked the photograph of the car in the country lane for itself, we also suggested that. It comes as quite a shock to realise how kitsch you can be when you're trying hard, perhaps, to be the opposite.

The Alberto's sleeve is an over conscious attempt at subscribing to 'tastefulness'. A satirical gross-out, in fact, as mushy as a chocolate box. This was a definite contradictory cover — not the way we imagined the record company would ever think to promote the Albertos at all. Nor what we thought that the public would expect — Alberto, the 'unexpected', so we designed the unexpected. Not so original perhaps but successful in a way because it was so like the sleeves we were satirising that record stores thought it was the real McCoy.

SHOCK ROCK DISC GETS THE CHOP
—Sunday People, May, 1976.

"The sleeve of a British pop group's latest record looks like the sort of L.P. you might buy mum for her birthday.

"On the record, being sold by Boots and W. H. Smith, a pretty Alpine scene with two cuddly cats gives the impression of folk songs for family listening.

"But, after the Sunday People stepped in, the two famous High Street chains were withdrawing the record from sale.

"Because the songs played by Alberto Y Lost Trios

1976 ALBERTO Y LOST TRIOS PARANOIAS

1971 BIRTH CONTROL FRONT COVER

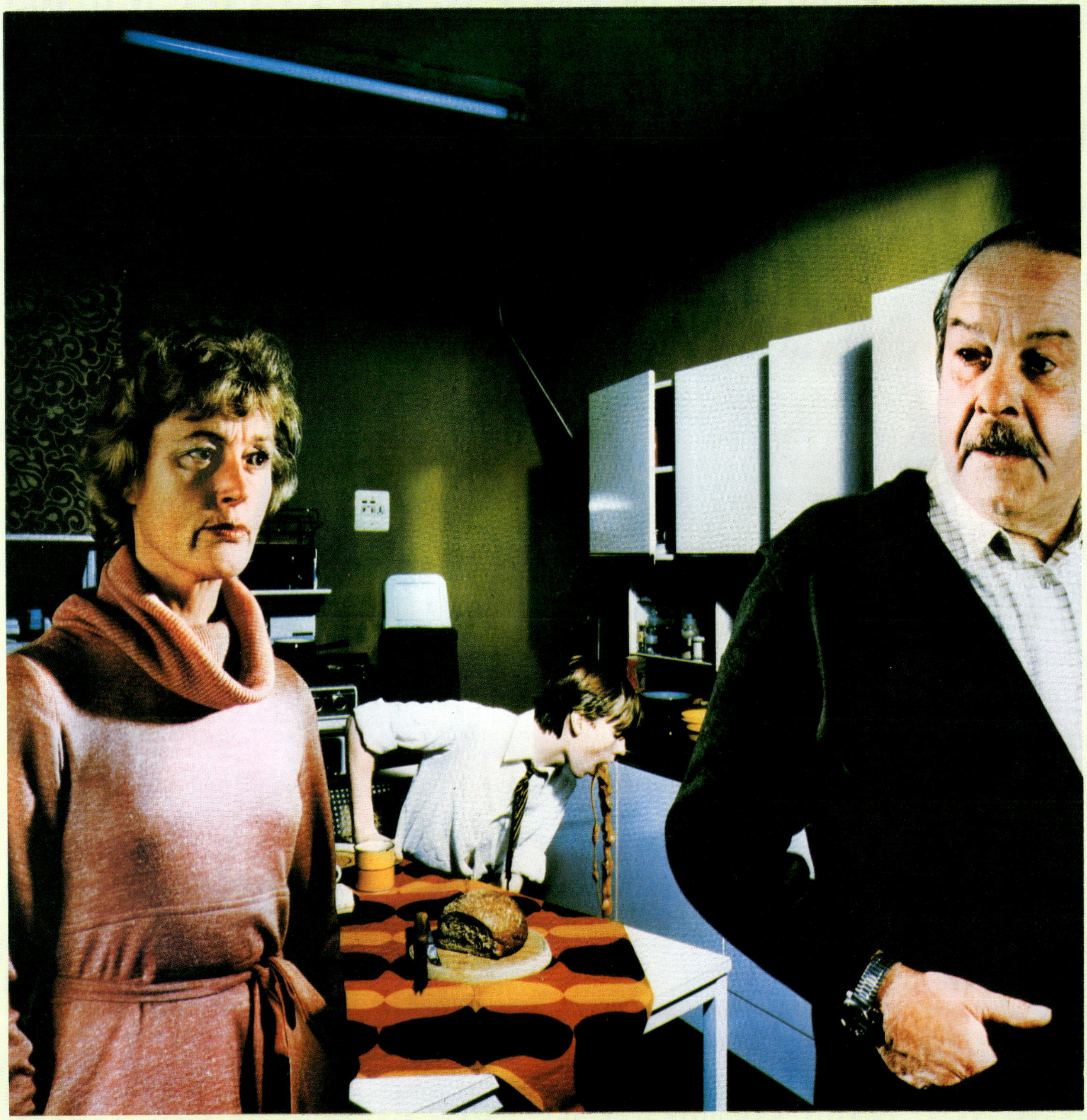

1977 CORTINAS 'DEFIANT POSE' SINGLE'S BAG

EDGAR BROUGHTON BAND ▷

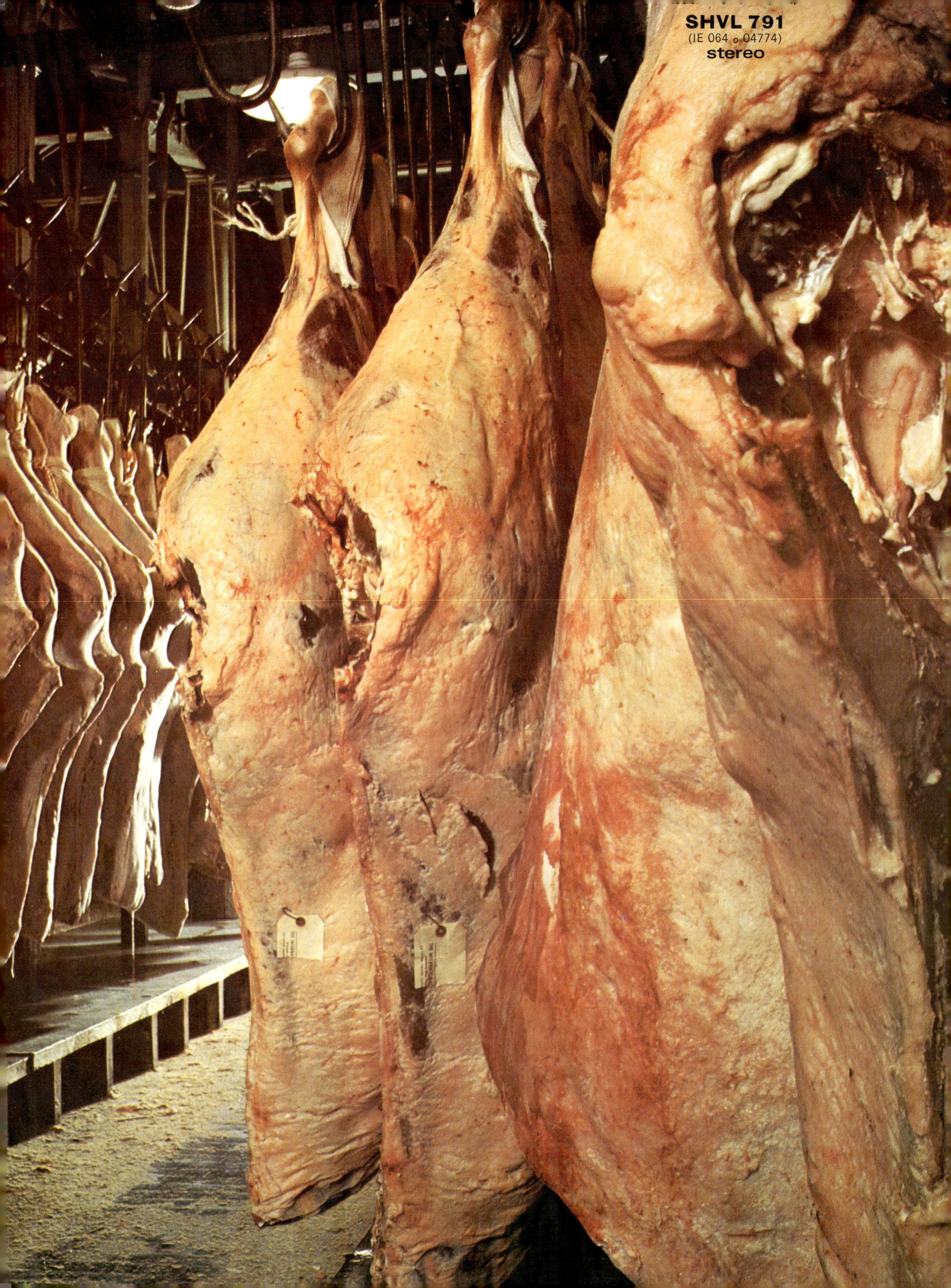
SHVL 791
(IE 064 o 04774)
stereo

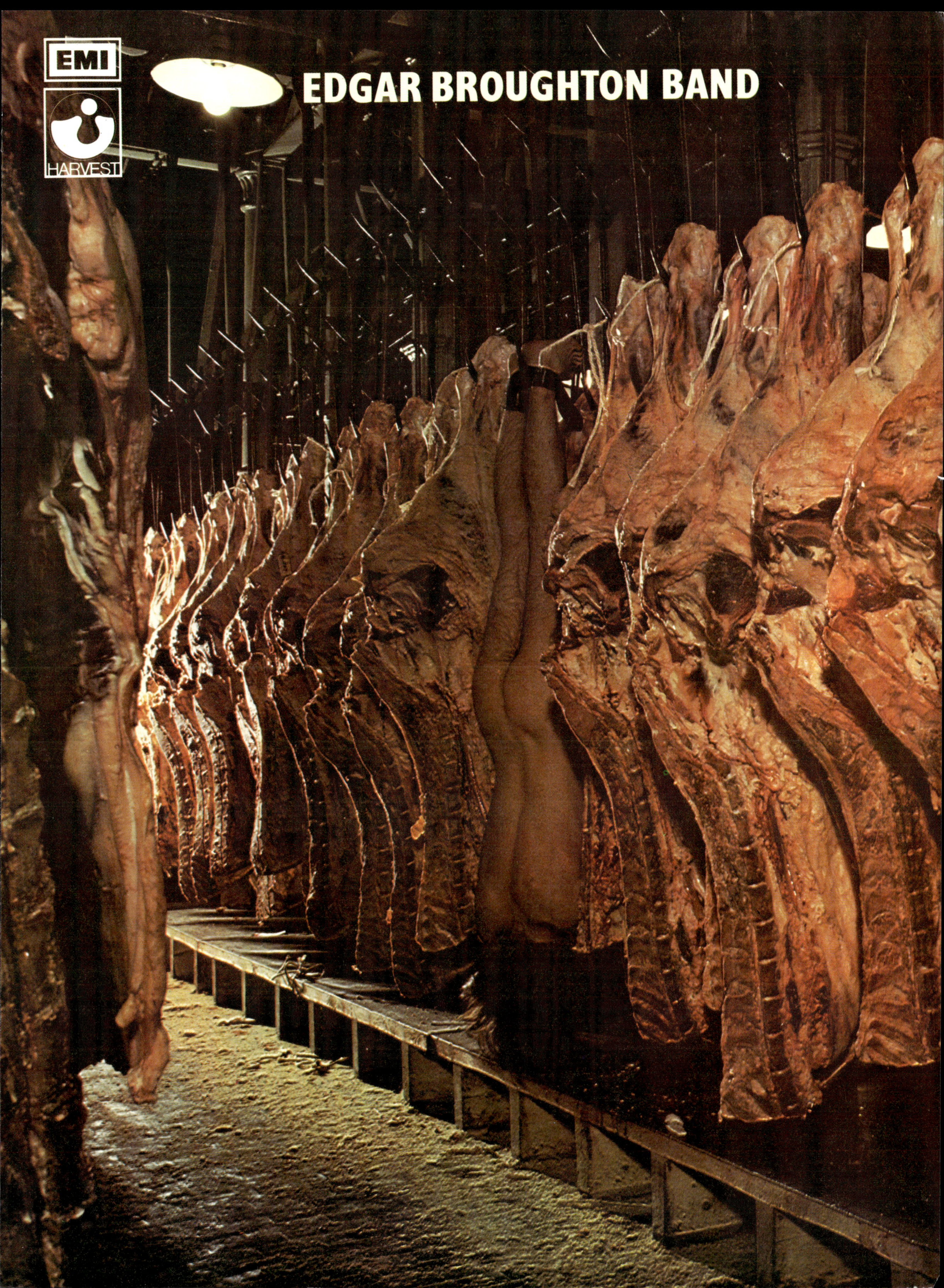
EMI
HARVEST
EDGAR BROUGHTON BAND

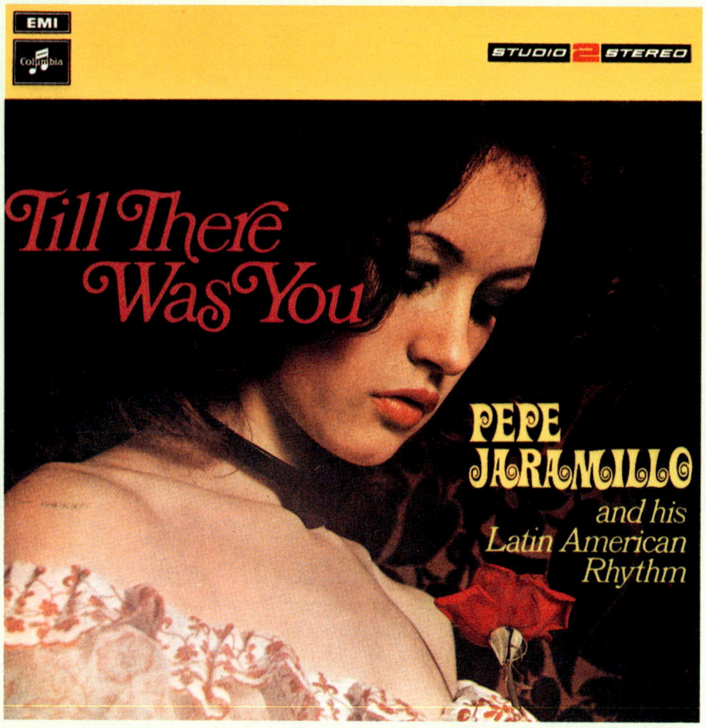

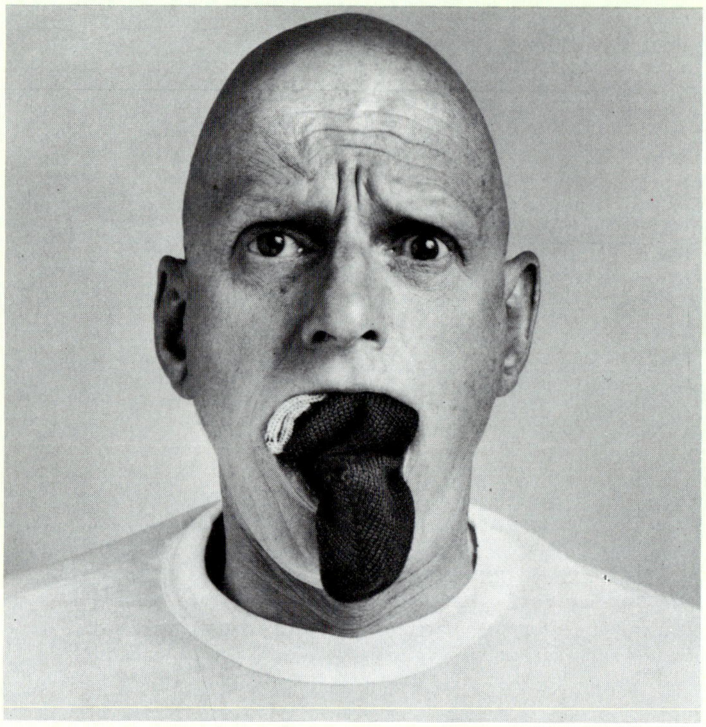

Paranoias, six lads from Manchester, are better suited to an ORGY.

"Titles like 'Torture You', 'Dread Jaws', and 'Dead Meat' feature lyrics about depravities like sadism, masochism, bondage and physical abuse of children — with four-letter words for good measure."

Pepe Jamarillo is middle of the road music. This sleeve is straight down the line and utterly tasteless as a result — it doesn't even work as a genteel piece of middle class tweeness. 'Birth Control' was simply considered offensive, but the Germans (it was a German band) thought it really weird. I was again exasperated by the English record company's inability to respond to the design's hidden depths — the mixed sexuality of its imagery. Have they no taste?

Edgar Broughton Band was greeted by the marketing director of EMI with cries of dismay. Pacing nervously up and down, clawing at his chest neurotically, he stomped away, describing it as one of the most disgusting things he'd ever seen. But then he didn't put the clappers on it because the band were, how should I say . . . very 'demonstrative'. Always saddened me that he never appreciated its Marxian qualities — the dehumanization of the assembly line.

'Tightly Knit' is an early design of ours and is a photographic rendition of the well known phrase 'put a sock in it'. Say no more. The photo for String Driven Thing is part of a domestic nightmare. Commonplace habits become horrendous, simple procedures appear impossible and the household objects seem to conspire against you. An everyday act as simple as cleaning the old choppers develops into a battle — the tube of squeezed toothpaste looms far larger than usual and the pendulous gooey paste is poised to engulf you. Sensual but repellent. 'Defiant Pose' for the Cortinas, a new wave band, is a singles bag which, I trust, speaks clearly for itself.

PEPE JARAMILLO 'TIL THERE WAS YOU'

CLIMAX BLUES BAND 'TIGHTLY KNIT'

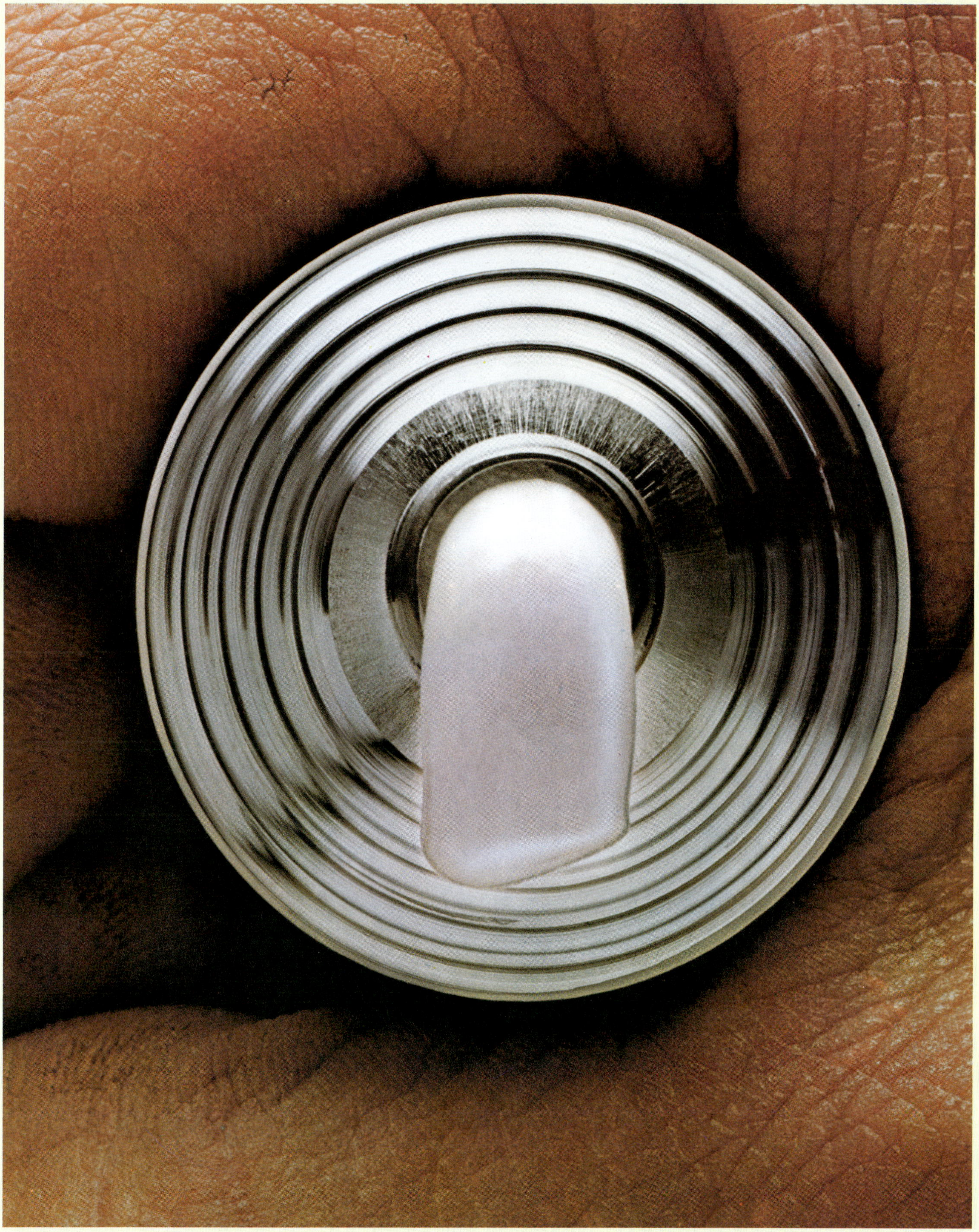

STRING DRIVEN THING 'KEEP YOUR HAND ON IT' FRONT COVER

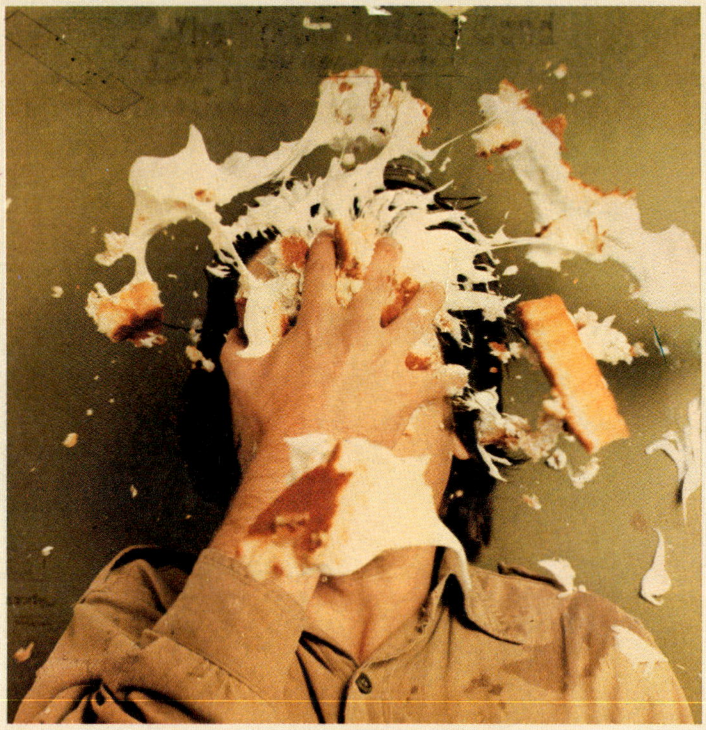

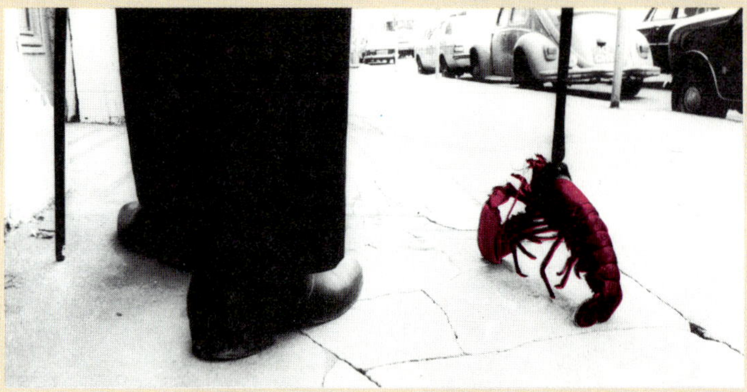

Like a recurring tune that a fellow cannot get out of his brain so some ideas just won't go away, even when they have been turned down by clients time and time again. Perhaps we should not be so surprised. Most of the ones here have been considered too unkind or too 'heavy'. Maybe the intended humour was not strong enough to overcome the logic of such a view. However, the time has come to reveal them to you, the public. At last.

When we begin a job we usually come up with three or four suggestions and these roughs are examples of how ideas are initially submitted and we have, therefore, left them in the state in which they were first put together. These designs were thought up at different times and have been shown for subsequent jobs when they were felt appropriate, hopefully not all at the same time and not to the same client twice! We can't always remember what has been shown and what hasn't, and have got ourselves occasionally into very embarrassing situations. I suspect that some clients would take it amiss if they knew they were being shown an old idea but I sincerely believe there is nothing so very bad about this because basically it's a question of appropriateness and if a band chooses a good and fitting design for themselves then it surely does them credit, no matter whose design it is and no matter who may or may not have seen it before. But it's hard to keep a good idea down especially if you really like it. I thought, for instance, that 'Ducks on the Wall' was a piece of genuine inspiration. It was born spontaneously in the middle of shooting a totally unrelated assignment. It wasn't intended for anybody in particular, nor for any specific project. It was admired but never used, remaining unloved till the end. (Pass the handkerchief.)

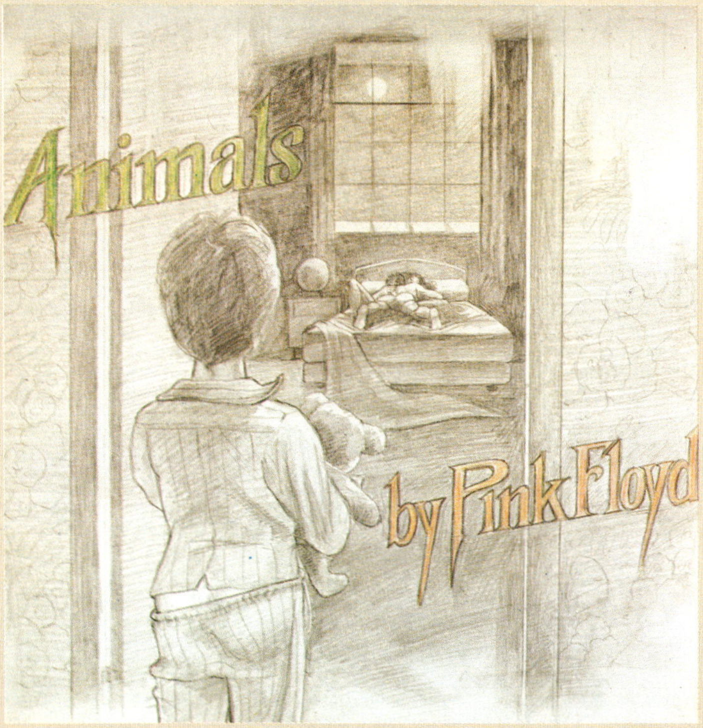

COIT IN THE ACT

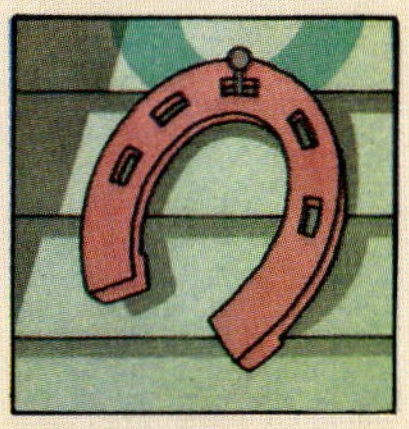

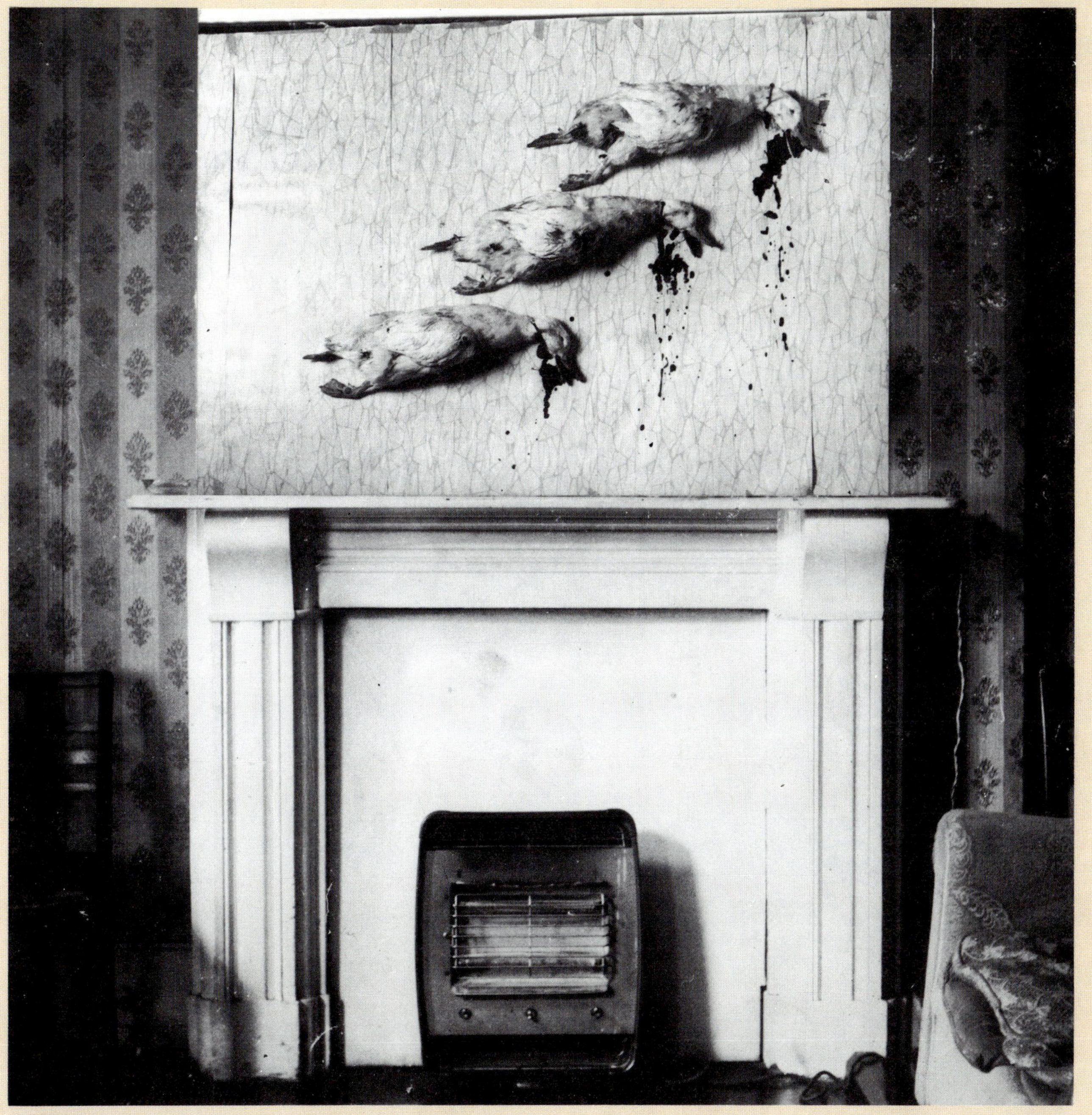

ART DUCKO

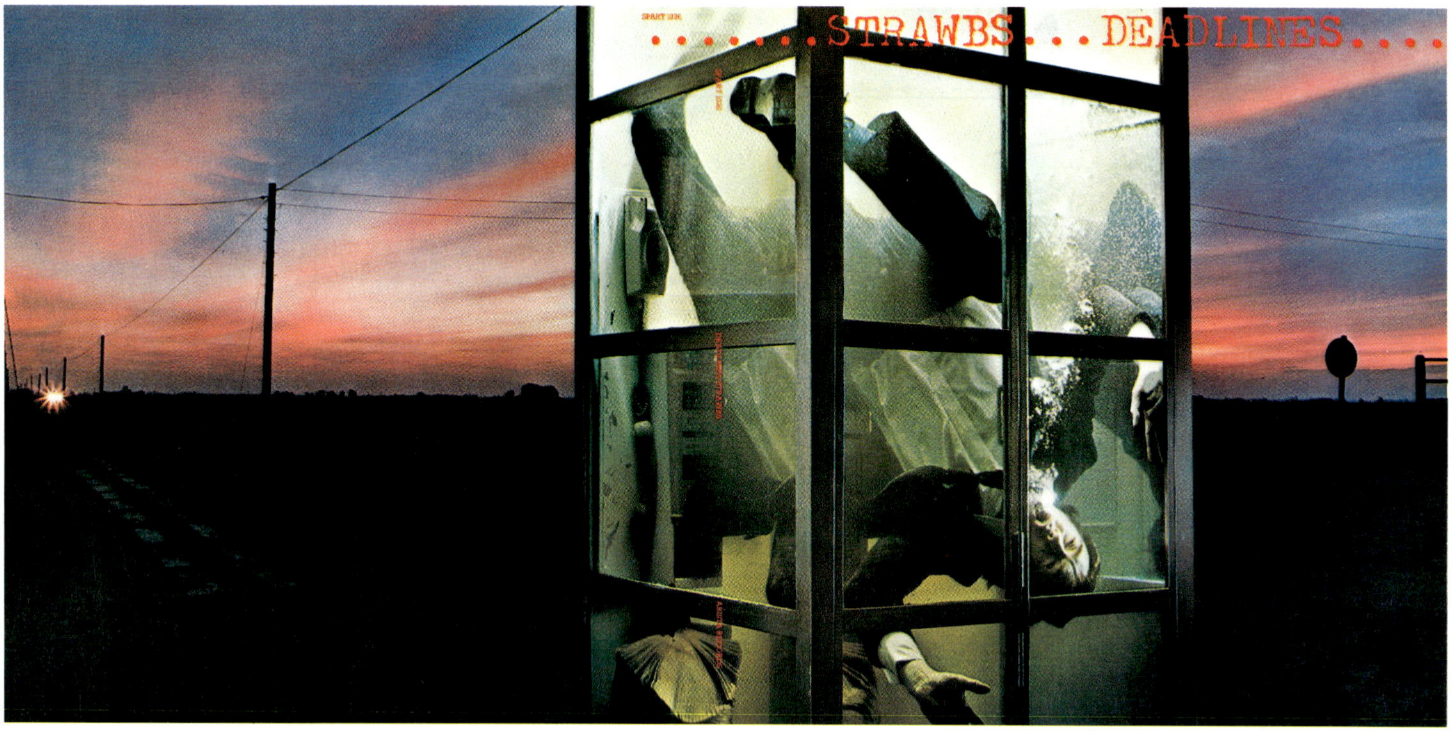

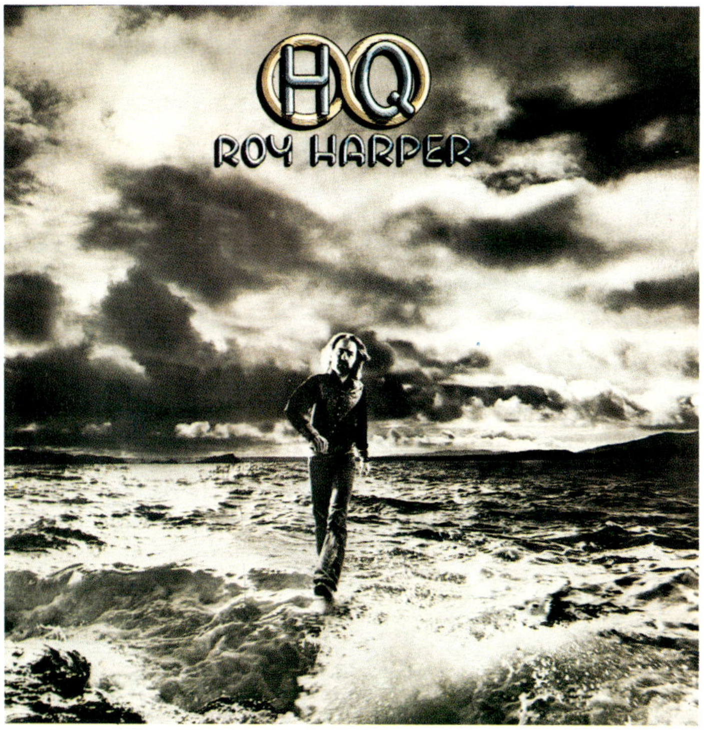

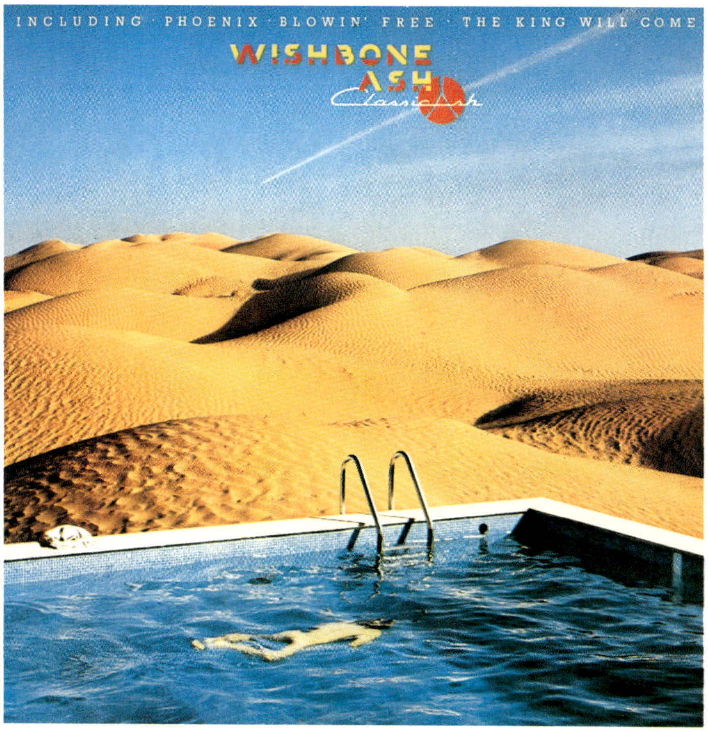

STRAWBS 'DEADLINES' ROY HARPER WISHBONE ASH

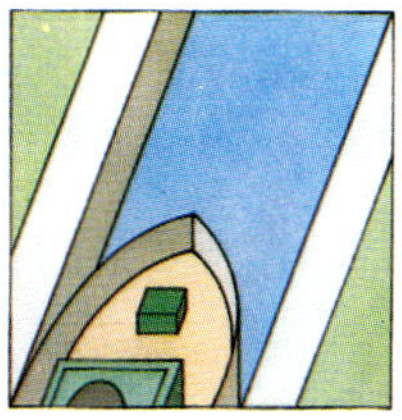

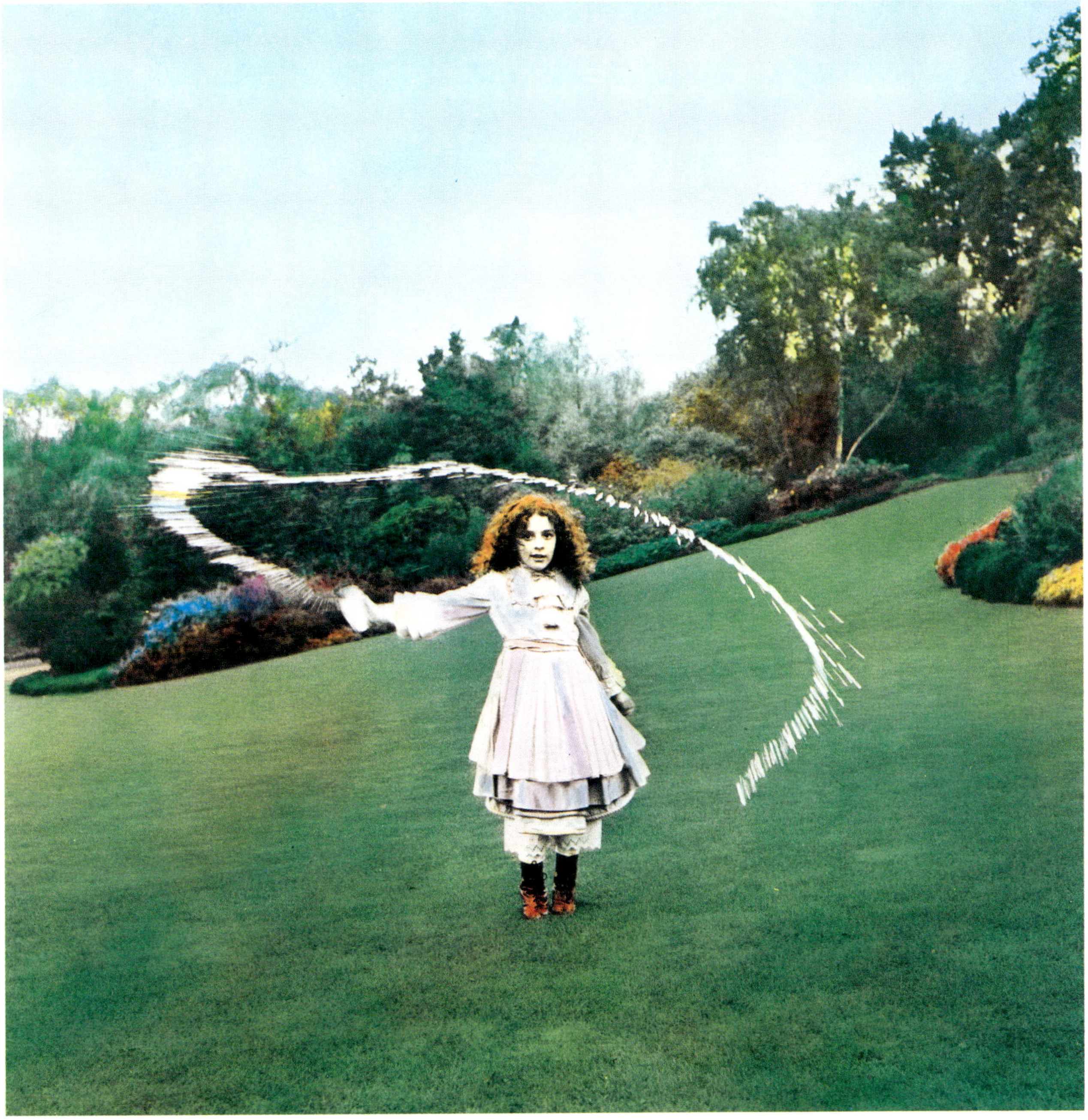

1971 TREES 'ON THE SHORE' CO-DESIGN JOHN BLAKE FRONT COVER

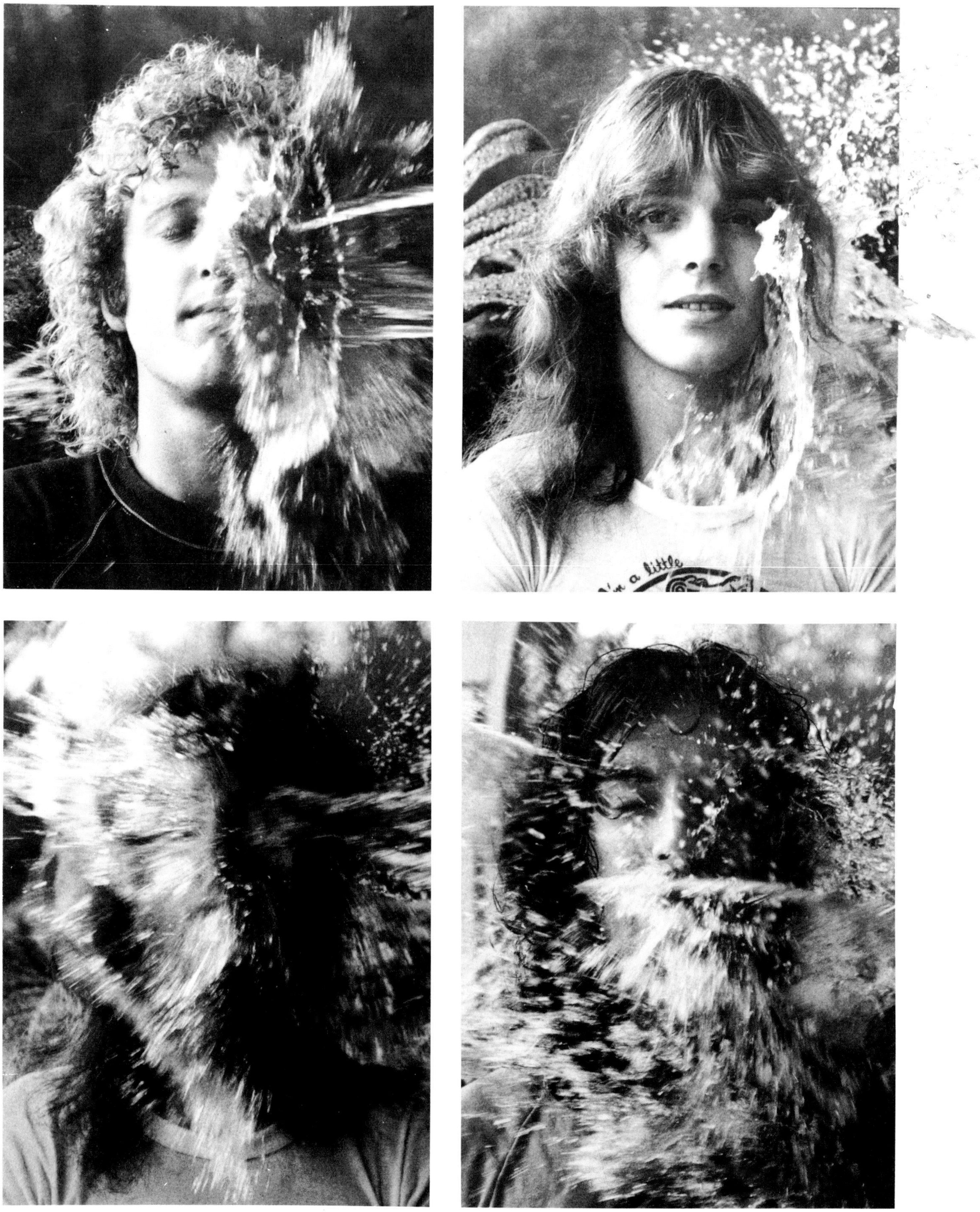

1974 PETER FRAMPTON 'SOMETHIN'S HAPPENING' FRONT COVER & DUST JACKET

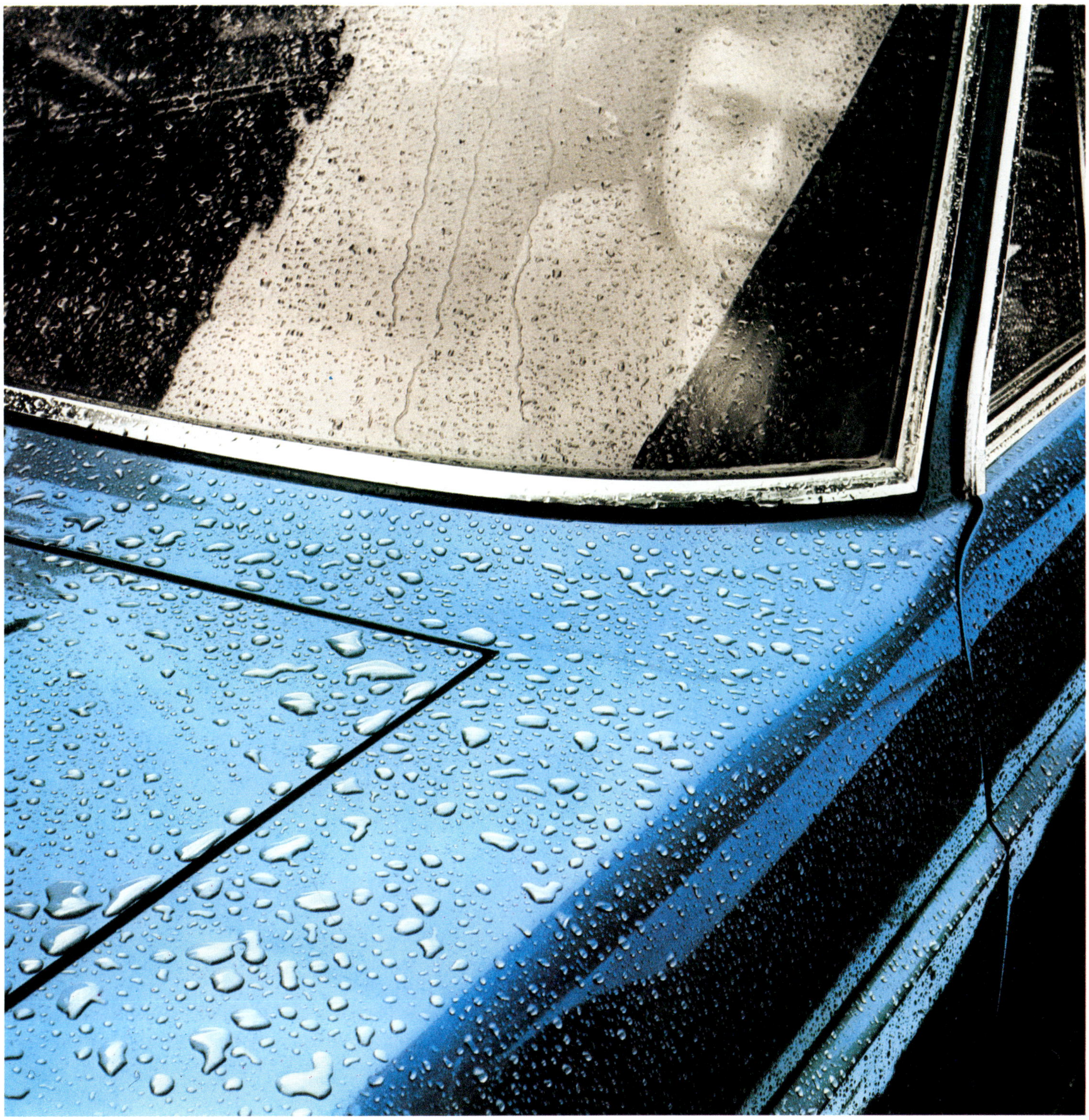

1977 PETER GABRIEL FRONT COVER & DUST JACKET

Pink Floyd first talked about this sleeve on their West Coast Tour in April 1975. At that point there was no specific brief because they didn't have a clear idea of what they were going to record. 'Shine On You Crazy Diamond' was a definite starter but the rest of the material was undecided. 'Shine On' began as an introspective piece — a few haunting bars from Dave and a lyric from Roger. The words were initially about Syd Barrett, but as the work progressed so they became more universal. When I read them they seemed to be about unfulfilled presence in general rather than about Syd's particular version of it — and he certainly had his own unique brand. The idea of a presence withheld, of the ways that people pretend to be present whilst their minds are really elsewhere, and the devices and motivations employed psychologically by people to suppress the full force of their presence eventually boiled down to a single theme — absence; the absence of a person, the absence of feeling.

Two whole months passed and it was still not cracked. I'd returned from the tour by this time and we were having plenty of late night discussions about it. We'd been searching for a powerful metaphor or symbol of absence. We were especially interested in the aspect of absence which involved pretence, something supposedly genuine but that was in reality as phoney as a Nixon denial. Roger was particularly critical of the music business at this time (Have A Cigar) and we finally came up with a handshake. Simple, clear and very familiar. An ordinary handshake can be a physical, touching presence, warm and definite, but it can as easily be a meaningless ritual. It is often an empty gesture, present but absent.

I remembered that Roxy Music's 'Country Life' sleeve so strongly displayed undercurrents of masturbation and lesbianism that it had been covered by an opaque green shrink wrap in the States in order to hide its alleged lewdness. This gave me the idea of covering the record and sleeve in a removable black (or blue) shrink wrap which would be similarly opaque and would hide the sleeve design from the public eye — the cover picture itself would be 'absent'. We chose to make the cover a normal single pocket affair, perhaps with a dust jacket, rather than a gatefold which was too expensive. Shrink wraps are compulsory in America and though they are normally transparent it seemed no real problem to make it black — modern technology could handle that, or so we thought.

The package structure was thus decided before the actual imagery. It also struck us that it would be nice, just for once, to separate art from commerce clearly — to do the sleeve without any commercial considerations in mind whatsoever (no writing, no name, etc.) because it wouldn't be seen. However, the outside needed some kind of labelling for identification, and so the sticker was born. The idea is that the shrink wrap is one cover for the trade, and the actual sleeve is another cover for the public. (The visual psychology is different; the experience of seeing it from three to ten feet in a shop is not the same at all as holding it in the hands at home when there is time to ponder over it and to scrutinize it closely.) This 'personal' design could be composed of very arty pieces, pertinent to the record, yet as obscure as we liked — hence studies in absence.

Now, there are four members of Pink Floyd and four separate 'faces' to the cover — the single sleeve (2) plus the dust jacket (2). It felt appropriate therefore, to use an idea we'd had previously involving nature's four elements — earth, air, fire and water. In addition, the four elements have mystical and alchemical references that would, in part, reflect aspects of the Floyd's music.

At the time we were also exploring frame breaks, ways of trying to suspend disbelief for a moment, as if a design were really in three dimensions instead of just on a flat surface (see Ummagumma, 10cc, etc.). And so we set about thinking up four pictures about absence, a different element featured in each design plus a frame break on the white surround, as though the cover itself was a piece of white card with a rectangular hole in it through which you looked at a slice of reality — namely the picture we would design.

I was explaining to George a particular notion I'd had about people who retreated and withdrew their presence from others. If they were to expose their full nakedness (their full sensitivity) to any experience their sense receptors might become overloaded and thus impaired, perhaps for ever. I reckoned that people were frightened of getting scorched at the nerve ends, of getting burnt, especially if they had been burnt once before. Like falling heavily in love, and then being suddenly jilted. "That's it," he said, "someone actually burning, someone on fire, the flames licking around them." Yes, I could see it, a startling image, especially if we were to do it for real! (And this can be seen in the sequence included at the beginning of this book.) And the person on fire could be a business man shaking hands with a colleague, standing in some slightly bizarre yet empty setting. It struck us, also, that 'getting burned' is a phrase used in and about the music business for not getting paid, or for not making a profit from some risky but colourful venture.

This was enough to provide an idea of how the sticker should look. A mechanical pair of hands shaking (Machine Song) which traverse a circle divided into quadrants (the four elements). The title appears round the outside and the illustration is very colourful, to stand out against the opaque cellophane wrap. In further group discussion we arrived at the diving man. This idea is a reverse of the imprint left on a bed by someone who has

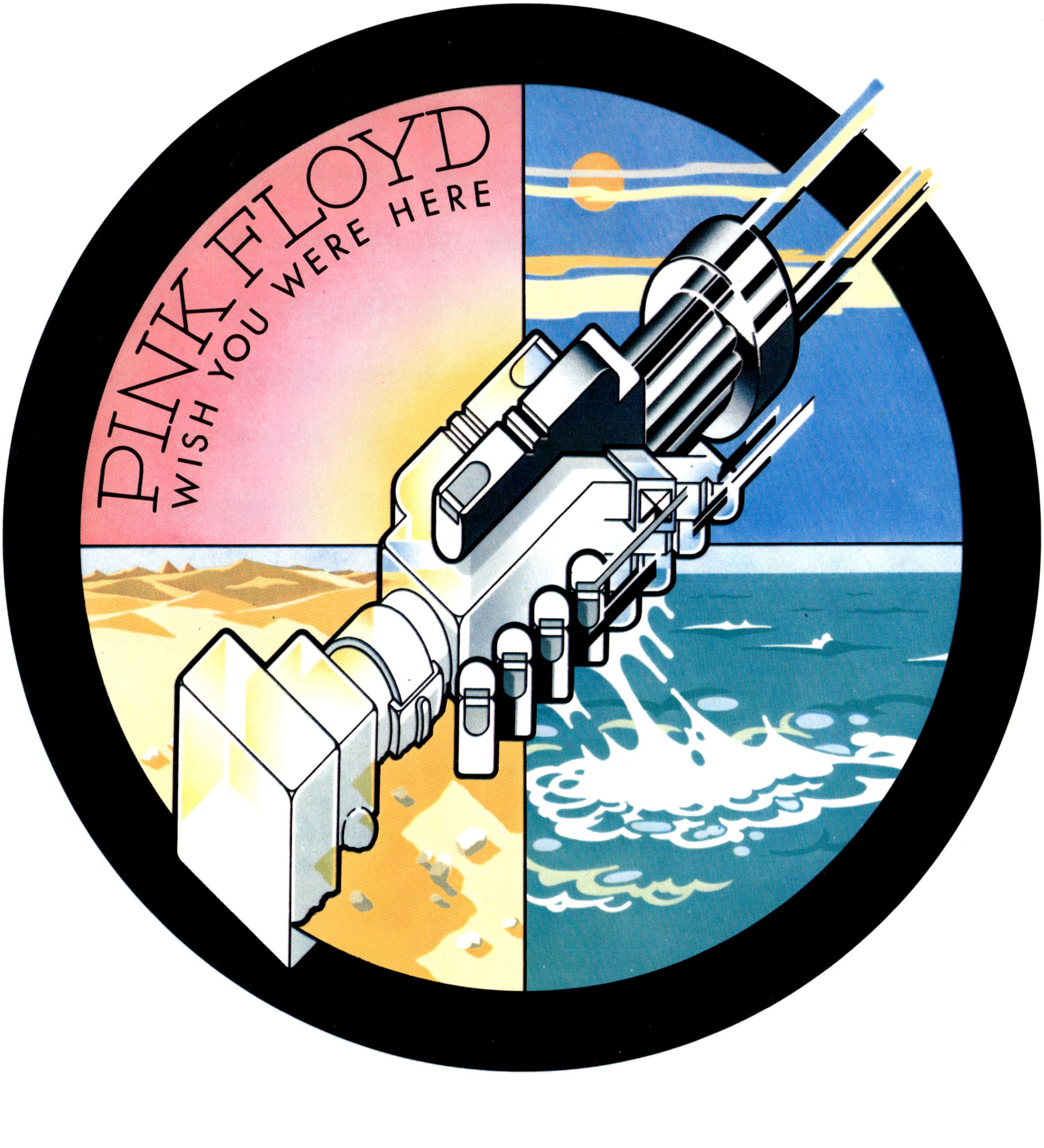

1975	PINK FLOYD 'WISH YOU WERE HERE'	ILLUSTRATION GEORGE HARDIE	STICKER

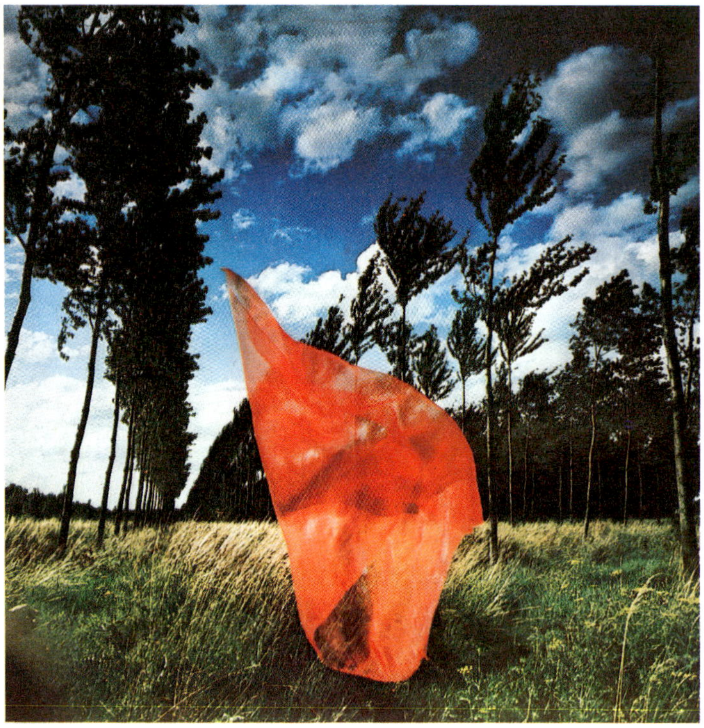

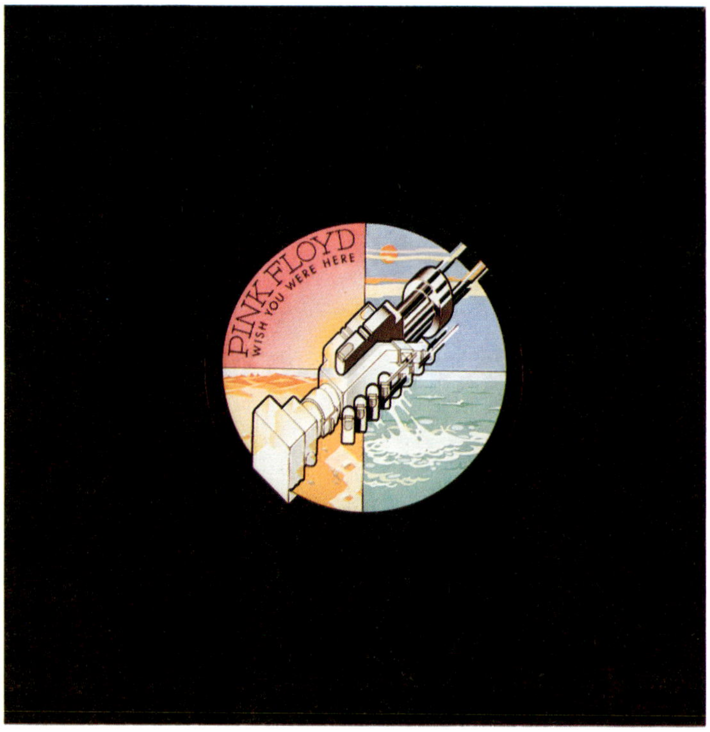

just vacated, where there is *trace* but no *presence*. In our picture there is a diver (presence) but no splash (trace). Also there existed this mirror idea that was, in fact, never used. It showed a couple kissing in front of a mirror; in the reflection the man is missing (his mind not on the job) and a wind or vortex blows through the room caused by his 'absence'. We shot it twice but it never really came off. The last study in absence was a salesman selling his soul. His physical presence is not there — no wrists, no ankles and no face. He is pushing forward a blank record (clear plastic) for he is, in fact, a Floyd salesman, his briefcase bedecked with appropriate stickers. The mirror shot was replaced by a pseudo mystical piece inspired by a line of lyric out of 'Machine Song'. It was about the arrival of a premonition, which if true would mean that its subject could not be there to receive it. Floyd thought it naive and were perhaps right, but it was a great photo and so it resurfaced for Kitsch (see Tasteless). Pity really, as I liked the reference to wind, blowing the newspaper up the country lane. John Blake suggested using a veil — symbol of absence (departure) in funerals and also a way of absenting (hiding) the face. This was the last shot. All the pictures were to be atmospheric like the record and the whole package was intended to have several meanings and to evoke, hopefully, several different moods commensurate with the breadth of the music. The rationale behind the pictures is only relevant for us and for those who want to know — the pictures have to be evocative on their own.

Now, the whole production cost plenty because we decided to shoot it for real and to do all of it in the States, bar the veil picture which was photographed in Norfolk. The photography took three weeks and was an exhausting adventure. The desert is the Yuma desert in Southern California. The town we visited was only a truck stop and everyone there seemed to be wired out on speed, driving dune buggies at breakneck speeds at night, their radio pole lights making them look like small sea craft as they plunged recklessly down steep troughs in the sand. Our cameras fell off one of these buggies and caused severe anxiety whilst we had to backtrack and find them. Lake Mono, for the diving man, was located only after extensive aerial reconnaissance of California in a private plane,

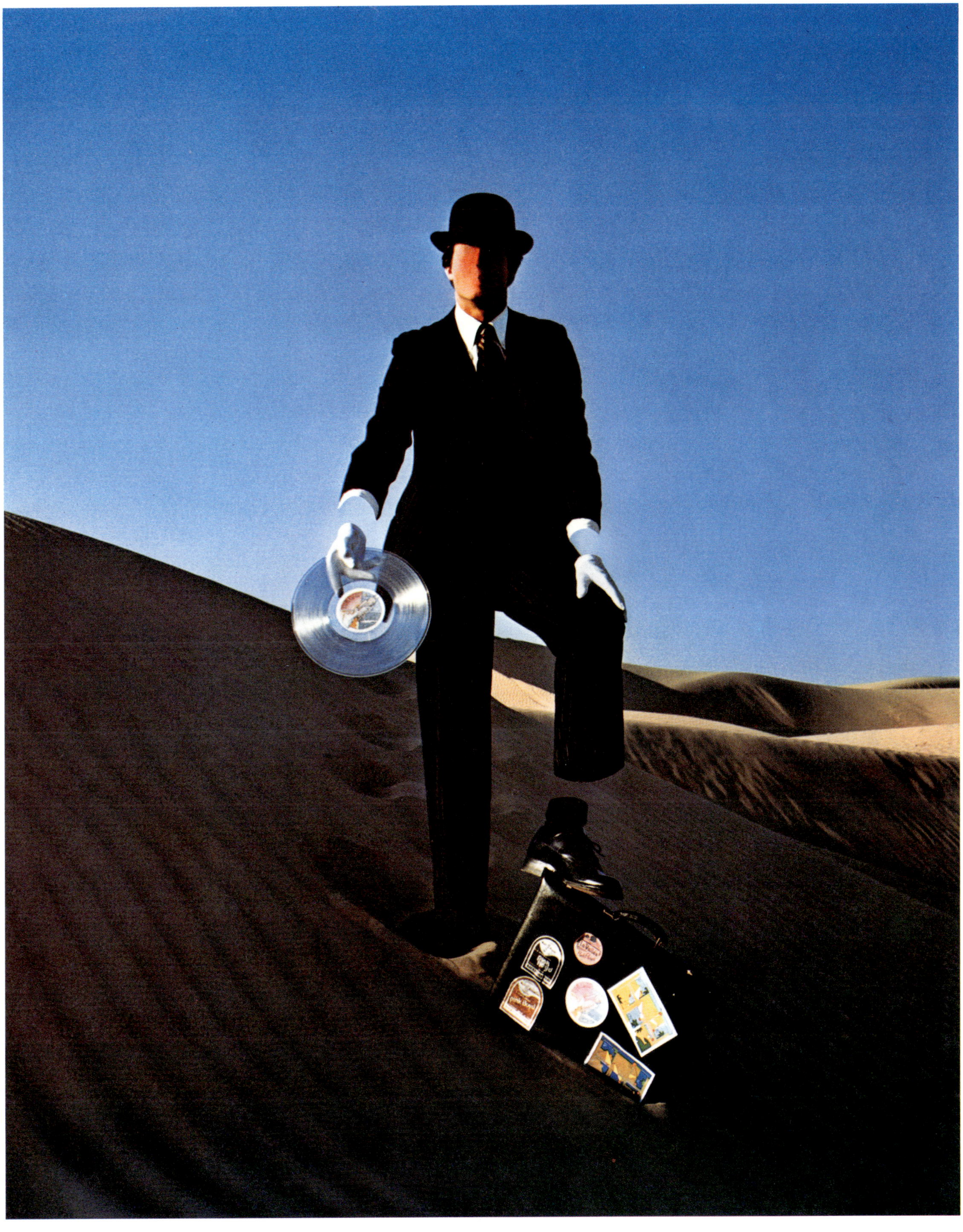

1975 PINK FLOYD 'WISH YOU WERE HERE' BACK COVER

but it was well worth it. The diver is performing a yoga headstand in the bucket shaped frame embedded on the bottom of a shallow part and remaining submerged for as long as humanly possible so that the ripples died away. The fire man was shot in Los Angeles at the Burbank Studios lot. It took a week to find the right location and arrange the stuntman and what with fixing the desert trip and looking for lakes, it was all hard enough . . . but then two days before the first shoot, coming back from an all-night party, Po's car burst into flames and was slowly burnt down to the chassis. Peter and Po got out alright but what an omen! Hipgnosis remakes Towering Inferno.

The black shrink wrap was not such good news for it turned out to be very difficult to produce and to cost an awful lot of potatoes. Added to which, the American record company couldn't for the life of them understand why we were covering up "such great" graphics. In England the shops hated it because they wanted to show the sleeve (especially without a record in it, for fear of pilferage) but when they took the shrink wrap off they couldn't put it back again — this was very frustrating because the cardboard sleeve had no name on it but the shrink wrap did. EMI omitted to send the dealers a whole load of empty sleeves for display.

The title was ours, as was the logical suggestion of a postcard, as an insert. The American version had a different photo of the fire man from the English one but there was no reason for this other than whim. If we had our time over we might have made the photo of the diver larger on the actual cover, and either the veil or desert man small to accompany the lyrics, and would probably have omitted the frame breaks. A satisfying but flawed piece of work and one of the better examples of us all working together — sharing the designing, shooting by Po and Peter, George doing all the graphics and me doing the artwork. One of the nicest things was that we showed the Floyd only this idea, mocked up as if shrink wrapped and they accepted it very graciously with a warm round of applause.

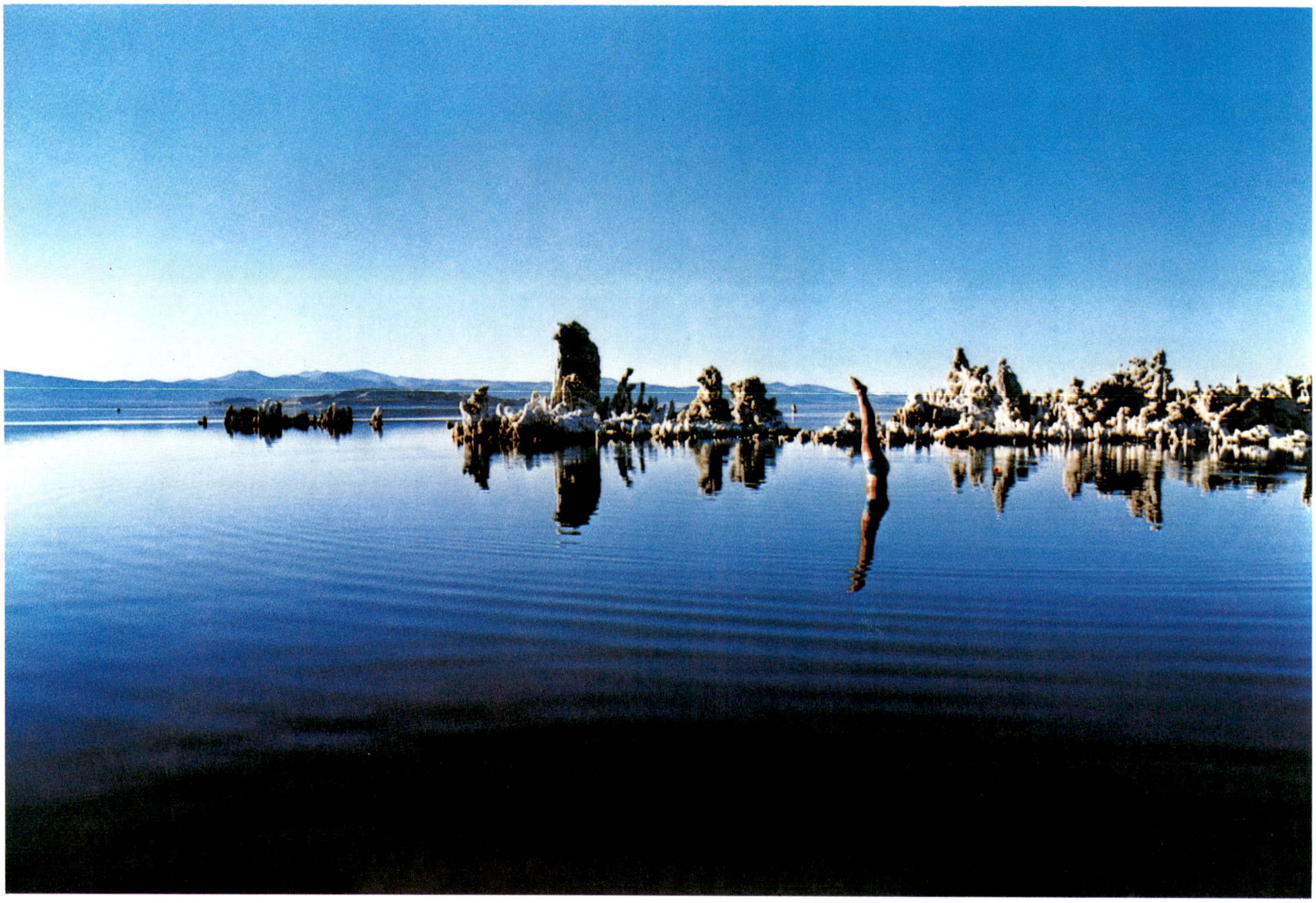

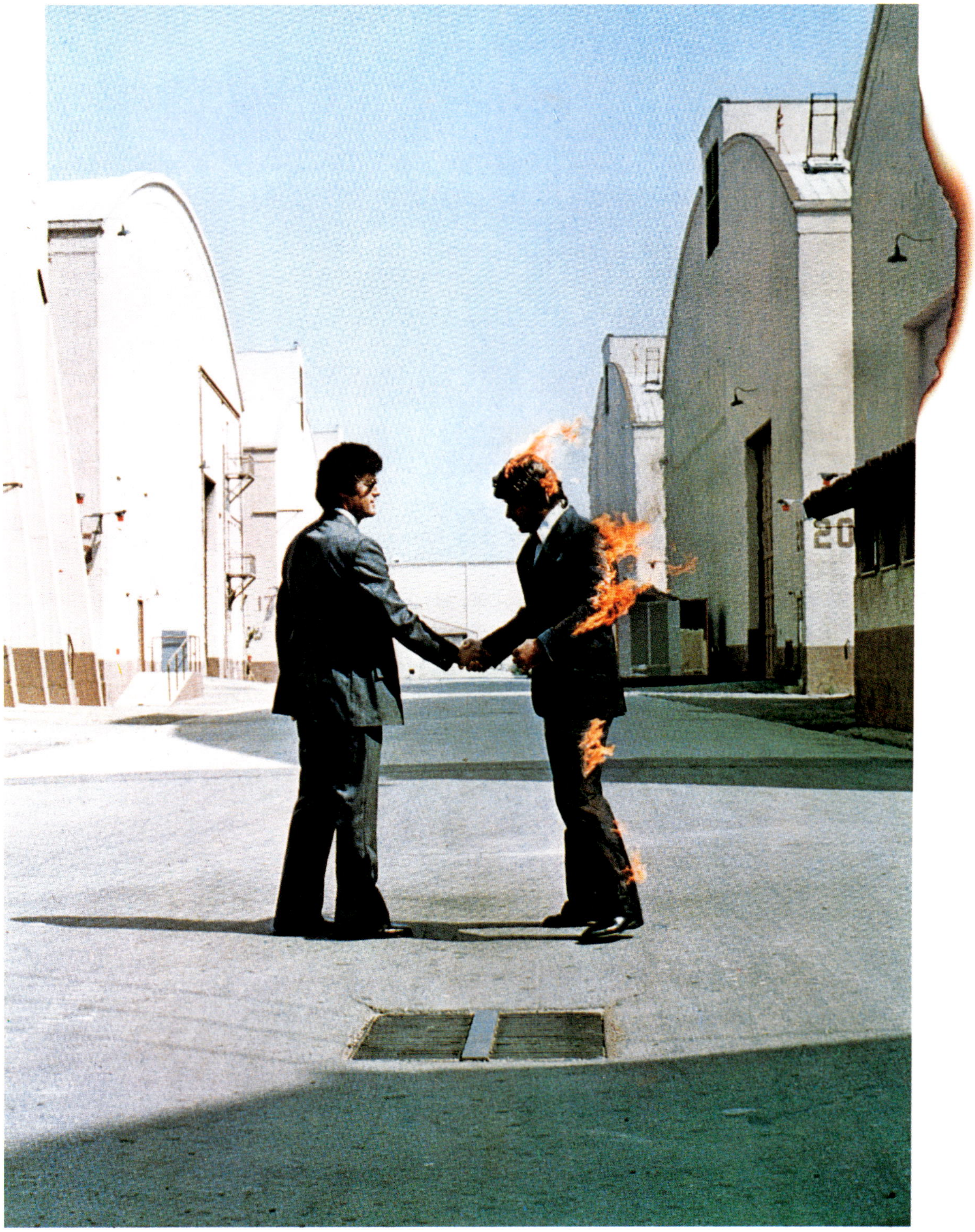

1975 | PINK FLOYD 'WISH YOU WERE HERE' | FRONT COVER

The following data is from memory; where it's incomplete is where we've forgotten the details. Designs originate in group meetings or are submitted by individuals to be refined in group meetings. In most instances the actual work is executed in continual collaboration, crosschecking on design features, and exchanging views at any time during completion. Divisions of labour and responsibility are therefore approximate; for example Flash 'Knickers' pg. 22-23 was designed and photographed by Po but the artwork was completed by Storm, whilst 'New England' pg. 21 originated from group discussion but was actually designed and photographed by Peter.

In this appendix we've shown the published items whereas in the book itself we've gone back to original artworks or films where possible. We have only used actual covers on pages of four or more or in the odd instance like Aynsley (pg. 86) where original artworks and negs have been lost.

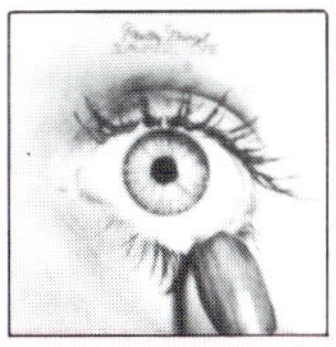

5 Pretty Things 'Savage Eye' 1975 Atlantic Records. Front gatefold cover Hasselblad 500c and 80mm lens + Proxar. Flashlit. Tri X f22 1/60th. Dev D76 sepia toned B/W hand tinted. Lettering Colin Elgie. Design/Photo Storm.

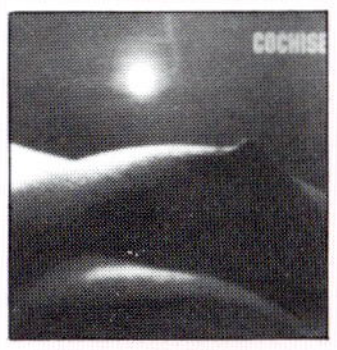

6 Cochise 'Cochise' 1970 UA Records. Front gatefold cover. Nude photo Nikon F 35mm lens infra-red proc as neg c-type print. Sky photo col. neg. Mamimya C33 80mm lens c-type print. Montage. Photos Po. Design Storm.

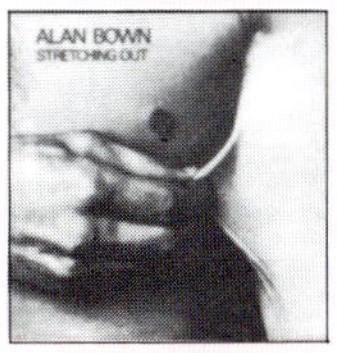

6 Alan Bown 'Stretching Out' 1971 Island Records. Front gatefold cover. ½ plate normal lens. Flashlit. Plus x. Photo Po from some work by John Blake in 1969.

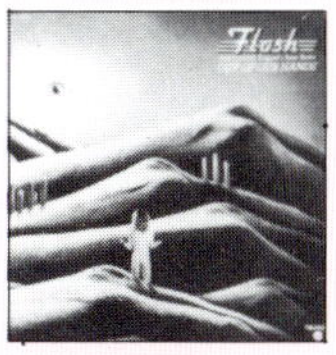

7 Flash 'Out Of Our Hands' 1973 Sovereign Records. Gatefold cover. Montage. Hasselblad 500c normal lens & proxar. Flashlit. Plus x D76. Photos Po. Design Storm.

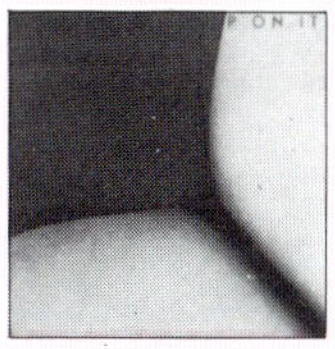

9 Montrose 'Jump On It' 1976 Warner Bros. Records. Front cover. Hasselblad 500c 150mm lens f8 1/60th flashlit. Plus x D76. Sepia toned. Hand tinted by Richard. Design Po. Photo Storm.

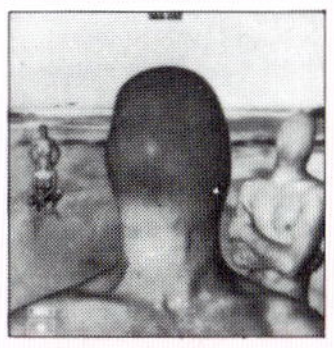

10 Toe Fat 1969 EMI Records. Front cover. Daylight Pentax 50mm and Mamimya C33 col. neg. c-type print. Montage and phase printing. Location N.Wales. Photos Po/Storm. Design Storm.

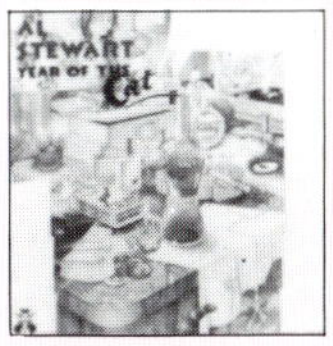

11 Al Stewart 'Year of the Cat'. 1976 Chess Janus Records. Front cover. Airbrush illustration on Kentmere printing paper. Drawn by Colin Elgie, Design Colin/Storm from an idea by George and Peter.

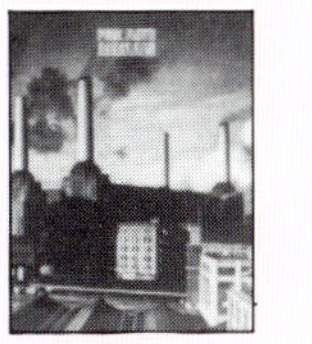

12 & 13 Pink Floyd 'Animals' Songbook 1977. Design Storm/Bush Hollyhead. Graphics by Bush and photos by H. Bartrop, R. Brimson, R. Ellis, C. Jones, A. Kim, C. Littledale, N. Tucker, P. Warfe, R. Whittaker and Hipgnosis.

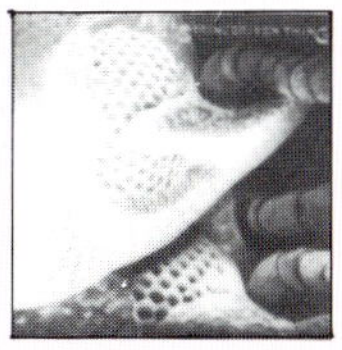

14 String Driven Thing 'The Machine That Cried' 1973 Charisma Records. Gatefold cover. Photos c/o Ministry of Agriculture and Fisheries. B/W montage. Photocopied and hand tinted by Phil Crennel. Design Po.

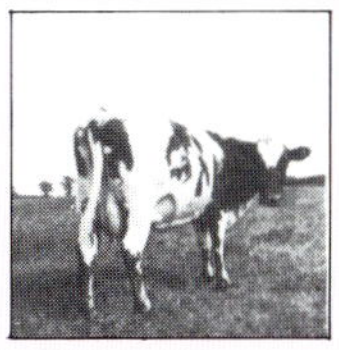

15 Pink Floyd 'Atom Heart Mother' 1971 Harvest EMI. Front gatefold cover. Daylight location Potters Bar. Mamimya C33 normal lens f11 1/60th Ektachrome. Photo Storm. Idea John Blake.

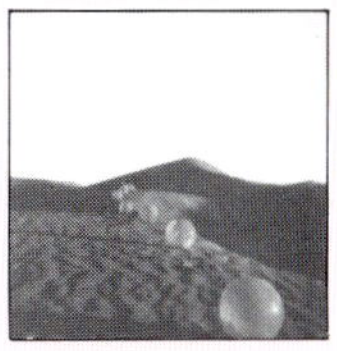

18 & 19. Nice 'Elegy' 1971 Charisma Records. Front gatefold cover. Hasselblad 500c normal lens Ektachrome f22 1/30th. Two transparencies joined. Location Fort Mamid, Sahara, Morocco. Photos Po/Storm. Design Storm.

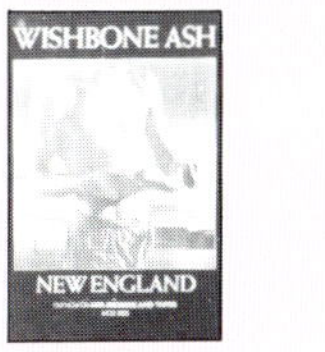

21 Wishbone Ash 'New England' 1976 Atlantic Records. Poster. Montage. Figure is flashlit. Hasselblad 500c normal lens f16 1/60th. Background Nikomat. Tri x pushed to 1000 ASA. Location California. Photos/Design Peter.

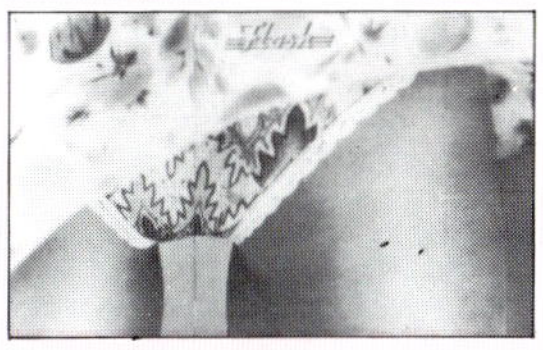

22 & 23 Flash 1972 Sovereign Records. Front cover gatefold. Hasselblad 500c normal lens. Flashlit f16 1/60th Tri x B/W hand tinted Maurice Tate. Design/Photo Po.

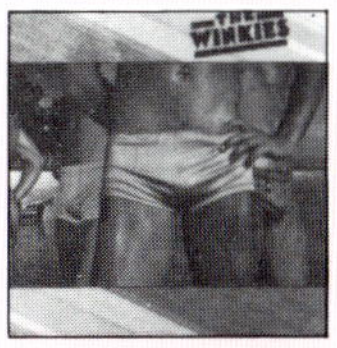

24 Winkies 1975 Chrysalis Records. Front cover. Hasselblad 500c normal lens. Flashlit + body filter. Kodacolour negative. Montage. Background library photo daylight. Photo Po/Peter. Design Storm.

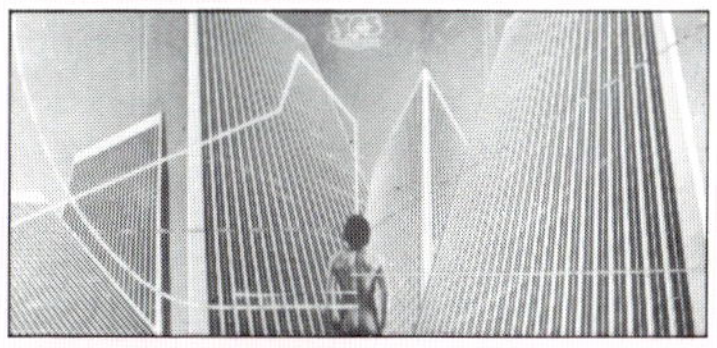

26 & 27 Yes 'Going For The One' 1977 Atlantic Records. Triple cover. Montage with lines dropped in and reversed out in tints. Buildings shot on Hasselblad 500c W/A + Brookes veriwide. Man flashlit Hasselblad + 80mm lens. Location Century City, L.A. Ektachrome transparencies. Photos Po. Design Storm.

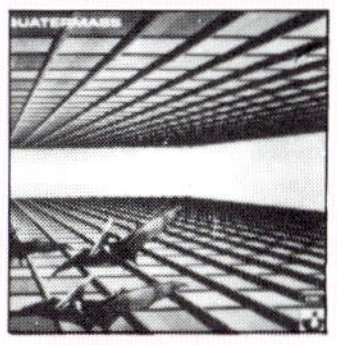

29 Quatermass EMI Records (Harvest). Gatefold cover. B/W montage and reversed print. 35mm Pentax 28mm lens Tri x f8 1/125. Location Barbican, London. Design/Photo Storm.

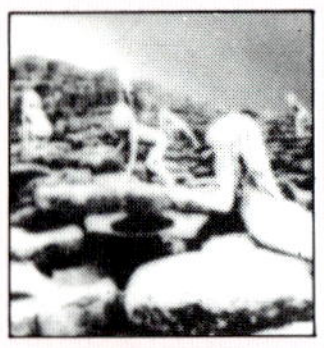

36 & 37 Led Zeppelin 'Houses of the Holy' 1973 Atlantic Records. Front gatefold cover. Hasselblad normal lens. Tri x f8 1/60 Dev D76. Hand tinted by Phil Crennel. Photos Po. Design Hipgnosis.

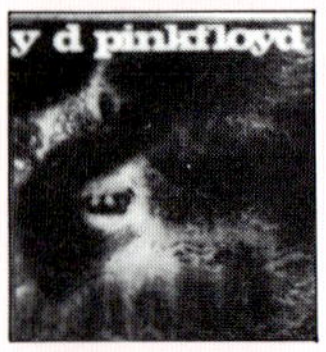

34 Pink Floyd 'Saucerful of Secrets' 1968 EMI Records. Single cover. Multiple c-type colour print superimposition printing Colin Mitchell. 35mm Pentax 50mm lens Kodacolour negative. Photos and design Hipgnosis.

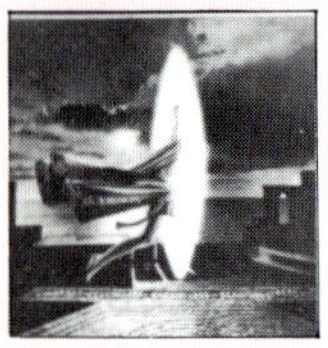

35 Al Stewart 'Past, Present & Future' 1973 CBS Records. Single cover. B/W montage and retouching by Terry Day. Hasselblad 500c normal lens. Tri x Dev D76. Location Minack Theatre, Cornwall. Photos Po. Design Storm.

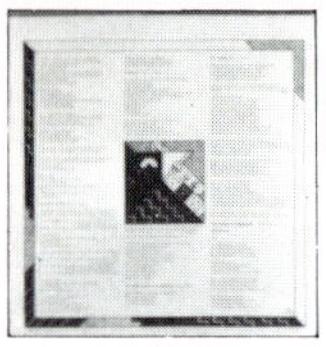

39 Genesis 'Lamb Lies Down on Broadway' 1974 Charisma Records. Dust jackets. B/W line rapidograph. Illustration/Design George.

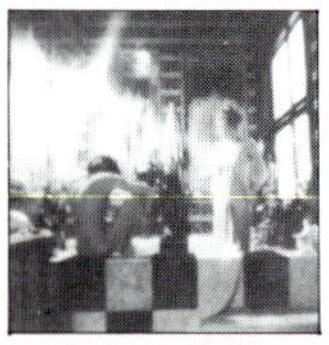

38 Humble Pie 'Thunderbox' 1973 A & M Records. Dust jacket. Hasselblad 500c 50mm lens. Ektachrome. Natural and artificial light f8 1/30th. Muslin over lens. Photo Storm.

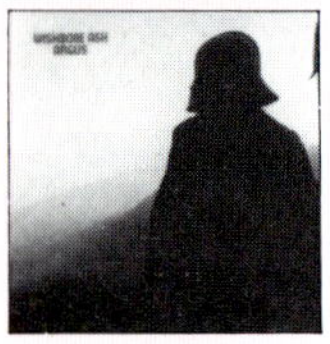

42 Wishbone Ash 'Argus' 1972 MCA Records. Front gatefold cover. Mamimya C33 64mm lens. Ektachrome. Internegatives c-type prints. Retouching Phil Crennel. Daylight. Location Provence, France, Photos Storm/Po. Design Storm.

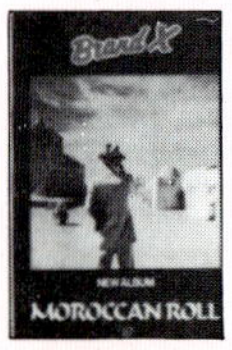

43 Brand X 'Moroccan Roll' 1977 Charisma Records. Poster. Hasselblad 500c 50mm lens. Ektachrome polaroid filter. Location Tunisia. Photo Peter/Po. Graphics George. Design Storm/George.

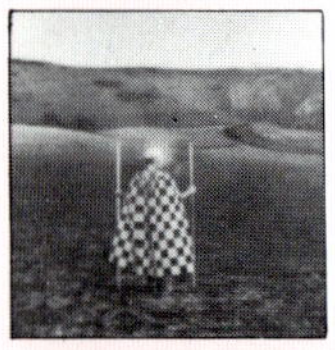

45 Uno Motors Records, Paris. Front cover. Hasselblad 500c normal lens. F11 1/30th Ektacolour negative c-type prints. Montage. Location Wilmington, S. Downs, England. Photo/Design Storm.

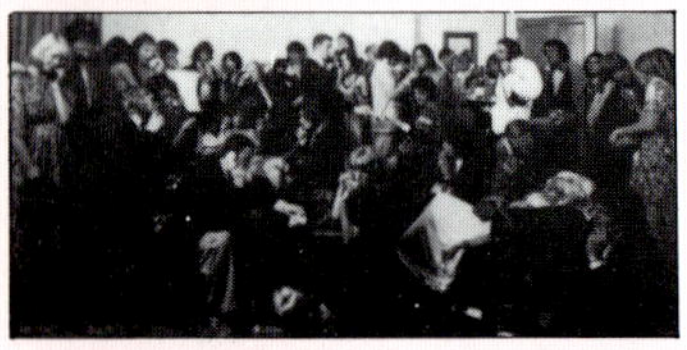

46 & 47 10cc 'How Dare You' 1975 Phonogram Records. Inside spread. Gatefold cover. ½ plate Ektachrome. Photo by Po assisted by Howard Bartrop. Idea George.

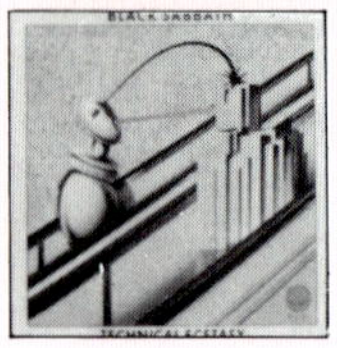

48 Black Sabbath 'Technical Ecstasy' 1976 Phonogram Records. (Vertigo). Front cover. Retouched illustration and photography. Hasselblad 500c 50mm lens Ektachrome. Dye transfer print. Robots designed by George, painted by Richard. Photo Po. Idea Storm.

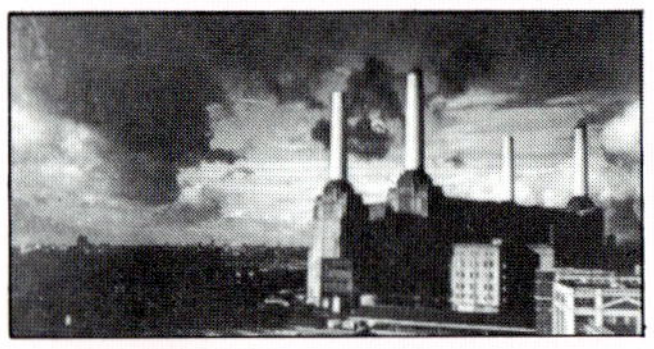

50 Pink Floyd 'Animals' 1977 Harvest Records. Front gatefold cover. Daylight. 5/4 Sinar. W/A lens Ektachrome. Location Battersea Power Station. Dye transfer strip-in. Photo H. Bartrop and Po. Design Hipgnosis from an idea by Roger Waters.

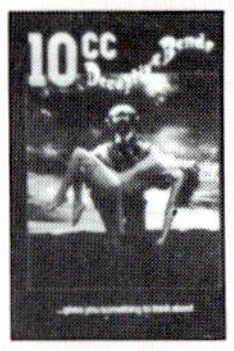

55 10cc 'Deceptive Bends' 1977 Phonogram Records. Poster. Hasselblad 500c normal lens. Ektachrome. Dye transfer strip in. Suits courtesy of Siebe Gorman Ltd. Photos Po/Peter + library material. Design Storm.

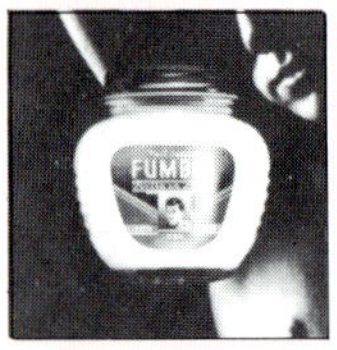

57 Fumble 'Poetry in Lotion' 1974 RCA Records. Front cover. Montage. Background Hasselblad 500c normal lens. Flashlit. Tri x sepia print. Bottle Hasselblad 500c normal lens + proxar. Ektacolour. Label by Colin. Photos Peter/Po. Design Storm/Peter.

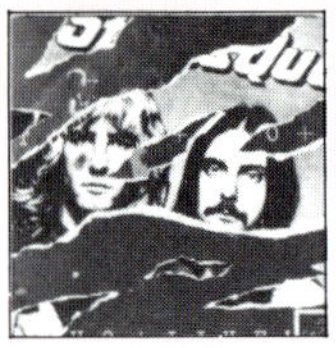

58 Status Quo 'Live' 1977 Phonogram Records. Front gatefold cover. Torn posters — B/W photo Terry O'Neill. Colour photo R. Ellis. Design Storm.

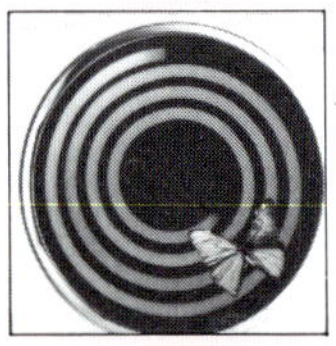

59 Solution 'Cordon Bleu' 1976 Rocket Records. Single cover. Front. Photos H. Bartrop. Dye transfer strip in. Design Storm.

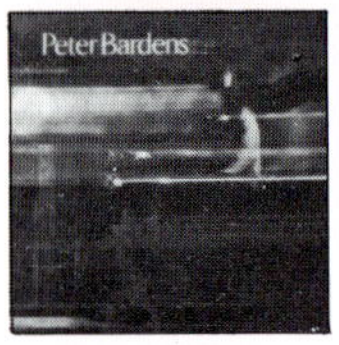

66 & 67 Peter Bardens Transatlantic Records. Gatefold cover. Nikon 35mm 105mm lens f4 1 sec, panning camera to one side halfway through exposure. Ektachrome uprated two stops. Shot live at the Roundhouse, London. Photo Storm.

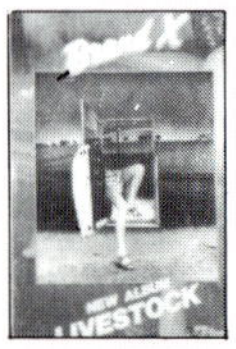

68 Brand X 'Livestock' Poster for live album. Car Hasselblad 500c 80mm Tri x D76. Border 35mm Tri x D76. Montage Richard. Graphics Alwyn Clayden. Photos Po. Design Storm.

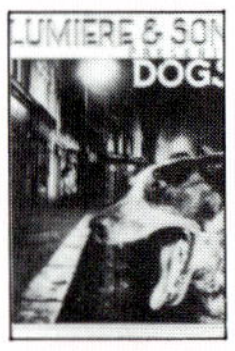

69 Dogs 1976 Lumiere & Son Theatre Troupe. Poster. B/W Montage. Hasselblad 500c normal lens. Night location f8 8 sec. Tri x D76. Dog flashlit f16 1/500 Tri x D76. Photos Peter. Design Storm.

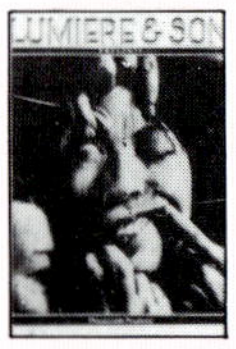

71 Passionate Positions 1977 Lumiere & Son Theatre Troupe. Poster. B/W. Hasselblad 500c 80mm lens f11 1/500th flashlit. Plus x D76. Photo Rob Brimson/Storm. Design Storm.

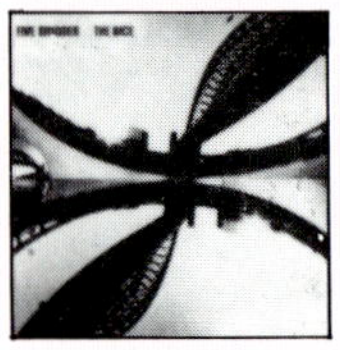

73 Nice 'Five Bridges' 1970 Charisma Records. Gatefold cover. 35mm Nikomat 9.6mm lens infra red transparency. Colour prints montaged together as mandala. Photos on location at Newcastle by daylight by Storm/Po. Design Po.

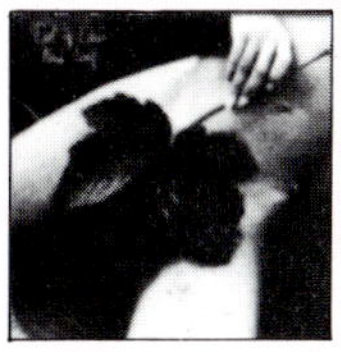

76 East of Eden 'New Leaf' 1971 Harvest Records. Gatefold cover. Photo by Gabi Naseman. Art direction by Hipgnosis. B/W 35mm Tri x with the leaf hand tinted green by Miss Naseman.

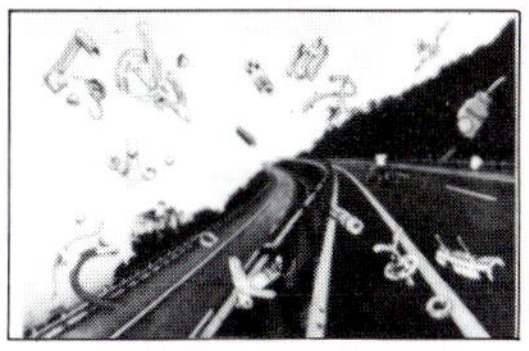

77 Bikes Poster 1975 Pink Floyd Knebworth open-air concert. Freddie Bannister Promotions. Bicycle parts drawn and airbrushed by George. Photo 35mm Nikomat Ektachrome daylight 28mm lens. Location Switzerland taken by Po. Design George/Storm.

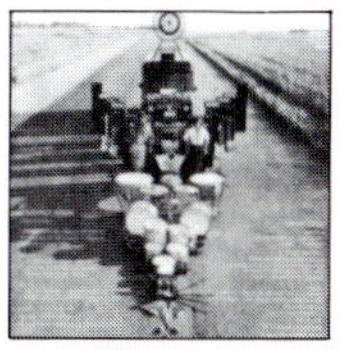

78 Pink Floyd 'Ummagumma' 1969 Harvest Records. Back cover of gatefold. Mamimya C33 64mm lens daylight Ektachrome. Location Biggin Hill, England. Photo by Po.

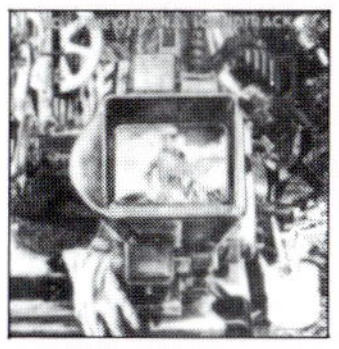

79 10cc 'Original Soundtrack' 1975 Phonogram Records. Front gatefold cover. Pencil drawing by Humphrey Ocean based on a photo by Storm. Two shots 2¼ Hasselblad normal lens Tri x lit by tungsten. Design Hipgnosis/Humphrey Ocean.

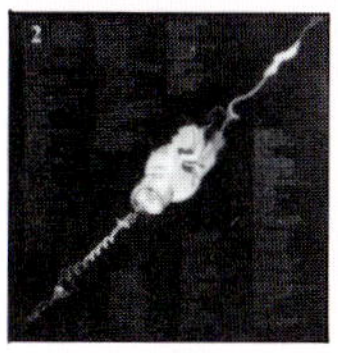

79 10cc 'How Dare You' 1976 Phonogram Records. Liner bag or dust jacket. Gouache and airbrush illustration and design by George Hardie.

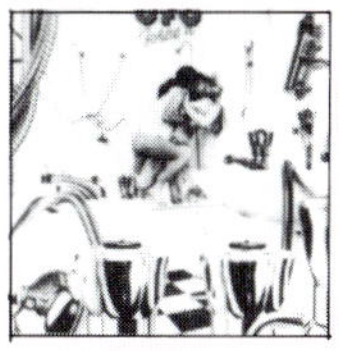

80 UFO 'Force It' 1975 Chrysalis Records. 20/30 Poster. Set built by Crispin designed by Michael Messenger. Hasselblad 500c 50mm & 80mm lens Ektacolour flashlit. Montage by Richard. Photos Po/Peter. Lettering R. Evans. Live photos courtesy Chrysalis Records. Design Storm.

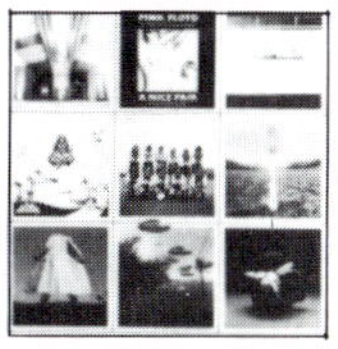

82 & 83 Pink Floyd 'Nice Pair' 1973 Harvest Records. Gatefold cover. Most of the B/W were shot on Hasselblad 500c normal lens Tri x both daylight and flash except 'Fork in the Road' 35mm Nikomat 24mm lens recording film. Colour work is also Hasselblad 500c normal lens Ektachrome. 'Laughing all the way to the Bank' designed and drawn by Bob Lawrie and 'Nip in the Air' drawn in pen and ink by Colin Elgie. Photos/Design by Hipgnosis.

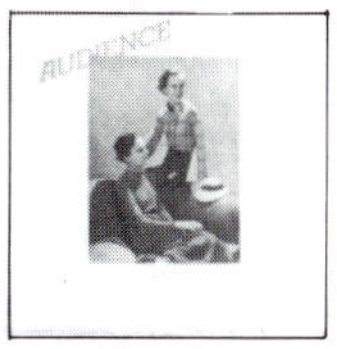

84 Audience 'Lunch' 1972 Charisma Records. Gatefold cover. This photo is literally snitched from an old book of knitting patterns circa 1930 and is an advert for a kind of cardigan. Graphics by George. 'Design' Storm.

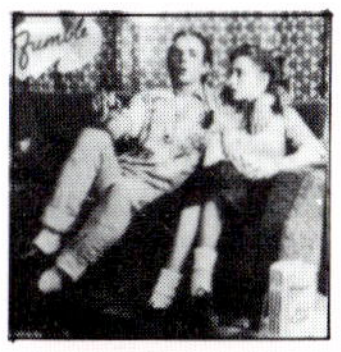

85 Fumble 1972 Sovereign Records. Gatefold cover. Photo taken on location at home of painter Dougie Fields on Hasselblad 500c normal lens f8 1/60th Ektachrome flashlit. Lettering George Hardie. Photo/Design Po.

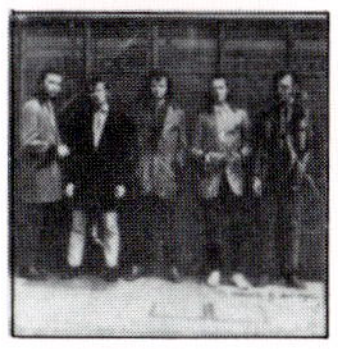

86 Aynsley Dunbar 'To Mum With Love' 1969 Front cover. Mamimya C33 normal lens daylight Tri x D76. Sepia toned print bent and creased on A/W. Location Southend public convenience. Photo Po. Design Hipgnosis from an idea by Bryan Morrison.

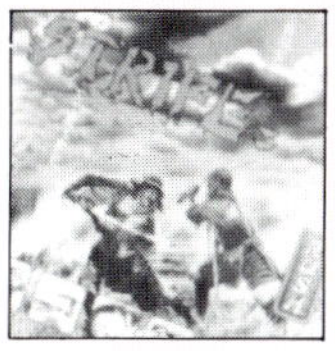

89 Strife 'Rush' 1975 Chrysalis Records. Single cover. Hasselblad 500c 80mm Tri x D76 hand tinted. Location Ely, Cambs. Daylight. Graphics R. Evans, Colin & John Blake. Photos Po. Design Hipgnosis.

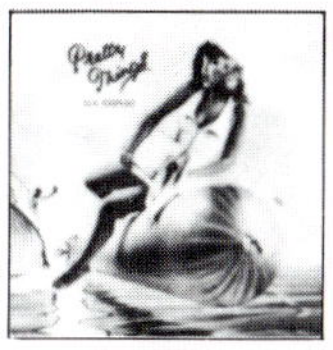

90 Pretty Thngs 'Silk Torpedo' 1974 Swansong Records. Front gatefold cover. Hasselblad 500c 50mm lens. Tri x D76 Montage and copy print. Hand tinting R. Manning. Photos/Design Po.

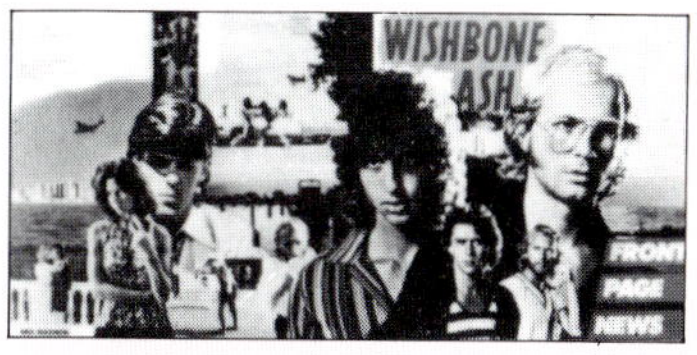

90 Wishbone Ash 'Front Page News' 1977 MCA Records. Gatefold cover. Location Miami. Nikomat + 50mm 35mm & 28mm lenses & Hasselblad 500c 80mm lens studio portraits. Ektachrome + Kodachrome. Photos Peter. Design Storm from an idea by Wishbone Ash.

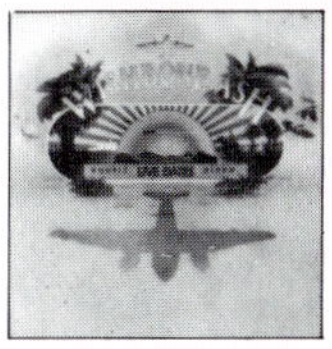

91 Wishbone Ash 'Live Dates' 1973 MCA Records. Front gatefold cover. Airbrush illustration by Colin Elgie. Design Colin/Storm.

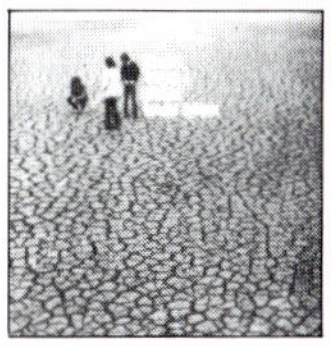

94 Marvin, Welch & Farrar 'Second Opinion' 1971 EMI Records. Gatefold cover. Hasselblad 500c 80mm lens Ektachrome f16 1/30th daylight. Location Tees Estuary, U.K. Photo Storm/Po.

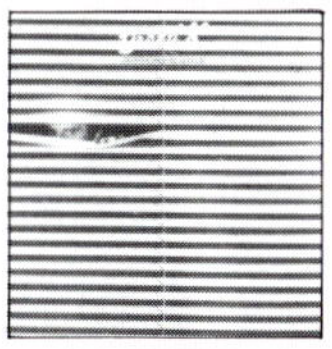

93 Brand X 'Unorthodox Behaviour' 1976 Charisma Records. Single cover. Hasselblad 500c 80mm lens f16 1/60th flashlit colour negative c-type print. Photo Po/Peter. Design Peter.

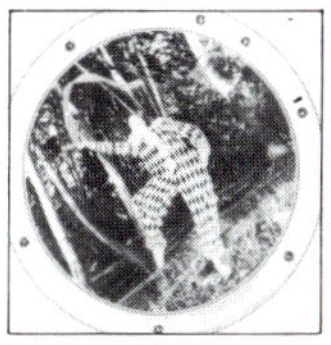

92 Rolling Stones 1976 Knebworth Open-Air Concert. Freddie Bannister/Five One Promotions. Circular poster. Hasselblad 500c 50mm lens Tri x 1/60th f8 flashlit and daylight. Montage and hand colouring by Richard. Location Epping Forest. Photos/Design Storm.

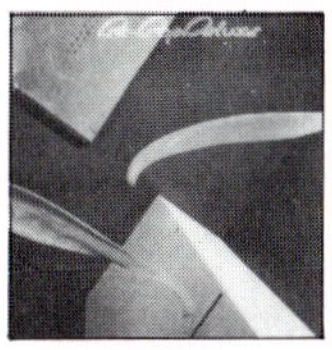

95 Be Bop Deluxe 'Drastic Plastic' Harvest Records 1978. Single jacket. Set photo Hasselblad 500c + 50mm lens flashlit at f16. Ektachrome (E6) uprated half a stop. Dye transfer strip in prints. Photo of paint Nikomat plus 50mm lens daylight uprated two stops. Lettering Geoff Halpin. Photo/Design Storm and Peter. Set built by John Whiteley.

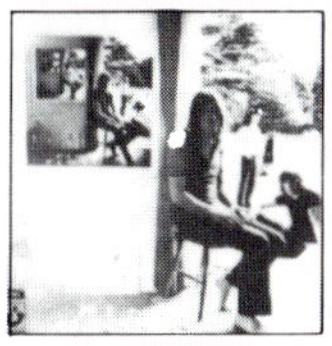

99 Pink Floyd 'Ummagumma' 1969 Harvest Records. Gatefold jacket. Hasselblad 500c 50mm lens colour negative daylight and flash. Montage. Prints by Colin Mitchell. Photos Po/Storm. Design Libby January/Storm.

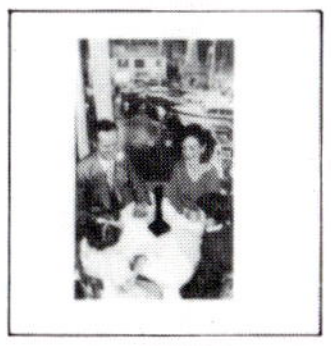

105 Led Zeppelin 'Presence' 1976 Swansong Records. Gatefold cover. Hasselblad 500c 50mm lens. Ektachrome flashlit. Background is Earls Court Boat Show. Dye transfer strip in. Retouching Richard. Photos Po/Peter. Object design & graphics George. Cover design Hipgnosis/George Hardie.

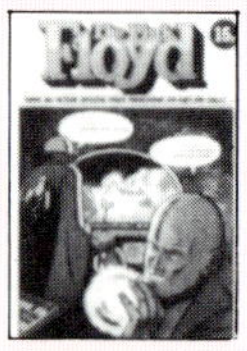

111 Pink Floyd Concert Programme 1975. Idea from Nick Mason. Illustrations by R. Evans, Colin Elgie, Joe Petagno and one other (?) Layout Hipgnosis/R. Evans.

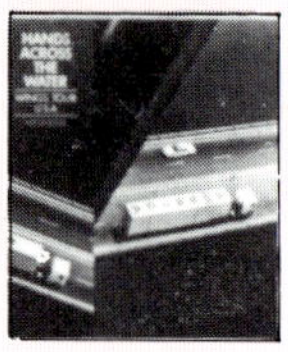

112 & 113 Wings 'Hands Across The Water' 1977. Book Dragons World/MPL. B/W photos by Po mostly Nikomat Tri x daylight 50mm + 28mm lenses on location in USA. Graphics George Hardie.

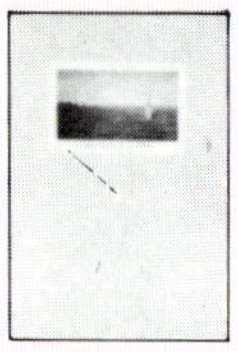

114 & 115 The Beatles Story 1977 Thames TV. Folio devised by George & Storm. Photos and illustrations by Rob Brimson, John Blake, George Hardie, Colin Elgie, Humphrey Ocean and Hipgnosis.

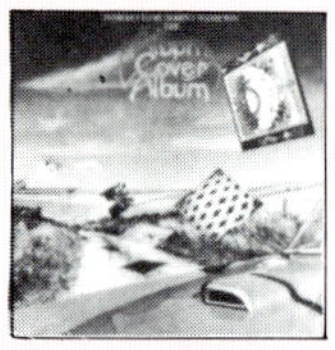

116 Album Cover Album 1977 Dragons World. 160 pg. colour book. Intro by Dominy Hamilton. Research Peter Christopherson & David Howells. Secretary Diana Korchein. Text editor James Slattery. Devised, designed and edited by Roger Dean & Storm.

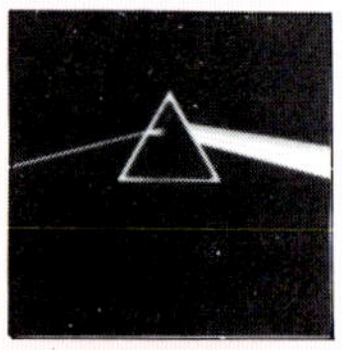

117 Pink Floyd 'Dark Side of the Moon' 1973 Harvest Records. Gatefold sleeve. Artwork is mechanical + airbrush by George Hardie. Design Storm.

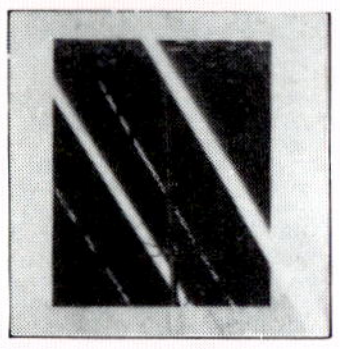

119 Unicorn 'Blue Pine Trees' 1974 Charisma Records. Single jacket. Location Sussex. Hasselblad 500c 80mm lens colour negative daylight. Prints by Colin Mitchell. Photo Po/Storm. Design inspired by a drawing from Malcolm Harrison of NTA Studios.

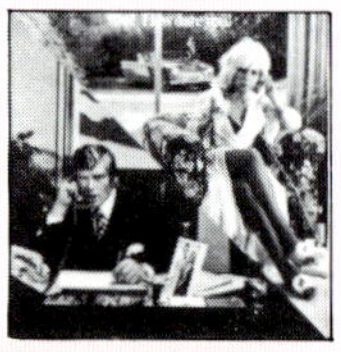

123 10cc 'How Dare You' 1975 Phonogram Records. Gatefold sleeve. On location. Flashlit 5 x 4 Ektachrome. Photos Po/Peter assisted by H. Bartrop. Design Storm/Peter.

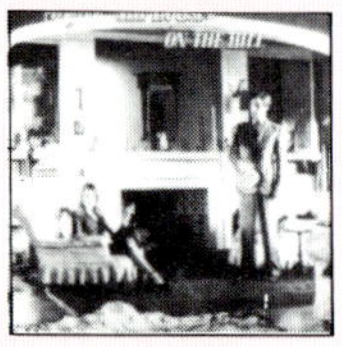

124 Audience 'House on the Hill' 1971 Charisma Records. Gatefold sleeve. Hasselblad 500c or Mamimya C33 with 50mm or 64mm lens Tri x Dev D76. Two prints montaged together. Hand tinting Maurice Tate. Photos Po. Design Hipgnosis & Howard Werth.

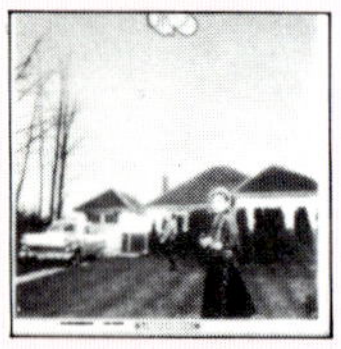

125 UFO 'Phenomenon' 1974 Chrysalis Records. Single jacket. Hasselblad 500c 50mm lens Tri x D76. Daylight location Esher, Surrey. Hand tinting by Maurice Tate. Lettering by R. Evans. Photo Po/Storm. Design Storm.

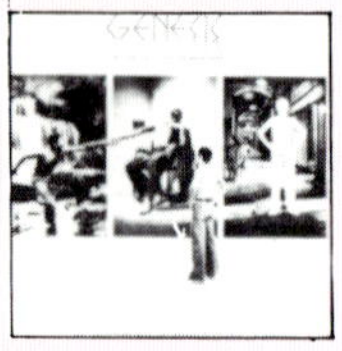

126 & 127 Genesis 'Lamb Lies Down on Broadway' 1974 Charisma Records. Gatefold sleeve. Photos by Peter, Po & Storm mainly Hasselblad 500c 80mm lens Plus x and Tri x D76. Studio and locations in Wales and beneath Roundhouse, Chalk Farm. Lettering George. Montage and retouching by Richard. Design Storm.

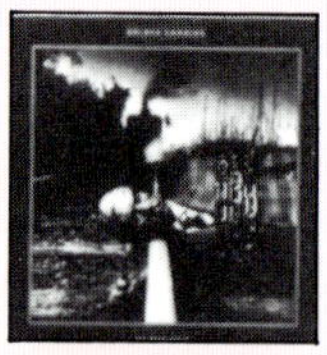

129 Golden Earring 'To The Hilt' 1975 Polydor Records. Gatefold jacket. Photos Peter & Po Hasselblad 500c 50mm & 80mm lenses. Also 5 x 4 work, assisted by H. Bartrop. Location studio and front projection. Montage by Richard. Design Po/Peter/George.

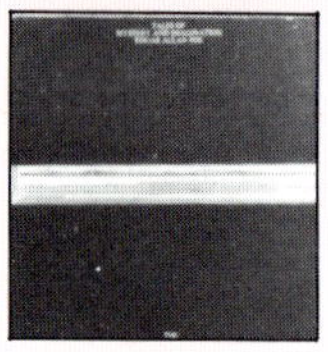

131 Alan Parsons 'E.A.P.' 1976 Charisma Records. Gatefold cover with booklet. Illustration George Hardie. Graphics and booklet by Colin Elgie. Photos Storm & Peter mostly on location in St. Pancras Station, London by available light and flashlight Tri x D76. Theme and design Storm.

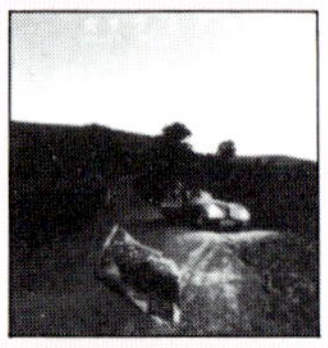

135 Heavy Metal Kids 'Kitsch' 1977 RAK Records. Single jacket. Location S. Downs. Hasselblad 500c + 50mm lens Ektachrome + Chromofilter. Dye transfer strip in. Photos and design Storm/Peter.

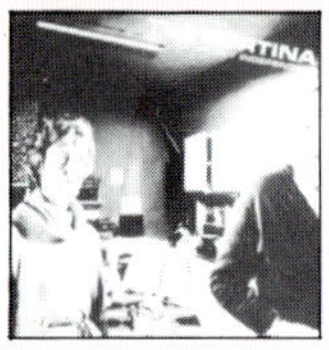

137 Cortinas 'Defiant Pose' 1977 Step Forward Records. Single's sleeve. Hasselblad 500c Ektachrome montage r-types. Photos by Peter. Design Storm/Peter.

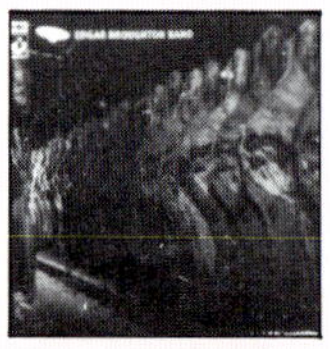

138 & 139 Edgar Broughton Band 1971 Harvest Records. Gatefold jacket. Hasselblad 500c + 50mm lens Ektachrome. Two transparencies joined. On location at Smithfield Meat Market flashlit f16. Photo Po/Storm. Design Storm.

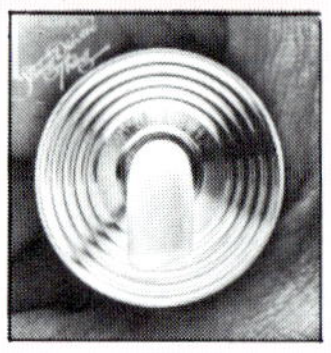

141 String Driven Thing 'Keep Your Hand On It' 1975 or 6 Charisma Records. Single jacket. Photo H. Bartrop. Graphics by Colin Elgie. Design Storm.

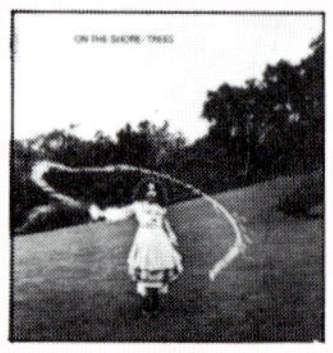

145 Trees 'On The Shore' 1971 CBS Records. Single jacket. Hasselblad 500c 50mm lens f8 1/60th daylight. Tri x D76. Location Golders Hill Park, London. Hand colouring John Blake. Photo Storm. Design John Blake/Storm.

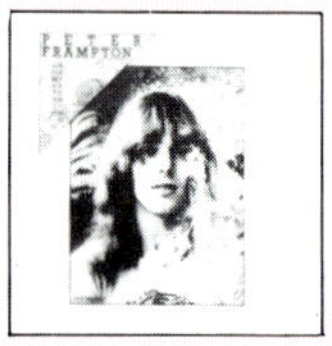

146 Peter Frampton 1974 A & M Records. Single jacket. Photos by Po. Hasselblad 500c 80mm lens Tri x D76.f5.6 1/500th daylight. Graphics George. Design Storm.

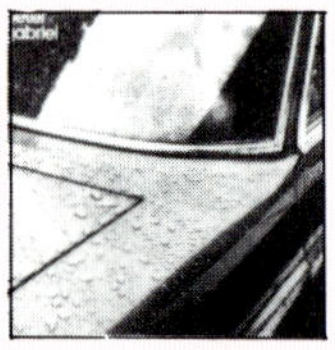

147 Peter Gabriel 1977 Charisma Records. Single jacket. Hasselblad 500c 80mm lens f22 1/15 plus x. Colouring and highlights by Richard. Photos & design Storm.

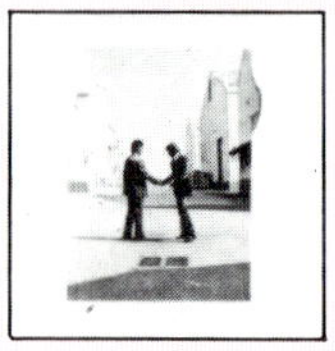

153 Pink Floyd 'Wish You Were Here' 1975 Harvest Records. Single jacket with cellophane wrap. Photos Po & Peter in California — Lake Mono, Burbank Studios and Yuma Desert. Hasselblad 500c 80mm & 50mm lenses Ektachrome. Nikomat 50mm + 28mm lenses Kodachrome daylight. Veil photo Storm/John Blake, Norfolk, U.K. Graphics George. Design Hipgnosis.

A.
Abbey Road Studios 44
Acupuncture 33
Alberto Y Lost Trios Paranoias 136
Album Cover Album 116
Anachronism 104
Argent 51
Art Deco 104
Art Nouveau 63, 76, 104, 128
Artwork 7, 8, 52, 56, 60, 63, 70, 88, 118
Artwork costs 72
Asbestos suit 49
Atlas Mountains 16, 20
Audience 70, 84, 104, 124
Airbrush 8, 28, 60, 62, 118, 120

B.
Bad Company 44, 72, 102
Band, The 44
Bardens, Peter 66
Barrett, Syd 44, 87, 96, 102, 103, 148
Battersea Power Station 50, 51
Beatles 42, 62, 110
Be Bop Deluxe 95
Bends 52
Birth Control 51, 136, 140
Black Sabbath 42, 43, 120
Blake, John 7, 51, 150
Blue Mink 63, 122
Bown, Alan 6, 7
Brand X 42, 43, 62, 68, 72, 93
Brief 52, 60, 74, 124
Broughton, Edgar 51, 138, 140
Budget 53, 70

C.
C-Type 8, 25
Cambridge 33
Capitol Records 44
Castaneda 118
Century City 25
Charisma Records 16, 20
Chrysalis Records 51
Clarke, Allan 49
Climax Chicago 63, 140
Cochise 6, 7, 8, 51
Collage 8, 25
Colour variance 54
Commercial design 75, 134
Consciousness Incorporated 87
Cortinas 137, 140
Creation 17
Crennel, Phil 8
Crystal Palace 51
Cubism 96
Cummings, Jeff 60

D.
Daddy Longlegs 25, 29
Dark Side of the Moon 20, 25, 60, 62, 81, 118
Day, Terry 8
Dean, Roger 110
Depth of field 98
Desert 16
Dirty Tricks 72, 128
Ducks on the Wall 140
Dunbar, Aynsley 86
Dye-cut 40
Dye-transfer 54, 70

E.
East of Eden 76
Effects – muslin 40
Effects – mottled 25
Effects – perspex 98
Effects – softar filter 102
Effects – wind machine 102
Elgie, Colin 33, 54, 60, 81, 88, 96, 131
Embossing 62
Emerson, Keith 16, 20
EMI 88, 140, 152
Evans, Richard 60, 62
Expenses 72
Exposure 8, 49, 104, 120
Expressionism 8

F.
Fees 70
Fishfryer 53, 98
Flash 7, 8, 22, 51
Flying saucer 124
Focus 25, 28, 40, 54, 98
Frame Breaks 152
Frampton, Peter 96, 106, 146
Free 88
Fumble 51, 57, 63, 85

G.
Gabriel, Peter 44, 147
Gale, David 70
Genesis 39, 40, 126, 128
Gilmour, Dave 44, 87, 148
Goatshead Soup 49
Going for the One 25, 28, 62
Golden Earring 104, 128, 129
Gorge du Verdun 49
Gouache 60, 63
Grain 8
Gravy Train 128

H.
Hagar, Sammy 17, 44, 96, 97, 110
Halpin, Geoff 60, 63
Hands across the Water 110
Hand colouring 8, 28, 33
Hardie, George 25, 33, 40, 60, 62, 63, 88, 96, 104, 106, 110, 128, 131, 148, 152
Harley, Steve 62, 96
Harper, Roy 44, 96, 144
Hawkwind 63
Headstone 63
Heavy Metal Kids 134, 135
Heroic myth 53
Hipgnosis personnel 33
Hollyhead, Bush 60, 63
Hollywood 98
Houses of the Holy 25, 28, 51, 63
Humble Pie 38, 40
Hydra 72

I.
Infra-red film 8, 25
Inner sleeve (liner bag) 40, 62, 63, 81, 106, 148

J.
Jagger, Mick 44
January, Libby 96
Jaramillo, Pepe 140

K.
Kentmere paper 62
Keylines 62, 63
Korner, Alexis 88

L.
Lake Mono 150
Lamination 62
Laser beams 42
Lawrie, Bob 81
Led Zeppelin 25, 28, 36, 70, 104-109
Light, available 98
Line screen 102
Live albums 58
Logos 56, 60, 63
Los Angeles 25, 152
Lumiere & Son 69-71

M.
Maharishi 110
Mandala 74
Manning, Richard 8, 33, 54, 106, 118
Mark-up 54
Marrakech 16, 20
Marvin, Hank B. 44
Marvin, Welch & Farrar 94
Marx 140
Mason, Nick 110
Matts 54, 62
McCartney, Paul 42, 110, 120
Mechanical 25, 56, 110
Mock-ups 54
Montage 7, 8, 25, 28, 54, 120
Montrose 7, 8, 9, 40, 41, 44, 51
Mooncrest 60
Morocco 16
Morrison, Bryan 87

N.
Naseman, Gabi 76
Newton-John, Olivia 44, 102
Nice 16, 18, 73
Nice pair 81
Nine days wonder 14
Nostalgia 104

O.
Obsession 104
Ocean, Humphrey 60, 62
Oedipus 96

P.
Page, Jimmy 106
Parsons, Alan 63, 74, 131-3
Paste-up 70
Past, Present & Future 118
Petagno, Joe 60
Pattern 74
Perspective 25, 96
Phased printing 8
Photocopy 8, 25
Photorealism 62
Pig, inflatable 50, 51
Pink Floyd 12, 15, 29, 30, 34, 44, 50, 74, 77, 78, 81, 82, 87, 88, 99, 110, 111, 117, 118, 124, 136, 148-53
Plant, Robert 104
Plate, printing 56
Poe, Edgar Allan 131
Polaroid 53
Portraits 96, 102
Presence 51, 104, 106
Pretty Things 5, 7, 40, 41, 49, 72, 90
Primary inks 25, 110
Print reversal 25, 62
Printing sleeves 56
Programmes 110
Psychedelia 81, 134
Punk 134

Q.
Quatermass 25, 29, 72

R.
Rapidograph 62
Reflector boards 53
Retouching 28, 33, 51, 56, 70, 120, 121
Retouching dyes 8
Reversed out 25, 62
Robots 42
Rolling Stones 42, 49, 92
Roughs 52, 53, 60, 70, 142

S.
Sargeant, Bob 96, 97
Sassafras 96, 97
Separation proof 56
Sepia 8
Shadows, The 44
Sharks 96, 98
Shearston, Gary 96, 98
Shops displays 74, 152
Shrink-wrap 51, 148, 152
Sleeve – manufacturing costs 72
Solution 59, 72
Sounds – Music Paper 106
Specified tints 25
Spectrum 118
Spotting 120
Status Quo 58
Stewart, Al 11, 35, 60, 63, 118, 120
Sticker 60, 148
Strange, Dr. 118
Strawbs 144
Strife 89
String Driven Thing 14, 140, 141
Stripping-in 50, 54, 70
Studio 44, 130
Studio set 95, 96
Superimposition 25, 88
Suspension of Disbelief 96
Swansong 60

T.
Tate, Maurice 8
10cc 40, 42, 46, 52-6, 60, 70, 79, 81, 96, 97, 123, 124, 148
Thames TV 110, 114
Toe Fat 7, 8, 10, 51, 88
Tolonen, Jukka 58
Trees 145
Tungsten 96, 98
2001 60, 104

U.
UFO 8, 14, 25, 28, 80, 124, 125
Ummagumma 88, 96, 148
Underexposure 25
Unicorn 118, 119
Uno 25, 28, 42, 45, 63
Uprating 102, 103

V.
Views 116
Vignetting 8, 120, 121
Visual psychology 148

W.
Watercolour 60
Waters, Roger 44; 118, 148
Welch, Bruce 44
Werth, Howard 70, 96, 98, 124
Wings 17, 40, 41, 110, 112, 118, 120, 121
Winkies 24, 25, 51
Wishbone Ash 17, 21, 25, 42, 49, 90, 91, 102, 124, 144
Wish You Were Here 44, 49, 51, 104, 106
Woolfson, Eric 131
Wright, Rick 110, 118

Y.
Year of the Cat 60, 62, 104
Yes 25, 26, 62, 72

Z.
Zagora 16

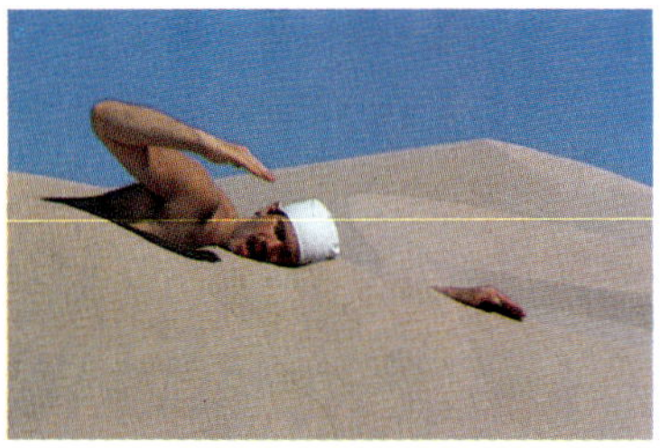

BOOK DESIGNED BY GEORGE HARDIE AND STORM THORGERSON
MATERIAL EDITED BY AUBREY POWELL, PETER CHRISTOPHERSON
AND STORM THORGERSON
GRAPHICS BY GEORGE HARDIE ASSISTED BY ALWYN CLAYDEN
TEXT WRITTEN BY STORM THORGERSON
(EXCEPT FOR LABELS BY COLIN ELGIE)
EDITED AND SUBTITLED BY DAVID GALE
SECRETARY JUDY REYNOLDS
PRODUCTION MARTIN DEAN
COLOUR REPRODUCTION BY
CASTLEMEAD LITHOGRAPHIC REPRODUCTION LTD